ENCOUNTERS

OF THE

SPIRIT

RELIGION IN NORTH AMERICA
Catherine L. Albanese and Stephen J. Stein, editors

ENCOUNTERS
OF THE
SPIRIT

Native Americans and
European Colonial Religion

Richard W. Pointer

Indiana University Press
Bloomington and Indianapolis

Portions of the author's article "The Sounds of Worship: Nahua Music Making and Colonial Catholicism in Sixteenth-Century Mexico" (*Fides et Historia*, Summer/Fall 2002) are reprinted herein by permission of Ronald Wells, editor of *Fides et Historia*.

Portions of the author's chapter "From Imitating Language to a Language of Imitation: Puritan-Indian Discourse in Early New England" (Laura Lunger Knoppers, ed., *Puritanism and Its Discontents*) are reprinted herein by permission of Associated University Presses.

Portions of the author's article " 'Poor Indians' and the 'Poor in Spirit': The Indian Impact on David Brainerd" (*New England Quarterly*, September 1994) are reprinted herein by permission of the publisher of *The New England Quarterly*.

This book is a publication of

Indiana University Press
601 North Morton Street
Bloomington, IN 47404-3797 USA

http://iupress.indiana.edu

Telephone orders 800-842-6796
Fax orders 812-855-7931
Orders by e-mail iuporder@indiana.edu

The paper used in this publication meets the minimum requirements of American National Standard for Information Sciences—Permanence of Paper for Printed Library Materials,
ANSI Z39.48-1984.

Manufactured in the United States of America

Library of Congress Cataloging-in-Publication Data

Pointer, Richard W., 1955-
Encounters of the spirit : native Americans and European colonial religion / Richard W. Pointer.
p. cm. — (Religion in North America)
Includes bibliographical references and index.
ISBN-13: 978-0-253-34912-5 (cloth : alk. paper)
ISBN-10: 0-253-34912-5 (cloth : alk. paper)
1. Christianity and culture—North America. 2. Christianity and other religions. 3. Indians of North America—Religion. 4. Church history—North America. I. Title.
BR115.C8P653 2007
261.2'97—dc22   2007002839

1 2 3 4 5 12 11 10 09 08 07

For Barb, with love

Contents

Foreword

Richard Pointer begins his new book with a classic narrative of exchange —Daniel Defoe's famed fictional account of the shipwrecked Robinson Crusoe and his newfound Carib companion "Friday," to whom Crusoe confides essential lessons from the Christian faith. The snapshot is thoroughly appropriate. Pointer sets out to excavate and explore a story that has, shockingly, been little told—if told at all—until recently. We say "shockingly" because any consideration of sociological and psychological dynamics makes it clear that human meetings are *always* occasions for exchanges of one or another sort, be the exchanges inquiring, hostile, enthusiastic, or seemingly neutral. Alternatives become available, and received practices become subject to comparison and decision in new ways. In Crusoe's case, Indian companionship helped to keep him going and sustain him in both physical and spiritual ways. It also, and perhaps surprisingly, helped him to come to terms with his own more or less conventional Christian beliefs more clearly as he tried to convey them to another.

What the Crusoe snapshot seeks to do, then, is to open the way for a serious discussion of the quintessential exchange situation when Europeans and Indians encountered one another in early America. The received story about that mega-encounter is decidedly one-sided. With a few nods to Squanto and Samoset and the "first Thanksgiving," it mostly tells a tale of the goods—material and spiritual—that Indians got from Europeans. Indeed, it was only in the latter part of the twentieth century, with the birth of the new discipline of ethnohistory, that descriptions of the Euro-Indian encounter came to be called the "Contact" and that questions began to be raised by a series of interpreters about what white culture got from the Indians.

If one raises this question in religious, or spiritual, terms, the ex-

pected research trajectory might be to search out the ways that European Christianity itself became Indianized in its "New World" context
or to track down outright examples of de-conversion from Christianity
and embrace of Indian faith. This is surely a tantalizing project and one
obscured by layers of denial added to other layers of lack of evidence.
Indeed, one of the biggest problems that any researcher faces in such an
endeavor is the one-sided nature of many of the sources—the leavings
and rememberings of mostly European white men of a certain social
class with certain interests and concerns. Yet if one raises the question,
for Europeans, in a different way, the trail can lead to a Crusoe-like
situation. Here a researcher can discover how European *Christian* faith
got changed through deepening and intensification because of Indian
encounter.

It is precisely this agenda that sets the intention of Richard Pointer as
he makes his way through the mixed sources available to him as he
creatively assembles them. He does, to be sure, notice the Indianization
of white Christianity when there are hints of the same. His compelling
first chapter, for example, narrates, among other things, the way that
Nahua Christian converts in sixteenth-century central Mexico changed
European church music. And indeed, recent musical renderings on easily available commercial compact disks reproduce this early American
music and document what Pointer is talking about. That noticed, however, much of the burden of Pointer's story is about how Europeans
repositioned themselves in relation to their Christian beliefs and practices because of Indian presence—how Europeans got clearer, sharper,
better in their own appropriation of the Christian message with the
Indians, as heaven-sent teachers, pointing the way.

This, of course, is *not* the only tale to be told. And many will want—and
rightly—more work on the subtle or not-so-subtle Indianization of white
beliefs and practices (an augmentation of metaphysical religion? an
embrace of Native American ceremonies as today among some New
Agers? a rejection of some or many aspects of Christianity? a combina-
tiveness that brought new and creative options for spirituality to whites
from Indian perceptions and deeds?). Even so, Pointer has worked well
with what he has found, and he has made bold moves in the direction of
discovery. Yes, he is telling us, Indians did affect white religion; and yes, it
matters. That he does this on a landscape that extends from central
Mexico to New France, in what is now Canada, is an added bonus of this
volume. Pointer's space is the space that the Religion in North America
series has wanted to foreground in its projects. It is the space of the North
American continent in which, today, three major political establish-
ments hold sway. As Pointer works, state boundaries fall away in a more

fluid situation in which the reigning exchanges concern not Canadians, Mexicans, and U.S. citizens but instead natives and outsiders from across the sea. Through a period from the 1520s into the 1790s, on a broad canvas that encompasses many cultures, Pointer holds this fluid situation together with the focused nature of his questions and his persistence in seeking answers. His work might be characterized as a splendid and challenging tease—asking other researchers to come aboard with him (and Robinson Crusoe and Friday) in a narrative voyage of discovery that is only at its beginning. Pointer's work invites other voyagers, other islands for visiting, and other narratives for result.

Catherine L. Albanese
Stephen J. Stein
Editors, Religion in North America

Acknowledgments

This rather short book has taken a rather long time, in fact a very long time. It began as a kind of idle wondering as I sat listening to Patricia Bonomi and Jon Butler discuss their, at that time, recent books on religion in early America at a session of the American Historical Association. Their conversation and works made clear that scholars were beginning to make significant headway in understanding how the encounter with Africans in early America had been important for the shape of Euro-American religion. It occurred to me to ask whether similar questions shouldn't be investigated regarding the encounter with Native Americans, especially since at that moment Indian historians were making a strong case that natives were much more central to early American history than previously thought. There started my journey into the world of "encounters of the spirit" among Indians and Europeans. David Brainerd caught my attention first, and thanks to the guidance and encouragement of eminent early Americanists Jim Merrell, Greg Dowd, and Mark Noll, I was off and running.

Though I never expected a sprint, neither did I envision the marathon of sorts this topic has required. Perhaps I should have anticipated better what uncovering even a portion of its complexities and nuances might demand. Fortunately, it has never failed to keep my interest, and it has taken me literally and figuratively across North America and across three centuries. Along the way, I have been fortunate to be aided by a whole host of willing and able co-laborers. Librarians and archivists at the following institutions were especially instrumental in assisting my efforts: Calvin College; Columbia University; Friends Historical Library, Swarthmore College; Hamilton College; Huntington Library; Massachusetts Historical Society; Moravian Church Archives; Newberry Library; New York Public Library; Santa Barbara Mission Library;

University of California, Santa Barbara; and Yale University. Special mention must be made of the assistance provided by the library staffs at my home institutions, first Trinity College (now Trinity International University), and since 1994 Westmont College. Their diligence in securing innumerable interlibrary loan items was foundational to my research. So, too, were sabbatical grants from Trinity and Westmont, as well as several additional summer research grants from Westmont. A summer seminar on Puritanism held at Calvin College and funded by the Pew Charitable Trusts was also extremely helpful. All the seminar's members taught me new things about early New England, but I am especially indebted to Laura Knoppers, Steven Pointer, and Timothy Hall. They and many other scholars have read portions of the manuscript and offered sage advice, including Jim Merrell, Greg Dowd, Mark Noll, James Axtell, David Hall, Michael Zuckerman, Alden Vaughan, Ronald Wells, Kristina Bross, Chris Densmore, Eric Seeman, Laura Stevens, and Bradley Gundlach. Stephen Stein and Catherine Albanese, series editors for Indiana University Press, have read the entire manuscript (more than once) and have made lots of valuable suggestions, most of which I heeded.

Closer to home, I am happy to acknowledge the aid and support of many of my Westmont colleagues. Grey Brothers and Leonor Elías provided specific help on chapter 1 through, respectively, their musical and language expertise. Student assistants Maria Grijalva, Chris Atkinson, and Jane Messah performed cheerily all the research, transcription, and translation tasks I set before them. Fellow members of the history department Shirley Mullen, Marianne Robins, Joan Meznar, Chandra Mallampalli, and Alister Chapman provided occasional sounding boards but more often steady encouragement to keep persevering with my Indian project. Other colleagues and their spouses—John and Anna Sider, Paul and Sharon Willis, Greg and Janet Spencer, Jim and Jennifer Taylor—have simply been the best kind of friends, dependable, loving, and funny.

Of course, my best friend and the one to whom this book is dedicated, Barb, my wife, has endured the marathon with me. That she has done so with her usual grace, compassion, and wisdom is not surprising, but it is nevertheless noteworthy and deeply appreciated. This book would simply have never seen the light of day had she not been my best critic and my best advocate. I am also deeply grateful to my three daughters, Katie, Kristyn, and Julie, not because they read the manuscript or helped with the research, but because as they have grown into adult women during the course of my work on this book, they have remained for me sources of unspeakable joy.

Thirteen years ago I made a deal with Vernon Nelson, the archivist for the Moravian Church. He let me do as much photocopying as I wanted as long as I promised to send my completed book to the Archives. Vernon is now retired, but his library's copy is finally on its way to Bethlehem.

ENCOUNTERS
OF THE
SPIRIT

Introduction

CASTAWAY ON AN ISLAND OFF THE COAST OF SOUTH AMERICA, ROBINSON Crusoe set about remaking his new world in the image of his old one. In the course of his two-decades-long solitary sojourn, nothing would fall outside his mimetic impulse, least especially the Carib native whom Providence eventually brought his way and called upon him to save. Crusoe named him, sheltered him, dressed him, taught him "everything that was proper to make him useful, handy, and helpful," and finally evangelized him. Once able to converse in English, the two spoke of higher things, spiritual things, and as they did, Crusoe's long-standing grief "set lighter" upon him and his "habitation grew comfortable . . . beyond measure." His stranded condition no longer appeared a curse but rather a blessing, for it afforded him the chance to save not just the life but "the soul of a poor savage." Crusoe implored his god to enable him to instruct the Indian, whom he called Friday, effectively in the ways of Christian faith. He quickly realized, though, that he had "more sincerity than knowledge" when it came to telling others of divine matters. Still, in the process of "laying things open" to the native, Crusoe gladly discovered that "I really informed and instructed myself in many things, that either I did not know or had not fully considered before, but which occurred naturally to my mind upon my searching into them for the information of this poor savage." So grateful was Crusoe for his own awakening that he confessed, "whether this poor wretch was the better for me, or no, I had great reason to be thankful that ever he came to me." Slowly but surely, Friday did indeed become the kind of "good Christian" Crusoe hoped for, indeed one "much better than I" in the Englishman's estimation. Over their three years together, the two carried on regular religious dialogues, Crusoe reading Scripture aloud and trying to explain it, Friday offering back "serious inquiries and questionings" that "made me [Crusoe] . . . a much better scholar in the Scripture knowledge than I should ever have been by my own private mere reading."[1]

By the time English Protestant dissenter Daniel Defoe penned those lines about a shipwrecked sailor and his indigenous compatriot, Native Americans and Europeans had been experiencing encounters of the spirit for more than two centuries. How much or how well Defoe understood the nature of those encounters, or the larger Atlantic world of which they were a part, is hard to say. His story clearly reflected the presumptions and prejudices of his homeland in the early eighteenth century. As a result, Friday the Indian was constructed according to standard English conventions about the Americas' native peoples. Yet somehow, perhaps unwittingly, Defoe captured an essential element of what happened religiously when natives and newcomers met: powerful effects were felt on both sides, and the flow of influence moved in both directions. Predictably, in the novel Defoe had Crusoe try to convert Friday to Christianity. The Indian, grateful for the Englishman's role in saving his life from his prior captors, eagerly submitted to his new "master" (that is what Crusoe had Friday call him) and willingly listened and conversed about questions of faith. Friday's eventual embrace of the Christian good news is presented as the capstone of a civilizing process Crusoe has benevolently put him through. No real surprises here for a reading public at least vaguely familiar with Protestant missionary efforts in the Americas. But the passages cited above suggest that Defoe knew at some level that more was going on in the religious exchanges between Crusoe and Friday (and perhaps more generally between Europeans and Indians) than simply the Indian's conversion. Crusoe, too, was being changed as he and the native engaged in spiritual talks. As Defoe imagined those encounters, he saw hope rise up to replace Crusoe's grief, and gratitude to God emerge to replace Crusoe's resentment. He also envisioned the Englishman as intellectually awakened to a greater biblical literacy and a deeper theological understanding. Some of those changes Defoe may have thought to be intrinsic to the act of evangelism. But it is noteworthy that he took pains to credit Friday himself for Crusoe's transformation. Thus, among the *Strange and Surprizing Adventures of Robinson Crusoe* was the discovery that the European and the Native American in the course of their encounter had each altered the other's religious life, not in duplicate manners or to comparable degrees but nevertheless in identifiable ways.[2]

This book will explore the dimensions of that "discovery" that to this point have been the roads less traveled by historians. While much attention has been and continues to be rightly devoted to understanding the European impact on the religious beliefs and practices of Native Americans, much less study has been made of how contact with Indians shaped and reshaped European colonial religion. That scholarly lacuna, though regrettable, is not difficult to explain. For centuries, a tale of European exploration and conquest was told in terms of a superior civilization supplanting native peoples and cultures who were bound, perhaps even providentially destined, to succumb and even vanish. Within such an equation, it was virtually impossible to imagine primitive tribes having an influence on enlightened Europeans, apart from introducing them to maize and moccasins.[3] By the 1960s and 1970s, new ways of rehearsing early American history had emerged that still emphasized European superiority, but this time only in terms of power and the raw pursuit of self-interest. The European invasion of America victimized Indians in every conceivable way.[4] Under such circumstances, natives were comparably powerless to leave an imprint on their conquerors. In the last quarter century, scholars have infused far more contingency into what happened in colonial America and have ascribed far more agency to Native American participants in that history.[5] We now see Indians as central actors in the drama of early America, certainly confronted by a host of difficult challenges but creative, resilient, and often courageous amid the new worlds made by and for them after the Europeans' arrival.[6] Adopting such a view has required historians to fix their gaze primarily on natives themselves, learning much more about the internal dynamics of their cultures and attempting to tell their histories with much deeper understandings of Native American perspectives. The results have been far richer portraits of the Indian peoples who populated North and South America before and after contact with Europeans. Scholars have come to see these peoples as important in their own right, not just for the roles they played in colonial (read European) history. Along the way, somewhat less interest has been shown in how Indians may have influenced Euro-Americans, perhaps out of fears that historians might either fall back into the old patterns of valuing natives only for what they can tell us about the traditional major characters of the story, the European newcomers, or adopt overly simplistic models of the nature of cultural interchange. This seems to be especially the case in treatments of early American religion, where comparatively few attempts have been made to note how the encounter with Indians may have affected whites.[7] Furthermore, presumptions of Euro-American intransigence to the native touch on religious matters have remained strong. Most colonists seem to offer little or no evidence of having had their faiths changed by Native Americans.

Yet greater awareness of Indian agency and greater appreciation for

Indian resourcefulness should point us in another direction. If Native Americans wielded considerable power in early America, so that their relations with Europeans were never a matter of simple subordination, then we might expect to find more complex patterns of dialogue, negotiation, borrowing, dependency, reciprocity, and violence in the long history of their interactions. Recent studies illustrate precisely those patterns in the economic, cultural, political, military, and diplomatic exchanges amongst native and European peoples. They make plain the substantial influence Indians exercised over the course and character of Euro-American lives. Why should we not expect something similar in the religious realm?

To be sure, steps in that interpretive direction have been taken in the last two decades amid a welcome flurry of interest in the religious encounters of Europeans and Indians in the Americas. In many respects, ethnohistorian James Axtell has led the way, particularly with his *The Invasion Within*, published in 1985.[8] Detailing the long course of French and English religious interactions with native peoples on the North American mainland, especially in terms of European missionary efforts, Axtell made a strong case for considering religion as a central component in the outworking of European-Indian relations. At the same moment when he and other Native American historians were insisting that Indians be seen as more crucial players in the overall evolution of early America, he was also demonstrating more specifically that religion was an essential element in the complicated interplay of multiple people groups. That book, Axtell's other writings, and the work of many other scholars have shown that few if any aspects of Euro-American–Indian contact did not have a religious dimension to them. All the stuff of life could have a religious significance or impact. One has only to think of native spiritual crises amid the epidemics caused by newly introduced European microbes or colonial pleas for divine protection and redemption following Indian raids to find ready examples. Furthermore, whether exchanging goods, negotiating treaties, contracting diseases, waging war, or making love, natives and colonists usually entered and interpreted their intercourse through worldviews that were fundamentally religious in character. In the words of Kenneth Morrison, "From first contact to the present, Native Americans have understood contact, and have responded to non-Indians, religiously."[9] For the early modern era, something comparable could be claimed for Euro-Americans. As a result, Indians and Europeans ascribed spiritual meanings, often engaged in some form of religious ritual, and saw spiritual and moral values at stake in virtually all the ways they interacted. The religious encounter, then, was far broader than native responses to Christianity and Euro-

American reactions to native religion. It entailed the whole array of native-newcomer interaction, for whenever and however those peoples and cultures touched one another, the character and effects of their contacts extended into the religious realm. Conceived in this manner, whatever else it may have been, the history of Indian-European relations was a rich religious tapestry.

Illuminating the various pieces of that cloth has absorbed the energies of a growing number of historians, anthropologists, literary critics, and religious studies scholars. Neal Salisbury, James Ronda, Daniel Richter, Gregory Dowd, Jane Merritt, and Joel Martin are just a few of the dozens of scholars who have deepened understanding of everything from Native American cosmologies to the complexities of Christian Indian identities and the distinctive appeal of Moravian women's outreach.[10] Out of that collective work come a number of themes or interpretive emphases that are foundational to this study. First is an awareness of the immense diversity of native peoples and cultures in North America. When combined with the varieties of Europeans and Africans who entered its bounds, the continent displayed a panoply of pluralism in the seventeenth and eighteenth centuries. Unfortunately, our later mental construct of three races has often veiled or reduced the scope of difference among, rather than simply between, Indians, Europeans, and Africans. Care must be taken, then, to avoid generalizations that speak in too sweeping terms about any of them. Put another way, this book will seek to appreciate the specificity of the lived experience of particular persons and peoples. Second, Native American responses to European culture in general and European religion in particular varied greatly. Christian precepts and practices evoked everything from violent resistance to tearful embrace among Indians. Their choices of how to respond were born primarily out of present needs and concerns, but usually with an eye to both the past and the future. To speak of Indian choice is to imply that the religious encounter was never a matter of mere imposition, even in cases where physical force was applied. Though the imperial context of the encounter must be kept in mind, how much Native Americans internalized of what Europeans strove to pass on of their faith depended ultimately on indigenous peoples' decisions.[11] They controlled their own hearts and minds, though the presence of the European "other," in whatever form, inevitably changed their worlds.

Was the same true for Euro-Americans? Did their responses to native ways and native religions vary? Were they in control of their own hearts and minds, especially since Indians did not try to convert them, at least not in the Western Christian sense of the word? Were they nevertheless changed by contact with the Indian "other"? The evidence from early

America suggests that we answer yes to all those questions. European immigrants, like natives, were free to differ in their reactions to the alien cultures they encountered, and they did. The range and nature of their responses may not have looked the same as those of their Indian counterparts, but neither side was uniform in reacting to the other. And both sides were affected by how the other responded to them. Many of the episodes to be described in this book show how colonists were affected by Indian responses to their overtures. For their part, Euro-Americans typically rejected or dismissed native practices and beliefs, but that was hardly the whole story. And even in their rejections, newcomers came to bear the mark of the encounter.

Figuring out why Indians and Europeans reacted as they did points to a third theme in the recent literature: the nature of religious encounters depended to a great extent on the relative cultural power each side possessed at that historical moment. Religious exchanges usually had a different feel to them when they took place within Indian country rather than in English, French, Dutch, or Spanish controlled territory,[12] or when they took place within what historian Richard White has called "the middle ground," a geographical and conceptual meeting space where "no sharp distinctions between Indian and white worlds could be drawn. Different peoples, to be sure, remained identifiable, but they shaded into each other."[13] In addition, the outcomes of those exchanges had much to do with the current cultural condition of a community. Significant suffering or vulnerability created the circumstances most ripe for religious assimilation or transformation, whether in individual lives or among whole groups. But it is important to note that many of the religious changes provoked by intercultural encounters were not of the wholesale variety. Subtle alterations were more commonly the case, perhaps especially among Europeans. For now, though, we have a much better sense of how that story played out among Native Americans, thanks to many studies of if, how, and to what degree they appropriated Christianity. Indians from Mexico to Canada proved remarkably capable of adding Christian elements into their existing religious systems or of building a Christianity that included important holdovers from their traditional faiths. Native religious blending or hybridity took many forms and expressed itself in both rituals and beliefs. Among peoples whose existing religions emphasized practice as much as if not more than conviction, this was essential.[14] Those who went furthest in adopting Christianity did so on their own terms. Like African American slaves, they made Christianity their own.[15]

A certain amount of religious hybridity of various forms appeared among European colonists as well. David Hall, Jon Butler, Richard God-beer, and historians of early modern Europe have demonstrated that folk religious beliefs and practices existed alongside Christian ones in the lives of some Europeans on both sides of the Atlantic.[16] Among such people, occasional direct or indirect contact with Native Americans (as well as with Africans) exposed them to an array of other ways of con-necting to the supernatural from which they could pick and choose. For other colonists, more sustained contact with Indians put them in posi-tions to fuse in some manner elements of the new with the old. Perhaps most substantially, many Euro-Americans had occasion to become fa-miliar with Indian medical cures and healing practices. Some settlers borrowed freely from native remedies, especially in moments when their confidence in their own physicians or medical techniques had ebbed. For Native Americans, all their efforts to heal physical ailments had an essential spiritual component. Colonial Protestant and Catholic leaders were quick to dismiss the spiritual power of Indian healers even when they acknowledged the value of Indian treatments, but not all Europeans accepted that conclusion. Some were willing not only to try native cures or preventative health methods such as sweat baths, but did so in the Indian fashion, with the appropriate rites and rituals.[17] Prominent among those who experimented in that manner were trad-ers, many of whom spent extended periods of time deep within Indian country and gained a familiarity with native ways few other Euro-Americans shared. Some of them lived rather fully in two worlds, able to move back and forth between them and to assume religious identi-ties, or at least to participate in the religious ceremonies, appropriate to each one. Their type of religious hybridity was quite fluid as they tended to adhere primarily to whichever faith dominated their surroundings in a particular time and place.[18] Euro-Americans taken captive by native warriors similarly spent much time in Indian communities. Axtell labels these men, women, and children "white Indians" and argues that they were "Indianized" to varying degrees. Changes in religious values and beliefs usually took longer than other forms of assimilation, so by no means did all captives experience them.[19] But for those who did, ves-tiges of Christianity likely remained part of their religious outlook, if not their ritual practice, even as they conformed to native spirituality.

While interesting and important, religious hybridity of any substan-tial sort characterized the experience of only a small fraction of the Euro-American populations of North America. The majority of colo-nists condemned white neighbors who took on any Indian cultural, let alone religious, ways. Fears of "going native" ran strong within colonial blood. Consequently, one will search in vain for whole communities of newcomers who proverbially went "Indian" religiously. Where Europeans became religious hybrids, they did so one by one.

What does that mean, then, for a study interested in understanding how European colonial religion was affected by its encounter with Native Americans? Must it limit its view to the margins of colonial society and colonial Christianity and conclude, even as Axtell has done, that overall within the European-Indian religious encounter "in North America the direction of religious change . . . was decidedly unilinear"?[20] Yes, if one is persuaded that comparatively dramatic and long-lasting changes are the principal, if not the only, alterations worth noting. But no, if one is willing to look and listen for more subtle, elusive, and temporary changes that impacted the religious lives of Euro-Americans. A good case for pursuing the latter course comes from the burgeoning scholarship on World Christianity.[21] Analyses of Western Christianity's expansion to Latin America, Africa, and Asia in both the early modern and modern periods underscore a fourth theme foundational to this book, and the one Defoe captured well: when European Christians met indigenous peoples, the flow of cultural influence and religious change moved in both directions.[22] Among many studies, the highly influential works of anthropologists John and Jean Comaroff and of historian Lamin Sanneh speak to this point. Although operating from very different theoretical frameworks and generally reaching quite different conclusions about the missionary enterprise, the Comaroffs and Sanneh illustrate that European Christians in Africa (and by implication, those elsewhere), and perhaps especially those involved in evangelism, engaged in spiritual encounters with native peoples that were fundamentally reciprocal and often mutually transformational. Sanneh explores this process particularly in relation to the vernacularization or the indigenization of Christianity within numerous African communities that occurred as missionaries and natives translated the new faith, literally and figuratively, into local idioms. Among other results, "All this translation activity concentrated attention on the vernacular, leading missionaries to a critical comparative perspective on the West while thrusting Africans into the world of literacy and the wider opportunities that represents." In light of those developments, he concludes that "[w]e may [should?] characterize the new [in terms of scholarly perspectives] interrelationship between missionaries and Africans as reciprocity."[23] Meanwhile, in *Of Revelation and Revolution*, the Comaroffs argue that "[a]t the frontiers of empire, expatriate 'colonial societies,' and those who made up their various cadres, tended—sometimes despite themselves—to be profoundly affected by the encounter with 'native' peoples

and cultures." Colonialism and the intercultural encounter (re)con-
structed colonizers both within colonies and "at home" in Europe.[24]
Thus, Sanneh and the Comaroffs, though disagreeing on how best to
understand mission history ("mission as translation" versus "mission as
cultural imperialism"), nevertheless both point toward a conception of
intercultural religious encounters as dynamic processes that altered all
the participants in important ways.

Similar conclusions have been reached by many recent students of
the religious encounters within Spanish America. One case in point is
the essays in *Spiritual Encounters: Interactions between Christianity and Native Religions in Colonial America*, edited by Nicholas Griffiths and Fernando Cervantes. Most of the articles in their collection study colonial
Mexico or Peru and demonstrate all of the themes highlighted in this
introduction, including, in Cervantes's words, "the essentially reciprocal nature of the interaction between Europeans and Amerindians."[25]
Griffiths is even bolder in announcing that "it is now broadly recognized
that the interaction of Christianity with Native American religions in
the colonial era (and indeed subsequently) was characterized by reciprocal, albeit asymmetrical, exchange rather than the unilateral imposition of an uncompromising, all-conquering and all-transforming
monotheism." While his confidence about the state of historiographical
consensus still applies better to studies of Latin America than of colonial
territories further north, a certain scholarly momentum in this direction
clearly exists. In this particular collection, unpacking the nature of reciprocal exchanges leads most of the contributors to focus once again
primarily on the "full gamut of native responses" to what the Europeans brought.[26] They teach us much about how indigenous peoples
interacted with the Christian "words, ideas, or objects" that missionaries and others introduced, but they offer far fewer hints as to what the
exchanges meant for Europeans. Just what does it mean to imagine that
Christianity and colonists "received" as well as gave amid the spiritual
encounters? In what ways were the exchanges reciprocal for Europeans? One suggestion comes in David Murray's essay on the colonial
northeast, in which he proposes that in the course of the encounter,
French and English newcomers made some adjustments or adaptations,
sometimes unconsciously, in the Christianity they presented. Murray
implies, and I concur, that within the encounter, a reciprocal process
beyond the control of the encounter's participants asserted itself and
made differences in the faiths of all.[27] Griffiths states the point similarly:
"In their endeavours to erect bridges between the two religions, Christians inadvertently compromised their message and—however inad-
missible and (consciously, at least) unthinkable such a phenomenon

might be—allowed some adaptation to take place on their side."[28] Though Griffiths implies a kind of universal opposition among Euro-American Christians to religious accommodation of any sort that I believe overstates the case, he does highlight one type of native impact on European colonial religion that this study intends to explore.

Other important insights into the reciprocal nature of the religious encounter in colonial British America are coming from a new generation of literary critics. Sandra Gustafson, Hilary Wyss, Laura Stevens, Kristina Bross, and most especially, Joshua Bellin, are not only offering new texts for, and new readings of, early American literature but propose a new form of criticism that places the encounter and reciprocal exchange at its center.[29] Bellin outlines an "intercultural literary criticism" that asserts "that texts must be viewed within contexts of encounter, that generative and destabilizing region in which cultures, peoples, languages, and literatures exist not singly but in relationship with their various others." Conceiving of interculturalism as what Françoise Lionnet calls the "process whereby all elements involved in the interaction [are] changed by [the] encounter," Bellin sees the religious dimension of Native American–Euro-American interaction as no exception. Hence, he writes, "refuse the image of a monolithic Christianity whittling away a monolithic heathenism, and a new picture emerges, strange yet certain: encounter affected every believer in America." Furthermore, he says, that encounter was a dynamic ground in which "neither Indians nor [Euro-American] Christians experienced . . . religious contact as a unidirectional replacement"; instead, within it, "diverse peoples—both curiously and combatively, and with both outsiders' and insiders' eyes—tested, interpreted, and (re)defined the beliefs of their others."[30]

Such conclusions undergird the spirit if not the specific methods of this study. My own training is as a historian, specializing in the religious history of early America. The approaches and instincts that have guided this work are those of a religious historian rather than a literary critic or an anthropologist, though I have benefited greatly from the studies of early America done by colleagues from many disciplines. The field of early American religious history itself has blossomed significantly in the last two decades, with many outstanding monographs and notable efforts to write synthetic overviews by Jon Butler, Patricia Bonomi, and Mark Noll.[31] Yet on the whole, neither their works nor the field in general has taken full, or even substantial, account of Native Americans. Indians and the encounters of which they were a part generally remain peripheral to the core narratives of early American religion. I am persuaded that such a mapping of our religious history needs to be altered. Even as early Americanists in general have repositioned natives to the center of what transpired, so students of early American religious history must do the same. This book is a modest effort to push scholarship in that direction.

It also in limited ways follows the impulse of some recent historians of religion to focus on what they call "lived religion." Concerned with how religion is actually practiced, and with the beliefs that inform those practices, the emphasis on lived religion widens the purview of the religious historian and breaks down the "oppositions between popular and elite, high and low, official and vernacular, the social and the religious."[32] Robert Orsi suggests, in words especially apropos for an exploration of intercultural religious encounter, that the quest to understand "lived religion" encourages "study of how particular people, in particular times and places, live in, with, through, and against the religious idioms available to them in culture—*all* the idioms, including (often enough) those not explicitly their 'own.'"[33] The chapters that follow seek to provide glimpses of the lived religion of Euro-Americans within the social and cultural contexts of the encounter with Native Americans.

Of all recent assessments of the religious encounter within early America, the one that comes closest, at least on the surface, to my enterprise here is Russell Bourne's *Gods of War, Gods of Peace*. Bourne's subtitle, *How the Meeting of Native and Colonial Religions Shaped Early America*, aptly summarizes the story he wishes to tell. His preface boldly asserts that "as the two peoples encountered each other across the centuries (1620–1830), their religions shuddered, gave good for good and bad for bad, and changed in order to survive." In the long run, "that change through interaction dramatically altered but did not blend the peoples' separate cultures, resulting in a strangely uncombined, uniquely American civilization."[34] While helpful in turning our eyes toward the multiple religious dimensions of European-Indian relations in early America, Bourne's work and what follows in these pages end up being strikingly different. Perhaps most importantly, he hopes to explain how the competition between religious systems in early America played a key role in shaping the formation of a distinct American civilization by the nineteenth century. By orienting our attention on later American culture, however, we run the risk of missing what might have been or might have seemed vitally important at that *present* historical moment. In my view, if the religious encounters of natives and Europeans were indicative of later American religious culture, they were so primarily in their reciprocal nature. As Catherine Albanese has argued, when peoples of different faiths have met one another on American soil throughout our history, they have engaged in mutual exchanges of "selves" and "souls"; they have all been givers and receivers.[35] That said, understanding the myriad meetings and exchanges of Native Americans and Europeans on their own terms and within their own peculiar historical contexts, rather than in relation to some future American identity or American culture, is my main concern, for it seems essential for doing justice to each particular religious encounter in early America. No doubt some of those encounters had long-lasting effects. But we do a disservice to those involved, and to what happened in early America itself, if we assign primary or solitary value to how the meetings of Indians and Europeans contributed to what was to be rather than what was.

To that end, then, my design for this book has been to research and write a series of suggestive essays (rather than an exhaustive survey) that in case-study or episode fashion look for the kind of effects encountering Indians could have on the religion, and more specifically the Christianity, of European colonists. Because of a desire to explore the diversity of ways in which Native Americans might have affected Euro-American religion, I have chosen to examine many different points of contact rather than to research and write about a single example. The theme or question that unites the volume is how did the encounter with Indians impact the religious lives of Euro-Americans? The six case-study chapters move more or less chronologically across the entire span of early American history from the 1520s through the 1790s. They stretch geographically from Mexico to New France, stretch culturally across a wide spectrum of native and European people groups, stretch denominationally across numerous Catholic and Protestant bodies and across a host of native religions, and stretch topically across an extensive range of religious thought and practice. They look at laypersons as well as those officially designated as religious leaders, the devout as well as nominal believers, individuals as well as whole communities, and missionaries as well as warriors, traders, settlers, diplomats, and many others. Specifically, chapter 1 explores how a musical partnership forged between European friars and Nahua neophytes in sixteenth-century central Mexico shaped the worship experience and spiritual condition of both groups. Chapter 2 examines how seventeenth-century New Englanders' religious identity was shaped by the mutual choice of Puritans and Native Americans to converse with one another in a vocabulary fraught with the notion of imitation or modeling. The next chapter traces how the religious encounter with Indians in the colonial southeast and elsewhere served as an important social context and intellectual stimulus for Euro-American theological reflection, construction, and refutation. Chapter 4 investigates the career of eighteenth-century missionary David Brainerd amid the Delaware Indians of New Jersey and Pennsylvania and argues that Brainerd's methods and mentality were profoundly shaped by the natives he encountered. Chapter 5 relates the stories of three Native American Christian preacher/teachers from mid-seventeenth-century New France, mid-eighteenth-century New York, and late eighteenth-century New York who were shaped in their ministries by the particular European Christian tradition (French Jesuit, German Moravian, English Congregational/Presbyterian) to which they belonged but who in turn influenced those bodies' notions of religious leadership. The final case study examines how Euro-Americans interpreted religiously the most prominent social reality they confronted in their encounter with Native Americans, the Indians' high death rate. While for most colonists the passing of Indians heralded a divine blessing of one type or another upon Euro-American aspirations, Quakers came to see the survival of Native Americans as a prime indicator of the fate of their "holy experiment" in colonial America and in the new republic. For them, live Indians, not dead ones, bespoke the lasting viability of the visions of George Fox and William Penn.

Together these chapters seek to shed light on a portion of early American religious history that has been not only hidden, but assumed not to exist. Fortunately, coming to understand the mutuality and reciprocity of encounters of the spirit may now require less of a leap of imagination than it did in the past. Most people in the twenty-first century who live and work outside their home culture readily admit that local peoples and ways invariably rub off on them. Contemporary Catholic and Protestant missionaries are often among the first to say so. But European colonizers of earlier centuries were far less willing to make that concession, and usually entered those situations resistant to being changed by indigenous neighbors. Receptive or not, though, European contact with native others altered both groups. For too long, that simple but profound reality has escaped our accounts of what transpired in early America, especially when the discussion has turned to early American religion. Redressing that oversight or omission, at least to the extent of enticing other scholars and the general public to be alert to the important roles played by Native Americans and to the reciprocal nature of religious exchange, is the hope of this project. If it succeeds, then in my view that will be one small step toward affording all those who were a part of the encounters of the spirit in early America their proper due.

1

The Sounds of Worship

Wɪᴛʜ ᴀɴ ᴏʀᴄʜᴇsᴛʀᴀ ᴛʜᴇ Jᴇsᴜɪᴛs ᴄᴏᴜʟᴅ ʜᴀᴠᴇ sᴜʙᴅᴜᴇᴅ ᴛʜᴇ ᴡʜᴏʟᴇ continent." That memorable line from Roland Joffé's 1986 film *The Mission* bespeaks music's presence and power in the encounter of indigenous peoples and Europeans in the Americas. Nowhere was that more true than in Spain's colonial territories.[1] Almost from the very start of New Spain and Peru in the early sixteenth century, missionary evangelists relied upon music as a valuable aid in the Christianization of New World inhabitants.[2] By the mid-eighteenth-century setting of *The Mission,* Jesuit priests and members of other religious orders were long accustomed to training up Indian youths in the musical way they should go. In the film, Father Gabriel, played by Jeremy Irons, is seen not only teaching a group of novice violinists and leading native choirs in a well-established mission church but also initiating contact with a band of previously hostile Guaraní Indians with nothing more powerful than the sonorous sounds of his oboe. Their curiosity is sufficient to grant him entree to their community, and thus begins a familiar process of pacification and Christianization within which singing and instrument playing assume vital roles. If not quite a universal language, music, in the words, images, and tones of this film, serves as a cultural bridge, a means to friendship, and an avenue to evangelization. It symbolizes and embodies the way of peace, love, and justice championed by Father Gabriel and stands in sharp contrast to the way of the sword that would ultimately overwhelm Jesuit and Guaraní alike. Music is a gift offered by one people to another. In this case, that gift is received and in turn reciprocated in a form far more glorious—the exquisitely beautiful, and in Catholic ears profoundly holy, sounds of Indian choirs.

Joffé's depiction of what the Jesuits and their music were about in the borderlands of Argentina, Paraguay, and Brazil is surely more heroic than historical. Like most accounts of the Jesuit *reducciónes* (reductions) in South America, it romanticizes, perhaps even utopianizes, what occurred.[3] More specifically, critics of *The Mission* have pointed out that in telling the story of Jesuit-Guaraní contact, the film renders the natives voiceless. Indian dialogue is rarely translated, no native character is named or developed, and no Guaraní are allowed to express any of their own cultural heritage or cosmology. The result is a film ultimately about Europeans contesting amongst themselves, told from a European perspective. Indians, as usual, are pushed to the margins.[4]

And yet like many European "texts" relating to New World encounters, this one still helps alert eyes and ears to important dimensions of European-Indian interaction, including ways in which contact with the Indian other may have changed the European. In particular, *The Mission* hints at how mission Indians' music making might have affected the hearts and minds of those European newcomers who heard it. Several poignant scenes give glimpses of the range of their reactions to neophyte singing. When a young Indian boy sings part of the Latin Mass before a papal legate sent to adjudicate territorial disputes between the Jesuits and colonial officials, Father Gabriel hails the sacred sounds as proof of the natives' innate spirituality. To the local don, however, the boy is no more than a parrot mimicking what his master has taught. For him this is simply more evidence of the natives' barbaric nature and need for subjugation. The legate, under strong political pressure to rule against the Jesuits, is later taken to Mission San Miguel, where he is greeted by an Indian orchestra and then escorted into the large mission church. There he stands amazed at the sights and sounds of a cavernous sanctuary being filled with harmonious native voices. He can only confess, "nothing had prepared me for the beauty and power of the limb [of the Catholic Church] I have come here to sever." Less articulate but no less moved are the Portuguese soldiers seen in *The Mission*'s dramatic conclusion. Sent to take possession of newly granted territory that includes the Guaraní homelands and the Jesuit mission within it, the Portuguese encounter violent resistance from the natives and some of the brothers. The invading Europeans battle on undeterred until they hear singing coming from the Indians' village. Women, children, and the elderly are gathered around Father Gabriel, standing courageously and singing hymns of their new faith. The soldiers pause in bewilderment and wonder. What are they to do to these fellow Catholics? They turn to their captain for direction. Bent on doing his duty and completing the conquest, he urges them to finish their task regardless of what they see and hear. What follows is wholesale slaughter and martyrdom. Father Gabriel and the Guaraní choir are silenced.

When taken as a whole, those scenes suggest that natives are not so voiceless in this film after all. They get to have a say, albeit it comes in the form of a song. What is perhaps most striking about the three episodes just summarized is that in each case it mattered who was doing the singing. If the music and texts the Guaraní sang were familiar to Europeans, the singers themselves were not. Encountering *Indians* performing plainsong chants or polyphonic anthems, in whatever language, at the very least got Europeans' attention; if the film is right, it had the power to do far more. In dramatizing such moments, Joffé, intentionally or not, points toward a much broader and longer story of Indian music making leaving its mark on the colonial Spanish from their earliest days in Mexico to their final days in Alta California.

Sixteenth-century Mexico provides perhaps the most opportune window for observing how that story played out in North America. Scholars have long recognized that music was an integral part of the religious encounter between the Spanish and the indigenous populations there. Works written up through the mid-twentieth century mostly emphasized the laborious efforts of friars to use music as a tool of doctrinal and liturgical instruction. The model presented was one of the Spanish as givers and the Indians as receivers.[5] Recent scholarship points toward the need for a different conception of the two sides' "musical interplay," one that sees give and take in both directions. During the last three decades, anthropologists and historians have transformed understanding of the peoples who inhabited central Mexico both before and after the Spanish arrived. Making much greater use of materials generated by Nahuatl-speaking Indians, scholars have moved away from describing the colonial encounter in Mexico as a matter of "straightforward clash, simple displacement, . . . [or] indigenous survival through isolation," at least in those places where natives and newcomers had lots of contact.[6] Instead, the picture is one of a complex set of interactions and borrowings.[7] If Nahuas quickly took to some of what the Europeans brought in the 1500s, it was because parts of Spanish culture resembled longstanding aspects of their own culture. Meanwhile, Franciscan, Dominican, and Augustinian friars did best when they helped perpetuate indigenous ways while bringing Nahuas into the Christian fold.[8] Indeed, some scholars go so far as to speak of the "Nahuatlization" of Christianity. Friars' openness to acculturation of that sort was greatest during New Spain's first four or five decades, when they enjoyed relative autonomy from state or ecclesiastical officials.[9] Conclusions such as these suggest new ways of imagining music's role in shaping the relationships and exchanges between Nahua and Spanish peoples in sixteenth-century Mexico.

In particular, I want to propose that from roughly the 1520s to the 1570s or '80s, Nahua musicians and European friars formed a musical partnership. Brokered by men from both cultural communities, rather than merely being imposed by the conquerors, it stemmed from each people's distinctive though not incompatible needs and wants. The partnership proved to be comparatively short-lived. Yet its impact was significant in both the short and long runs. Multiple generations of later Spanish Catholic missionaries were inspired by New Spain's first friars and took music with them as a tool of evangelism around the world. Indigenous peoples across multiple continents thus came to have their own musical exchanges with European newcomers. More immediately, the Spanish-Nahua musical partnership left its mark on both its major participants—friars and Indian musicians—and those on its periphery— colonists and other Nahuas. The lives of natives and Europeans alike, including their religious lives, were simply different because of it.

A New World of Music

Central Mexico was a land filled with song and dance long before the Spanish arrived. Nahuatl records and early Spanish accounts testify to the important place music, and those who performed it, occupied within preconquest native society. All young adolescents, regardless of sex or social class, attended *cuicacalli*, "houses of song," where they were diligently instructed in the songs and dances that filled Nahua rites and festivals.[10] Adult musicians in Nahua culture were held to high standards but also accorded high status. They formed something of a professional class whose task was to compose and perform music appropriate for the hundreds of different religious and cult ceremonies that dotted their calendar throughout the year.[11] As part of a whole hierarchy of religious specialists, musicians had their talents called upon for the opening of new temples, coronations, funerals, battles, and a host of other occasions.[12] Whatever the event, what was sung, played, or danced had some connection with the divine. In the Nahuas' sacralized culture, music had no life apart from rituals infused with religious content. According to Fray Toribio de Benavente, commonly known as Motolinía, one of the earliest Franciscan friars in Mexico, Aztec "festivals of song and dance . . . were organized not only for the delight of the inhabitants themselves, but more especially to honor their gods, whom they thought well pleased by such service."[13] Such occasions were highly communal. The music performed sought to express the deepest disappointments and greatest achievements of whole villages or towns. Even when soloists sang or played, their goal was collective rather than self-expression. Perhaps fittingly, their names went unrecorded, swallowed up in testimonies describing a people, not a person.[14]

With such a high calling, it is no wonder Nahua musicians trained rigorously. Proper service to the gods and the community demanded near perfect performances. Moreover, some of the very instruments upon which they played were thought to be divine. Nahuas considered the *teponaztli* and the *huehuetl,* their two principal types of drums, to be earthly manifestations of gods sent here in temporary exile.[15] Playing them improperly or moving to their sounds inexactly in a public setting could apparently have dire consequences. At least that is the impression conveyed in several early missionary reports. Bernardino de Sahagún's *Historia General de las Cosas de Nueva España,* written in the 1540s, claimed that if a singer, player, or dancer erred, "then the ruler commanded that they place in jail whoever had done the wrong; they imprisoned him, and he died."[16] Even if the stakes were not ordinarily that high, there is little doubt that indigenous musicians and the communities they served took their work very seriously.

It is equally clear that performers and listeners alike also delighted in their work. Nahua festivals could be both solemn and joyous occasions. Whatever the mood, singers, players, and dancers usually carried on for hours, if not days. Their sounds and movements literally set the tone of community praise and lament.[17] Crowds eagerly gathered to watch and sometimes join in the music making. Motolinía reported that amid a fiesta "the people hearing the beginning of the kettle drums all feel the singing and start to dance." The people's movements were so well synchronized that "all the dancers from Spain that see this are astounded."[18] Local nobles went one step further. They hired professional singers to be part of their households. Caciques wanted to hear not only the old songs but new compositions commemorating the great acts of their leaders, past and present, according to Dominican missionary Diego Durán.[19] Just that type of music was being written and sung as late as the 1550s. Cult songs (*xochicuicatl*) reappeared in Mexico City during that decade, hailing the memory of fallen warrior ancestors.[20]

By that time, Spanish conquistadors and padres had had more than a generation to take stock of the Nahuas and their music. The reverse was also true. Hernán Cortés's entourage had included several fine musicians whose talents were immediately showcased. Their minstrel songs quickly caught the attention of central Mexico's indigenous peoples. So, too, did the centrality of music within Spanish worship.[21] Bernal Díaz's account of the expedition's early days indicates that Fray Bartolomé de Olmedo "who was a fine singer, chanted Mass" on the first Sunday following their reaching shore.[22] When Motecuhzoma's representatives arrived to negotiate with the aliens, the Indian diplomats were likely struck by Cortés's insistence that talks be delayed until a makeshift altar could be constructed and worship offered to their Spanish god. The words and symbols of that Catholic ritual no doubt seemed strange, if not bizarre, to native eyes and ears. But the fact that it was *sung* might very well have seemed appropriate and proper to peoples long accustomed to approaching their gods in song.

It is not surprising, then, that when the Spanish began their Christianization efforts in earnest following their military victory in the early 1520s, they wasted little time in exposing the Nahuas more fully to the sounds of their faith and that many Nahuas responded with interest and enthusiasm. On the Spanish side, as the first groups of friars arrived, they brought with them not only a fair amount of musical expertise but an expectation that music would pervade their daily religious life in the New World as it had in the Old. They also anticipated that music would be among the means employed to pass on Christian faith to New Spain's indigenous peoples. Even so, they were not quite prepared for the extent of native musical ability or the speed with which Nahuas warmed to Catholic sacred music.[23] Friars were naturally delighted to find so many willing listeners to their chant. By 1540, Mexico's first bishop, Fray Juan de Zumárraga, gleefully reported to Emperor Charles V that "experience teaches us how much the Indians are edified by it [church music], for they are great lovers of music, and the religious who hear their confessions tell us that they are converted more by music than by preaching, and we see them come from distant regions to hear it."[24] On the Nahua side, music-filled religious ritual was one among many elements of Spanish religious practice and belief that were sufficiently akin to native patterns to give them an air of familiarity and, as a result, a relatively high degree of acceptability. Alongside other common features such as sumptuously decorated temples, a yearly round of feasts and processions, and close links between religious and political authority, sacred music making struck Nahuas as both appropriate and valuable. What is more, according to James Lockhart, "for the people of preconquest Mesoamerica, [political or military] victory was prima facie evidence of the strength of the victor's god. One expected a conqueror to impose his god in some fashion." In other words, Indians assumed they would be taught what to believe and how to practice their new rulers' faith. As a result, Lockhart says, "after the Spanish conquest, [the Nahuas] needed less to be converted than to be instructed." He claims that even the friars defined their work more often in terms of teaching than evangelism.[25]

Even if Lockhart overstates the case, there is plenty of evidence that the newcomers were eager teachers and the natives were generally receptive students. Clearly that was the case with respect to music. From the time the first missionary friars arrived in the Valley of Mexico, the Spanish wanted Nahuas not only to hear church music but to sing and play it. For reasons to be explained more fully below, neither they nor the Indians were content with having the latter be simply passive observers of Catholic rites. Both peoples wanted Indian neophytes to become active, contributing participants in the transformed religious life of Mexico. Efforts in that direction were already well under way by the time Zumárraga sent his letter to the emperor, thanks primarily to Pedro de Gante, one of the first three Franciscans sent to work specifically among the Nahuas. Arriving in 1523, Fray Pedro, a lay brother, first learned Nahuatl, the principal native language, and then established schools for Indians at Texcuco and Mexico City where natives were taught music alongside other European subjects. The results were, in de Gante's view, nothing short of remarkable. Within nine years he confidently reported to Charles V that "without falsifying I can say that there are . . . singers who could sing in your majesty's chapel choir, so good that perhaps if it is not seen it will not be believed."[26]

Other friars rapidly followed Pedro's example and invested much time and effort in instructing Indian youths. Fray Martín de Valencia made a point of "recruiting" the children of caciques and other noble families. He thought that isolated in a monastery, they might be freed from "heathen influences" and thereby freed to learn "not only how to read and write, but also how to sing both plainchant and polyphonic music." Literacy in a European tongue, including musical literacy, might make Nahuas more receptive to, not to mention more knowledgeable about, the new faith. Beyond that, such literacy would allow Indians to become far more active participants in the daily religious life of Catholic communities. With that object in mind, Martín and his colleagues taught the children "how to sing the canonical hours and how to assist at Mass."[27] Before long, missionaries in Indian villages large and small were training native choirs and orchestras. Their singing and playing became a familiar part of Catholic worship across colonial Mexico and, as Fray Pedro indicated, a source of not inconsiderable pride for their teachers.

All this instruction took place alongside or in the midst of the creation of parishes, or more technically *doctrinas*, across central Mexico from the 1520s onward. *Doctrinas* were communities in which a church and clerical residence were located. Sometimes they were placed in existing Indian towns; others created new settlements. They served as the headquarters of Spanish Catholic activity in a local area and were typically surrounded by outlying villages, *visitas,* which often had their own churches but rarely if ever resident priests.[28] As more and more natives embraced the new faith, *doctrinas* functioned less as missionary outposts and more as normal parishes.[29] Virtually all the parishes for the first fifty years were headed by either Franciscans, Dominicans, or Augustinians, the three mendicant orders that dominated the Mexican church in the sixteenth century. The Franciscans were especially prevalent in central Mexico, establishing close to forty *doctrinas* outside Mexico City by 1570. The assigned friar or friars oversaw a host of activities but had to rely on indigenous church staff to carry out much of the parish work, both within the *doctrina* and in the neighboring *visitas.* A whole array of *teopantlaca,* "church people," performed various tasks, led by the *fiscal de la iglesia,* steward of the church's resources. Nahuatl and Spanish records testify to the fact that native church musicians were a regular part of that staff, along with sacristans, constables, deputies, and custodians. Choirs and orchestras usually consisted of boys and men under the direction of the *maestro de capilla,* the choir master, who in most parishes was himself an Indian.[30] Adult cantors and instrumentalists often filled multiple church positions and with the *fiscales* exercised important religious and social leadership. According to one recent assessment, they "prepared the dying for confession or death; helped them write their wills; administered baptism in the absence of the priest . . . taught catechism and announced the feast days . . . kept the register of alms and offerings, and watched over the cult objects and ornaments of the church."[31]

Just how ubiquitous Nahuatl musicians and music making became in New Spain's churches may be gauged from statistics provided by music historian Robert Stevenson. Based on an estimated number of printed copies of a new choirbook, the *Graduale Dominicale* (it contained the plainchant for all Sunday and feast-day Masses), which appeared in the 1570s, Stevenson calculated that there could have been as many as "a thousand [Indian church] choirs with singers trained to sing the full service in the elaborate plainsong version" of this gradual. Since the European population in New Spain at the time was only about 15,000, the vast majority (Stevenson says "nearly all") of the 10,000 or more singers who made up those choirs had to have been Indians. While Stevenson's estimates seem very high in light of a total native population of about 325,000 in 1570, church records from Mexico City confirm the difficulty of coming up with Spanish singers, even in places where colonists were clustered. Perhaps only at the cathedrals of Puebla, Guadalajara, and Mexico City did European voices hold forth. Elsewhere friars relied upon Nahuatl singers and players to join with them in producing the sounds of worship.[32] And that they did. As one contemporary source put it, even in the tiniest villages, handfuls of native cantors gathered daily in the church to sing the hours.[33]

Thus, Spanish and Nahuas found common cause or at least common ground in sacred music making. Delving deeper into why people on both sides of the cultural divide were willing and able to do so will shed light on their respective motives but also the effects of their participation on the other.

SINGERS AND PLAYERS APLENTY

For the Nahuas, whatever degree of coercion the Spanish employed in getting their "cooperation" with other parts of their colonial agenda was largely absent when it came to musical participation—so much so that church and state officials encountered an unanticipated problem: an overabundance of native singers and players willing to serve the church. The issue was significant enough to be addressed at the first church council held in Mexico in 1555. Its provisions made the excess plain:

> The great number of Indians who spend their time in playing and singing obliges us to apply a remedy and to place a limit on all this superabundance. . . . Because of the vast number of churches which have sprung up everywhere in our archdiocese, proper regulation has proved difficult. . . . No more Indians than are absolutely necessary shall be permitted to become choristers.

The synod proceeded to lay down rules aimed at controlling the quantity and quality of Indian musicians:

> They should be few in number, and should live lives that are without blemish or spot. They moreover should know the doctrines of our holy faith and the traditional customs of the church. They should be married and not bachelors, and they should be persons who know how to give sound instruction in doctrine to those who are still ignorant. . . . The Indian singers shall be examined by the clergy who know the native languages, and shall not be permitted to sing songs that remind the people of their old idolatrous customs; they shall sing nothing that savours of heathenism or that offends against sound doctrine.[34]

Such regulations give hints as to what it was about native music makers that concerned the church hierarchy.

An even plainer view of the situation may be found in a letter of Emperor Philip II to New Spain's religious leaders in 1561. He set down in no uncertain terms the nature of the problem and its ill effects:

> Because of the cost of maintaining the present excessive number of in-strumentalists who consume their time playing trumpets, clarions, chi-rimias [a double-reed wind instrument] . . . and other kinds of instru-ments, an inordinate variety of which are now in use in the monasteries, . . . and because the number of musicians and singers is reported to be increasing constantly in both large and small towns, . . . and because very many of those reared to sing and play on instruments soon become lazy scoundrels whose morals are reported to be extremely bad, . . . and be-cause in many places they do not pay tribute and resist lawful authority, we require a reduction in the number of Indians who shall be permitted to occupy themselves as musicians.

Apparently no quick fix was in order, for in 1565 the second Mexican church council asked the emperor for further help in abating the num-ber of Indian musicians.[35]

Why were so many Nahuas and other Mexican Indians attracted to a life of church music making in the postconquest era? One explanation offered at the time claimed that it had to do with continuing preconquest patterns. Bishop Sebastián Ramírez de Fuenleal argued that natives were accustomed to according special social status to musicians within their communities and perpetuated that custom under Spanish rule. That status, combined with at least occasional exemption from Spanish taxation (another parallel to earlier Nahua practice), gave singers and players social and economic privileges few other Indians enjoyed.[36]

Fuenleal might have also pointed out that for some natives, those privileges represented a significant step up. Particularly after mid-century, more and more musicians came from common families eager to experi-ence some social mobility.[37] Furthermore, the hours Indians spent in musical instruction, practice, and performance for the church were hours not spent in other forms of labor (sometimes for the church), few if any of which held much appeal. However demanding and harsh Spanish and Nahua choirmasters may have been (corporal punishment was almost certainly employed by some), it is unlikely they made the task of learning music (and the Christian doctrine implanted in it) less appealing than tilling soil, tending cattle, building roads and churches, mining silver, or a host of other physically draining jobs.[38] Moreover, the work of making a joyful noise unto the Lord was not so time-consuming. Philip II's com-plaints imply that at least some Indian musicians had plenty of leisure time, enough to act in un-Catholic ways with local women.

Virtuous or not, the participation of men and boys in the church choir or orchestra certainly made them visible within missionized Indian villages, and all the more so in places where they got to wear elaborate robes. While it would be stretching the point to claim a celebrity status for these musicians, it certainly can be said that they received more attention than their peers, and not just from women. Friars typically spent at least several hours every week in the company of their singers and players, instructing, practicing, performing, and worshiping together. A description of the services sung by Indian choristers in Augustinian communities hints at the close and frequent contact among them: "Every morning the cantors sang the *Te Deum* and the Hours of the service of the Holy Virgin. In the afternoon they sang vespers and complines in the same service, except on feast days, when they sang the first vespers of the solemn ceremony. Every Friday after vespers and complines they sang the *Benedicta*, and on Saturdays the salute to the Holy Sacrament."[39] Church music making gave native performers greater access to the (new) leading religious authority figures in their towns and hamlets, the friars. Probably more than Indians enlisted to aid missionaries in other ways (church janitors, decorators, gardeners), musicians caught the eyes and ears of those powerful enough to change their lives, and not just when they were singing their notes or playing their tunes. They were entrusted with key parish responsibilities that enhanced their value in the minds of their priestly overseers and their peers.

Social prominence, upward mobility, less taxing work (both economically and physically), more free time, higher responsibilities, and greater access to the community's power elite may have been reasons enough to motivate and explain the flood of native church musicians in New Spain by the mid-sixteenth century.[40] But cultural and religious factors should also be considered. As noted earlier, for Mexico's indigenous peoples, the opportunity to perform music for a spiritual ceremony allowed for some semblance of continuity with the past in a world otherwise turned upside down. Those who had been temple singers prior to the conquest likely welcomed the chance to continue their work, even if for a different religious hierarchy. Aspects of what the friars wanted from their church musicians accorded with Nahua custom, including accompanying priests in elaborate processions and following a regular pattern of daily prayer and penance (canonical hours).[41] Native families from the 1520s on may have encouraged sons to seek such roles for the sake of maintaining a link to ancient religious practices. Since for the Nahuas religion was likely as much a matter of practice as belief, there was much to be said for carrying on the tradition of approaching the divine in song, even if the texts, tones, and rhythms of Spanish sacred music were markedly different from their own.[42] And at times, what Indian musicians played or sang was not alien to their musical past. During the early decades of Spanish rule, Nahuas may have sometimes been allowed to use native instruments in Catholic rites. As they marched in church processions, for example, natives likely played their own drums and bells, adding to the festive character of such occasions. As time went on, some within the church hierarchy hoped to exert more control over the sounds of worship, including placing limits on sounds introduced by the Spanish themselves. Hence, by the 1550s, some ecclesiastical officials attempted to curtail if not eliminate trumpets, *chirimias,* and *vihuelas de arco* (a guitar-like instrument played with a bow), all European instruments, from use in churches and replace them with organs "so that the noise and clamor of the other instruments may cease."[43] Meeting at the first Mexican synod, they sought to limit such free expression, worried that it strayed too far from what Europeans in the Old World considered liturgically acceptable. But its efforts went for naught, as church orchestras using a wide range of European instruments continued to perform through the rest of the century, even in the archbishop's own cathedral in Mexico City.[44] Furthermore, friars from early on encouraged the development of a Nahua Christian hymnody. Set to familiar native tunes and rhythms, and likely accompanied by native instruments, the Nahuatl poetry that resulted celebrated traditional Christian events or themes but also incorporated "images and stylistic conventions in use before the conquest—flowers, butterflies, *quetzal* feathers."[45] Such compositions lent a native flavor to some of Mexico's sixteenth-century sacred music and, as will be shown below, proved capable of conveying multiple layers of religious meaning.[46]

At some level, pure aesthetic pleasure may have also kept natives singing and playing, before and after the council's regulatory actions. According to one caustic Spanish source, the Indians "liked Mass best when it was an instrumental concert as well."[47] The Nahuas had not conceived of music as art prior to the Europeans' arrival. Under the tutelage of men such as Fray Pedro de Gante, however, elite natives were exposed to examples of the best European art-music of the time and likely gained an appreciation for the music itself apart from its connections to particular religious or cultural contexts.[48] Such a development would not be terribly surprising among peoples who placed such a high premium on musical preparation and performance. Sixteenth-century missionary sources repeatedly reported on what they took to be the delight of natives in producing and consuming church music, whether in regular services, processions, or plays. The friars hoped, of course, that the neophytes in their choirs and orchestras would find spiritual joy alongside aesthetic satisfaction in what they performed. No doubt some did. How many is hard to tell. More certain is the fact that Mexico's Indians simply liked to make music. If Spanish conquest meant doing so under the auspices of the Catholic Church, many natives were prepared to say "so be it."

That was true even when the economics of church musicianship turned against them. As mentioned above, cantors and instrumentalists were at times exempted from the tribute payments other Indians had to make to the Spanish crown. That privilege was never entirely secure, and it came under increasing attack from state officials, especially when the numbers of musicians grew far beyond what those officials deemed necessary.[49] In 1561, Philip II insisted that native singers and players pay the tax alongside their peers. Reducing the number of musicians and getting the remnant to share the tax burden became twin policies of colonial administrators. Mexican bishops sympathized with that agenda but also recognized the economic conundrum facing Indian music makers. The latter's wages were so low that a year's income would barely cover the cost of the tax. As the bishops told Philip in 1565, "the small payment they [Indian musicians] now receive almost always is insufficient for them even to eat, much less pay tribute." Moreover, even with the tax exemption, most native musicians had found it necessary to supplement their income through other forms of work, and in the process, devote much less time to their churchly role. The bishops' recommended solution was to curb the number of musicians so that each one could be paid a salary adequate to eliminate the need for a second job. Concentrating available funds into the hands of a more select group of natives who could conscientiously perform their tasks as church singers and players was not a wholly new idea. A generation earlier, before the glut of musicians had arisen, Bishop Zumárraga made a case to Emperor Charles V that choir members be paid a royal stipend that would free them from other work and allow them to gain the requisite expertise "so that the Masses may be celebrated with befitting solemnity." Fray Alonso de Paraleja echoed that sentiment in 1569 from Guadalajara. He wanted the state in Spain to pay church musicians a stipend of ten pesos annually. Such an act, he promised, "would be accounted a deed glorious in the sight of God, and would enhance our work with those who still remain heathen."[50]

Indian musicians would have undoubtedly welcomed better pay, something perhaps more on a par with what Spanish and creole singers were earning in Mexico City. One sample of native singers found them being paid an annual salary (two pesos) equal to only one percent of what those European and Euro-American musicians received. Efforts to get state officials to improve their lot were usually fruitless. Certainly that was the case in 1576 when a group of Indian singers petitioned Viceroy Martín Enríquez to be excused from paying the tribute. Enríquez sharply denied their request and told them that all Indians had to pay the tax regardless of their low wages or service to the church.[51]

Despite such hardships, Indian peoples in Mexico remained eager to fill the ranks of church choirs and orchestras. The large numbers of native musicians cited earlier are thought to have been active in the 1570s, after the tax exemption had been revoked, and in the midst of plagues that substantially reduced the overall native population. Neither that policy nor imperial pronouncements demanding a cutback in the number of Indian singers and players netted that result. Gabriel Saldívar's study of 123 Mexican towns found an average of 11.2 native church musicians per community. Considering the fact that many of those places numbered in the hundreds, not thousands, of people, it seems clear that plenty of Indians across this colonial territory wanted to sing and play for the church.[52]

A SPLENDID WORSHIP

It also seems clear that their churches wanted and needed them. For everything that has been said so far regarding the pluses that attracted them and the hardships they were willing to endure, Indian musicians would never have been so plentiful or so prominent if friars had not wanted or at least been willing to have it that way. It is important to recognize that the regulatory efforts of emperors and councils to limit the numbers and instrumentation of Indian musicians described above were comparatively peripheral to the experience of most parishes in central Mexico. The main story of the Spanish encounter with neophyte music makers in the sixteenth century involved friars and, secondarily, settlers, not rulers and bishops. As regular clergy took up residence in Nahua territory, so too did Spanish traders, farmers, and officials.[53] Understanding something more about those clerical and lay Europeans' day-to-day efforts to carve out a satisfying life, including a religious life, for themselves, as well as those they came to live beside (the latter was a concern of at least the friars), will help explain further why music was such a crucial part of what Nahua and Spanish shared and exchanged.

Like most immigrants, those Europeans who came to New Spain in the sixteenth century brought along or hoped to reproduce elements of the world they had left behind, including their religious world. The account provided earlier of Cortés's hasty efforts to create the right setting in which to perform the Mass, minimalist though they were, reflects an important aspect of what the newcomers carried with them— a religious sensibility concerned with form as well as content. Both before and during the Catholic Reformation in the sixteenth century, Spanish believers experienced an intensified religiosity that manifested itself in a wide variety of ways, including a desire "to establish firmly the sense of the sacred, not only in services and sacraments but in the physical environment of churches themselves."[54] The place of worship was to be hallowed. All its sights, sounds, smells, and actions were to reflect the presence of the divine and aid the worshipper in her spiritual devotion.[55] While similar desires drove Christians elsewhere to make their churches more austere, in Spain the impulse usually went in the opposite direction. Worship spaces and the services performed in them became increasingly "vivid and dramatic." Churches were adorned from head to foot, so to speak, and an air of pageantry sometimes accompanied the celebration of the liturgy and other religious feasts. Elaborately dressed priests and altars joined with choirs, incense, paintings, and dozens of other religious ornaments to create an aesthetically rich and often spiritually satisfying worship experience. Increasingly popular church processions allowed common folk to carry the church's splendor and their own spiritual devotion out into the streets.[56]

While Cortés's aide, Fray Olmedo, could hardly have reproduced all of that in his first few days in Mexico, his long line of spiritual successors there certainly tried. Missionary priests and church officials set out to bring to New Spain as much as possible of the *material* of Spanish Catholicism, as well as its spirit. The result was dozens of sumptuously decorated (inside and out) churches and monasteries. The Augustinians seemed particularly fond of large-scale construction and ostentatious decor.[57] One Augustinian friar reported to Philip II that their "churches are adorned with bells, statues, and retables [giant screens], and have [musical] instruments and organs in the choir. The sacristies are filled with jewels, silver, and ornaments; they are clean and well cared for, offered and consecrated to the King of Heaven, to honor Him in divine worship."[58] Bishop Zumárraga hoped that his New World cathedral "in every detail of appearance and appointment would equal that of the parent church at Seville." To that end, Zumárraga devoted four years worth of diocesan income.[59] According to French historian Robert Ricard, a typical Sunday Mass in sixteenth-century New Spain saw the church and altar "brilliantly illuminated, and . . . decorated with all possible ornaments: tapestries, green boughs, gladioli, iris, and mint, with which the floor was covered also."[60] Such was the splendor of some, though certainly not all, of Mexico's new places of worship.

Why were members of mendicant orders so eager to build churches and convents whose look and feel seemingly stood at odds with their own vows of poverty? Was it simply a matter of spiritual pride and oneupsmanship among competing religious orders? Did Indian villages seek to outdo one another in the grandeur of their churches, in a manner reminiscent of medieval European towns building taller and taller spires?[61] While all of those factors may have played some role, the friars themselves claimed that the luxurious decorations were warranted because such accoutrements were an effective tool of evangelism. They helped establish a sense of the sacred and were awe inspiring. "Ornamentation and pomp in the churches," wrote one missionary, "are very necessary to uplift the souls of the Indians and bring them to the things of God, for by nature they are indifferent to internal things and forgetful of them, so they must be helped by means of external appearances."[62] Vivid images in murals and religious paintings, along with lavish material objects, so the argument went, captured natives' attention and gave padres a chance to work on their souls.[63] Such alternative teaching tools were especially important while friars were still learning native languages.[64]

For much the same reason, priests wanted to match the beauty of their buildings with sumptuous services. In their view, whatever could be done to enhance the solemn pomp of religious ceremonies ought to be employed. Most of them came from a Spain where, in the first half of the sixteenth century, lay attendance at Mass was irregular and lay behavior at Mass was often unruly. They certainly did not want those patterns to be duplicated in New Spain.[65] The challenge, then, was to attract natives to religious services and teach them appropriate church manners. Very quickly friars recognized that Nahuas, like lay worshippers in Spain, were accustomed to elaborate feasts and ceremonies. While at one level the prospect of catering to this taste disturbed friars (would natives remain or become as doctrinally ignorant as most Catholics in Spain?), at another level they rapidly accepted the notion that to interest the natives, especially in the early stages of evangelization, they would have to put on a better spiritual spectacle lest the new faith pale in comparison to the old.[66] Their long-term hope was that Indians would eventually come to find Christian joy and beauty in Catholic worship. In the meantime, though, they needed to do something to capture Nahua attention. They also hoped to deter natives from maintaining or resuming ceremonial practices the newcomers deemed idolatrous. To that end, then, Spanish friars willingly gave Christianity in sixteenth-century Mexico a celebratory quality. Services, processions, plays, and feast days let Indians witness and participate in the splendor of the church and her god.[67]

That splendor was never more magnificently put on display than in

1559, when New Spain paid tribute to the memory of Charles V. A contemporary account written by Francisco Cervantes de Salazar, a professor at the recently established University of Mexico, provides vivid detail of the event. The ceremony began with a mammoth procession which made its way solemnly from the viceregal palace to the Church of San José in Mexico City. At the front were some two thousand Indians, including more than two hundred caciques. They were followed by the Spanish archbishop and a host of other church officials and clergy. At the church a throng of some forty thousand onlookers met the procession. Finally inside (the procession lasted two hours), Indians and Europeans took their places and the service commenced:

> The cathedral choirmaster began by directing one of his choirs (his singers were divided into two antiphonal choirs) in the singing of the invitatory, *Circumdederunt me,* by Cristobal de Morales [a leading Spanish composer of church music]; and then the other in the singing of the psalm, *Exultemus,* also by Morales. Both settings by Morales are polyphonic throughout, and the choirs sang them with utmost sweetness.

Next came a series of antiphons and psalms sung by combinations of eight cope-bearers, the antiphonal choirs, a chorus of friars and clergy, and a boy choir. The service later included the singing of "Morales's polyphonic setting of *Parce mihi Domine* . . . the beauty of which enthralled everyone." To conclude the ceremony, "the cope-bearers began the psalm, *De profundis,* during which the clergy and friars prepared to form the recessional. At the conclusion of *De profundis,* the singing of the response, *Libera me,* aroused the deepest devotion. The response completed, the archbishop . . . and all the choristers . . . joined in the final prayer; the vigil service thus came to an end with profoundest solemnity."[68]

Magnificent services in magnificent churches. The Spanish who came to Mexico in the 1500s were realistic enough to know that such an ideal could be actualized only on rare occasions and in few places. Nevertheless, they expended enormous energies and resources in trying to create places of worship and times of worship that would woo New Spain's native peoples to Christian faith.

A MUSICAL PARTNERSHIP

At least that is what the Spaniards on this side of the Atlantic liked to tell themselves and those on the other side of the ocean about the motives behind their actions. What did not get mentioned much was their desire for sacred spaces and sacred moments that would satisfy their own spiritual yearnings. Priests, soldiers, government officials, and settlers all brought religious preferences and needs with them. Those varied within and between the groups. But all had been shaped principally, if not exclusively, in Old Spain or elsewhere in Europe. Coming to the New World afforded an opportunity to transplant familiar religious ways, although for the reform-minded Franciscans, it was also a chance to leave behind some of late medieval Europe's longstanding religious problems. What took form as the Catholic Church in Mexico in the sixteenth century, then, was not solely a product of missionary strategy. It was the result of immigrant Europeans' wanting their own souls fed in ways that had become for them not only customary but normative.[69]

At a practical level, reproducing aspects of their Old World religious culture was certainly easier said than done, whether at the Church of San José or at remote *visitas*. To have any hope of achieving it across New Spain in general required the cooperation and participation of thousands of Nahuas and other native peoples. The Spanish could certainly not have pulled it off on their own, starting with the construction of places of worship. Recent studies of central Mexico demonstrate that the Nahuas, like indigenous Catholic converts elsewhere, often built their own churches and sometimes even financed them.[70] For example, Nahua aristocrats Don Juan Iñica Actopán and Don Pedro Izcuicuitlapico covered the costs of constructing the massive Augustinian convent of San Nicolás in Actopán.[71] At one level, such indigenous contributions might be explained away as mere products of Spanish pressure. After all, Indians were sometimes "assigned" to build churches, and in 1563 Spain passed legislation requiring that natives in all of its colonial possessions pay one-third of the cost of any new churches constructed. Given their limited resources, that payment almost always came in the form of labor.[72] But a growing number of scholars, including Serge Gruzinski and Gauvin Bailey, believe that something more was going on here, something more akin to a partnership between friars and Indians. As Gruzinski puts it, "the composite architectural style, with its ever-increasing juxtapositions of romanesque, gothic, moorish and plateresque elements, was the fruit of the shared labor of monks and Indians."[73] That partnership may very well have extended to how churches were adorned inside. Although this is still a matter of debate among art historians, some are persuaded that there were sixteenth-century Mexican church interiors where European and indigenous styles blended or coexisted.[74]

Some kind of partnership certainly occurred when it came to the church's music. Of all the elements of sixteenth-century Spanish Catholic worship that the European newcomers wished to transfer, music may have been the most difficult, or at least the one with which friars needed the most help. Getting churches built required much native labor, but once the church was completed, priests did not have to rely on most of those workers again. Equipping churches inside with the right accoutrements and decorations usually meant gradually importing large numbers of European-made religious objects. Even when native artists were allowed to make contributions, their work was episodic.[75] Not so with Nahua church musicians. What friars and their parishes needed out of them was continuous service, for without them, the sound of Catholic worship in New Spain would have been, figuratively speaking, barely audible, and a radical departure from European worship. With virtually all parishes manned by either a single friar or a handful of them, and with friars often out itinerating, services without Indian choirs and orchestras would have been typically limited musically to plainsong chanted by a solo voice.[76] That voice, however good, could not begin to match the richness and diversity of musical expression that some Spanish Catholics were accustomed to hearing when they went to church. If the Mass in Mexico was going to sound anything like what it had at home, friars would have to recruit, train, and maintain groups of Indian singers and players.

That, of course, is precisely what they set about doing. And with good results from their point of view. Before long, as was noted above, Nahuas were singing a wide range of Spanish sacred music and accompanying it on European instruments. The singing of the Daily Office, Sunday masses, feast day services, processions, religious plays—all these occasions and more saw Indians producing the sounds of worship that friars and other Europeans wanted to hear. Without Nahua participation, that would have been possible in only a few times and places in sixteenth-century New Spain. But with their musical help, it became the case that Catholic worship in colonial Mexico took on more, not less, of a familiar Spanish feel.[77]

That reality was no mean accomplishment, nor was it an inevitable byproduct of the Spanish presence in central Mexico. Instead, it was a consequence of, on the one hand, the friars' recognition that to win Nahuas over to their spiritual agenda, or at least to gain a modicum of native cooperation, required negotiation, compromise, accommodation, and concession, and on the other hand, Nahua willingness to play along literally and figuratively. The result was a musical partnership struck up at the initiation of the friars but entered into by European and native peoples out of their own motives and for their own purposes.

To make that partnership work, that is, to get Indians to perform the sacred music the Spanish wanted to hear for the sake of everyone's souls, they had to offer natives some meaningful rewards. Some of what the Spanish offered came in the form of the political and economic benefits already discussed. Within most parishes, choir members functioned as part of local Christian native elites charged with overseeing church and community activities. They were typically given positions on parish and town councils, where their responsibilities included getting other natives to attend and participate in Mass and serving as the eyes and ears of the priests among their peers, especially when friars were away.[78] Certain economic advantages, such as elevated social status and tax breaks, came alongside this partnership of political and ecclesiastical authority. It is noteworthy that most friars do not seem to have agreed with state and episcopal commands in the mid-sixteenth century to reel in or eliminate some of those tangible benefits. On the contrary, when tribute payments were insisted upon, Franciscans applauded the practice of *doctrinas'* having two choirs and two orchestras so that the groups could alternate weekly, thereby freeing up participating natives to work at other jobs to earn enough to pay their taxes. The friars went so far as to say that "it would be cruel for us to allow them [Indian musicians] to serve continuously in church, doing nothing but singing. They are all so long-suffering that we feel conscience-stricken not to give them any financial aid."[79]

Friars took a mixed view of attempted crackdowns on what may be considered another type of concession, allowing Nahuas to sing and play and dance as they wished. That much music making of purely native design went on without Spanish knowledge is highly likely.[80] But how much native musical license friars actually encouraged, tolerated, or ignored is difficult to say. In retrospect, any amount seems likely to have done more to draw Nahuas into, rather than push them away from, the Catholic fold. At the time, however, knowing where to draw the line on how far to accommodate indigenous musical styles and ideas was no simple task. What should be permitted within religious services? What types of actions should be allowed within church buildings or church courtyards? What limits, if any, should be set on native music within the community as a whole? Such questions vexed Catholic clergy throughout the sixteenth century and beyond. No uniform position or policy emerged in the 1500s. Certainly most friars worried about religious activities maintaining a proper amount of solemnity. To that end, they tried to keep Indian dancers from performing as part of Christian rites or made sure that religious plays "safely encased indigenous processions and dances within orthodox Christian parables and narratives."[81] An ecclesiastical order of 1539 implies that some wanted to go much further in restricting Indian music. It suggested that the lyrics of all native songs be scrutinized and native singing and dancing be limited to certain times of the day when it would not interfere with their attendance at worship services.[82] But that pronouncement is hardly the whole story, for there is evidence that state and church officials took an interest in and even a liking to some native performances. In fact, local friars' efforts to exercise occasional control over indigenous music seem to have occurred alongside a more general endorsement of Nahua singing and playing and appear timid in comparison with the more thoroughgoing restrictions legislated by church councils and the Spanish crown. Those higher bodies' *repeated* attempts from the 1550s on to limit or prohibit the use of certain instruments in worship services and the occasions when Indians would be allowed to dance indicate that Nahuas were in no hurry to comply.[83]

How to respond to native impulses and preferences in the context of carrying out their mission drew friars into what proved to be a challenging and risky game of give and take with Indians over music. That was most dramatically illustrated perhaps by the complicated interplay of native and Spanish wills and wits over another persistent European fear—Nahua inclusion of non-Christian elements in sacred song texts. By the time Dominican Diego Durán repeatedly warned his fellow missionaries in New Spain in the 1580s "against allowing idolatrous intrusions into Christian festivals, songs, and dances," friars and Indians had long been addressing the issue, sometimes together, sometimes apart.[84] The problem arose in the wake of efforts to allow Mexico's Indians to sing their new faith in their old languages. Rather than teaching only Latin texts or forcing natives to learn Spanish rapidly, friars were often eager and willing, as indicated earlier, to have Nahua converts singing new Christian lyrics to familiar native tunes. They no doubt hoped that this would speed the neophytes' embrace of Catholic doctrine. To that end, Franciscan Pedro de Gante, as early as the 1520s, began to compose Christian texts for native songs. He was followed in that activity not only by other friars but by Nahua converts themselves, who were writing hymns for use in worship services by the 1530s.[85]

While such compositions likely facilitated the neophytes' sense of ownership of the new religion, the songs were by no means an unmitigated blessing from the standpoint of effective Christian evangelism. The problem lay in the art of translation, for whether done principally by friars or natives, it was always approximate and ripe for miscommunication. As in their preaching and teaching, friars composed hymns that sought to communicate Christian truths through employing terms already familiar to natives. They borrowed Nahuatl words and concepts that ideally allowed for accurate correspondences between Christian themes and native understandings. But given the wide differences in Indian and European cosmologies, that approach was bound to create a fair amount of ideological confusion and to allow for, purposefully or not, holdovers or reinsertions of traditional native belief.[86] While the friars understood that vernacularizing Christianity was a key to their missionary efforts, they also had persistent doubts about the consequences of allowing native agency.[87]

When the Spanish became aware of suspect texts, their principal impulse was to substitute new words or whole new compositions for those deemed inappropriate. Yet revision itself was still no guarantee that natives would receive the Europeans' intended message. Take, for example, Fray Bernardino de Sahagún's hymn collection, *Psalmodia Christiana*, published in 1583 but composed between 1551 and 1566. It constituted the most thoroughgoing missionary effort of the century to produce a native Christian hymnody. Its Nahuatl hymn texts focused on major biblical themes and lives of Christian saints. If predictable in that way, Sahagún's collection is less so in other ways, according to an analysis by John Bierhorst. He asserts that the *Psalmodia* was influenced by, and in turn influenced, a group of ninety-one native compositions now known as the *Cantares mexicanos*. The latter were mostly postconquest songs whose texts and meanings evolved dynamically in the same decades Sahagún was working on the *Psalmodia*. While Sahagún worried about the pagan character of some of the *cantares*, he was still willing to borrow some of their native vocabulary, poetic form, and even metaphorical imagery for his own hymns. Sahagún almost certainly did not realize how tricky this was, especially if Bierhorst is right in arguing that the *Cantares mexicanos* are best understood as "ghost songs," a traditional Aztec form in which "warrior-singers summon the ghosts of ancestors in order to swell their ranks and overwhelm their enemies." In the context of the mid-sixteenth century, their veiled message, "hidden from missionaries and even from younger, acculturated Aztecs," went something like this: "waves of incoming Mexican revenants . . . will establish a paradise on earth in which Mexicans, while embracing Christianity, will enjoy superiority over Spanish colonists or at least rise to equal status." Bierhorst notes that many of the *Cantares* employed Christian language and allusions, helping them to offset some of the lingering clerical suspicion. But close textual analysis reveals that even those seemingly "safe" stories were reframed into a native cosmology by Nahua composers.[88]

The *Cantares mexicanos* demonstrate native ingenuity and resilience, and make clear that Nahua music, stylistically and thematically, continued after the conquest, albeit in a transformed mode. Creative Indian musicians ensured, as another scholar has written, that "the hymns accompanying the celebrations of the young church simultaneously evoked the memory of ancestors, the valor of warriors, and the pre-Columbian paradise as well as the new Christian deities, the saints, the Virgin, and the Holy Ghost."[89] Anthropologist Louise Burkhart's recent translation and study of a late sixteenth-century Nahua religious play gives further evidence that natives could put their own stamp and their own spin for their own purposes on the Christian stories they sang and dramatized. She asserts that in this case, the native interpreter made subtle but important changes in a play originally authored by Spaniard Ausías Izquierdo Zebrero. The Nahua drama's "alterations and elaborations, by revealing what the Nahua author accepted and what he saw as inadequate or inappropriate for his purposes, constitute a cultural critique of the Spanish model, and through it of Spanish culture and Christianity more generally."[90]

Were the Spanish friars too naïve or too patronizing in their views of Indian abilities to recognize and curtail such native license? Perhaps, but if it has taken till very recently for historians to unveil Nahua designs, sixteenth-century clergy can hardly be faulted too much for missing them. Frankly, the instincts of Sahagún, Durán, and other friars that something more was going on in native hymns and performances than met the eye or the ear was on target.[91] To their credit, more of them in the first half-century of New Spain, beginning with Pedro de Gante himself, were inclined to try to channel rather than throttle their charges' musical impulses. Confident that their evangelistic work was a critical element in the outworking of God's millennial plan and that all would be well, the first generation or two of mendicants in Mexico were inclined to give natives the benefit of the doubt and to make allowances for what other Spaniards deemed native excesses.[92] While it is too exuberant to claim that "instead of controlling the flood [of excesses], the missionaries joyfully let it run," it can be argued that de Gante and others caught on to how vital a role song and dance played for natives in communicating their deepest values and beliefs.[93] Such a crucial form of cultural expression could not be ignored or suppressed. Instead, through instruction, inclusion, and a process of compositional invention and reinvention, friars attempted to tailor, as best as they could, postconquest Nahuatl music making into an acceptable article of Christian worship.

Moreover, when they observed Indians performing sacred music, friars and other European newcomers typically went the next step and construed Nahua acts positively. Consider, for instance, religious plays such as the one described by Burkhart. For friars and other Nahuatl-speaking non-Nahuas, the principal message of such theater in the sixteenth century was the simple fact that natives were appropriating and disseminating the Christian Gospel. They read Indian performances as a tangible sign that the work of Christianization was going forward.[94] Fray Motolinía said as much in his description of a religious drama staged by the Tlaxcaltecas in the late 1530s. The play depicted the expulsion of Adam and Eve from the Garden of Eden. Its climax came when the humans were escorted into exile by a group of angels. At that moment, according to Motolinía, "they sang together a polyphonic setting of the psalm *Circumdederunt me*. This was so well performed that no one who saw it could keep from weeping bitterly."[95] On that occasion, the tragedy of the Fall was expressed in a song of lamentation sung in a native language; Indian performers depicted biblical characters for an audience who two decades earlier had not heard the name of Christ. Motolinía's tears that day were of both sorrow and joy—sorrow over the human predicament, joy over what he took to be Nahuatl knowledge of their sinful condition.

The same was true more broadly of how friars and other European newcomers read Indian sacred music making in general. Priests gave some form of rudimentary instruction in singing the new faith to almost all the Indians they encountered. In an era when Franciscans and other mendicants wasted little time in administering baptismal water, a neophyte's ability to recite the Pater Noster, the Ave Maria, the Credo, and a few other basic texts gave some kind of proof that Christian truth had taken hold in them.[96] As friars watched that much more select group of Nahuas trained to perform as church choirs and orchestras do their work, on the whole they could not help but be pleased at how the cause of Christ was advancing. Indian singers and players, especially in those moments when they exercised their musical gifts within a divine service, gave Europeans some of the best evidence they could find that their evangelization labors had not been in vain. Nahua musicians, and particularly the cantors, were typically exposed to dozens of musical texts filled with Christian teaching. As they played and sang them, friars responded not only with pride in their own teaching prowess but with spiritual satisfaction at the musical witness being offered. In the absence of developing a native priesthood and in the face of well-founded fears that Indians persisted in their traditional beliefs and practices, friars were all the more reliant on groups such as native church musicians to be an ongoing reminder that Christianization was occurring.

DEPENDENT EUROPEANS

To speak of friar "reliance" on Nahua performers may seem odd in light of the relative distribution of power within the colonial setting. Clearly, the newcomers had the upper hand in most respects. But as with much else during the early stages of Indian-European interaction in North America, a considerable amount of Spanish dependence on indigenous peoples took place amid the musical partnership I have been describing. As we have already seen, friars depended on Nahua musicians to exercise significant if subservient local authority in support of the friars, as well as to help create religious services that were closer to the Spanish Catholic ideal of worship they brought with them. So, too, did native singers and players provide friars with what the Spaniards took to be spiritual success stories. As Nahuas lifted their voices and instruments in spiritual song, they testified, sometimes beautifully, to the presence and the power of the Church within New Spain.

Indian musicians in sixteenth-century Mexico may also be seen as helping to fill the need for fellowship among a class of European men accustomed to living and working in community.[97] As they took up their posts in the New World, most friars went from living within close-knit groups of likeminded brothers with whom they shared almost all in common to serving virtually by themselves amid alien villagers with whom they shared almost nothing in common. What is more, their former lives had been dedicated at least in part to communal performance of the Daily Office. The rhythms and routines of each day had been set by the texts and tones of the sung liturgy. Music was the medium of collective praise and petition; it pervaded the friars' daily existence and indelibly shaped their spirituality. Little wonder, then, that once in New Spain, they worked so hard to train a cadre of native church leaders, and especially church musicians, who could assist them in performing at least some of the liturgies that had been part of their prior spiritual practice. Friars surely wanted Nahuatl cantors to be spiritually transformed and doctrinally instructed by the music they taught them to sing. But friars also needed Nahuatl cantors to be surrogate brothers, singing and playing alongside them as a body for the sake of the parish and the priests. Indian boys and men who did so helped reduce the newcomers' sense of isolation, anxiety, and alienation. Though clearly not equals to the padre in any manner that fellow mendicants had been, native singers and players supplied much needed fellowship for friars whose lives were often solitary. Preparing and performing worship liturgies gave priests and musicians common work that bonded them together at least in those moments. Sharing in the production of sacred sounds, though no doubt fraught with plenty of conflict, tension, and anger, nevertheless afforded friars and natives frequent occasions for constituting a communion that, however different, was still some kind of substitute for what these Europeans had left behind.

The argument for Spanish religious dependence upon Nahua church musicians may be extended one step further. Even when friars knew that their choir and orchestra members were not all living up to Catholic ideals, Spaniard and Indian alike were still capable of being spiritually fed by what those musicians produced—the music. As previously suggested, Indians in comparatively large numbers were attracted to the role of church musician for a variety of reasons, many of which had little to do with the state of their own souls. If they were like most other natives in central Mexico, they picked and chose among all the elements of the new faith, appropriating those aspects that fit their needs best, and melding them onto their existing belief system and patterns of behavior.[98] Sometimes they acted like good Catholics, and sometimes not. Friars were no doubt regularly dismayed by what singers and players did or did not do. Yet when it came to what native musicians contributed to worship services, ultimately it did not matter what their moral or spiritual condition was. What mattered was the music itself. Its efficacy as a source of spiritual inspiration, comfort, edification, instruction, or nourishment depended far less on how holy natives were and far more on the power of music itself to move hearts and minds.

Spanish testimonies from the period make it clear that the music was often capable of doing just that. To return to Salazar's account of the commemorative ceremony for Charles V, he peppered his description with numerous references to the impact of the music on the enormous audience that day. The first two choral anthems began the vigil "with a devotional fervor that elevated the minds of everyone present." Later musical selections contributed to a feeling of "utmost solemnity" and "aroused the deepest devotion." A Mass sung the next day was performed "with such great fervor and pathos that tears involuntarily started in the eyes of those present."[99]

Sacred music nurtured the souls of European newcomers in Mexico. When Franciscans in the colony told a visiting inspector in 1568, "all the beauty of the music lifts their spirits to God and centers their minds on spiritual things," they were referring to the Nahuas.[100] But they could have said the same thing about themselves. In supplying most of the church music that filled New Spain's churches and monasteries in the sixteenth century, Indian musicians gave friars and the other Europeans who heard them a vital part of their spiritual diet. It may not be an exaggeration to suggest that in a way analogous to most priests' reliance on natives to provide their physical food, so they and other Spanish newcomers depended on native singers and players to provide an essential element of their spiritual sustenance.

The musical exchanges from Nahua to Spaniard in central Mexico

illustrate well, then, Stafford Poole's contentions that "the evangelization of New Spain was not just a one-directional matter. The friars
absorbed as well as instructed. The result was a phenomenon in the
sixteenth century that has only been recognized and accepted in the
twentieth: the missionary who is missionized."[101] Another way to put
it, in line with the overall argument of this book, is to say that Indian
sacred music making had an important impact on the religious experience of European newcomers in Mexico. Thanks to native participation, music-filled services, sometimes extremely simple, sometimes in-
credibly elaborate, became customary in New Spain from early on. As
Indians sounded out prayers, hymns, litanies, and anthems, musicians
and music alike left their mark on the souls of those who had come to
save them.[102]

To say as much is to point to the remarkable character of the musical
partnership formed between Nahua and Spanish. Born out of the needs
and wants of people on both sides of the cultural divide, it was multidi-
mensional and multifunctional. At its most pragmatic level, it entailed a
sharing of political power, ecclesiastical clout, and social status. At its
most spiritual, it contributed to the religious nurture and communal
well-being of European and Indian alike. At its most surprising, it proved
capable of articulating and sustaining more than one cosmology. In that
way, the partnership must be seen as having a will of its own, not fully
controllable by newcomer or native. In the end, it both gave an important opportunity for religious and cultural expression and allowed for
both the transplanting of European styles and customs and the continuation of some preconquest Nahua musical traditions. The striking
result was worship services throughout central Mexico in the sixteenth
century that were both more Spanish and more Nahuatl than they
otherwise could have been. Indian singers and players who learned and
performed a full array of imported church music made it possible for
Europeans to hear many of the sounds that they associated with Old
World worship. But these same musicians also sang well in their own
language and continued to play native instruments. As they brought the
distinctive vocal accents of their tongue and the particular musical
blends of their instrumentation into the church, they indigenized the
sounds of worship in New Spain.

A FADING NOTE

The kind of musical partnership that developed among the Spanish and
the Nahuas beginning in the 1520s seems to have lasted in central

Mexico for only five or six decades. Thereafter a number of changes set in that assured its decline.[103] For one thing, the Spanish crown became increasingly intrusive in New Spain's church affairs as early as the 1550s and especially after the *Patronato* was codified in 1573. Philip II and his successors afforded the mendicant orders far less elbow room than they had previously enjoyed.[104] A spirit of restraint was also communicated through the creation of the Holy Office of the Inquisition in the Spanish dominions of the Americas in 1570. For a brief time (1577–81), all works in whatever language, including Sahagún's, that detailed traditional native religious beliefs and practices were banned.[105] The religious orders themselves became less adventuresome theologically and otherwise in the wake of the Council of Trent's (1545–63) effort to homogenize Catholic belief and practice. Also, by the last quarter of the century, secular priests, rather than friars, oversaw more and more parishes.[106] The former simply did not have the same attachments to church music or to church musicians, and seemed content with the mere appearance of Christian faith among their native charges.[107] Many of the secular priests were Mexican-born Spaniards whose families and friends gave them a ready-made network of communal contacts.[108] Although as *criollos* (creoles) they were discriminated against by native-born Spaniards (*penisulares*), they did not need nor were they inclined to rely upon Nahuatl church staff nearly so often or for nearly so much as earlier generations of missionary friars. And even if they had, it would have been increasingly difficult to do so in the wake of disease-induced massive Indian population losses.

For those Indians who remained, the years after 1600 brought more imposed constraints. In the face of ongoing native resistance to Christianity, regular and secular clergy alike resorted to various forms of religious compulsion. Under such circumstances, "partnership" no longer described well the relationship of priests and natives. Negotiation might be said to have continued, but the terms were far different from what earlier Nahuas and friars had worked out. The result, according to most accounts, was a growing discord between the two groups. Whatever harmony they had previously enjoyed went flat.

Even so, members of Spain's mendicant orders remained convinced that music could be a valuable tool in reaching indigenous peoples, so along it went with Franciscans, Jesuits, and others as they carried the gospel into the far corners of colonial Spanish America during the following three centuries. What had happened among the Nahuas in the first half century of Spanish rule came to be looked upon as a model of music's evangelizing and catechizing potential. Fray Antonio de la Ascensión gave eloquent testimony to that point following his trip along the coast of Alta California with Sebastian Vizcaíno in 1602. Impressed by the singing of the Chumash, Ascensión recommended that it would be advisable "to bring from New Spain minstrels, with their instruments and trumpets, that the divine services may be celebrated with solemnity and pomp." The Carmelite priest also thought it would be wise to recruit native musicians:

> Choose from among the Indians some of the brightest, selecting among the young men and boys such as appear the most docile, talented and capable; that they should be taught and instructed in the Christian doctrine and to read the Spanish primers, in order that along with the reading they may learn the Spanish language, and that they may learn to write and sing, and to play all the musical instruments; because a good foundation makes the edifice firm, and according as care is given in this matter to the beginnings, so will the middle parts and the ends be good.[109]

It would take the Spanish almost another two centuries before they returned to Upper California in force. When they did, Fray Antonio's advice still seemed sound. So it was that in Spain's final major colonizing effort in North America, Franciscans in Santa Barbara and the other twenty California missions turned to music, even as their earliest forebears on the continent had, to woo and win native peoples through the sounds of worship. And they, in turn, were changed by Indian singers and players whose voices and instruments continued to penetrate European souls.[110]

2

A Language of Imitation

In February 1629, Governor Matthew Craddock of the New England Company wrote a letter of instructions to John Endecott, leader of the first wave of planters in what soon became the Massachusetts Bay Colony. Craddock reminded Endecott that "the main end of our Plantation" was to "bring the Indians to the knowledge of the Gospel." That end could be more quickly achieved if Endecott kept a "watchful eye over our own people," for their behavior would be the key to winning Indians to Christ. English settlers should "live unblamable and without reproof, and demean themselves justly and courteous towards the Indians, thereby to draw them to affect our persons, and consequently our religion."[1] A second letter two months later from all the company governors in London reiterated the same point. The governors expressed the hope that there might be "such a union" among all those involved in planting the colony "as might draw the heathen by our good example to the embracing of Christ and his Gospel."[2] Craddock and his colleagues apparently believed that if transplanted English Puritans could practice what they preached, Native Americans would be enticed to follow their exemplary lives and accept Christianity.

Like the Spanish in sixteenth-century Mexico, the English who arrived in Massachusetts Bay in the early seventeenth century would eventually employ a variety of means in hopes of attracting local Indians to their faith. Numerous historical studies have examined the Puritan "errand into the wilderness" and have made it clear that drawing the native peoples of southern New England to the gospel in the seventeenth century never was as high a priority nor as easy a process as the colony founders anticipated. However loud actions might speak, the messages received by Native Americans were not always the ones Puritans intended, nor did early Puritan behavior in many cases communicate much besides disdain, antagonism, and hostility toward their native neighbors, especially in the wake of the outbreak of the Pequot War in 1636. The religious encounter in New England as elsewhere was always a subset of the larger story of European-Indian relations. Consequently, something more than being the good example that Craddock prescribed was called for if Puritans were to see any natives come to Christian faith. At the very least, words would also be necessary to convince Indians to change their ways, and not just any words would do the job. Eventually, no one knew that better than John Eliot, the most renowned of the Puritan missionaries to natives. "The *first step* which he [Eliot] judg'd Necessary," according to later Puritan minister Cotton Mather, "was to learn the *Indian* language." Eliot recognized that natives "would never do so much as enquire after the Religion of the strangers now come into their Country, much less would they so far imitate us as to leave off their beastly way of living . . . unless we could first address them in a *Language* of their own."[3] Eliot labored long and hard from the 1640s through the 1680s to master the Massachusett tongue so that he could deliver in word and deed calls for Indians to follow English Christianity and civility. His messages made explicit what Craddock had hoped natives would discover on their own—that the Massachusett should leave the old ways and the old wisdom behind and pattern themselves instead on the biblical models embodied in New England Puritanism.

Massachusett men and women were hardly the only natives told to imitate the Englishmen's ways. Pequots, Narragansetts, Nipmucks, Wampanoags, and all the other Indian peoples with whom Puritans had contact heard the newcomers speak that same message.[4] Simply put, Puritans wanted to re-create Indians in their own image. Whatever else they had in mind in relation to natives, a central part of the Puritan project was an exercise in imitation. They endeavored to have Native Americans not only follow but duplicate their lead in embracing the Christian gospel and living in communities dedicated to biblical principles and English cultural ways. While the Puritan impulse to transform Indians has been repeatedly studied, too little note has been taken of the fact that that desire was rooted in a mindset, and often communicated in a language or vocabulary, rife with the notion of imitation. Even as Puritans sought to pattern their lives after first-century Christianity and described themselves as imitators of "ancient things," so they repeatedly told Indian peoples to remodel their worlds after the Puritans. Interestingly, natives often responded in kind by employing words and deeds rich with "imitative" substance. Whether they heeded the call to convert, merely pretended to, or made clear their contentment with their traditional ways, the Native Americans of southeastern New England spoke back to Englishmen in a similar "language of imitation." The result was a discourse, and especially a religious discourse, between Puritans and Indians in the middle decades of the seventeenth century grounded in a mental framework of imitation and punctuated by the motifs of pattern, model, and example. On the English side, that language originated from Puritan views of themselves; imitation was at the heart of their religious self-identity. It was natural for them to frame their hopes and fears about Indians in a familiar vocabulary. But Native American peoples seem also to have resonated with the idea of imitation as they underwent significant cultural transformations in the wake of the English arrival.

While clearly only one element of a much larger religious discourse, this language of imitation embodied and constructed Puritan aims, assumptions, and anxieties.[5] As they presented their ideas in it to natives and as natives communicated their responses back, often in the same vocabulary, Puritans were refashioned by this language's use. In particular, Puritans' religious identity, their sense of self, was shaped by the ways Native Americans spoke in word and action with them about models, examples, and patterns. Such a claim reinforces Jill Lepore's argument that words were "at the center of the encounter between the Old World and the New, between the European 'self' and the native American 'other.'"[6] It also follows, with an important twist, a line of scholarship that has long suggested that contact with Indians impacted the Puritan self or Puritan selves, as those within the movement assumed many different religious identities across time and space, both in England and across the Atlantic.[7] Building primarily upon Richard Slotkin's *Regeneration through Violence*, a book that insists that Puritans projected their own worst qualities and fears upon Indians and then regenerated their own selves through destroying those native peoples, a broader argument has developed that sees Puritan migrants to the New World as determined not to have their identity changed by their new surroundings. Puritans "worried that conquering the American wilderness and coming into contact with American Indians would alter . . . [their] English culture and their sense of themselves as English people." As they interacted with Native Americans, Puritans "defined themselves in opposition to Indians." What Indians were, they were not. What was deemed Indian savagism thus clarified for Puritans what it meant to be civilized. Meanwhile, Indian defeats, depopulation, and displacement clarified for Puritans what it meant to be divinely chosen. Still, second- and third-generation Puritans had occasions for self-doubt when God used natives (of all people) as the instruments of divine judgment upon them. And plenty of fears could still be aroused among late-seventeenth-century Puritans about being "Indianized." In the end, most Puritans "did not become Indians, but they did become something other than what they, or their ancestors, had been."[8]

That interpretation highlights the oppositional dimensions of Puritans' concepts of, and interactions with, Native Americans. The Puritan bent toward destruction of all things native certainly waxed strong at particular moments, and left its mark upon Puritan identity. But there was another side to the coin, the "imitative" side, on which Puritan desires bent toward reproduction (in a religious/cultural, not biological, sense) rather than extirpation. And if on the one hand the godly wanted, at best, to keep Indians at arms' length, on the other they wanted natives to get close enough to them to copy the Puritans' every righteous move. The language of imitation was a critical vehicle for the expression and working out of that latter impulse. Examining its content and applications, as used by both natives and Englishmen, seems important, then, for opening another window onto how the encounter with New England's indigenous peoples shaped the Puritan self.[9]

IMITATING LANGUAGE AND MODELING PEOPLES

Before speaking to one another of imitation, Indians and Englishmen first had to imitate speech. Initial contacts in the late sixteenth and early seventeenth centuries between coastal natives and English fishermen and traders involved efforts to communicate with signs. Without a common language, Europeans and Indians improvised with gestures in hopes the other would understand their intended meaning. Body language, material gifts, and mimicked sounds were all employed. The case of English merchant John Guy's first encounter with Beothuck Indians is illustrative. When Guy's small trading party in 1612 came upon a temporarily vacated Beothuck village, the English took great care to make sure that the natives knew they had been there, not by stealing anything but by moving all the Indian goods into a different cabin and leaving behind gifts of food and beads. Guy's intent was to win Indian trust, a necessary first step for beginning and carrying on trade relations. His strategy proved effective for before long, two canoes of natives approached the white traders, and through a series of reciprocal flag wavings and shouts, the two sides initiated face-to-face contact. A single Englishman and two Beothuck left their vessels and moved toward one another imitating the gestures of the other. When they met, gifts were immediately exchanged to the delight of all. After another Englishman went ashore, "all fower togeather daunced, laughing, & makeing signes of ioy, & gladnes, sometimes strikeing the breastes of our companie & sometymes theyre owne."[10]

As Stephen Greenblatt has explained, the display and interpretation of signs, the exchange of gifts, and the bartering of goods were all critical modes of communication in these early cross-cultural encounters. They in turn paved the way for the learning of language. Europeans were usually inclined to speed up the process of language acquisition by taking Indians back to Europe, often against their will. There they expected that the natives in childlike fashion would quickly assimilate the Europeans' language through imitation. Linguistically equipped Indians would then be returned to the Americas to serve as interpreters and guides.[11] Something like this happened in the case of Squanto. One of over twenty Indian captives of English sea captain John Hunt, Squanto ended up at the English home of merchant John Slaney where he learned at least a modicum of English. Once back in New England, that language skill allowed him to become an important go-between or negotiator when Pokanoket sachem Massasoit decided that it was a good idea to establish friendly relations with the newly arrived English Pilgrims in 1621.[12]

By the time the much larger Puritan migration occurred in the next decade, some members of each southern New England tribe were conversing well enough with the English (and the Dutch for that matter) to carry on complex diplomatic and trade relationships. Cross-cultural communication expanded apace despite English reluctance to learn much of the Ninnimissinuok's Algonquian languages.[13] Native dialects generally baffled settlers and reinforced European assumptions about the barbarism of native cultures.[14] Nevertheless, sustained exchange with New England's indigenous population convinced many Puritans that though savage, the Indians were educable and capable of both recognizing the superiority of English ways and mimicking them.[15] Whether they would do so automatically (if the English set good examples), as Matthew Craddock had presumed in 1629, or only after instruction, the same facility natives had shown in learning English would likely manifest itself in other ways. William Wood's early account of New England, published in 1634, offered one practical example. He noted the uncanny ability of Narragansett pipe makers to "imitate the English mold so accurately that were it not for matter and color it were hard to distinguish them." Wood expected the region's Indians to learn other "mechanical trades," given their "quick wits, understanding apprehensions, strong memories, . . . [and] quick hand[s] in using of the ax or hatchet." Still, native males would have to overcome their penchant for idleness for either them or the English to benefit. Wood hoped that as Indian men had "learned much subtlety and cunning by bargaining with the English," so "good example and good instructions" from the English might "bring them to a more industrious and provident course of life."[16]

While clearly ethnocentric, Puritan pronouncements about the natives' need to follow English models are understandable from a people whose collective religious identity was bound up in the notion of imitation.[17] Governor John Winthrop's sermon aboard the *Arbella*, "*Model* of Christian Charity" [my emphasis], presumed that they themselves would be the exemplar, at least according to Perry Miller's version of the Puritan errand. Winthrop called them to be a holy commonwealth whose light would shine to all nations, but especially to England. Someday the land and the church that had forsaken them might be stirred by their example to complete the reformation begun a century earlier.[18] They could draw inspiration from places such as Calvin's Geneva, where sixteenth-century Reformed Protestants had made their own attempt to establish a model community. For the Puritan "city on a hill" to flourish, however, they would also need to do their share of imitating. As T. Dwight Bozeman has emphasized, Puritans were strong biblical primitivists committed to the power and exemplary authority of an ancient and first time. The Old and New Testaments laid out precedents for church and society that were now to be restored. Human additions to scriptural patterns, what the Puritans called "inventions," were to be stripped away in the return to biblical simplicity and purity.[19] Competing versions of Christianity as well as other belief systems were similarly disdained as "invented religions." So Roger Williams (admittedly a marginal Puritan himself) thought Indians "having lost the true and living God their Maker" had "created out of the nothing of their owne inventions many false and fained Gods and Creators."[20] Today historians recognize that European (including Puritan) views of Native American religions (and much else) were themselves "inventions."[21] But in the seventeenth century, Puritans saw themselves not as originators or innovators but as imitators of the originals set down in the biblical narrative.

Puritan approaches to scriptural interpretation reinforced their imitative bent. Puritan hermeneutics included an "exemplary" reading of the Bible, alongside literal and typological interpretations of passages, in which exegetes would identify "scriptural examples as 'patterns for imitation.'" As E. Brooks Holifield has explained, Puritans "often read biblical episodes as precedents that permitted or required a course of action." Ministers such as Thomas Shepard were persuaded that even the smallest details of believers' lives might be guided and governed by the principles and patterns embedded in biblical stories.[22]

Whether wishing to be the imitated (as in models of Christian charity) or the imitator, New England Puritans operated within a mindset and language caught up with imitation. That Puritans repeatedly brought that theme into their discourse with Native Americans is therefore not surprising. Before examining that discourse more closely, however, it is worth noting briefly that the Indians of southern New England may have been similarly inclined to speak among themselves and with Englishmen about what patterns they should follow.[23] They were accustomed to conceiving time as "the constant re-enactment of tradition," a sort of perpetual dance in which new waves of dancers continually joined the circle and learned to imitate the steps of those more experienced. This "taken-for-granted character of day-to-day interaction" within Indian communities was becoming far less sure by the 1630s and 1640s, however, as the English presence gradually made it increasingly difficult for natives to count on the dance continuing unabated. Following a smallpox epidemic and amid the Pequot War in 1636–37, for example, Narragansett sachem Miantonimi decided that the best way of protecting his people and their social order was to act more "like an English leader" (and less like his forefathers?) and to place "himself and those associated with him within the English system of rules and government."[24] By 1641, in the face of new circumstances, including English violations of earlier agreements, Miantonimi sought to reverse his earlier act of political imitation and urged the Montauks to unite with them against the English "for so are we all Indians, as the English are, and Say brother to one another, so we must be one as they are, otherwise we shall be all gone shortly, for you know our fathers had plenty of deer and skins, our plains were full of deer, as also our woods, and full of turkies, and our coves full of fish and fowl."[25] Miantonimi's plea for pan-Indian cooperation to rival English unity embodied yet another departure from past Narragansett action. Even more telling though, as anthropologist Kathleen Bragdon has pointed out, was his appeal to the *past*. This appeal reflects a growing tendency among the Ninnimissinuok to view time historically, that is, as a progression of change. Native communities wrestling with the prospect that time as they had understood it would not be endless thus had their own reasons for talking with Puritans about ancient ways.

PURITAN PRESCRIPTIONS

More often than not, when Puritans employed the language of imitation in speaking or writing with or about Indians, they did so in a prescriptive manner. Most typically natives were encouraged, much as lay Puritans were, to follow some good Puritan model. The usual admonition was to heed the righteous example of the local minister. But this style of discourse proved flexible enough for the English to use it to cover a variety of other "imitative" relationships. Sources reveal at least four other prescriptive applications within Puritan-Indian dialogue during the mid-seventeenth century. One involved Puritans upholding themselves as faithful followers of good models in their relations with Indians. Or to put it another way, they presented themselves not only as good models but as model followers of good models. At other times, Puritans placed emphasis on converted Indians as positive examples for newcomers and natives alike to emulate. The lives and deaths of Christian Indians were nothing less than powerful sermons to be heeded by all who heard or read them, including Englishmen back home.[26] Just as readily, however, Puritans warned all Englishmen against the bad models set by unredeemed natives. Colonists needed to guard themselves against the temptation to "go native" and adopt the pagan practices of their Indian neighbors. Conversely, all natives were told not to pattern their lives after one or another of the all too readily available models of native or English wickedness in New England.

Puritan dexterity in communicating through a language of imitation may be seen through sampling each of these prescriptive uses. When it came to being told to emulate Puritan ways, few groups of Native Americans heard the refrain more often than Eliot's band of praying Indians at Natick, Massachusetts. Eliot's outreach to Indians began in the mid-1640s, after a full decade and a half of very few proactive efforts in the colony to Christianize natives, despite the founders' high-sounding intentions. At roughly the same time, Thomas Mayhew, Jr., started a missionary work among the Wampanoags on Martha's Vineyard. Mayhew befriended a Wampanoag named Hiacoomes, and the two proceeded to teach one another their languages, and from there, aspects of their respective faiths. An important breakthrough for Mayhew's mission came in 1645 amid a second recent lethal outbreak of smallpox among the Wampanoags. Strained to the breaking point by the epidemic, "Wampanoags sought out medical attention from Mayhew, who brilliantly, and quite consciously it seems, played the role of Christian powwow the Indians had cast for him." When several of the natives that Mayhew attended to, including the son of a sachem, recovered, the English pastor won a larger hearing for his Christian message. In years to come, Mayhew and some of his successors on the island would continue to show an adaptation to native ways and a tolerance of native traditions not typically associated with Puritans.[27] That is because the more famous John Eliot took a different tack, at least in the early years of his ministry.

In concert with most other Puritans, Eliot believed that if Indians were ever to embrace Christianity, they would first need to be civilized. As he explained it, "That which I first aymed at was to declare & deliver unto them the Law of God, to civilize them, which course the Lord took by *Moses*, to give the Law to that rude company because of transgression . . . to convince, bridle, restrain, and civilize them, and also to humble them."[28] Such a process would require not only native adoption of English cultural ways but also close imitation of certain scriptural models. That dual agenda may help to explain why Eliot pursued the seemingly paradoxical strategy of keeping his Massachusett charges "at a physical distance from the English while also transforming them into as close a resemblance to English people as possible."[29]

To that end, Eliot established Natick as the first of his "praying towns," isolated Native American communities that he hoped and prayed would become bastions of Christian civility. As with later praying towns, Natick's formation reflected Eliot's, and more broadly the Puritans', own strong impulse to imitate biblical patterns. Eliot instructed natives to construct political and ecclesiastical forms explicitly modeled on precedents found in Exodus 18. Convinced that Indian ways were inadequate in both church and state, Eliot implored these Massachusett men and women to refashion their community life along Old Testament lines.[30] Beyond that, the twin goals of Christianization and civilization Puritans set out for the Massachusett required that they imitate English ways in matters of individual faith as well as in their dress, hair length, architecture, farming, and much more.[31] Eliot's latest biographer, Richard Cogley, has concluded that he was most concerned with Indians changing culturally in three main areas: personal grooming, sexual behavior, and settlement patterns. Cogley finds that over the long run, Eliot came to tolerate many traditional native ways within the praying towns.[32] But the pressure to comply with Puritan demands was always strong and confronted Native American converts with fundamental changes in their mental and behavioral universe. For example, moving to Natick and remaining there imposed a significant spatial reorientation to the land upon natives, and strictly enforced observance of the Sabbath restructured natives' relationship to time.[33] How far the Puritans expected Indians to go in copying them is suggested in Charles Cohen's analysis of Massachusett church confessions. Indian neophytes were instructed in the elaborate morphology of conversion that New England Puritans had worked out, another sign of their penchant for models.[34] Despite the fact that Waban, Nishohkou, Ponampan, and other Natick residents made confessions in 1652 that echoed "the cries of contrition standard in Puritan narrations," they were turned down for membership. They failed again in 1654. Only in 1659, when their spiritual narratives resembled those of English saints even more closely, did these converts win acceptance into Eliot's Roxbury congregation and the eventual right to form their own church.[35]

Of course, the rendering of Indian conversion narratives into English by Eliot and other English translators and scribes was itself an exercise in imitation and a lesson in the vicissitudes of intercultural communication. Daniel Richter has perceptively identified many of the challenges involved. Even assuming that Eliot intended to give an accurate record of what the Natick people said, "an Indian-language oral performance that comes down to us only in European words written by European hands remains problematic. Even under the best of circumstances, translation is a tricky art, dependent not only on the linguistic aptitude of the translator but on the ability to make subtle cultural references comprehensible in foreign contexts." Different cultural idioms made the work of translation far from straightforward, and in the case of 1652, Eliot was functioning as both translator and transcriber. Besides slowing down the delivery of Indian confessors that day, his written record then and later had no way of capturing the "tears and laughter . . . [nor] the verbal emphases and body language that convey much of the emotional content of the speakers' messages." When that is combined with the complexities of Puritan theology that natives were suppose to articulate and the subtleties of Puritan rhetorical conventions with which natives were to comply, it is no wonder that Natick confessions did not measure up to Puritan standards on the first and second go-rounds.[36]

In all of this, Eliot seems to have been at least partly aware of the difficulties he faced. So, Hilary Wyss has written, "Eliot was . . . in the disconcerting position of attempting to represent Algonquian language through the systems and structures familiar to Anglo-Americans just as he came to terms with differences that could not be accounted for within those structures."[37] Whatever the linguistic and cross-cultural challenges on his side, though, Eliot sincerely and resolutely believed that native imitation of English, Puritan, and biblical patterns was possible and would serve the best interests of the Massachusett and the kingdom of God. In retrospect, it is also possible to see that his imitative project also sought to confirm his own and his community's religious identity. If Eliot "could turn his converts into a people whose values and choices mirrored his own . . . [natives would become] more understandable to himself," and those converts could serve as powerful evidence of New England's vital role in God's redemptive activity.[38]

With such a goal, Eliot and other Puritan leaders on both sides of the

Atlantic not surprisingly took Ninnimissinuok who embraced Christianity, whether or not church members, and quickly upheld them as model saints. "Sagamore John" was one of the first, celebrated because "he desired to learne and speake our [English] Language, and loved to imitate us in our behaviour and apparrell, and began to hearken after our God and his wayes."[39] Other natives progressed even further in the faith. Early converts of Roger Williams, Thomas Mayhew, Jr., and John Eliot became familiar figures to English readers who followed their spiritual journeys in tracts detailing missionary work in the 1640s and early 1650s. Wequash, Hiacoomes, Waban, and an elderly native referred to simply as "an Old Man," were portrayed as dedicated believers worthy of English imitation.[40] So, too, were Nishohkou and Robin Speen. The deathbed testimonies of their young children provided examples of the fruits of Christian fathering at its best.[41] Massachusetts minister Thomas Shepard "frequently chided his countrymen for being outdone [in piety] by the Christian natives." Stephen Marshall and a group of English Puritan pastors went even further. They admonished their charges to "let these poor *Indians* stand up as *incentives* to us . . . who knows but God *gave* life to *New England,* to quicken Old . . . ?" Model native lives could function in Marshall's words as an *"Indian Sermon"* to inspire or goad on the English to holier actions.[42] And for him and some other English ministers, Christian Indians could "do more than call England to repent and purify itself. They [could] trouble the status of English Puritans as a chosen people and England as a chosen nation" by illustrating the fact that God had moved the scene of his principal activity across the ocean.[43] Back in New England, as early as 1651 Eliot believed that Natick as a whole could serve as something of a city on a hill for other native communities, if not for his homeland. In response to requests from other groups of New England Indians for evangelists, he expressed confidence that "the worke which wee now have in hand [in Natick], will be as a patterne and Copie before them, to imitate in all the Countrey, both in civilizing them in their order, government, Law, and in their Church proceedings and administrations."[44]

Thirty years later Eliot and the Mayhews were still publishing accounts of Indian lives transformed by grace, and of faithful natives "dying in Christ."[45] Eliot's final tract, entitled *Dying Speeches,* recorded the parting words of eight praying Indians. Though more somber than most of his earlier works, it perpetuated the figure of the "dying Indian saint" and countered the contemporary assertion, expressed especially in wartime, that "all Indians were instruments of Satan."[46] Overall, the positive portrayals of Massachusett and Wampanoag men and women in missionary publications belie claims that Puritan views of Native Americans were wholly negative.[47] Individual Indians could be as holy or devilish as anyone else. When Puritans set out to destroy Indian ways, in most cases it was probably less because they were Indian and more because the newcomers perceived them as wrong and displeasing to God.[48] On the other hand, it is clear that when Englishmen extolled the merits of Indian believers for others to follow, it was usually the natives' saintliness and not their Indianness that the English had in mind.[49] Furthermore, in the wake of events such as King Philip's War (Metacom's War) in 1675–76, it became difficult for even pious New Englanders to appreciate any Indians, praying or not. Amid that conflict, it seemed that there were only preying Indians, despite Eliot's claims to the contrary.[50] No wonder second- and third-generation New England Puritans were more inclined to hail the missionaries rather than the natives as exemplars, although even the missionaries came under attack during the war.[51]

During quieter times, the work of the first generation in evangelizing Indians, as with much else that it did, was celebrated as a worthy model to follow.[52] This was only one of a number of ways in which Puritans either encouraged each other to imitate or told themselves they were already imitating biblical models in their relations with Indians. That pattern was set even before any systematic attempts at evangelization. Following the Pequot War of 1636–37, Captain John Underhill legitimated the killing of native women and children amid the conflict by pointing to the biblical example of King David's war against the Geshurites and other enemies of Israel. He and other Puritan chroniclers believed that these "biblical accounts gave divine sanction and precedent to unrestricted warfare."[53] When missionary efforts to the Massachusett did begin, they were likened to the New Testament acts of the apostles in spreading the gospel, whether one considered native peoples as Gentiles or long-lost descendants of the Jews.[54] By the 1650s, Roger Williams was able to appeal to the Puritans' reputation (at least among themselves) for treating Indians well to dissuade colonists from going to war with the Narragansetts.[55] Later Puritans hailed the exemplary lives of redeemed Indian captives such as Mary Rowlandson and Hannah Swarton. Their narrative accounts of physical survival and spiritual salvation amid harrowing circumstances followed in the literary tradition of a representative life, a genre well-suited for a people enamored with imitation. Their experiences became lessons for their neighbors that the same sovereign god who had preserved Daniel and Jonah was still at work in their world.[56]

Puritan fears of being literally carried away by Indians were part of a longstanding, broader concern that contact with natives might "Indianize" them. Here the language of imitation took the form of negative prescriptions against native cultures and any influence they might exert on English newcomers. Colin Calloway has suggested that from the earliest settlement, New England Puritans "worried that . . . their American experience threatened to give colonists a new identity," one they did not want.[57] Jill Lepore goes even further and insists that the "colonists' greatest cultural anxiety . . . was the fear that they were becoming Indianized." Such fear was not entirely unwarranted, for some New Englanders throughout the seventeenth century had incorporated Indian ways into their lifestyles. Lepore suggests that Puritan anxiety was especially acute during the bloody fighting of King Philip's War, when the English worried that their tactics too closely resembled those of their cruel foes. Puritan histories of the war became instruments of reassurance that their own actions had in fact been justified and that they had remained Englishmen throughout the conflict.[58] The words of those narratives added to a long line of Puritan defenses against Indianization, for as Alden Vaughan and Edward Clark have explained, "Puritan society had abundant legal and social structures against imitating or admiring the Indians' 'prophane course of life.' Indian ways were to be shunned, not emulated."[59] When those strictures were not obeyed, the results were disastrous, at least according to Increase Mather. "God is greatly offended," Mather wrote in the 1670s, "with the *Heathenisme* of the English People. How many that although they are *Christians* in name, are no better then *Heathens* in heart, and in Conversation? How many Families that live like *profane Indians* without any *Family prayer*? . . . Now there is no place under heaven where the neglect of *Divine Institutions* will so highly provoke and incense the displeasure of God as in *New-England*, because . . . *Religion is our Interist* and that which our Fathers came into this Land for."[60]

Mather was hardly alone in raising the specter of divine judgment on New England if the right models were not followed. Nor were such warnings addressed only to the English. Indian listeners had plenty of opportunities to hear Puritans telling them to flee from the pagan paths of their fathers, or else. And they were to avoid the "prophane and ignorant" example of the bad sort of Englishmen as well.[61] The sins of immigrants were the last thing faithful Puritans wanted the Ninnimissinuok to mimic.

Native Responses

What did the native peoples of southern New England think of all this Puritan advice offered up in the language of imitation? How did they respond to the Puritan calls to imitate them at a time when their worlds

were undergoing dramatic change? Answering those questions re-
quires us first to ask whether it is possible to find authentic native voices
and perspectives within the Euro-American–generated written sources
of the seventeenth century. In the absence of unmediated Indian materials, is there any hope of recovering what Ninnimissinuok actually
thought and said, or what they intended by their actions? While appropriate skepticism continues to be expressed, recent historians and literary critics of New England have argued that it is possible to detect natives speaking in these texts.[62] For example, within the missionary
tracts and other pamphlets produced by Eliot and fellow supporters of
Indian evangelism, native converts expressed themselves through the
recorded questions they asked, as well as in their conversion narratives,
sermons, dialogues, and dying speeches. All of those various forms of
religious discourse were used by Puritan writers to further their own
purposes. But that did not altogether preclude Native Americans from
speaking their own minds. And when they did, they, too, in one way or
another, could employ the language of imitation. Sprinkled throughout
the discursive forms present within Puritan publications is evidence of
Indians operating from an "imitation" mindset and using the familiar
motifs of pattern, model, and example to express their responses to the
Christian message. In addition, the same motifs appear in certain kinds
of Indian actions that were similarly intended to communicate what
natives thought of the gospel and the English.

Before examining those materials and events, it is worth noting that
Puritan *descriptive* accounts of the one to two thousand Indians who
converted to Christianity between the Puritans' arrival and King Philip's
War also made use of the language of imitation.[63] The first groups of
Massachusetts who came to hear preaching and who were willing to
have their children catechized were quickly held up as a sign "that in all
probabilitie many *Indians* in other places, especially under our jurisdiction, will bee provoked by this example in these" to desire Christian
instruction.[64] Later praying Indians were commended for following
godly English models in Sabbath observance, administration of the sacraments, church discipline, and family prayer.[65] Even more striking are
the cases in which the English noted the Indians' ability to mimic their
oral modes of religious expression. Europeans had long marveled at
how the peoples of the Americas could rapidly imitate new languages.[66]
In seventeenth-century New England, the Massachusett and other Indian groups proved adept at echoing the substance and style of Puritan
religious discourse. In the 1640s, for example, Thomas Shepard reported on how quickly native children learned catechetical answers,
largely because they mimicked the responses given by more experi-

enced catechumens.[67] John Eliot was not disappointed to find that Massachusett preachers and teachers he had earlier evangelized now followed his instruction style in trying to win over fellow natives. "They imitate me," Eliot asserted; the "manner of my teaching them" through inductive questions and answers was borrowed intact.[68] Similarly, as natives became more familiar with Puritan conversion narratives, they "conformed their speech [conversion narratives] to patterns accepted by the missionary [Eliot] and Praying Indian communities."[69]

They also apparently imitated Puritan styles of public prayer. When Governor John Endecott attended a worship service in Natick, he was brought to tears by an Indian prayer despite not understanding most of it. What he admired was the way it had been offered with "such reverence, zeale, good affection, and distinct utterance." Endecott knew a good prayer when he heard one, even if spoken in an incomprehensible tongue.[70] Pastor Richard Mather had a similar experience listening to and watching Natick residents offer spiritual testimonies. Though again understanding little of what they said, Mather and others "heard them perform the duties mentioned, with such grave and sober countenances, with such comely reverence in gesture, and their whol carriage, and with such plenty of tears trickling down the cheeks of some of them, as did argue to us that they spake with much good affection, and holy fear of God, and it much affected our hearts."[71] Lack of comprehension did not keep men such as Endecott and Mather from "using native speech patterns to distinguish a 'good' Indian from a 'bad' one." As Jane Kamensky has noted, "good Indians were good speakers, cherishing rules for right speaking similar to those the English prized. Pliant, generous, polite, respectful—some Indians spoke in ways that confirmed their 'civility,' " and apparently also their Christian faith.[72]

In all those cases southern New England Indians showed that they knew the right forms to use in conversing with Puritans and God, at least from the Puritan perspective. But were natives merely parrots, mimicking back to the English what they wanted to hear in the way they wanted to hear it? Was the Puritan emphasis on imitation producing only mindless puppets or feigned converts? Puritan concerns about "mere" imitators were strong and will be discussed below. For now, though, it is important to note that a scholarly consensus has emerged that some Ninnimissinuok did choose to embrace Christianity, but did so on their terms and tailored their new faith into what best suited their needs. Neal Salisbury has concluded that "on a human landscape utterly transformed by English colonization, some Indians found in Christianity a basis for reordering their lives materially, politically, and spiritually. Rather than entailing a loss of Native cultural identity, Christianity . . .

may have actually served to sustain and reinforce that identity for some Indians." Daniel Richter adds that "Natick Christians were not simply parroting back the judgments of their English missionaries." They instead constructed a Christianity that "laid claim to their Native identity." As Indians had occasions to testify about their Christian spiritual journeys, they put their own thematic stamp on their experiences, themes drawn from native spiritual and moral values such as the importance of maintaining harmonious relationships and the greater significance of action over belief. Daniel Silverman similarly suggests that Wampanoag converts "were not blank pages waiting to be filled by their missionaries with absolute Christian truths. They sought out dissenting opinions and probed the faith's gray areas and contradictions, whether their missionaries liked it or not." Moreover, the natives' "tenacious . . . questioning left missionaries with little choice but to teach . . . [their] doctrines within an Indian framework." That often meant that these Indians, in tandem with Thomas Mayhew, Jr., "filtered Christian teachings through Wampanoag religious ideas and terminology." Together they sought out points of commonality or overlap between the two belief systems, what might even be called places of imitation in the sense of their being analogous claims. From there they built an understanding and practice of Christianity that preserved some elements of traditional Wampanoag belief and culture even while they "embraced many of Christianity's novelties."[73]

Active craftsmen of distinctively Ninnimissinuok brands of Christianity, then, southern New England's Christian Indians partially but by no means completely fulfilled Puritan hopes that they would "adopt European models of living, thinking, and worshipping wholesale."[74] They and their Christianity were by no means mere duplicates of New England Puritanism. Instead, they engaged in what Lamin Sanneh in another context has called "a real indigenous discovery of the gospel."[75] Historically, Christianity has taken hold most firmly among new populations when the Bible and its message have been vernacularized. Colonial New England proved to be no different. As Christianity was translated into the cultural idioms and forms of the Wampanoags, Naticks, and other New England Indians, it became something some of them were willing to own. The rigor with which natives interrogated the new faith is testament to the seriousness with which they undertook this process and is particularly evident in their voluminous inquiries into the meaning of specific biblical passages. The missionary journal of John Cotton, Jr., lists dozens of the questions he was asked during his ministry on Martha's Vineyard in the 1660s and '70s. They show "the profound significance his charges placed on correctly understanding and performing the new rites they were supposed to observe (such as baptism) and the new behavioral code they were expected to follow."[76] In other words, Wampanoags and other Indians thought long and hard about the things and people they were being asked to imitate. Take, for example, two of the earliest recorded questions asked by the Massachusett as mission work began among them in 1646. One was, "Whether English men were ever at any time so ignorant of God and Jesus Christ as themselves?" After some deliberation, the Puritan pastors deduced that what lay behind that query was Indian observation of Englishmen who acted "wickedly and loosely." The ministers tried to clarify that natives needed to follow the example of other Englishmen, those who "know Christ, and love Christ, and pray to Christ." A few weeks later Massachusett listeners asked another question in the same vein: "How come the English to differ so much from the Indians in the knowledge of God and Jesus Christ, seeing they had all at first one father?" Thomas Shepard and the other ministers tried to make a case that the English had descended from sons of Adam who had heeded God's counsel whereas "Indians forefathers were a stubborne and rebellious children, and would not heare the word, did not care to pray nor to teach their children, and hence Indians that now are, do not know God at all." The pastors once again conceded that "many English men did not know God [either] but were like to . . . drunken Indians." All needed to repent. But beyond that, these Puritans were not willing to go in their explanations of why the religious fortunes of English and Indian were so different "because it was too difficult." Greater Puritan facility in "their owne [native] tongue" would be necessary to review biblical history with Indians and have them find their own fathers in it.[77]

Native questions such as these show Massachusett not only trying to sort out the Puritan call to imitation, but framing their inquiries in that mindset and language. What model were they to follow when sinful English behavior clearly complicated and compromised Puritan appeals? If sons and daughters were to use the ways of their fathers as exemplars, as Ninnimissinuok had strongly believed for generations, how could they and the English differ so dramatically in their religious ideas if, as the Puritans claimed, they all had the same earthly father? Had later natives failed to follow the wisdom of their original father? Those southern New England Indians who eventually constructed their own indigenized forms of Christianity did so only by working through these and other conundrums of imitation.

Puritan missionary writings indicate that the English got accustomed to hearing Indians talk back to them about patterns, models, and examples. Sometimes even nonbelieving natives seemed to know of the need to follow the right rhetorical models in talking to or about the Christian god. At least that is how John Eliot depicted one such Algonquian-speaker in his *Indian Dialogues,* a series of fictional conversations based on his long experience of trying to convert the Massachusett and de-signed, among other things, to train native missionaries to evangelize fellow Indians more effectively. Peneovot was spiritually moved by the counsel of Waban, who encouraged him to pray for other natives and for God's work in the world as a whole. "I feel your heart to answer your words like an echo," said Peneovot. But his imitative impulse needed guidance: "I am ignorant of fit words in prayer, and therefore I do request of you, first do you pray, and set me a pattern." After spending the night in prayer together, Waban pointed the new convert beyond any mortal model: "Christ himself hath set us an example, who spent whole nights in prayer."[78]

Eliot's construction of Waban as a model convert and teacher who had learned to imitate the language of imitation logically flowed from Puritan hopes and observations. Eliot made Waban who he wanted him to be. Similar acts of invention took place in representing Indian figures such as Philip, a character based on the Narragansett sachem. In the *Dialogues,* he initially resists Christianity but eventually sees the light.[79] Whatever liberties Eliot took with the end of the story (and within five years of writing this, Eliot did see a very different end—the real Philip went to war with the English), he may have been most historical in recording the kinds of objections Philip and others voiced to the evange-lists' overtures.[80] After all, if Eliot hoped the *Dialogues* could prepare native missionaries well, he would have to portray the verbal ex-changes they could expect to encounter with recalcitrant brethren as realistically as possible. Though fictional, then, those exchanges let us hear reasonably reliable Indian voices, voices that in the *Dialogues* reveal that Indian resistance to Puritan evangelism could be voiced as elo-quently in the language of imitation as any embrace of the new faith had been.[81] Very likely, the Ninnimissinuok derived such language in part from their cultural traditions and needs. But they also might well have appropriated it from listening to Puritan pleas and then turning them on their heads in discontented replies.

Indian opposition in the language of imitation manifests itself in the *Dialogues* in two principal ways.[82] On the one hand, natives responded to Puritan calls that they leave their old "fleshly" ways behind by in essence retorting, "Why should we follow the examples of your fathers rather than our own?" To do so would be an act of intellectual ar-rogance and cultural disobedience. As one Indian "kinsman" explained it, "Our forefathers were (many of them) wise men, and we have wise men now living. They all delight in these our delights. They have taught us nothing about our soul, and God, and heaven, and hell, and joy and torment in the life to come. Are you wiser than our fathers?" Another sachem pointed the finger directly at natives themselves: "As for this new way of praying to God, I like it not. We and our forefathers have through all generations lived in our religion, which I desire not to change. Are we wiser than our forefathers?" To deviate from long-set patterns of belief and practice would "make trouble and disturbance unto us [and disrupt] those old ways in which we and our forefathers have walked." Better for the Indian and Englishmen alike to follow the separate sets of ancient wisdom passed down to them. Or as one native woman put it, "we are well as we are."[83]

Eliot's fictional Indians were not even always sure about how ancient or wise Puritan Christianity in fact was, and they used the language of imitation in a second way to say so. In words that cut to the heart of Puritan identity as biblical imitators, an Indian pointedly asked why he and others could not "think that *English* men have *invented* these stories to amaze us and fear us out of our old customs [my emphasis], and bring us to stand in awe of them, that they might wipe us of our lands, and drive us into corners, to seek new ways of living, and new places too?"[84] To be accused of *inventing* their faith was for Puritans the strongest indictment possible. It was the very weapon they used against Catholics, Baptists, Antinomians, and all other religious opponents. As Dwight Bozeman has put it, in the Puritan "world of discourse, no combatant's thrust could gouge a deeper wound."[85] In a later dialogue, Philip used the same verbal knife: "I pray tell me what book that is? What is written in it? And how do you know that it [the Bible] is the Word of God? Many say that some wise Englishmen have devised and framed it, and tell us that it is God's word, when it is no other than the words of wise men."[86] No wonder Piumbukhou, a Christian Indian, felt compelled to respond to such accusations by insisting, "The Book of God is no *invention* of Englishmen [my emphasis]." He and other native Christian apologists were well trained to defend Puritan views of Scripture and to warn against all those who would "add their own wicked inventions unto the pure and perfect Word of God."[87]

Among those "wicked inventors" were Catholic missionaries. Puritan denunciations of their Jesuit competitors give interesting hints of a third general type of Indian response to Puritan admonitions to imitate them, one that fell between positive embrace and outright opposition. In the *Indian Dialogues,* native evangelists Anthony and William deride "popish teachers and ministers" for on the one hand keeping the Bible from their proselytes, and on the other hand adding to the Scriptures.[88]

What they (and Eliot) feared were shallow "converts" who not only were taught false doctrine but whose Christianity was only a "mere imitation" of the real thing. Puritan leaders throughout the century insisted that in contrast to Catholic methods, they offered Indians the "whole Bible" and a *"Thorough-paced Christianity"*; anything less and they would not have "imagined our Indians *Christianized.*"[89] With pride, they sarcastically remarked that "wee have not learnt as yet that [Catholic] art of coyning Christians, or putting Christs name and Image upon copper mettle."[90]

And yet Puritans clearly worried about how deep the Ninnimissinuok were drinking at the waters of English religion and civility. How many of the natives who appeared to be following the newcomers' ways were merely playing a role rather than internalizing a message? When Matthew Craddock expressed his hope that Indians would "affect" Puritan Christianity and culture, he surely used that word to mean "to be drawn to" or to "have affection or liking for." But was it possible that some natives could "affect" the English in the more negative sense of that word, that is, "to put on a pretence of; to assume a false appearance of, to counterfeit or pretend"?[91] Certainly some New Englanders thought so. Concerns over Christian Indian hypocrisy started early and lasted through the century. Roger Williams worried that if he or other ministers concentrated on teaching Indians to observe church ordinances without their first experiencing a "true turning to God," natives could not help but be like the baneful "million of soules in England" who were brought into the church without "the saving work of Repentance."[92] Williams pointed the finger at himself for the Indians' predicament: "woe be to me if intending to catch men . . . I should pretend conversion and the bringing of men . . . into a *Church-estate,* . . . and so build them up with *Ordinances* as a converted Christian People, and yet afterward still pretend to catch them by an after conversion."[93] Others were more inclined to point the finger at the Indians themselves. Increase Mather rehearsed the story of Squando, "a strange *Enthusiastical Sagamore* . . . who some years before pretended that God appeared to him." After that supposed divine visitation, Squando had left off his evil ways and "with great seeming Devotion and Conscience" practiced the Christian disciplines of prayer, attendance at worship, and Sabbath observance. Recently, however, he had led an attack on the town of Saco, thereby revealing "himself to be no otherwise then a childe of him, that was a Murtherer and a Lyor from the beginning."[94]

Squando's deception had been too subtle for Puritan detection. That was not always true. Sometimes there was no mistaking Indian mimicking for the real thing, as when during King Philip's War a band of warring Nipmucks entered a Congregational church and mockingly "made an hideous noise somewhat resembling singing." They shouted derisively at nearby soldiers to "Come and pray, & sing Psalmes."[95] Such "theater" might have reminded Puritans of the satirical attacks leveled in print and on stage against their forebears in England and in the colonies.[96] That kind of overt deceit could be easily countered, linguistically if not militarily. Far more pernicious were cases such as Squando's, where a believable Christian facade masked political intrigue. Missionaries such as Eliot, the Mayhews, and Daniel Gookin became accustomed to defending the validity of Indian conversions, perhaps to allay their own fears as well as those of others. There were always plenty of nay-sayers "who were suspicious of Indians' motivation for converting, and even well-wishers doubted Indians' ability to understand Christianity fully." Supporters in England especially needed to be repeatedly convinced that natives "were really learning and internalizing God's truths, not simply memorizing and parroting catchphrases in the manner of the hated papists."[97]

Missionaries also got used to dispelling suspicions of the sort Eliot reported in 1653 when the praying Indians were rumored to be "in a conspiracy with others, and with the *Dutch,* to doe mischief to the English." Eliot called the accusations "groundless" but indicated that his own course of action was accordingly more cautious thereafter.[98] Far more serious accusations that all praying Indians were dissemblers in their faith and political loyalties got leveled during King Philip's War. The knowledge that some Christian Nipmucks stood against the English in the war convinced many colonists that no Indian could be trusted, least of all praying ones. Thereafter, Christian Indians and the missionaries who tried to defend them received hostile treatment from both sides in the war.[99]

Puritan anxieties over the authenticity and depth of Indian imitation thus fueled, and were fueled by, a recurrent English belief that Indians of all types were secretly plotting against them. Time and again in seventeenth-century New England, rumors circulated that natives were about to attack. English vulnerability to such rumors and misinformation stemmed in part from their ignorance of native languages and from the difficulty of verifying information. Not understanding what Indians said or fear of misinterpreting their signs left Puritans suspicious. They were inclined to believe the worst, succumbing in the process to the "mere imitations" of the truth embodied in those rumors. Such a fate was ironic for a Puritan people convinced that "right speech" (including truthful speech) was crucial for the godly social order they wished to maintain in New England. Whatever the case, shrewd Indian leaders such as Uncas, a

Mohegan sachem, took advantage by repeatedly spreading stories that his enemies, the Narragansetts, were conspiring with the Mohawks against the English.[100]

That other equally shrewd Indians engaged in religious forms of mere imitation in interacting with the English there is little doubt. The Ninnimissinuok knew their own needs and proved capable of using the words and deeds of "imitation" to suit their own ends, whether in playing a role, constructing a Christianity of their own, or rejecting Puritan models altogether.[101]

Changed Selves

Puritans and Native Americans were equally adept, then, at using what I have called the language of imitation. Whether consoling or cajoling natives, Puritans usually spoke in a prescriptive manner that appealed to good models and bad, to communicate what they wanted Indians to do and who they hoped Indians would be. Their quest was nothing less than to change Indian identity internally and externally. The native responses described above show something of the results of their efforts. In turn, whether confessing or critiquing Puritanism, natives spoke back to the English in ways and words that made equally effective use of "imitation" in one form or another. Their goal was to find the best means to continue as viable communities amid the immense disruptions of the seventeenth century. In the process, whether intending to or not, they, too, affected critical aspects of the religious identity and practice of their conversational partners. Puritan self-understanding was altered by the encounter with Native Americans in a language of imitation.

In identifying the ways in which that happened, it is perhaps first worth noting that the Puritans' very preoccupation with imitation reveals much about their values and view of the self.[102] For the godly, the upholding of models meant that life was to be derivative, not innovative. Direction about those things that mattered most in life had been set out long ago in the Bible. The task before individuals and the whole community was to follow, or more precisely, to recover; little value was placed on the act of discovery. Fidelity to communal testimony or declarations was therefore far more important than individual expression, no matter how creative. How one measured up to community standards was what counted. Puritan introspection consequently entailed regular evaluation of oneself against an external standard, not a self-invented one. And given the perfection of that standard or model, there was little chance that a person or a group could fail to see their inadequacies. By nature, then, the Puritan bent toward imitation produced a discontented self, one routinely brought low by the high examples set out before it. Confession, contrition, and humility were postures the godly were to know well.

Even so, Puritans were entirely capable of self-righteousness and self-congratulation, as their spiritual diaries and relations with Indians attest.[103] By setting themselves up as the religious and cultural model natives were to follow, Puritans were bound to inflate their own sense of superiority. Moreover, in the Puritan mind, no matter how low they needed to be brought, Native Americans needed to be "reduced" that much more.[104] The language of imitation proved immensely useful in conveying that message. More broadly, it allowed Puritans to fit their encounter with Indians into the same "imitative" framework within which they understood themselves. Put simply, Indians were to imitate them as they imitated the "first ways" laid out in Scripture. From the Puritan perspective, what they asked of natives ran parallel to what they asked of themselves. Being able to communicate for several decades with Indians about religion in a language whose central theme was at the core of who Puritans thought they were and what they thought they were doing therefore reinforced Puritan self-perceptions as imitators and the imitated. And whenever Indians appeared to learn their lessons well, those self-perceptions were all the more confirmed.

But the story was a good deal more complicated than that. For one thing, in retrospect, it is clear that what Puritans asked of natives was not what they asked of themselves but instead its precise opposite. Rather than recovering the purity and simplicity of some "primitive" past, the Puritan call to convert to Christianity and English ways typically demanded that the Ninnimissinuok break with their past, be innovative and adaptive, and stand at odds with their traditional community and its standards. For Indians to undergo the kind of thoroughgoing transformation that the Puritans wanted required that they embrace the very values that Puritans usually rejected for themselves. That irony seems to have escaped most colonists, and as a result, it contributed to the misunderstanding and miscommunication that plagued cross-cultural relations so often.

Amid the upheavals of the seventeenth century, some southern New England native people heeded English pleas to convert, but as noted before, they did so on their own terms and not in strict accord with Puritan prescriptions. They found ways of continuing to imitate their native past even while embracing the essentials of Christian faith. Among Puritan missionaries, Thomas Mayhew, Jr., caught on to this reality more quickly than John Eliot, but in the end even he allowed for a number of native adaptations to Puritan Christianity. Doing so meant abandoning or at least compromising the sweeping project in imitation with which Eliot in particular had begun. Long-term interaction with natives showed just how hard it was for one people to mimic another, even among fellow believers. Such a conclusion surely sobered Puritan primitivists in their own hopes of duplicating the New Testament church. On the other hand, Puritans supportive of Indian missions clearly took heart from whatever were deemed genuine signs of transformation within Indian hearts. Where a native life or words mirrored the grace-filled Puritan, colonists found striking evidence of God's activity in New England. Such Christian Indians, as noted earlier, were held up as models to Englishmen everywhere and, according to Kristina Bross, "helped shape the belief, at a time of spiritual, economic, and political crisis in the colonies [1640s–'60s], that New England had a place and purpose in God's plan that was special to itself but intimately connected with events in Old England."[105] Puritans' sense of chosenness, a critical aspect of their identity, waxed and waned in the seventeenth century for a wide variety of reasons, but among them was how many praying Indians followed Puritan exemplars and how well they did so. Altered evangelistic strategies, a sobered primitivism, and a firmer belief in their special part in God's kingdom work were all, then, changes in Puritan religion precipitated by the particular ways natives chose to become imitators of Christ.

Cases of "mere imitation" in which Indians simply pretended to embrace Puritan ways clearly affected Puritan identity as well, troubling it in several ways and, in the process, eroding New Englanders' already minimal interest in Indian missions that much more. Such mimicking, carried on by natives for their own reasons, might in retrospect be seen as a subversive form of imitation. As James Axtell has put it, "in the face of great need or desire, some Indians were capable of masterly dissembling, even over long periods of time."[106] When Puritans occasionally "discovered," sometimes after fatal consequences, that one or more Indians had feigned civility or Christianity, they were forced to question their own ability to read others. Their self-confidence about knowing the truth got shaken and their insecurities intensified. Under such circumstances, suspicions could run rampant. For many Puritans, it became easier to dismiss all natives as beyond the pale. Having been manipulated and deceived by some natives, they branded all as enemies, at least in the tumult of war, and saw most as legitimate targets of violence. At a minimum, it meant keeping up one's guard against an untrustworthy lot. In the long run, such distrust of their native neighbors killed the Puritan missionary enterprise (after King Philip's War) for two generations as New Englanders preferred annihilating Indians over evangelizing them. Those who had worked hardest at and cared most about Indian Christianization continued to hold out the possibility that natives could be genuinely changed. But even they were forced to consider that within the imitative world Puritans and natives had constructed, no one might be quite who they seemed.

Resistant Indians who had rejected Christianity all along knew how to make that precise point. When Native Americans, consciously or not, employed the language of imitation to ward off Puritan approaches, they leveled attacks where Puritans may have been the most vulnerable. Charges that Christianity was a "human invention" and the Bible a work of clever Englishmen could not be simply dismissed as pagan nonsense. They came too close to expressing doubts Puritans had about themselves, if not about the Bible. Those doubts were especially acute during times of crisis, when Puritans wondered individually and collectively whether God had abandoned them.[107] Were they in fact inventors of human religion rather than imitators of biblical faith? Were they no different from those in the Church of England from which they had fled? Or from those dissenters who threatened to spoil the purity of the church in colonial New England?

For Puritans to hear Indians express what other discontents with Puritanism had said on both sides of the Atlantic was for Puritans to come face-to-face then with their own religious identity. That identity was multifaceted and multifaced. Among the images included in the Puritans' self-portrait were depictions of themselves as the chosen of God, as imitators of the primitive church, as wise discerners of the truth, and as righteous exemplars of biblical Christianity. Puritan sources suggest that each of those images could just as easily be complicated or compromised as confirmed in the course of conversing with Indians in a language of imitation. No natives responded to the Puritans' imitative project exactly according to the ideal Puritans set out. And even if they had, Puritans would have likely retained residual doubts about their authenticity. The most important change they wanted to see in natives was an inner transformation of the heart brought about by divine grace, not simply an external copying of Christian actions and speech accomplished by human effort. Gauging whether a heart had been genuinely renewed was notoriously difficult, and Puritans were a worrisome people. The same anxiety that many of them expressed about their own salvation (in the absence of a strong doctrine of assurance) extended to their assessment of the state of Indians' souls. By its very nature, then, the Puritan quest to have the Ninnimissinuok mimic them was bound to be disquieting. At best, native converts might give Puritans sufficient hopes to balance their doubts about the converts' spiritual conditions. Beyond them, it left Puritans wondering if Indians were appropriating what was most essential in the Puritans' imitative message, worrying that false imitation was as likely as true imitation, and writhing under the attacks in word and weapon of natives who charged that Puritans were anything but what they claimed to be.

Perhaps those facts alone were reason enough for Puritans to grow even more leery of reaching Indians with the gospel in the last quarter of the seventeenth century. By that point, English settlers were less sure about the founders' imitative project for themselves or for the region's native peoples. And they worried that their own behavior during King Philip's War had been far from exemplary.[108] If Ninnimissinuok did "affect English persons" in the wake of the conflict, Indian actions would likely be a far cry from the Christian civility Matthew Craddock originally envisioned. That was one form of mimicry that Puritans could do without.

3

A Scene of New Ideas

A CENTURY AFTER PURITAN-NINNIMISSINUOK MEETINGS AND A FEW HUN-
dred miles to the west in central New York, Taunewhaunegeu had had
quite enough of the Reverend Samuel Kirkland. It was bad enough that
the minister had come and destroyed rum belonging to his wife. Now
Kirkland harangued him about "Temperance, Righteousness, & Judge-
ment" for a good two hours. In typical Oneida fashion, Taunewhaunegeu listened carefully and nodded assent along the way. Then at the end
of their talk, he made it clear that he wanted Kirkland to pay for at least
half of the wasted liquor. When the missionary refused, the native went
off to ponder his next move. He came back the next morning and insisted
that Kirkland pay up. Tempers flared and a fight broke out. The minister
and two others wrestled Taunewhaunegeu to the floor and bound his
arms and legs. The same fate followed for the Indian's wife when she
arrived and "raged with more Violence." "I hate you and all English
Ministers," the native man cried out. "You are a good for nothing fellow,
a Villain, a Mischief Maker, a servant of the devil. . . . By your continual
talk of sin, sin, sin . . . You are a Plague to me, you give me all this trouble.
My sins now all lie before me as fresh in my remembrance as tho' they
were committed yesterday." Taunewhaunegeu kept up his insults for the
rest of the morning, what Kirkland later described as "the most disagree-
able Breakfast I ever had in my life," and the feud went on for several
more days. As Kirkland tried to make sense of what had happened, his
head was spinning with theological questions. Is this what happens
when sinners are made aware of their evil hearts? Should ministers
expect to be attacked for pricking sinners' consciences? For those ministers "called into Christs vineyard, what kind of a call [is] that?" The
whole encounter with Taunewhaunegeu, Kirkland wrote in October
1767, "has opened to me such a scene of new Ideas I know not where to

stop." As for the Oneida, for the moment at least, he just wanted the missionary to leave his body and soul alone.[1]

By that point in the long history of European-Native American interaction, most knew that Taunewhaunegeu was not likely to get his wish. For whether it was Kirkland or some other group of Euro-Americans, Oneidas could count on whites continuing to disrupt their lives. That had now been true for native peoples for more than a century and a half in British colonial America and for three centuries in the Americas as a whole. When Europeans moved outward to Asia, Africa, and the Americas beginning in the fifteenth century, little stayed the same. Separate precontact worlds largely gave way to a host of new realities. Trade networks, political alliances, disease environments, agricultural techniques, and cultural identities took on altered shapes and colors amid the diverse relationships developed among Asians, Africans, Native Americans, and Europeans. So, too, did the religious worlds and the religious outlooks of all these people groups. The scene of new ideas that crowded in upon Samuel Kirkland's mind as a result of this one encounter was indicative of the broad refashioning of the sacred realm and religious mindsets that accompanied intercultural contacts in the early modern world.[2]

How that story played itself out within the particular religious ideas and theologies of Euro-Americans in the North American colonies in response to their encounters with Native Americans is a complicated tale.[3] For a long time historians have been persuaded that colonists as a whole offer little testimony to religious beliefs overturned or theologies transformed because of contact with natives. As quoted earlier, James Axtell's conclusion that religious change moved only in one direction has held sway, maybe especially with respect to religious ideas.[4] The so-called white Indians he has studied only seem to be the exception that proves the rule. Their choice to become thoroughly assimilated to Indian ways, values, and beliefs is striking precisely because it contrasts so sharply with the typical colonist's aversion to and dismissal of native religious notions.[5]

Recent books on the history of theology in early America reinforce the impression that Native Americans mattered little for Euro-American belief systems. Comprehensive works by E. Brooks Holifield and Mark Noll have illuminated many of the broader social, political, and intellectual contexts that molded the character and evolution of religious thought among Europeans in colonial America, for both trained theologians and average settlers. Together they make a strong case that in early America, as Holifield puts it, "theologians ruled the realm of ideas," and as Noll puts it, "social and political events [brought about] grand shifts in theological conviction."[6] In other words, theology mattered greatly in early America, and context mattered greatly for theology. Yet neither book gives much attention to the role of cross-cultural contacts, especially between Europeans and Native Americans, in that historical process. At a time when other historians have been making a stronger and stronger case for the centrality of those contacts for most other dimensions of early American life, it seems appropriate to ask whether this may have also been true for religious thought in the colonies. Is it possible that the encounter with Native Americans precipitated colonial "theologizing"—that is, formal and informal attempts to formulate and express religious convictions? Such theologizing, as I am using the term, went on whenever colonists reflected upon religious matters, whether orally or in writing, whether in systematic scholarly treatments or in personal narratives, whether purely for themselves or for others.[7] As Robert Orsi has argued, scholars must recognize "the creativity and improvisational power of theology as a component of lived experience" and must be attuned "to the practice of *theologizing* in determinate circumstances."[8] Might the interaction with Indians have been an important, and heretofore largely overlooked, social context or intellectual problem shaping the newcomers' religious reflections and beliefs?[9] Or more simply put, did Indians prompt Euro-Americans to think about God, the devil, and other supernatural matters? If so, when did the encounter with Indians provoke such white theologizing and why? What were the main theological questions being raised and what kinds of answers were being given? And did interaction with natives ever *change* Euro-American theology?

To explore those questions and to gain a sense of the breadth of theological issues and theologizing moments that accompanied the intercultural religious encounters, this chapter will draw examples from many different points of contact, rather than examining a single extended episode, as was done in chapters 1 and 2. To give some definition to our inquiry, a few boundaries will apply. My focus will be on European colonial Christianity, which although not the only religion brought to the colonies by Europeans, was the dominant one. Chapter 2 has shown examples of the types of theological questions that arose when Euro-Americans interacted with Christian Indians. Puritan sources detail hundreds of inquiries from praying Indians on scriptural interpretation, Christian doctrine, and spiritual practice.[10] Most of the examples I will cite here involved seventeenth- and eighteenth-century encounters of Euro-Americans with non-Christian Indians. This was the more commonplace experience in colonial America, given the relative size and isolation of Christian native communities. In addition, I will draw the most extensive illustrations from the colonial South, a region well known for the weakness of its religious institutions and the preoccupation of its settlers with trade, profit, slavery, and war. Seeing how relations with Native Americans there prompted whites to theologize should clue us to how much this was happening elsewhere.

To begin our exploration, it is necessary to put aside two potentially limiting assumptions. First, the scarcity of newcomers who became theologically "Indianized" in a thoroughgoing fashion must not be interpreted to mean that interaction with Native Americans made little or no difference for colonists' religious views. There were plenty of other ways in which Indians might have had an impact on whites' religious thinking short of radical transformations. Whenever natives prompted Europeans to reflect upon, renew, expand, reinforce, revise or rethink their Christian convictions, they influenced colonial theology, broadly defined, in early America. Second, it is important to avoid the presumption that the religious encounter of Indians and Europeans was no broader than missionary efforts to evangelize Native Americans. As argued throughout this book, while those efforts were certainly a central part of the encounter, it is also true that all the principal ways natives and whites interacted in the colonial era, including trade, diplomacy, war, disease, and slavery, could have religious dimensions or meanings for both sides. A variety of factors made that true, including the natives' fundamentally spiritual view of reality, the "world of wonders" cosmology of some of the newcomers, and the inclination of all to link religion and morality. Naturally, participants on both sides defined the religious meaning of particular contacts according to their own beliefs, and the religious dimension of a particular event was not necessarily the same for European and Indian, though there were times when whites and natives made efforts to find shared meanings and interpretations of certain actions.[11]

To characterize how encounters of the spirit with Indians affected colonial Christians' religious thought, it is helpful to borrow a framework from historian James Merrell. In assessing the profound consequences for Indians of contact with Europeans, he has persuasively argued that nothing less than a new world "emerged in several overlapping stages" for Native Americans as immigrant microbes, traders, settlers, and missionaries left their successive marks.[12] Something of a similar pattern of overlapping stages or acts may be seen to have occurred as Indians left *their* marks on colonists' religious beliefs. And if they did not create a whole new religious world for Europeans, they certainly made the old one different. These acts were distinguished less by chronological sequence than by the character of the contact between natives and newcomers, and could vary between European Catholics and Protestants. The first stage occurred when Europeans of whatever stripe took seriously the physical existence of Indians. Columbus's contact with Caribbean natives initiated centuries-long debate, including theological debate, over who Indians were. By merely being, the Americas' indigenous peoples gave Europeans plenty to think about. Even more food for thought appeared when newcomers "saw" Indians act. As they witnessed native behavior firsthand or, more commonly, heard about it at second or third hand, colonists sooner or later had to fit Indian actions into European views of the world, even when they were inclined to dismiss what natives did out of hand. During this second stage of cultural interaction, Euro-Americans often misunderstood much of what Native Americans intended by their actions. This may have been especially true when natives performed explicitly religious rituals. But accurate or not, white efforts to "read" Indian life many times entailed some form of religious reflection. Because Catholics in the early modern world "honored sight as the most important sense for acquiring knowledge of the divine," they may have been especially prompted to theologize as they looked upon native behavior, literally or figuratively. Amid the Counter-Reformation's reassertion of the spiritual worth of a wide range of religious rites, Catholics in Spanish, French, and English colonies celebrated the value of images, processions, and dramas in conveying religious truth and emotion, and in turn were struck by the ritual power (and in their view, often the pagan perversity) of the native ceremonies they encountered.[13] Protestants faced the same challenges in interpreting Indian behavior. They struggled to comprehend that for natives all acts had a sacred quality and that religious practice was often more important than religious belief. Yet while Protestants sometimes took careful note of Indian actions, they were often more inclined to pay serious attention to native spiritual convictions, and when they and other newcomers did, a third stage of cultural interaction occurred. Early modern Protestants typically privileged mind over body, so they were struck most forcefully by what Indians said rather than by what they did. When they learned what Indians thought about ultimate things, and particularly in face-to-face settings, Protestant migrants were constrained to theologize. Catholic missionaries, especially in New France, also worked hard to discern native worldviews, and Jesuits in particular were adept at learning key elements of native belief systems.[14] Indians were often reluctant to disclose their deepest convictions to whites, who in turn repeatedly proved to be poor listeners or slow learners.[15] Still, Native American–European dialogue about theological matters was never so rare or so inconsequential as to leave no imprint on colonial minds. Instead, within this third act of the drama of cultural exchange, as during the other two, contact with Indians left colonists thinking about and responding to a diverse set of religious questions, issues, and problems.

Just what those questions, issues, and problems were defies easy categorization. It is difficult to generalize about an extraordinary range of interchanges extending over several centuries. Yet at the risk of imposing too much order, it may be helpful to identify three main sets of theological queries with which Europeans wrestled as a result of their contact with natives.[16] One of these sets corresponds roughly to each of the three stages of cultural interaction described above. In the first stage, as Europeans considered the very existence of Indians, reflection centered on how to situate natives within the cosmic drama of Christian redemption. In the next act, when newcomers watched or learned of native rituals and practices, attention focused on discerning the role of Indians within the theological meanings of colonial America and on assessing the validity of the Europeans' own Christian identity. In the third stage, amid exchanges over beliefs, colonists' religious thought turned to questions about the reasonableness of Christianity and ultimately the very nature of God. Examining how and why these sets of issues arose for Europeans in the wake of meeting Indians will allow us to see more of the ways natives reshaped European colonial religion.

Lost Tribes and Needy Souls

Most sixteenth-century Europeans saw the world through the eyes of Christian faith. For them, few events lacked theological significance. The "discovery" of Native Americans was no exception. Alongside discussions of the political, diplomatic, economic, and geographical value of the Americas went talk of how to make sense of their inhabitants in the light of Christian revelation. Who were these peoples? Where did they come from? What was their nature? Such queries were difficult and potentially disconcerting. They received immediate and prolonged attention from Europeans on both sides of the Atlantic, in part because of their need to fit new information into existing schemes of religious belief. In fact, the sheer number of people who addressed these issues in the sixteenth and seventeenth centuries gives, as Olive Patricia Dickason has suggested, "an indication of the seriousness accorded the theological problems posed by the mere existence of people in the New World."[17]

She and numerous other scholars have detailed the broad array of theories contrived to explain Indian origins, including the provocative hypothesis that natives were related to the ancient Hebrews and could very well be the Ten Lost Tribes of Israel.[18] Among the colonists who toyed with that possibility in writing were Puritans John Eliot, Roger Williams, Samuel Sewall, and Cotton Mather, Swedish Lutheran John Campanius, Quaker William Penn, French Catholic Antoine Lamothe Cadillac, Huguenot-turned-Anglican Francis Le Jau, Moravian Count Nicolaus von Zinzendorf, and Presbyterian Charles Beatty. Jesuit Pierre de Charlevoix disagreed with the theory, but the sixty-plus pages he devoted to the issue in his 1744 history of New France suggests how carefully he and his contemporaries considered the matter.[19]

Among settlers in the colonial southeast, two Jamestown residents weighed in on the subject of Indian origins within five years of its 1607 founding. Robert Johnson's *The New Life of Virginea* and William Strachey's *Historie of Travell into Virginia Britania* both asserted that Native Americans' ancient ancestors were the wayward offspring of Noah. For their sins, God had laid a "heavie curse and punishment upon them" that persisted for several millennia and helped to explain the devilish practices they saw in native religions. Yet now God's wrath was abating and his grace was opening a door, the English arrival, by which he might "rescue the brand from burning and the prey from the Lions teeth." God had brought the English to Virginia to tell Indians of "the true God, and the waie to their salvation."[20]

Johnson's and Strachey's conjectures on the possibility of Indian salvation illustrate that no less care was given to pondering the Native Americans' place in the history of redemption than to their biblical origins. They and other early commentators on Virginia, including Robert Gray, William Crashaw, Daniel Price, and Richard Eburne, wondered in print about how receptive natives might be to the gospel.[21] Would any Indians come to Christ? Might they someday come in large numbers, and if so, when? Why had God hidden the light of the gospel so long from these peoples? Was there any chance that they had once had the truth? If Indians were Jews, would success in converting them signal the advent of the prophesied mass conversion of the Jews? If they were not Jews, would widespread success in converting them have to await the Jews' conversion and be a part of the prophesied mass conversion of the unbelieving Gentiles? English reflection on these and related questions, as with the inquiries about Indian origins, began almost as soon as they and other Europeans knew of the natives' existence and continued throughout the colonial era. And how persons answered one set of questions could dramatically affect how they answered the others. For example, John Eliot's embrace of the Lost Tribes theory made him much more optimistic about the chances of gaining numerous Indian converts. Meanwhile fellow pastor John Cotton's belief that the natives were heathen Gentiles and not Jews persuaded him that evangelism of New England Indians would reap few souls for the foreseeable future.[22]

Logically prior to any discussions of Indian redemption by Christian believers in Europe or the colonies was the presumption that Indians needed saving. Harsh assessments of the Indians' fallen nature became commonplace. Even those colonial Christians who gave more positive depictions of Indian cultures shared in the assumption that natives by nature were sinners in need of saving grace. Indian nobility or innocence did not extend so far as to eliminate their need for Christ, although some observers marveled so at native women's ease (in their view) in childbirth as to wonder whether Indians were immune from Eve's curse.[23] At best, newcomers underscored natives' sinfulness in the context of affirming their equal humanity with non-Indian peoples and condemning European self-righteousness. Roger Williams used poetry to convict his white readers:

> Boast not proud English, of thy birth & blood
> Thy brother Indian is by birth as Good
> Of one blood God made Him, and Thee & All
> As wise, as faire, as strong, as personall.
> By nature wrath's his portion, thine no more
> Till Grace his Soule and thine in Christ restore
> Make sure thy second birth, else thou shalt see,
> Heaven ope to Indians wild, but shut to thee.[24]

A century later, Jonathan Edwards's prose in *Original Sin* made something of the same point. He insisted that the gross "ignorance, delusions, and most stupid paganism" of Indians prior to contact with Europeans demonstrated that human beings in their natural condition moved away from rather than toward truth and virtue. Native Americans, like all persons, were innately depraved. But if anything, their familiarity with sin paled in comparison with their European counterparts', despite the latter's exposure to divine truths: "The poor savage Americans are mere babes and fools (if I may so speak) as to proficiency in wickedness in comparison of multitudes that the Christian world throngs with."[25]

Edwards's Calvinism, as mediated by his own contacts with Indians, led him to place natives and Europeans on the same footing with respect to original sin.[26] So, too, did it lead him to place them on the same plane with respect to Christian redemption. Elect from all nations were to be a part of Christ's kingdom. As suggested previously, determining how and when Christ would gather Indians into his flock occupied colonial minds long before Edwards. Like him, however, most white Christians who addressed the question considered it a matter of prophetic interpretation. By the time he offered his own conclusions in his sermons on the history of the work of redemption in the 1730s, much eschatological musing about the Indians' role in the last days had already gone on among French Catholics and English Protestants.[27] New Lights and Old Lights continued the discussion during the Great Awakening and the Seven Years' War. Both groups thought that the coming kingdom would include Christian Indians, although the visions each had of what that kingdom would be like contained little if any room for Indians to continue native ways.[28]

The prospect of sharing eternity with even Anglicized Indians certainly did not appeal to all, or perhaps most, Euro-Americans. But it nevertheless suggests how the presence of natives in the here and now provoked colonists to take them into account even when considering the eschatological future. The Indians' place in colonial America was simply too prominent for European newcomers not to take stock of them. Early on, Europeans began thinking about how and where their Christian beliefs could, or would have to, make sense of the existence of Indians. The millennialist ponderings of the 1760s indicate that they worked at that task a long time.

What emerged from those European colonial reflections were efforts to fit Indians into the four grand acts of the biblical drama—creation, fall, redemption, and coming kingdom. Answering questions about the Indians' origins, nature, and destiny meant bringing natives "on stage" and assigning them roles. Or perhaps it would be more accurate to say that Indians appeared on stage and forced colonial Christians to give them parts. In general, natives were told to join the vast chorus of humanity, created by God in the beginning, stained by the sin of Adam and Eve, redeemed (if part of the elect) by the blood of Christ, and judged by God in the end. Occasionally, they were even put in the spotlight, as when cast as Israel's lost tribes or as harbingers of the millennium. Whether Indians were seen as major actors or bit players, however, by their very existence they came to have a presence within colonial Christian theology. That presence is a clear sign that during what I have called the first stage of cultural interaction between Indians and Europeans, natives did indeed leave their mark on colonial religious thought.

NATIVE ACTIONS AND GOD'S PLANS

When Columbus observed Taino men fasting from food and women for twenty days and then gathering gold with little effort, he instructed his own crew to confess their sins and to take communion before searching for the precious metal. He apparently reasoned that if native rituals could produce such good fortune, God would be even more inclined to favor those in a state of Christian grace.[29] Thus began a long history of Indian actions provoking European thought about matters sacred and profane. When soldiers, traders, settlers, and missionaries confronted native deeds and their consequences, they interpreted them according to what they already believed. That was no simple process, if for no other reason than the fact that Indian behavior was extraordinary and diverse. Colonists employed their religious imaginations to greater or lesser degrees. Some settled for a single, universal view of Indians as "heathen savages." For them, as James Axtell has argued, observing natives principally served to sharpen their religious concept of heathenism.[30] But that was hardly the whole story. The ebb and flow of political, military, economic, and religious relations among Indians and whites evoked a much wider array of theological probings and pronouncements among other colonists. As they learned of native ways and encountered them in travel, trade, treaties, war, mission work, and much else, Euro-Americans found themselves facing a host of religious questions that tested their intellectual wits and spiritual commitments.

Take, for example, the challenge presented by Indian nakedness. Columbus and his successors encountered many indigenous peoples who showed no shame in going without clothes and resisted European efforts to dress them. Traditional Christian teaching asserted that following Adam's original sin, nakedness and shame went hand in hand. What were they to make of natives whose behavior and attitudes fell outside this assumption? Did this effect of the Fall somehow not apply to native inhabitants of the Americas?[31]

Ruminations on those matters hardly consumed European attention, especially in those moments when Europeans were eyeing native bodies. But they were part of a larger pattern of Indian actions prompting Euro-American theological reflection. Certainly that was the case whenever the Christian newcomers tried to pass on the gospel to natives. Whoever took on that task, whether formally designated missionaries or not, needed to work out at least an elementary theology of missions that could inform their mission strategies. Mission methods if not mission theology almost always underwent some adjustment if and when Europeans actually got around to missionizing. Contact with both resistant and receptive Indians prompted evangelists to tailor their message and methods for greatest effect, a subject to be explored in greater depth in chapter 4. For now it is worth pointing out that missionary exposure to what they perceived to be Native American religious rites was an especially provocative impetus to Euro-American theologizing. A prime example comes from the French Catholic missionaries who worked among various Indian peoples in the southern Mississippi Valley in the late seventeenth century. They were pleased to find that the Taensa, Tunica, and Natchez cultures possessed recognizable religious elements such as houses of worship, priests, and idols. In their eyes, that was an improvement over what earlier missionaries had encountered among natives in Canada, where indigenous religious life seemed more elusive. Father François-Jolliet de Montigny and others were persuaded that missions' work might proceed more smoothly in this new setting. They believed they could build upon the foundational religious understanding these Indians already possessed.[32] Yet not all of the religious activities of these peoples pleased the Catholic fathers. Jesuit missionary Paul Du Ru expressed particularly strong disapproval of native mourning rituals and burial practices. The sounds, smells, and spirit of these ceremonies struck him as cultic and pagan. He was confident that the priests would be able to dissuade Indians from their magic, but his anxiety suggests that he also felt threatened by the competing ritual system on display in front of him.[33] Such anxiety would have been enhanced by the mere frequency with which missionaries saw Indians having to mourn, for as they made contact with native peoples throughout the South (and elsewhere), death was an ever-present reality. Young and old alike succumbed to disease, war, and slave raids, and priests were there to witness the consequences. At a practical level, the prevalence of Indian death shaped whom the missionaries evangelized and what they could do. In this case, the French Catholics chose to leave the Arkansas behind primarily due to their depopulation and instead concentrated their efforts further south among the more numerous Tunica. Even among them, though, "the priests settled for baptizing dying children."[34]

Under such circumstances, Euro-American Christians could not help but wonder about God's purposes for Native Americans and for missionaries in the New World. Chapter 6 will look more thoroughly at how they responded to the scope of Indian death in early America. For the moment, it is sufficient to say that French priests in the South were forced to ask themselves why Indians were dying so much, whether the divine was involved, and what spiritual role they might have within such hard-pressed communities. Fathers La Source and St. Cosme bemoaned the decline of the Arkansas: "This beautiful nation of which much is spoken is nearly all destroyed by war and by sickness."[35] How were they to understand these events in the larger framework of divine sovereignty? Was this a product of God's judgment, the work of the devil, or simply a human tragedy that the Almighty permitted? And what did God have in mind for the future of native peoples and the priests themselves? Was their spiritual calling to evangelize natives going to be negated before they ever had a chance to fulfill it?

Many of those same questions emerged for larger numbers of Euro-American Christians, lay and clergy, in the context of events that were part of the contest for empire in colonial North America. As the English, Dutch, French, and Spanish vied for power, native peoples became engaged as allies, enemies, and neutrals in the often bloody struggles. Amid the tumult, Euro-American Christians pondered how God might be working out his providential plan for the future of the continent. At a more earthly level, European success regularly depended upon the strength of their alliances with Indians. Meanwhile, European fears regularly stemmed from the threat hostile Indians posed. Few events aroused more fear—or more theologizing—than when Indians took colonists captive. The rise of the captivity narrative itself as a literary genre in the colonial era is a telling indication of the religious reflection provoked by this form of encounter with natives. The captivity of Eunice Williams, as retold by historian John Demos, seems especially revealing. Demos makes clear that the 1704 attack on Deerfield, Massachusetts, by a French and Mohawk war party precipitated immediate and long-term reflections on the religious meaning of the captives' fates. Minister John Williams, Eunice's father and fellow captive, led the way in trying to make sense of God's purposes for himself, his family, and his community in these harrowing circumstances.[36] While held in Canada, he received a letter from Cotton Mather telling him that God had called Williams to glorify the Lord there and that the calamities in Deerfield had stirred a religious awakening among New Englanders. If this somehow explained Williams's own predicament in 1705, it was of little use in understanding Eunice's choice thereafter to remain among her native captors. Why had God allowed a small, impressionable child to be taken in the first place, and especially by Indians? Was her refusal to come home a prolonged punishment from God upon New England for its sin? Why had all their petitions to men and God not delivered her? For the next two generations, John and other Williamses, along with much of the rest of New England, prayed and preached about Eunice in hopes that the native manners and Catholic faith that she had received from her Mohawk captors might finally give way. In the end, their concerted quest for her "redemption" proved futile. But their efforts nevertheless demonstrate how deeply disquieting contact with natives could be for the religious thinking of large numbers of colonists.[37]

Other instances of political and military disquiet with Indians in early America similarly gave rise to colonial theologizing. In the mid-sixteenth century, Spanish debates over "the rights to the rewards of conquest," including whether it was legitimate to enslave Indians who were not war captives, were framed in theological terms.[38] A century later, King Philip's War not only wreaked havoc upon southern New England in the 1670s but demanded that Puritan leaders such as Increase Mather offer some kind of explanation for what had happened. Mather's providential view of history pushed him beyond analyses of failed diplomacy and land encroachment to spiritual causes. What had stirred God to inflict this bloody conflict on the colonies? Why had so many settlers suffered at the hands of heathen warriors? What did God intend to teach his people through their affliction? What was New England's future, and what did it really mean to be a chosen people? Mather's narrative history blamed the war on the sins of the second-generation Puritans. Greed, spiritual lethargy, hatred of the Indians, and a general failure to be faithful to the goals of the first generation aroused God's wrath. The war was his judgment on unrepentant Englishmen, and Indians were the divinely chosen means of carrying it out. Native attacks punished New Englanders according to God's purposes. Whether they knew it or not, Philip and his allies, however much servants of Satan, were also instruments of the divine will.[39] In addition, Mather said, they could stand as an object lesson to colonial Christians of what happens when God withdraws his glory from a people. Indian darkness could paradoxically be a beacon to Puritans of what might befall them if they remained disobedient.[40]

Society for the Propagation of the Gospel missionaries Francis Le Jau, Gideon Johnston, and William Treadwell Bull reached many of the same conclusions about the Yamasee War in South Carolina in 1715. They were sure that the devastating native attacks that killed hundreds of settlers through the course of that year were God's righteous judgment upon a wicked colony. Like Mather, these Anglicans rehearsed the sins of the settlers, which in this case included exploitative trade practices that impoverished Indians and the failure to evangelize effectively either natives or African slaves. Unlike Mather, however, Le Jau and the others were not inclined to see the Yamasee as merely devilish doers of the divine will. They were instead a truly oppressed group whose revolt was understandable. Modern historians can identify other causes of the war, but it remains noteworthy that in the midst of the conflict, the colony's would-be spiritual and moral leaders affixed blame squarely on white shoulders and upheld the justice of Indian resentment.[41]

This was not the only time that Francis Le Jau found Carolina Indians in the right. As he observed their customs and lifestyles in the years after his arrival in the colony in 1707, he became convinced that there was much to admire. In fact, Europeans would do well, Le Jau thought, to follow native examples. He told his superiors in Britain that the Indians "do make us ashamed by their lives, conversation, and Sense of Religion [though] quite different from ours; ours consists in words and appearance, theirs in reality. I hope they will soon worship Christ." He was especially impressed by "their sense of justice and their patience."[42] Few of his fellow Carolinians shared Le Jau's sympathetic reading of native cultures or his sincere interest in converting them to Christianity. But across early America in the seventeenth and eighteenth centuries, other minority voices similarly expressed respect for aspects of Indian behavior and in some cases found them positively Christian.

One case in point was Native Americans' contentedness with lives of simple pleasures and few material goods. Watching Delaware Indians in and around Germantown, Pennsylvania, convinced Mennonite pietist Francis Daniel Pastorius that although these natives had never "heard the teaching of Jesus concerning temperance and contentment, yet they far excel the Christians in carrying it out." He thought that settlers should "not hesitate to learn contentment from these people, that they may not hereafter shame us before the judgment-seat of Jesus Christ."[43] John Lawson's *An Account of the Indians of North Carolina* complimented them for similar virtues and ascribed moral superiority to the natives: "They are really better to us, than we are to them; they always give us Victuals at their Quarters, and take care we are arm'd against Hunger and Thirst: We do not so by them (generally speaking) but let them walk by Our Doors Hungry, and do not often relieve them." Europeans imagined themselves as far above Indians in moral and religious character, but in reality they possessed "more Moral Deformities, and Evils than these Savages."[44] Pastorius, Lawson, and others wondered how those outside of Christ could act so much like him.[45]

Some who pondered that issue were brought back to the question of Indian origins, and none more so than James Adair. His four decades of trading among the natives of the colonial southeast became the basis for his *History of the American Indians,* published in London in 1775. Adair dedicated almost half of his long treatise to marshaling twenty-three arguments "in proof of the American Indians being descended from the Jews." He built his case primarily on the parallels he found between Indian ways and ancient Hebraic practices. Native American social organization, languages, concepts of time, marriage and purification rites, burial practices, names for God, religious leaders, places of refuge, and much else all resembled or echoed Jewish custom and belief. Taken together, Adair insisted, the evidence was convincing that Indians were not ordinary pagans; they were descendants of God's chosen people.[46]

Even if his readers were not persuaded by his arguments about Indian origins, Adair thought they served another valuable purpose: "[the arguments] at the same time furnish the public with a more complete INDIAN SYSTEM of religious rites, civil and martial customs, languages, &c. &c. than hath ever been exhibited, neither disfigured by fable, nor prejudice."[47] Adair was overly sanguine about his own objectivity (he had strong prejudices against the French, Catholics, and his political opponents in South Carolina), but there is no doubting his genuine desire to counter fanciful notions of Indian ways. His long experience as a trader had taught him that accurate knowledge of native cultures was essential for good relations, and that, ultimately, is what he hoped his book might contribute toward, for the sake of the British, the colonists, and the Indians. Nothing was more frustrating, then, than seeing relations sour because of white stupidity or arrogance. Unfortunately, in Adair's view, the men sent to evangelize Chickasaws, Choctaws, Cherokees, and other southeastern natives fit that description. He minced no words in condemning the quality of missionaries in Indian country and their ill effects:

> Many evils are produced by sending out ignorant and wicked persons as clergymen. Of the few I know,—two among them dare not venture on repeating but a few collects in the common prayer. . . . The very rudiments of learning, not to say of religion, are wanting in several of our missionary Evangelists; the best apology I have heard in their behalf is, "an English nobleman asked a certain bishop, why he conferred holy orders on such a parcel of arrogant blockheads? He replied, because it was better to have the ground plowed by asses, than leave it a waste full of thistles."[48]

Adair placed the blame on church officials (in this case, the Church of England) in positions to select missionary candidates. How could they appoint and ordain "illiterate and irreligious persons to the service [?] . . . That court . . . which sends abroad stupid embassadors to represent it, cannot be reasonably expected to have success, but rather shame and derision." The "blind guides" sent out to minister to Indians and whites were an indication of how indifferent their superiors were to the spiritual needs of colonial America. Finding themselves on their own, religiously neglected laypersons were prone to conclude that they knew more than the clergy. When that happened, they started teaching on their own, and challenged ministerial authority. The net result was "they rend the church asunder; and, instead of peace and love, they plant envy, contempt, hatred, revilings, and produce the works of the flesh, instead of those of the spirit."[49]

"Not so act the uncivilized Indians." Adair proceeded to contrast native practice in selecting spiritual leaders: "Their supposed holy orders are obtained from a close attention to, and approved knowledge of their sacred mysteries. No temptations can corrupt their virtue on that head: neither will they convey their divine secrets to the known impure." Such wise, and by implication more "civilized" and "Christian," conduct was "worthy to be copied, by all who pretend to any religion at all, and especially by those who are honoured with the pontifical dignity, and assume the name of 'Right reverend, and Most reverend Fathers in God.' "[50]

Adair's biting criticism of the white religious establishment and admiration for Native American customs did not keep him from believing that Indians still needed to be civilized and Christianized, and that the former process would precede the latter. Standing in the way of either of those transformations, according to numerous colonial observers, was some supposedly Christianized Europeans' corrupting influence on Indians. If Adair the trader attacked missionaries for their dubious impact on natives, he was perhaps only responding to the long litany of complaints missionaries had lodged against traders during the prior two hundred years.[51] Clergy were hardly alone, though, in leveling such criticisms. In fact, no one spelled it out more plainly than naturalist and colony surveyor John Lawson after his travels in North Carolina in the early eighteenth century: "Most of the Savages are much addicted to Drunkenness, a Vice they never were acquainted with, till the Christians came amongst them." Far from showing natives "the Steps of Vertue, and the Golden Rule . . . [we] daily cheat them in every thing we sell, and esteem it a Gift of Christianity, not to sell them so cheap as we do to the Christians, as we call our selves." Lawson could not help but ponder aloud "where is there to be found one Sacred Command or Precept of our Master, that counsels us to such behaviour?"[52] Unfortunately for Lawson, his own arrogant and threatening words a few years later precipitated his Tuscarora captors to execute him.[53]

Alan Gallay's recent book on the Indian slave trade in the colonial South confirms that Lawson's concerns about trader behavior were shared more broadly. If Lawson focused on the liquor trade, others were upset over the commerce in native slaves. A combination of political, economic, religious, and moral factors prompted South Carolina's proprietors, governors, and local assembly all to make numerous attempts to regulate that trade more effectively, but their efforts met with little success. Self-interested traders, many of whom served in the colonial government, consistently won out over those committed to some higher principles of justice or at least some greater degree of fair play in interactions with natives.[54]

It would be stretching the point to suggest that sorting out the morality of Indian-European relations grabbed the attention of large numbers of newcomers in colonial America, though Gallay's study suggests that it may have occurred more often than we thought, when political, diplomatic, and moral interests converged.[55] What can be said is that it happened often enough to see it as part of a broader process in which colonists wrestled with fundamental religious and moral questions as a result of their living in a world where native actions had consequences for them. When Indians took captives or when war broke out, settler thoughts turned especially to the workings of divine providence. What was God's intention for the new settlements in America, and what part were Native Americans to play in that divine plan? When whites negotiated peace treaties, trading rights, and land deals with Indians and then failed to honor them, a small minority of Euro-Americans voiced concern about the meaning of justice and the Christian call to righteousness.[56] How would God look upon those who cheated or exploited native peoples? When newcomers observed the harmony and simplicity of Indian lives, most interpreted it as a sign of native backwardness and preferred the prospects of "civilization." But to some Euro-Americans, material acquisitiveness seemed more evil and less necessary for contentment. Could Christians learn from heathen Indians how to live more virtuously? When natives turned greedy for European guns and rum, or when Europeans enslaved both native friends and enemies, new fears were raised about the corruption of colonial society and the consequences of sin. How long would God withhold his judgment, or what form would his judgment take? When Indians joined colonists in confessing Christ, visions of a coming millennial kingdom came quickly to mind, and renewed predictions of prophetic fulfillment quickly to tongue. What might Christians do to assist the outpouring of the Holy Spirit upon early America?

In all of this and more, whether Europeans and Indians were battling, betraying, or baptizing one another, their contact provoked colonists to theologize. Nominal as well as pious colonial Christians responded to what they saw and heard of Indian actions with plenty of knee-jerk comments and impetuous remarks. At other times, though, Euro-Americans were prompted to consider carefully a range of religious issues that native behavior and Indian-colonial relations set before them. As suggested earlier, those issues might be clustered into two main concerns: evaluating what their interactions with Indians revealed about God's providential plan for colonial America, and discerning the meaning and validity of their own Christian identity, individually and collectively. Efforts to resolve those issues, as with making sense of the Indians' physical presence, became ongoing projects within early America and reveal that during a second stage of cultural interaction colonial religious thought once again felt the native touch.

INDIAN MINDS AND A REASONABLE FAITH

Indians also left their mark on newcomer thinking when Euro-Americans encountered Indian minds. Though often hard to separate from the types of contacts just discussed, there were numerous occasions throughout early American history when newcomers and natives went beyond observing one another's behavior and carried on a fuller dialogue over religious ideas. Such dialogue is hardly surprising given the religious worldviews that permeated the cultures of all these peoples. European traders, political agents, and missionaries usually initiated those conversations, and as noted earlier, natives were often reluctant to reveal their deepest beliefs. Nevertheless, there were countless times in the course of colonial history when people discussed and debated sacred matters across the cultural divide. Sometimes those exchanges merely aimed at satisfying intellectual curiosity or represented friendly banter. But much of the time, a desire to persuade or "convert" the other animated the discussion.[57] Crucial to how those discussions proceeded was the fact that overall, Indians and Europeans approached conversion from very different points of view, and neither side fully understood the other's position. From the Native Americans' perspective, the goal of what might be called "conversion" was usually to persuade the European to acknowledge the legitimacy of their beliefs, not to have the white Christian actually embrace their faith. Even when Indians brought Europeans into their world through captivity and adoption, the "process of conversion did not focus on the spiritual condition of the captive per se" but instead aimed to "render a stranger more predictable and useful" through cultural assimilation.[58] Furthermore, when it came to responding to offers to convert to Christianity, receptive natives typically believed that it was possible and appropriate to graft certain Christian beliefs and practices onto their existing religions, even when it meant holding plural truths. More resistant Indians even more explicitly communicated a belief in multiple truths by telling Europeans that natives and whites were products of separate creations and on different paths to the afterlife. In their minds, what was spiritually true depended on a person's tribe and culture. European Christian colonists usually brought a vastly different set of assumptions about conversion to their talks with Native Americans. Whether or not formal apologists or evangelists for Christianity, they typically operated from the belief that Christian truth was absolute, universal, and exclusive. To accept Christianity was to dispose of all alternative beliefs and practices. Becoming Christian was an "either-or" proposition for the newcomer, not a "both-and." They presumed that Native Americans, like all peoples, should embrace the new faith they offered and leave their paganism behind.

Given such contrasting understandings of conversion, and more broadly, religious truth, it is no wonder that dialogue over those matters gave rise to much religious reflection by participants on both sides. While a comprehensive survey of that interaction is not possible, sampling a few illustrative episodes will highlight some of the dominant theological questions that emerged for Euro-Americans as they encountered Indian minds.

Traveling among the Cherokees in 1758–59, Presbyterian pastor William Richardson had a series of conversations with natives that reveal many of the issues those encounters could evoke. Richardson had been commissioned by Virginia Presbyterians in the wake of their recent participation in the southern colonies' phase of the First Great Awakening. They were eager to send out ambassadors who could share the Christian good news with their native neighbors to the southwest. Richardson found Cherokees and other Indians not so eager to discourse on religious matters, but when they did, he often got more than he bargained for. One group of older men asked him when he had arrived from heaven, since he told them that he had come "to teach them what he [God] would have them do." Richardson dismissed the question as a sign of Indian foolishness, and in the process missed their challenge to his spiritual authority. One younger Cherokee was blunter; he asked accusingly if Richardson "was not come to tell them lies." Standing Turkey, a Cherokee leader, wanted to know if the minister's Bible could tell his people "where their Enemies were, how many, if they shou'd defeat them & how many they should lose." Supplying that information would make Richardson a "great man" in Cherokee eyes. At the same time, of course, even if he could predict the future, that skill would only put him on a par with other powerful conjurers. On several other occasions, Richardson's descriptions of God's perfections and people's moral duties prompted his native hearers to ask "where . . . is the white man who does so?" Richardson could only reply that some whites did and some (especially traders) didn't. That was clearly not good enough for one Cherokee man, who, after patiently listening, told Richardson that neither he nor the town desired "to hear that Talk."[59]

William Richardson did not know Native Americans well. Like many colonists, his contacts with them were episodic not sustained, sometimes cordial but rarely intimate. Yet his experiences with the Cherokees reveal many of the most important questions posed for colonial religious thought through dialogue with Indians.[60] At the simplest level, Richardson was forced to keep thinking about how best to carry out his missionary task. But that query opened onto a host of other more complicated matters. As he moved among native villagers listening to what they said and hoping to be heard, Richardson, like hundreds of other priests, ministers, and lay workers throughout the colonial era, was forced to reflect on how to make his message plain and appealing. In this case, his on-the-job training produced a range of strategies both practical and philosophical. Midway through his trip he noted, "[I] hope by conversing familiarly with them, giving them small Presents, inviting them to eat with me, smoking with them, [and] going to their Town House to ingratiate myself with them to hear me in private . . . if not in public & so it may answer, with the blessing of God, in some measure the End of the Mission." In the weeks that followed, he made additional useful discoveries, including the wisdom of not challenging the work of local conjurers and the benefit of having pictorial representations of biblical stories. Richardson principally sought to find some common intellectual ground from which to build a case for Christianity. His main appeals came to rest upon the claims that he and the Cherokees shared beliefs in an overruling divine being and in a human moral conscience that told people that obedience to God was the right thing to do. If they repented of those things "their Reason" told them were wrong, God would look favorably upon them.[61]

What Richardson and the Cherokees considered "reasonable" turned out to be two different things, however. Their reluctance to embrace his message left him wondering about the nature of conversion, the eternal fate of those who did not hear the gospel, the relationship between "Christianizing" and "civilizing," and the spiritual knowledge of the "natural man." The Cherokee responses noted above made sure that Richardson's thinking did not stop there, though. Through their exchanges over divine matters, they questioned his claims to speak and hold religious truth. They challenged him to display his own and his god's spiritual power. They dismissed his religious authority as a laughable boast. They undermined his assumption that once presented, the rational truth of Christianity would be evident and persuasive to native hearts and minds. In short, the Cherokees' quick wit and sharp tongues sent Richardson away to consider the basic grounds of his Christian faith and ministerial calling. No wonder he concluded after five months that he was ill suited for the missionary life.

The Cherokee encounter with Richardson continued a contest of minds and wills over conversion between Native Americans and Europeans in the colonial South (and elsewhere) that stretched back to the sixteenth century. While it is already evident that numerous issues came up amid that religious dialogue, a centerpiece of contention was what Brooks Holifield has recently called "the reasonableness of Christianity." Holifield argues that "a majority of [Christian] theologians in early America shared a preoccupation" with "the quest for reasonableness." That is, they wanted to demonstrate the consonance between orthodox Christian claims and human reason so as to substantiate Christianity's truthfulness. That goal often took them in the direction of searching for rational evidences that could confirm "the uniqueness and truth of the biblical revelation."[62] Holifield's concern is with tracing the overall evolution of theological scholarship in colonial America. As a result, his focus is on formal theological writings. But his emphasis on the colonists' widespread interest in showing the rationality of Christianity may be applied to the theologizing Euro-Americans such as Richardson were forced to do on the "frontlines" as they exchanged religious ideas with Native Americans. Whether Indians listened passively, spoke approvingly, or offered strident rebuttals to Christian claims, European newcomers strove to show natives and themselves the reasonableness of their faith.

Holifield sees the quest for reasonableness as emerging with the first-generation Puritans and as later developing from a variety of factors, including the challenge of deism in the late seventeenth and eighteenth centuries.[63] Yet it is possible to see this intellectual impulse at work even earlier in some of the first encounters European Christians had with New World inhabitants and as thereafter arising often when conversion was at stake. Though not usually producing formal theological writings, these cross-cultural dialogues may nevertheless be recognized as an important additional social and intellectual context that prompted colonists to wrestle with the reasonableness of their Christianity.

Throughout the colonial era, many European Christians who spoke to Indians about religion imagined, at least initially, that a clear, logical presentation of Christianity's doctrinal claims would yield native intellectual assent. The sheer rational force of Christian truth would counter native errors and convince Indians to turn to the gospel. Church authorities in Europe, especially early on, presumed that Indian evangelization and conversion would proceed with ease.[64] A very early example of this type of thinking from within the colonial South may be found in the efforts of Father Juan Rogel to evangelize the Calusa off the coast of Florida in the late 1560s. Rogel came to concentrate his efforts on the local Calusa cacique, who he later named Don Felipe. Over the course of their interactions in 1567 and 1568, Don Felipe proved to be politically astute. He recognized that it was in the self-interest of the Calusa to align with the more powerful Spanish and to embrace their accompanying Christianity. But he would do so slowly and as piecemeal as possible so as not to lose his credibility with his own people or his forebears, who, though dead, still exercised important spiritual influence in the community. Felipe asked the Jesuit to begin to teach him "the law of the Christians." Rogel established a meeting place and time each day where the cacique and any other interested Calusa could hear him teach. The priest set up a cross in that spot and there with the help of an interpreter began to instruct them on how to recite the Lord's Prayer and the Hail Mary. With those prayers under their belts, the natives would know how to speak to God and how to ask him for their needs. Rogel soon moved on to basic doctrinal exposition, starting with the concept of the oneness of God and his roles as the creator and sovereign over the whole universe. He told Calusa of God's omnipotence and of the order of creation, culminating in the creation of men and women and the human soul. Felipe and other Calusa agreed with the missionary's claims about God's oneness and rule over creation, but thereafter the priest's words seemed more and more fanciful. Worth particular disdain were Rogel's notions about the immortality of the soul: "They laugh at me when I tell them in the catechism lessons that all the souls of as many men as there have been in the world are alive in heaven or hell and that they cannot die."[65] The Calusa had their own well-developed ideas about the human soul, or rather souls, for they believed that each person had three souls, one of which remained with the physical body following death and could be communicated with by the living. Natives went to their sacred burial grounds and there conversed with ancestors, who supplied wisdom about events current and future.[66]

Father Rogel was determined to "undeceive them of their errors and idolatries and evil customs and wicked laws." How to do so proved increasingly complex. Any illusions he had that the Calusa would immediately see the light of Christian truth now had to be tempered. He appreciated the fact that Felipe and others let him know which parts of the Christian message were just too hard to believe. Beyond the immortality of the soul, these included the resurrection of the dead and the invisibility of the divine. Rogel told his superiors what strategy he was now employing: "this is the method that I am following with them, striving to understand what are the things in the articles of our holy Catholic faith that give them the most difficulty; and with respect to them, putting them through reason on the right road to believing them."

Rogel believed that a rational examination of the disputed points would lead Calusa to recognize the reasonableness of Christianity's claims, even its most extravagant ones, and therefore its truthfulness. If the right arguments were marshaled and the right evidence presented, Indians could be persuaded to change their minds and their ways.[67]

One weapon in Rogel's rhetorical arsenal was the native's inclination to be awed by written truth. When Felipe asked him how he knew what God had revealed, he explained that it had been written down at the time God had spoken it and preserved ever since. According to Rogel, Felipe acknowledged "that the things we [Christians] have in our law [the Bible] have a much greater semblance of truth than did theirs even though they appeared more difficult and obscure." That was because written truth was unchanging, whereas Calusa law was entirely oral and changed much as it was transmitted from generation to generation. Later Native Americans would come to question Felipe's assessment, but for now it gave Rogel hope that the cacique "became more inclined to accept this truth about the immortality of the soul and the resurrection of the dead."[68]

Still, Rogel "always saw a great resistance in him [Felipe] to believe this article," and as time went on, the Jesuit confessed that the task was beyond his strength. Calusa attachment to their beliefs was "so fixed . . . that there is need for special favor and help from God in order to persuade them of the immortality of the soul and the resurrection of the dead and the reward and punishment of the next life." Rogel began to realize that the natives' reasons for believing in their own worldview transcended *reason*. As they argued over each other's religious symbols and exchanged accusations of idolatry, the Calusa, from the missionary's point of view, "saw that the things I am telling them make sense and that they cannot do the same for theirs because they are clearly false and evil." Yet they told him "that their forebears had lived under this law from the beginning of time and that they also wanted to live under it, that I should let them be, that they did not want to listen to me." How was he to proceed if Indians acknowledged the rationality of Christianity but still refused to believe it? Little wonder that Rogel was in "great doubt and perplexity because of not knowing whether this man [Felipe] may be persuaded to believe that the things of our holy Catholic faith are true and become aware of the lies and deceptions of his sect."[69]

As Rogel's time among the Calusa ended, he remained convinced that the conversion of Don Felipe would be the key to future evangelistic success among these natives. In his view, Calusa deference to the dictates of their cacique was sufficiently great to ensure that they would follow suit if and when he fully embraced the new faith. By that point, Felipe himself had tried to teach Rogel how best to missionize his people. On one occasion he had encouraged the Jesuit to focus his energies on Calusa children. They had not yet developed the familiarities with and loyalties to Calusa rites that adults possessed. After all, it was "a very troublesome and difficult thing for men to change who have been accustomed from their infancy with one manner of living . . . [to] undertake another very different one. And, consequently, my [Rogel's] wanting to strip old men and men of adult age of all their customs and make them perfect Christians was not possible of achievement." Rogel was not prepared to give up his efforts to convert Calusa adults, but he did alter his strategies. Besides offering small material rewards for talking with him, the priest largely gave up the practice of going to the cross and preaching to sparser and sparser numbers of Indians. Instead, he extended an open invitation to natives to come to his room in the fort and there to look at his books and images, and eventually to discuss "the things of our holy faith with them in clear language." Rogel found this method "more productive" for "with some coming and others going almost the entire day, they have given me something to think about in this [exercise]."[70]

That was hardly the only thing the Calusa had given Juan Rogel to think about during and after his time with them. Their responses to his evangelism were perplexing. What were he and his superiors to make of native dismissal of certain central Christian claims? The Spanish could (and did) explain it simply as evidence of the devil's sway over Indian minds, but Rogel's firsthand encounter with Calusa prompted him to reflect more deeply on the matter. What made gospel truth plain to him but not to them? Why were they willing at times to acknowledge its truthfulness but not give up their own contrary beliefs and practices? Did the Calusa possess sufficient reason to recognize the truth? Was Christianity as reasonable as he thought when he first arrived?

The issues provoked in the encounter between Jesuits and Calusa in the 1560s would reappear countless times over the next two centuries as Europeans and Indians exchanged religious ideas. Whites' presumptions about the superiority of their Christian faith met stiff resistance from many natives, who instead preferred to preserve belief in the creation stories, vision quests, revelatory dreams, guardian spirits, and other aspects of their traditional faiths that had long provided meaning and stability for their peoples. That choice struck most Euro-Americans as fanciful at best, devilish at worst. Folks on both sides of the cultural divide liked to laugh at the other's beliefs. Still, the question of why so many Indians chose to remain outside the Christian fold hung over colonial Christianity, perhaps especially within England's mainland colonies, where missionary success was particularly limited, though Catholic authorities grew disillusioned as well.[71] How were Christian believers to explain native reluctance to see this world and the next as they did?

Answering that question prompted further reflection on the "reasonableness of Christianity" amongst Euro-Americans. Colonists offered numerous practical reasons for the paucity of Indian converts, including their own lack of evangelistic efforts.[72] But some also offered more "theological" responses that tried to take stock of both the reasonableness of Christianity and the reasonableness of Native Americans and their ways. The most prevalent explanation for resistant Indians, and therefore the one noted most often by other historians and not in need of great elaboration here, suggested that native sinfulness and native savagery were to blame for their unwillingness to accept the Christian gospel. Only when Indians gave up their cultural ways and values would they be in a position to understand and embrace Christian truth. In other words, they needed to be "civilized" before they could be Christianized, or as some newcomers were wont to put it, Indians needed to be "reduced to civility."[73] Foolish native cultural pride in savage practices was destructive and irrational and needed to be replaced by the enlightened ways of Euro-Americans. Anglican minister Charles Inglis summarized this view in 1770: "it is necessary to civilize Savages before they can be converted to Christianity; & that in order to make them Christians, they must first be made Men."[74] For Inglis and those of his ilk, Native Americans might begin to enter the Christian fold more readily once they had grown into men; that is, once they had become more rational beings. The right use of their reason would eventually allow them to see the truthfulness of Christianity, for the latter accorded perfectly with the former. Based on those assumptions, most whites (and particularly Protestants) who sought to share the gospel with Native Americans from the seventeenth through the nineteenth centuries emphasized the necessity of Indians' undergoing a sweeping cultural transformation as part of their path to Christianity.[75]

Some other Euro-Americans were not so sure about this, however. Ridicule and indifference toward native beliefs and values, or an undervaluing of Indians' rational abilities, seemed an inadequate response to what these whites had personally heard and seen as they interacted with Indians. From their minority perspective, Native American reason had arrived at plenty of truth, for they were repeatedly struck by how close rather than by how far native convictions were to central Christian teachings. As a result, in the eighteenth century, a small group of colonists offered an alternative assessment of native religious ideas that served to confirm the colonists' own faith in the universality of Christian truth but at the same time granted some legitimacy to native spirituality and morality.

To arrive at that conclusion, these Euro-Americans made use of natural theology (consciously or not) to make sense of why sometimes what Indians said resonated with their convictions. Natural theology was not a new idea per se in the 1700s, but it gained greater popularity and utility in the wake of the deist challenges to standard Christian doctrine that arose in the late seventeenth century. As Brooks Holifield explains it,

> The claim of the natural theologian was that reason, reflecting on either the visible world or the workings of the human mind, could produce evidence for the existence of a transcendent God apart from the revelation in scripture or the tradition of the church. What distinguished natural theology from "natural religion," the religious ideal of eighteenth-century deists, was the further claim that natural theology pointed toward and confirmed truths above the capacity of reason to discover—truths accessible only through special revelation.[76]

When some Euro-American Christians heard pagan Indians express what sounded to them like the truth, they used natural theology explicitly or implicitly to explain how and why that was possible.

Good examples appear in accounts written by English trader John Long and Indian agent Conrad Weiser based on their long contacts with Native Americans. Both attested to a native spiritual wisdom that was real and instructive precisely where it squared with Christian teaching. In the 1740s, Weiser relayed a series of instances that had shown him that the Iroquois and their neighbors had a "united trust in God" and sometimes even made "united appeals to Him." That was enough for Weiser to assert that "we must certainly allow this apparently barbarous people a religion," a religion that in Weiser's stories resembled Christian claims about the divine character. He recounted one occasion in the 1730s when he came upon an Indian acquaintance, Anontagkeka, en route to Onondaga. Both men were traveling to the same destination, but the native had no provisions for the long journey. When asked how he expected to survive, the Onondaga replied that "God nourished everything that was to live, even the rattlesnakes, although they are wicked animals, so also will he take care of him and provide that he should reach Onondago alive." Weiser recalled the native's certainty that God was "with the Indians in the wilderness, because they alone relied upon his timely care; while the Europeans, on the contrary always took bread with them." Within a day or two, Anontagkeka was well supplied, and he reached Onondaga three days before Weiser.[77]

Long's travels among the Indians of the upper Great Lakes likewise revealed to him the natives' special awareness of God's providential care. His own brushes with danger had made him realize that whites were too prone to credit their "own sagacity and foresight" for escape or deliverance. Meanwhile, Indians thought "more properly," saying that "it is the Master of Life from whom we derive that presence of mind which has extricated [us] or procured us relief." Moreover, natives asked God for their "daily support," attributed to him their military victories, and even thanked him for the courage to endure torture with composure and defiance. For Long, watching and listening to the faith of the Chippewas served to remind him of familiar Christian truths, ones he sought to pass on to his Euro-American readers.[78]

Conrad Weiser and John Long were persuaded that although Native Americans had been deprived of access to the Bible and the presence of the church, Indians had nevertheless arrived at many of the core convictions of the Christian faith, thanks to the workings of human reason. Most likely through their close connections to the natural world, natives had rightly deduced the overruling presence of the divine and his righteous character. Such conclusions no doubt bolstered these whites' confidence in Christianity's truthfulness and suggested that the intellectual distance between Christian and native belief systems was not as great as most of their peers thought.

William Bartram's *Travels through North and South Carolina, Georgia, East and West Florida* as well as his other writings gave readers at the end of the eighteenth century an even more sympathetic interpretation of native religion's and native morality's consonance with Christianity, thanks to the influence of natural theology and the author's Quaker beliefs. Published in 1791, the book related naturalist Bartram's travels through the colonial South in the 1770s and his many encounters with the region's Indians. Bartram presented one early meeting with a Seminole warrior as especially formative for his thinking. The two came upon one another on a trail in Florida. The Indian was heavily armed; Bartram was not. The latter feared for his life given the native's angry countenance and intimidating gestures. But Bartram's bold offer of a handshake was eventually reciprocated, and the Seminole let him go on his way. Bartram imagined what the native might have been thinking ("the silent language of his soul") as he extended mercy to the white traveler: "White man, thou art my enemy, and thou and thy brethren may have killed mine; yet it may not be so, and even were that the case, thou art now alone, and in my power. Live; the Great Spirit forbids me to touch thy life; go to thy brethren, tell them thou sawest an Indian in the forests, who knew how to be humane and compassionate." Bartram explained the warrior's behavior as the product of a natural virtue rooted in belief in a just God. Once he found out that this particular Seminole was reputed to be "a noted murderer" and had been "outlawed by his countrymen," Bartram spent more time "seriously contemplating the behaviour of this Indian" toward him. How could it be denied, he concluded, "that the moral principle, which directs the savages to virtuous and praiseworthy actions, is natural or innate?" Native Americans had not been in a position to receive formal moral education. Hence, "this moral principle must be innate, or they must be under the immediate influence and guidance of a more divine and powerful preceptor, who, on these occasions, instantly inspires them, and as with a ray of divine light, points out to them at once the dignity, propriety, and beauty of virtue."[79]

If Bartram could derive all that from one "silent," momentary exchange with a Seminole (perhaps as a Quaker he was used to the power of silence to communicate), he was eager to glean much else from natives when he had the chance to visit with them more fully. Yet as he made his way from one native community to the next, he kept coming back to the same essential conclusion: the moral virtue he saw in the Seminole and in southeastern Indians in general was nothing other than the divine presence, what Quakers called the Inner Light, residing in native hearts and minds. With such an angle of vision, Bartram construed all types of Indian practices and beliefs as worthy of admiration and usually convergent or compatible with Christian revelation.[80] He recounted, for example, how one young, beautiful Seminole woman had married a white trader and then used her beauty to beguile him out of all of his possessions. Bartram concluded that here was "an instance of the power of beauty in a savage, and their art and finesse in improving it to their private ends." But the story did not end there, for the fact that her father and the men and women of her village "condemned and detested" her actions showed "the virtue and moral conduct of the Siminoles, and American Aborigines in general." That virtue he once again linked to "the divine principle which influences their moral conduct, and solely preserves their constitution and civil government."[81]

Unlike most of his white contemporaries, Bartram was disinclined to think that natives needed European civilization to become Christian. In fact, he was disinclined to think they needed "civilizing" at all, at least not with respect to moral knowledge. He told his readers, "If we consider them [Indians] with respect to their private character or in a moral view, they must, I think, claim our approbation, if we divest ourselves of prejudice and think freely. As moral men they certainly stand in no need of European civilization." Still, Bartram found that the Indians he traveled among were "strongly inclined to our modes of civilization" and more importantly for him, they admired "our Religion & would be pleased to have Missionaries sent, to introduce & teach it to them." Already they appeared to him "more sincerely religious than we ourselves" for they kept "strictly & and I may say holy the Sabbath Day, in all their Towns."[82]

Bartram's Indians were not "noble savages" for he found in them the same mix of virtue and vice that other human beings and societies presented.[83] Yet thanks to the divine light illuminating their minds, Seminoles and other natives already believed in many of Christianity's reasonable tenets and could be expected to progress toward a fuller embrace of the faith if treated properly. For Bartram, as for Conrad Weiser and John Long, the substantial common ground he believed existed among native religions and his own Christianity showed that a divinely inspired human reason was active and well in pointing native and newcomer alike toward the way of righteousness.

For all their sympathy for native faiths, men such as Bartram, Long, and Weiser still hoped that Indians would learn and accept the distinctive claims of the Christian message. The idea that existing native religious beliefs were sufficient for Indians, as Christian ones were for the European, was not an intellectual option these men considered. Yet this is precisely what some Indians had claimed when presented with the Christian gospel. In the seventeenth century, to such representatives of Christianity as Roger Williams in New England, Johannes Megapolensis, Jr., in New Netherland, and Jean de Brébeuf in New France, various Native American peoples said that natives had their religious ways and whites had theirs and they were content to leave it that way. Why couldn't whites do the same? Indian prophets in the mid-eighteenth century articulated a similar "separate" theology during the natives' great awakening.[84] What were white Christians to do with such radical ideas? Stalwarts of colonial Christianity such as Puritan John Eliot and Moravian David Zeisberger may be found promptly rejecting Indian pluralism and reaffirming Christian exclusivism. But further toward the margins of colonial Christianity and the edge of colonial society, the matter got murkier. Might there be some validity to what natives claimed? Time spent with natives in Indian country pushed at least handfuls of Euro-Americans to confront that possibility.

Take, for example, the case of Indian captive William Henry. Living among the Seneca, he spent long hours with an old sachem, Canasatego, learning the art of Indian eloquence and discussing matters of religious belief. Those talks clearly taxed Henry's thinking; he even wished in retrospect that he had listened more carefully to the sermons of his youth. Canasatego wondered about Henry's belief that there was only one great God, suggesting instead that there were many more, for "every country has its great good Manitta [Manitou], who first peopled that country." The Seneca chief also unveiled an elaborate creation account of the Five Nations, complete with an explanation of how evil entered their world. While impressed with his friend's rhetorical style, Henry responded with what he no doubt hoped would be a persuasive appeal to rational evidence. He said that there was "great uncertainty" about a story passed on orally from one generation to the next by women. In contrast, the Christian account had been written down "by direction of the great spirit himself" in a book that had never been altered and was therefore "undoubtedly the truth." However much Seneca women and all oral cultures might have been offended, in Seneca eyes Henry's reply was primarily rude for contradicting Canasatego. Henry caught on to that fact when the sachem asked him, "you see I always believed your stories, why do you not believe me?" What Henry had a harder time comprehending was Canasatego's ability to hold plural truths. And when several younger Senecas tried to encourage the chastened Henry by ironically telling him that his "stories indeed might be best for white people, but Indian stories were undoubtedly best for Indians," Henry walked away wondering about "the miserable darkness these poor creatures labour under."[85]

William Henry came face to face with natives whose logic told them that it made sense that religious truth could vary from one people to the next. For Henry to accept that view would have required him to cease or at least suspend his belief in the reasonableness of Christian claims to be the exclusive truth. Henry was not prepared to go down that road, but other colonists who entered Indian country *were*, to one degree or another. Amid his wide travels in the *pays d'en haut*, fur trader Alexander Henry not only observed but at least on one occasion participated in a native ritual. When at one point he was taken captive by the Ojibwas, they exposed him to a shaking tent ceremony held to invoke and consult the Great Turtle about their future. When opportunity came for individuals to ask the spirit about their personal futures, Henry "yielded to the solicitations of my own anxiety for the future: and having first, like the rest, made my offering of tobacco, I inquired, whether or not I should ever revisit my native country?" The shaman put the question to the spirit, the tent shook, and Henry got his answer: he would return safely home. Overcome with gratitude, the trader "presented an additional and extra offering of tobacco." Then, with his anxieties relieved,

Henry returned to watching closely "to detect the particular contrivances by which the fraud was carried on" (why was that tent moving?) but made no discoveries. Henry's mind had to live with the mystery even while his heart had been pacified.[86]

Alexander Henry's experience portrays a kind of mental shifting between worldviews as he got swept up in the tent ceremony and then reverted quickly (at least according to what he wrote for Euro-American readers) to the doubts about native religion with which he had arrived. If Henry's shifting was relatively momentary, other visitors to Indian country seemed capable of a more sustained attachment to native ways of perceiving reality. Among them were many of the French *coureurs de bois,* unlicensed participants in New France's fur trade. As these men moved back and forth from European settlements to Indian communities, some became adept at living in two worlds. To the chagrin of French religious and political officials, the *coureurs de bois* went "native" in a host of ways, as they "dressed in the fashion of the Amerindian, tattooed their arms, legs, and faces, greased their hair, strolled bare-legged through town, smoked tobacco, raced canoes, spoke tribal dialects, adopted native names, married according to native custom, . . . and raised their métis children *à la façon du pays.*" Perhaps most disturbingly to colonial authorities, these traders also participated in native religious ceremonies, rites that had been repeatedly denounced by missionaries. As they joined with natives in the sacred acts that accompanied the hunt, war raids, or the arrival of winter's first snow, they found it possible either to suspend their Catholic beliefs and practices (however strong or weak) or to mix them with Indian rituals. Historian Daniel Scalberg has concluded that "while few French fully adopted Indian cosmology, many of them integrated Native American rituals into their Christian belief system." So, for example, military commander Pierre de Troyes reported in the late seventeenth century that traders made tobacco sacrifices at the local natives' sacred place. But de Troyes also reported that those same traders were in the habit of baptizing any unbaptized passersby at that same location. Such men were apparently comfortable with trying to blend components of two different systems of religious belief and practice without worrying about logical consistency. And while hardly models of Catholic piety, many of them upon their return to colonial towns resumed participation in the mass "to assure . . . salvation by the use of sacraments."[87]

Though certainly not commonplace in colonial America, fur trader behavior represents a type of religious hybridity that occasionally emerged when Europeans and Indians met. Native Americans were much more often the ones who adopted Christian elements into their belief and ritual systems, but the reverse could also take place when Euro-American Christians dwelt in Indian country. While such Christians were among native folk, their lives more than their words communicated another type of response to the unwillingness of many natives to embrace Christianity fully. For those whites, Christianity's reasonableness extended to Indian country, but there it had to take second place to or at least share the limelight with native understandings of the supernatural. Native American religions, and native lives in general, had their own genius and validity. At least within their world, Indian faiths could be as satisfying and compelling as anything Euro-Americans had to offer them. As a result, some traders and even more white captives assimilated to Indian life to the point where they were able to "share unconsciously the values, beliefs, and standards of Indian culture."[88]

Those Indianized newcomers represent the extreme edge of what might happen when Euro-Americans encountered native ways and beliefs. Their choices may be linked to what has already been said about the other types of responses colonists made when confronted with natives who preferred to retain their own faith amid contact with Christians. The long dialogue in colonial America over conversion went in directions that sixteenth-century Europeans such as Juan Rogel would not have expected, at least not before his own experiences with the Calusa. Presumptions that Indians would be easily persuaded into the kingdom of God through rational argument proved problematic and got complicated by native minds, which had their own logic. Christian evangelists such as William Richardson were still hoping to find common ground on which to build a convincing case for the gospel two centuries later. But most of his compatriots had long since decided that Indians would first have to become much more like them culturally and intellectually before they could recognize the reasonableness of Christianity. Still, other Euro-Americans believed that the divine light had already shined brightly enough upon Indian communities to produce religious and moral practices that were Christian-like. If that were true, Native Americans surely had a shorter distance to travel to see the full light of God's revelation in Scripture and in the person of Jesus Christ than most colonists thought.

All these perspectives show Euro-Americans theologizing in the wake of conversing with Indians about religious truth. Though not always the case, those confrontations usually involved a covert hope if not an overt effort to see the other convert in some sense. On the European colonist side, the array of questions and issues that talking with Indians evoked centered in one way or another on the reasonableness of Christianity, a topic their most religiously astute members were already accustomed to reflecting upon. In the face of Indians' compelling narratives, biting humor, and reasoned responses, providing a defense of their faith and sorting out just how reasonable Christianity was became more difficult. Proving they had the corner on religious authority or spiritual truth was not so straightforward as it once had seemed, at least for some newcomers. Furthermore, if during the first two stages of cultural interaction Europeans primarily had to figure out who *Indians* were in God's scheme for humanity in general and colonial America in particular, in the third stage confronting Indian beliefs forced them to figure out who *God* was in both the native's scheme and their own. What was God's nature? How did he act? What did he demand of human beings? To whom had he revealed himself and how and why? Enough Euro-Americans cared sufficiently about those questions to suggest that during a third stage of cultural interaction, colonial religious thought was transformed by its encounter with Native Americans.

THEOLOGIZING MOMENTS

If Samuel Kirkland's physical and intellectual tussle with Taunewhaunegeu opened up a "scene of new Ideas" in his mind, so much more did the long religious encounter with Native Americans open the minds of Euro-American Christians as a whole. As natives and newcomers came to know of one another, it was not just the natives who were forced to rethink old verities and consider new ideas. That colonists far more often than not held on to the essentials of their existing Christian beliefs after confronting Indians has for too long been taken as proof that contact with Indians made no difference in their thinking. On the contrary, throughout the three stages of cultural interaction described above, meeting Indians stirred Euro-Americans to theological reflection, construction, and refutation. Around their core convictions, white Christians wrestled with the theological implications of natives' being, behavior, and beliefs. Confronted with the Indians' existence, European minds addressed questions about Native Americans that were broad, relatively abstract, and impersonal. They were also framed by the Europeans themselves. Europeans decided what needed to be explained about the New World inhabitants and how to do it, unencumbered by much native input. And yet, by merely being, Indians came to have a presence within the newcomers' Christian theology. In the two other stages of cultural interaction, natives had more of a chance to speak to whites, both in deed and in word. Indian actions touched colonial thinking at many points, as reflected in the multiple images of natives within the immigrants' religious vision; among other things, natives could be Satan's underlings, God's instruments of judgment, models of virtue, victims of white injustice, or paradoxical beacons of darkness. All such characterizations were connected to Euro-American efforts to sort out what God intended for colonial America and how whites and Indians fit into his plans. While some Native Americans willingly shifted their own conceptions of what the divine was about to views compatible with white Christianity, many others remained tied to belief systems that, to one degree or another, stood outside European claims. Listening to Indians express their own faiths and question that of whites pushed newcomers to consider what it would take for natives to see the reasonableness of Christianity. Native challenges could cut to the heart of personal belief, raising questions about the very nature of God. Whether colonists groped for answers, offered stout defenses of their faith, or crossed over to the Indian side, they indicated that exposure to native notions could stretch and sometimes unsettle their religious minds. Surely such encounters of the spirit with Native Americans must be seen as leaving clear marks upon colonial religious thought and, therefore, as giving an important social and intellectual context for early American Christian theologizing. Not to reach that conclusion would be to ignore a vital component in the lived experience of thousands of colonists and to perpetuate a too narrow view of what happened when Indians and whites met.

4

"Poor Indians" and the "Poor in Spirit"

Fʀᴇsʜ ᴏɴ ᴛʜᴇ ʜᴇᴇʟs ᴏꜰ ʜɪs ᴍᴏsᴛ sᴜᴄᴄᴇssꜰᴜʟ ᴍᴏɴᴛʜ ᴀs ᴀ ᴍɪssɪᴏɴᴀʀʏ evangelist, Presbyterian David Brainerd headed off into the Pennsylvania interior in September 1745 to visit Indian villages along the Susquehanna River. There he spent nine days observing and conversing with natives more different than he had anticipated from the Indians he had lately seen awakened to Christian faith at Crossweeksung, New Jersey. Brainerd found his attempts to "instruct and Christianize" the inland Indians to be "all to no purpose." Once back in Crossweeksung, however, his preaching brought "a season of comfort to some in particular" and "numbers were affected with divine truths." He could not help but take note of the contrast: "Oh, what a difference is there between these and the Indians I had lately treated with upon Susquehanna! To be with those seemed like being banished from God and all his people; to be with these like being admitted into his family, and to the enjoyment of his divine presence!"[1]

Brainerd's distinction among varied native responses to his evangelism reveals an understanding many other Euro-American Christians probably grasped intuitively and modern Indian historians have recently emphasized: Native Americans already living on the European-dominated side of the cultural divide between Indians and colonists were far more likely to embrace Christianity than those still living in Indian country.[2] That deceptively simple insight nevertheless adds considerable sophistication to our current appreciation of colonial Christianity's divergent appeal among Indian peoples. But even something more can be gleaned from Brainerd's brief reflection: his own emotional and spiritual conditions were apparently affected by the character of his contact with Indians. Natives were seemingly making differences in how close Brainerd felt to God in particular moments. Broader study of

Brainerd will confirm the fact that as he interacted with Delawares and Susquehannas, they came to impact his mind, body, and soul. While such a claim may no longer seem surprising, until recently, interpreters of Brainerd, beginning long ago with Jonathan Edwards, have minimized or ignored any native influence. In spite of Brainerd's daily contact with Mahican and Delaware Indians for much of his brief adult life, Edwards and later observers for two and a half centuries considered Native Americans virtually irrelevant to the story of Brainerd's real historical significance.[3]

Pushing Indians aside in such a manner, as noted previously, has been a longstanding tendency among historians of European colonial religion, who have been inclined to treat natives as at best part of the set, and at worst entirely offstage, in the colonial religious drama. Brainerd provides a particularly interesting case study of this interpretive bent and allows for a narrowing of focus in this chapter to a single life, after a series of rather sweeping chapters that examined longer and broader episodes in the religious encounter of natives and Europeans. In one sense, he is a logical choice for scrutiny since he came to exert an enormous influence on later generations of missionaries and on Anglo-American evangelicals in general, thanks to the editions of his *Life* put out most famously by Jonathan Edwards but also by John Wesley.[4] Moreover, his work among Indians in the 1740s allows for a snapshot of colonial encounters of the spirit amid the "great awakenings" of that decade, arguably the most important religious events of the eighteenth century. On the other hand, Brainerd does not seem like a promising candidate for discovering much Indian influence. For one thing, as a number of historians have pointed out, his private diary, especially as edited by Edwards, is far more attuned to his own spiritual journey than to natives or even his own evangelistic techniques.[5] His gaze is usually, and sometimes tortuously, inward. In addition, Brainerd seemingly made few if any cultural accommodations to Indian ways, at least that he self-consciously acknowledged. Compared to the Moravian men and women who lived and ministered among some of the same native peoples, he demonstrated far less cultural sensitivity and nuance. Thus, he was largely oblivious to the ways Indians may have been shaping him. Yet to say that is not to say this process was not occurring, as Brainerd himself noted in the passage quoted above. Indeed, it did happen, sometimes in spite of Brainerd. The diary itself, as Laura Stevens puts it, "reveals this influence in spite of itself."[6] Close attention, then, to that text and Brainerd's public missionary reports is warranted, both because of his surprising importance within eighteenth- and nineteenth-century Christianity and because of the unexpected nature of what they unveil about his encounter with Native Americans. If we can see how the religion of someone like Brainerd was shaped by Indians, perhaps there is a better chance that we can see that influence more clearly on other Euro-Americans in early America.

A Dismal Call

By the time Brainerd made that trip to the Susquehanna Indians, he was already an experienced Indian missionary by eighteenth-century colonial standards, even though he had been in the "field" only two and a half years. Evangelizing Indians had never been a major concern of the first colonial churches in English North America, and it was even less of one by the late 1600s. A generation later, the fledgling efforts of Anglican missionaries from the Society for the Propagation of the Gospel, renewed interest among some New England Congregationalists, and the more focused initiatives of newly arrived Moravians had sparked increased Protestant competition for native souls; nonetheless, Indian missions were still a low priority for the colonial church, and few young men felt called to serve Christ's kingdom among Native Americans.[7] Such indifference stemmed from a host of factors, not the least of which was the broader culture's desire for expediency. Often, as James Merrell has commented, "it proved easier to kill Indians than convert them." But Merrell and others have also pointed up that Indian resistance cannot be ignored as another crucial explanation for the scarcity of missionary ventures.[8] With comparatively few exceptions, Indian peoples throughout the colonial era did more to shun than embrace the whites' religion. Missionaries and native converts both found themselves swimming upstream against powerful cultural currents. No wonder so little was happening.

And no wonder David Brainerd responded so soberly when the prospect of evangelizing Indians was first presented to him in the fall of 1742. Having grown up in Haddam, Connecticut, a village along the Connecticut River where colonists had occasional contact with the surviving remnants of the neighboring southern New England Indians, young David undoubtedly overheard more than one story about bothersome or pitiable natives.[9] While studying at Yale College (1739–42), the young man absorbed accounts of John Eliot and the Mayhews, as well as stories about New England's many Indian wars, all of which, however told, would have left their mark. Norman Pettit suggests that Brainerd inherited Eliot's view of Indians as "doleful creatures," and certainly the young man would have been aware that many Indians had notoriously little interest in the Christian gospel.[10]

It is highly unlikely, then, that David Brainerd's attitudes toward Indians could have been very sympathetic. Altered circumstances had prematurely forced him to choose a vocation, however, and working among Indians was one option that presented itself. In November 1742, Presbyterian pastor Ebenezer Pemberton invited him to New York City to meet the colonial commissioners of the Society in Scotland for Propagating Christian Knowledge. Since his expulsion from Yale ten months earlier for accusing tutor Chauncey Whittelsey of having "no more grace than a chair," Brainerd had spent much of his time agonizing over God's plan for him.[11] In the three years since his conversion, he had mostly imagined himself preparing for a life as a New England pastor and scholar. Pemberton's offer consequently left him "much concerned" and prompted intensified prayers for divine guidance. His New York meeting went well enough to generate a job offer, which he accepted. But far from relieving his anxiety, the prospect of a life spent "gospellizing the heathen" overwhelmed him with a sense of his own "great ignorance and unfitness for public service."[12]

Brainerd was depressed, not enthused, by his calling, a reaction explained largely by his melancholic spirit, lack of self-confidence, and ongoing disappointment over unfulfilled scholarly ambitions.[13] Yet his conception of Indian missions, a conception partially created by Indians themselves, seems also to have played a role. As he prepared to take up his first assignment for the Scottish society, a sense of doom settled over his farewell to loved ones: "Took an affectionate leave of friends, not expecting to see them again for a very considerable time, if ever in this world." So awesome was the task ahead that the already modest Brainerd was humbled, prostrated: "I saw I was not worthy of a place among the Indians, where I am going, if God permit: I thought I should be ashamed to look them in the face, and much more to have any respect shown me there. . . . I thought I should be ashamed to go among the very savages of Africa."[14]

The Scottish society assigned Brainerd to be a supply preacher to white Christians at East Hampton, Long Island. He spent six weeks there pastoring the Congregational church. But he also saw firsthand the poverty of both the neighboring Indians (Niantics, Mahicans, Pequots, and Narragansetts) and Presbyterian minister Azariah Horton's attempts to convert them. Horton's methods of evangelism included public preaching and teaching, and one-on-one visits for spiritual counseling, approaches Brainerd would later employ in other missionary settings. At Horton's invitation, Brainerd preached several times to the Indian congregation, and to good effect according to the settled minister. Horton noted that his guest's preaching had been "attended with

Power for enlivening the Children of God, and the further awakening such as were under Conviction. He Spent the evening in giving them Instructions, Encouragements, Admonitions, according to their circumstances."[15] Brainerd himself made no mention in his diary of that particular occasion (February 22, 1743) but did comment on a return visit two weeks later (March 9). In an oft-quoted passage from his journal, Brainerd admitted his sense of "flatness and deadness" after seeing Horton's parishioners at Montauk Point. He struggled to preach to them twice that day but was preoccupied with the "blackness" of his own soul and the thought that he was not fit "to speak so much as to Indians."[16] While Brainerd's comments suggest a religious self-centeredness, their focus is broader, for they encompass not only his private thoughts but the realities reflected in the faces of the natives who stared back at him. Indians were, without a doubt, "poor" in every sense of the word, and going among them meant moving not only to the geographic margins of colonial society but to the religious margins of the colonial church.[17] While Brainerd's obvious distaste—his flatness and deadness—at the prospect of working with Indians partakes of the racist sentiments typical of white colonists, he does not share the swelled pride that, according to James Axtell, characterized the English response to relations with Native Americans in general.[18] Brainerd departed from the Long Island Indians with a broken spirit rather than an inflated ego. Direct contact with natives had done far more to intensify his self-loathing than to deepen his cultural bias.

THE MISSIONARY AS STUDENT

Not yet twenty-five, David Brainerd was poised to assume his first missionary post without benefit of formal training or experience. His uncompleted Yale education and his year as an itinerant preacher (he had spoken a few times to Indians) were all he could draw upon as he readied himself to embark on his assigned task—evangelistic work along the Delaware River. Now came word from the commissioners of the Scottish society, however, that tensions on the Pennsylvania frontier were too high to risk sending a new missionary. Instead, Brainerd was to head north to extend the ministry of John Sergeant, evangelist and teacher to the Indians at Stockbridge, Massachusetts.[19] Sergeant, a veteran missionary, a former Yale tutor, and the individual who had recommended that the society place a missionary among the Delaware Indians after his own visit with them in 1741, was a logical mentor for Brainerd.[20] Brainerd arrived in the Stockbridge vicinity in early April

1743, disheartened by the change in plans and ill prepared to minister to a small group of Mahican Indians living in Kaunaumeek, a small town on the New York–Massachusetts border, about eighteen miles from Albany and twenty miles from Sergeant.

Over the course of the following twelve months, Sergeant taught Brainerd many of the standard strategies English missionaries traditionally employed in evangelizing Indians: establish a school to teach native youths Christian morals, manners, and doctrine; suppress any "heathenish" practices, such as "idolatrous sacrifices" and "savage" dance; tutor Indians in how to pray, how to sing the Psalms, and how to observe the Sabbath; gather your charges into a single town, keep them there year round, and instill in them the work ethic of the English yeoman farmer; garner the support of native political leaders and discredit the spiritual authority of powwows; and learn the Indians' language while also teaching them English as quickly as possible.[21] Always a good student, Brainerd rapidly absorbed and implemented the lessons Sergeant and the Stockbridge mission had developed. In the long run, however, much of what Brainerd learned from Sergeant proved useless. For example, Brainerd's arduous efforts to learn one Algonquian dialect were wasted, for it could not be understood by the Algonquian and Iroquoian speakers of New Jersey and Pennsylvania among whom he spent most of his career.[22]

If much of what Brainerd the student learned in his year at Kaunaumeek was ultimately irrelevant, the same cannot be said of what Brainerd the teacher drew from his students. Ever since Europeans had arrived in the New World, Native Americans had offered them numerous lessons of lasting value.[23] Most colonists, and Brainerd was among them, never plainly acknowledged their debts. With or without Brainerd's awareness or acknowledgment, however, his first sustained contact with Indians revealed a host of truths about himself, his work, his faith, and his "people."

Some of those truths merely confirmed what Brainerd had previously been told or seen for himself. Missionary evangelism was a lonesome task with few rewards. New England Indians had been "reduced" to economic want. Neighboring whites were unsympathetic both to natives and to native missions. And breaking down Indian "prejudices" against Christianity was prerequisite to planting the gospel.[24]

Other lessons were fresh and unexpected. Brainerd's experiences among the Housatonic Valley Indians altered his view of material plenty. Six weeks after his arrival, he noted that he lived "poorly with regard to the comforts of life: most of my diet consists of boiled corn, hasty pudding, etc. I lodge on a bundle of straw, and my labor is hard and extremely difficult."[25] Even after moving into a cottage of his own, Brainerd's surroundings were spare by white standards. While at first a cause for complaint, Brainerd's own condition and the Mahicans' more straitened circumstances eventually prompted him to issue increasingly strident denunciations of lives devoted to "worldly pleasures."[26]

Feeling as if the world had rejected him (and in October he received a final rejection of his appeal of his case at Yale), Brainerd now in turn rejected the world. Whether he was praying for his own death, which would free him for immortality, or for the advent of the millennium, which would free all of God's chosen, one thing was clear: Brainerd desperately wanted to escape from the miserable world he then inhabited. How fully the Kaunaumeek Indians shared in Brainerd's discontent is impossible to say. But sharing even partially in their impoverished lives clearly deepened his alienation from "all earthly pleasures and profits."[27]

Naturally, what Brainerd desired most for the Mahicans was that they embrace Christianity. Their warm reception and willingness to listen to him preach initially provoked expectations of quick conversions.[28] When these failed to materialize, Brainerd gradually realized that native hospitality and deference to his spiritual leadership were no guarantees that regeneration (as he understood it) had taken or would take place in any individual Indian lives. Wishful thoughts about instant success gave way to more modest hopes that, slowly but surely, God "was preparing his way into their souls." As he looked back on his work during that year, he soberly concluded that "as there were many hopeful appearances among them, so there were some things more discouraging."[29] Ironically, when Brainerd decided to leave Kaunaumeek for the Forks of the Delaware, it was the Mahicans who warned him that the far distant tribes he now went to serve "were not willing to become Christians, as they were."[30] The truth of that lesson lay before him.

Defining Success

It was not long before Brainerd discovered on his own what the Mahicans had suggested about natives living on the other side of the cultural divide. On his way to Pennsylvania, he stopped at Minisink, New York, and met with a group of Munsees. His efforts to win a hearing for Christianity were mocked by the local "King" and rebuffed by a "rational" Indian who criticized Christianity as a corrupting rather than a purifying influence. They preferred to "live as their fathers lived and go where their fathers were when they died," the Indians informed Brainerd. To his request for a return engagement, they replied that they would be "willing to see me again as a friend, if I would not desire 'em to become Christians."[31]

Daunted by his failure to persuade the Munsees, a gloomy Brainerd arrived at the Forks of the Delaware and Lehigh Rivers unsure of how to proceed with his ministry. What he soon learned about the Indians he had waited a year and a half to evangelize only intensified his discouragement. Most immediately, only a smattering of the Delaware still lived in this part of Pennsylvania. Most of the area's Lenape Indians had been forced in the previous seven years to migrate westward to native towns along the Susquehanna River. They had been no match for the combined forces of white land hunger, government deceit, and imperial politics. White encroachment on Indian lands had been legitimated in the infamous Walking Purchase of 1737. Five years later, the Pennsylvania government had demanded that its Six Nations allies exert additional pressure on the Delaware to move. The few dozen who remained at the Forks thereafter lived in scattered villages and struggled to maintain some semblance of the life previous generations had enjoyed while also taking on some of the trappings of European culture.[32] What in recent memory had still been Indian country was now rapidly being absorbed into the Anglo-American world.

David Brainerd was there, of course, to change, not to support, Indian ways. He expected, or at least hoped, to pass on the dual gifts of Christianity and civilization. Supporters of his mission, including Brainerd himself, imagined that natives would be the beneficiaries of his human benevolence and the far greater reward of God's love.[33] The extent of his "reform" agenda as well as the character of the Indians he encountered is revealed in a letter to Ebenezer Pemberton, written six months after Brainerd's arrival at the Forks. The evil influence of irreligious whites certainly compounded "the difficulties that attend the Christianizing of these poor pagans," Brainerd conceded. Colonial traders in particular were inclined to think that missionaries were bad for business; historian James Merrell says that they "swore at, beat up, even 'tried to excite the Indians to kill' missionaries."[34] But most obstacles to the gospel, Brainerd insisted, were erected by the Delaware themselves. He enumerated them: the Delaware's strong attachment to "the customs, traditions, and fabulous notions of their fathers"; their ability to defend their religious faith; their awe for their powwows; and their "roving" lifestyle. Brainerd assumed that each of these features of native life would have to be altered if Christianity were to take hold among the Lenape.[35]

Despite his discouragements, however, Brainerd was able to report some modest success. The Forks Indians had often been willing to listen to him preach, and some of them had renounced "their old idolatrous notions" and were trying to persuade others to do likewise.[36]

Yet such a simple account belies the intensity of Brainerd's struggle with the question of missionary "success," both in the six months preceding and in the six months following his correspondence with Pemberton. He arrived in Pennsylvania in May 1744, and ordination a month later by the Presbytery of New York confirmed his call. Living among mostly Dutch and Irish colonists at Hunter's Settlement, Brainerd had to ride up to twelve miles each way to visit the Indians in the Forks area. He would preach to them in the "King's house" or, more privately, converse with those "much disaffected to Christianity." When apart from those he had been called to serve—and that was a good deal of the time, roughly nineteen weeks out of the thirteen months he spent in the Forks—he labored to translate prayers into the Unami Delaware dialect and to locate lands where the natives "might live together and be under better advantages for instruction," and further away from the ill influence of colonial settlements.[37] Notably absent from his activities were any sustained efforts simply to observe Delaware life, let alone participate in it, tactics used effectively by his Moravian competitors in Pennsylvania.[38] Instead, he felt compelled to disrupt native ceremonies and to dare local powwows to inflict their worst spells upon him.[39]

Feeling the "weight and difficulty" of his work, Brainerd understood that his "whole dependence and hope of success seemed to be on God." The task of Indian conversion "appeared 'impossible with men,' yet with God . . . 'all things were possible.'" Divine possibility increasingly consumed Brainerd. As early as July, he wrote that "of late all my concern almost is for the conversion of the heathen; and for that end I long to live." By late July, he thought he could be content never to see any of his old friends again "if God would bless my labors here to the conversion of the poor Indians." In October he took his first trip inland to evangelize the Susquehanna Indians, again prompted by his growing passion for Indian converts.[40]

Still, with no sure signs that any native souls had been or were about to be won, Brainerd was plagued by doubts: perhaps God was "not able to convert the Indians before they had more knowledge"; perhaps he did not exist at all. Such thoughts were quickly repressed, but anxieties would occasionally reemerge and find expression. "I feel as if my all was lost and I was undone for this world if the poor heathen mayn't be converted," Brainerd confessed to one friend.[41] With such meager results, Brainerd wondered about his own worthiness as a minister. From Scripture and much evangelical preaching, he had been taught to believe that the success of a ministry depended to a large extent on the spiritual adequacy of the pastor or missionary. It was hard for him to avoid concluding that if natives were not welcoming the Christian good news, it must be because of his own spiritual failings.[42] As fall turned to winter, no real progress could be reported. There were a few bright moments in December, but as 1745 began, the Delaware continued to participate in native feasts and dances, and some simply "refused to believe the truth of what I taught them." On Sunday, January 27, Brainerd recorded that he "had the greatest degree of inward anguish that almost ever I endured: I was perfectly overwhelmed, and so confused, that after I began to discourse to the Indians, before I could finish a sentence, sometimes I forgot entirely what I was aiming at." He attributed his distress to "vapory disorders, melancholy, spiritual desertion, and some other things that particularly pressed upon me . . . the principal of which respected my Indians."[43]

Native American resistance, along with a developing case of tuberculosis, brought Brainerd to something of a breaking point in early February 1745. For two days he experienced hellish depression and confusion. Relief came on the third day in the form of a revised understanding of what it meant to be a successful missionary. Brainerd wrote in his diary, "God was pleased to hear my cries, and to afford me great assistance; so that I felt peace in my soul; and was satisfied that if not one of the Indians should be profited by my preaching, but should all be damned, yet I should be accepted and rewarded as faithful; for I am persuaded God enabled me to be so."[44] Selfless execution of missionary duties, in Brainerd's new view, was an appropriate criterion for judging his or any other evangelist's success, even in the absence of an impressive tally of born-again souls.

Six months later, in Crossweeksung, New Jersey, Brainerd finally witnessed that ingathering of repentant Indians for which he had long hoped. At that point, he reverted to his earlier position of valuing results over devoted service. Ironically, however, many of Brainerd's eighteenth- and nineteenth-century evangelistic successors adopted the view Brainerd had arrived at in despair. Joseph Conforti has persuasively argued that Brainerd's example and words inspired later missionaries to place as much, if not greater, emphasis on their personal quests for holiness as on the salvation of non-Christians. For them, a missionary's success was to be measured not by the number of his converts but by the faithfulness of his sacrificial service in the cause of Christ.[45]

But while Brainerd's influence on the evangelical missionary movement has been recognized by historians, that of the Delaware Indians has not. They were the chief cause of Brainerd's much-noted soul searching. Their occasional responsiveness fueled his zeal for converts. Their more frequent hostility sparked his long journey into night. They prompted him to reassess why he was among them, whether he was a worthy minister, and what he could accomplish. They provoked him consciously and unconsciously to wonder about the nature of God and his power. They left him perplexed and perturbed about the workings of native life and thought. And they aroused in him feelings of love and hate toward himself and toward those he had come to serve. Through it all, forgotten Delaware men, women, and children molded the character of the young missionary. In so doing, they made their own inadvertent contribution to the spread of Christianity around the globe.

DEPENDING ON INDIANS

In June 1745, David Brainerd visited the Delaware at Crossweeksung. There he found a much more receptive audience for his Christian message, and within six weeks, a spiritual awakening had dawned among his native listeners. Indian conversions became a regular, if not quite commonplace, occurrence, and Brainerd poured himself into the work of pastoring and catechizing the new believers. He quickly sensed the need for a more permanent home for his emerging congregation, and he set about acquiring lands where the Christian Indians could live in peace and grow in faith. By the following May, he helped them move to Cranbury, New Jersey, and the work of creating a Christian Indian town began in earnest. Brainerd spent the next six months overseeing the community's spiritual and "worldly" concerns. Then, fighting ever worsening tuberculosis, he left Cranbury in November 1746, hoping to recuperate in New England so that some day he could return to his people. But apart from a brief visit the following March, Brainerd never again saw his congregation.[46]

Much of the story of the Christianization of the Crossweeksung Indians conforms with recent historical findings about natives and missionaries. As "Settlement Indians," these Delaware were more susceptible to Christian evangelism than their brethren in the Pennsylvania interior. By the 1740s, their ranks were depleted, their lands mostly appropriated, and their culture largely in disarray. They lived in a colony where English ways dominated and where Indian ways were less and less visible. On the whole, the contest of cultures had inexorably pushed New Jersey's natives toward an increasing dependence upon whites. Within such a context, embracing Christianity was a logical, although not inevitable, choice for resident Indians and destroying native traditions a common practice among those doing the Christianizing.[47] Expressing a cultural arrogance all but universal among the English settlers, Brainerd publicly berated members of his own flock as ungrateful, indolent, slothful, and lacking "the spirit of a man."[48]

Still, the story of David Brainerd's sixteen months among the New Jersey Delaware has enough interesting twists and turns in it that it would be unwise, and unfortunate, to make it conform to type. For example, whereas most Native American groups more readily adopted the economic than the religious practices of the English, Brainerd's Indians found Christianity much more to their liking than the work ethic he tried to drill into them.[49] Repeatedly complaining about having to attend to the Indians' secular affairs, he bemoaned their reluctance to become the "laborious and industrious" self-sufficient farmers he envisioned. In fact, virtually all of Brainerd's virulent remarks about the Native Americans with whom he was acquainted concerned their work habits. What he saw were idle Indians too willing to depend upon him for their worldly well-being. What he failed to see was that such a willingness was likely a reluctance for, and an attempt to retard, a far more thoroughgoing dependence upon English ways.[50]

Brainerd's private diary and public journal for 1745 and 1746 suggest that he was often blind to another major twist in the story: his own growing dependence upon Indians. Hidden but not absent in his writings are clues that while he remained thoroughly English and Christian, his relationships with Indians increasingly shaped everything from his evangelistic method to his psychological health.

The most important of these relationships during his years in Pennsylvania and New Jersey was Brainerd's association with his Indian interpreter, Tunda (Moses) Tatamy, hired soon after Brainerd arrived in the Forks of the Delaware. Tatamy was an extraordinary Indian. He was well known in the area not only as a skilled interpreter but as a private landowner and an experienced "cultural broker" who facilitated negotiations between various Indian groups and the Pennsylvania government. He also knew the ways of Christian missionaries, having spent time two years earlier with Moravian leader Count Nicolaus von Zinzendorf, who found that Tatamy "spoke English well" and "had regulated his housekeeping much in the English style."[51] Once employed, Tatamy soon became indispensable to Brainerd, who described him as "well fitted for the business of an interpreter." Brainerd appreciated the native's "acquaintance with the Indian & English languages; & likewise with the manners of both nations."[52] Having little or no facility in the Delaware languages and being committed to a brand of Christianity dominated by words rather than images, symbols, or rituals, Brainerd rightly saw his missionary effectiveness as directly dependent on his translator. On one occasion he acknowledged, "my interpreter being absent, I know not how to perform my work among the Indians."[53]

Tatamy's importance in Brainerd's life and ministry steadily grew in the two and a half years they spent together. A critical turning point came when Tatamy experienced the new birth. According to Brainerd, the native had been evidencing signs of strong interest in Christian faith for many months, the very sort of preparation for conversion the missionary believed was customary and in line with other evangelicals' teaching on the matter. What is more, it had been true in Brainerd's experience. Brainerd therefore proceeded cautiously in administering baptism, wanting to be sure that Tatamy did in fact have an experiential knowledge of the gospel.[54] He and his wife became the first Indians Brainerd baptized; their children were sprinkled several days later. With this event, and the outbreak of a revival among some Delaware shortly thereafter, Brainerd's earlier frustrations that his interpreter's doctrinal knowledge was insufficient and his tone indifferent now gave way to an enthusiasm for his colleague's ability to appreciate and replicate the missionary's sermonic style and substance.[55] Soon Tatamy was extending his role. Amid the revival in Crossweeksung, the native took "pains night and day to repeat and inculcate upon the minds of the Indians the truths . . . taught them daily." Indeed, Tatamy was doing so much spiritual mentoring that Brainerd found it necessary to remind him frequently to avoid setting himself up as a "publick teacher."[56] By the last of the four evangelistic trips the two made together into the rugged Pennsylvania interior (August 1746), however, Brainerd had instructed Tatamy and five other Christian Indians to spend a day talking with the Delaware residents before the missionary began his evangelizing. Apparently, Brainerd had come to rely on Tatamy to clear a spiritual as well as a physical path through the alien forest.[57]

Brainerd's appreciation for Tatamy was, although limited, completely genuine. In his public journal, Brainerd described the native as a "great comfort" and a "great instrument of promoting this good work among the Indians."[58] He also referred to Tatamy by name, the only native so acknowledged in any of his writings.[59] At the same time, Brainerd never thought of Tatamy as anything but an Indian. Brainerd's repeated attempts to recruit a white colleague to assist him and to provide the opportunity for Christian fellowship makes plain the limits of his friendship with Tatamy and thus with natives in general.[60] Still, the Indian interpreter was a crucial presence for Brainerd. Experientially acquainted with divine truths and highly assimilated to English ways, Tatamy represented precisely the kind of Christianized and Anglicized

Indian Brainerd set out to create. No wonder Brainerd felt comforted by Tatamy. He was living proof that, with God's grace, the ideal could be realized.

As Tatamy helped translate Brainerd's message into Indian languages, he and other natives, individually and collectively, helped determine what that message would be. The evangelist noted immediately that he had struck a responsive chord with the Crossweeksung Indians in early August 1745 when he preached a "milder gospel," one devoid of terror and focused instead on "the compassion and care of the Lord Jesus Christ for 'those that were lost.' "[61] Brainerd's one extant sermon, dating from 1742, indicates that he was already familiar with emphasizing God's compassion in the work of salvation before beginning his missionary efforts. But native responsiveness no doubt shaped his preaching tone and tenor.[62] It is also possible that Tatamy's earlier contact with Moravians, known for their stress on Christ's sacrificial love, may have influenced him to counsel Brainerd on how to present the good news.[63] In any case, for the rest of the month, the missionary drew on scriptural texts revealing the "comfortable" rather than the "dreadful truths of God's Word" in his daily revival preaching. As more and more Indian hearts were "melted," he became convinced that native spiritual concern "was never excited by any Harrangues of Terror, but always appear'd most remarkable when I insisted upon the Compositions of a dying Saviour, the plentiful Provisions of the Gospel, and the free Offers of divine Grace to needy distressed Sinners." [64] Not surprisingly, Brainerd used the same texts (and probably the same sermons) when he traveled in September to the Forks of the Delaware and on to Shamokin and Juniata, Indian towns further into Pennsylvania's backcountry.[65] Once back in Crossweeksung, he continued to reorient his preaching and teaching toward those themes natives preferred to hear.[66]

Studies of Delaware culture by Herbert Kraft, C. A. Weslager, and Anthony F. C. Wallace suggest that Lenape sensibilities were more suited to receiving a "milder gospel."[67] Just how clearly those sensibilities were communicated or how fully Brainerd understood them is impossible to say. At the very least, though, the Indians' words and actions made him aware that concepts of sin, guilt, divine anger, and eternal punishment were especially foreign to their vocabulary. And once aware, Brainerd made concerted efforts to tailor his evangelism accordingly.[68] If his sermons' biblical texts are any indication, he now concentrated his preaching on the suffering and atoning work of Christ. He even tried to build on native religious beliefs occasionally. For instance, what "very aged Indians" taught him about their ancestors' notion that "something of the Man . . . would survive the Body" became a means for explaining the other-worldly focus of his own message to Indians who were otherwise accustomed to conversing with whites only about this-worldly matters.[69]

Brainerd's remarkable encounter with a nativist preacher on one of his visits to Juniata shows just how far his contacts with Native Americans could move his own thinking. One of a number of leaders who stressed the need for pan-Indian cooperation and a return to ancient native ways, this reformer was part of what Gregory Dowd has called the "Indians' Great Awakening."[70] Brainerd rehearsed how upon meeting this man "none appeared so frightful or so near akin to what is usually imagined of infernal powers; none ever excited such images of terror in my mind." Dressed in animal skins and a wooden mask, and dancing about with a rattle, he "came near me [and] I could not but shrink away from him." Brainerd proceeded to see the native's sacred space, "a house consecrated to religious uses, with divers images cut out upon the several parts of it." An earlier Brainerd might have ended the encounter there, with quick denunciations of the Indian's devilish idolatry. Instead, the Brainerd who was now accustomed to conversing with natives entered into an extended dialogue with him about their respective spiritual journeys and beliefs. Not surprisingly, both men found elements of the other's faith with which to disagree. But Brainerd's account of the incident placed more stress on the discovery that there was also much common ground, both experientially and theologically. Each man had gone through a heart change, a conversion, several years earlier, and then felt God's call to proclaim the truth they had found to other needy souls. Both were disheartened when Indians failed to heed their message, both were perceived as "precise zealot[s] that made a needless noise about religious matters."[71] Brainerd reported those parallels without feeling the need to pronounce who or what was in the right. Whether that silence constitutes "a tentative and partial recognition of native systems of belief," as one recent scholar has suggested, is debatable.[72] But it surely shows a level of respect and tolerance for certain Indian ways that a younger, less native-wise Brainerd would never have demonstrated. And that change, that maturity, was a product of his contacts with Indians.

With all that said, what touched Brainerd the most in this specific encounter was the reformer's manner with him. As a good Edwardsean, Brainerd believed that the proof of a person's regenerated heart was in the pudding of their religious affections. When the missionary wrote that "he treated me with uncommon courtesy, and seemed to be hearty in it," Brainerd was testifying to the genuineness of this preacher's kindness and hospitality. Brainerd's conclusion that "there was something in his temper and disposition that looked more like true religion than anything I ever observed amongst other heathens," bears witness to his willingness to acknowledge the presence of holy affections or their likeness in whomever they might be found, a willingness that was once again the fruit of his face-to-face interactions with Indians.[73]

As a consequence of his encounters with other native religious leaders, Brainerd may have also borrowed or adapted native oratorical methods. Sandra Gustafson has argued that as he observed and competed with local powwows, "Brainerd quietly adopted their performance strategies in an effort to persuade his listeners and exert authority." He could not acknowledge such borrowing, even to himself, given typical Christian fears of being tainted by any type of pagan idolatry. Nevertheless, when Brainerd went off to pray in the woods alone or sweated profusely amid delivering a sermon, his actions may have been sufficiently analogous to native religious customs of vision quests and healing rituals to gain him a closer hearing from his Indian audiences.[74]

When native souls were saved in the summer of 1745, Brainerd, like any good Calvinist, was quick to credit God. But that is not to say that he did not derive deep personal satisfaction from his role in the process. For the first time, his ministry had borne tangible fruit, and he finally had a congregation he could truly call his own. Feelings of warm affection evolved on both sides, leaving Brainerd less emotionally disabled than perhaps at any other point in his adult life.[75] By December 1745, with twenty Indian families living within a quarter mile of his cottage, he had ample opportunity to nurture his flock. Individual Indians moved him with their struggles for faith, and he delighted in going from house to house teaching and counseling and in gathering Indians in his home for singing and Bible study. Emotions often ran high as pastor and laypersons wept together over the conditions of their souls.[76] By the following spring, Brainerd felt a wonderful closeness with his people: "My heart was knit to them. . . . And I saw in them appearances of the same love. This gave me something of a view of the heavenly state; and particularly that part of the happiness of heaven which consists in the communion of saints: and this was very affecting to me."[77]

The spiritual pilgrimages of the Indian conjurer, the woman in "great distress," and the "one who had been a vile drunkard" bespoke the amazing work of God's grace among the New Jersey Indians.[78] So, too, did the testimony of "one weary heavy-laden soul" whose account of "God's dealing with his soul" Brainerd found "abundantly satisfying" and "refreshing." This native described how he had often heard the missionary say that people must recognize their helplessness to do anything on behalf of their own salvation. He imagined that once he was humbled, God "would then be well pleased with him and bestow eternal life upon him." To his surprise, however, having become aware of his inability to save himself, he "felt it would be just with God to send him to eternal misery." Preoccupied thereafter with his own sinfulness, the Indian had come to one of Brainerd's evening services, and amid the invitation to sinners, his heart saw "something that was unspeakably good and lovely, and what he had never seen before." That "unspeakable excellence" was "the way of salvation by Christ." The regenerate native now believed that it was "unspeakably better to be saved altogether by the mere free grace of God in Christ, than to have had any hand in saving himself."[79]

In a real sense, Brainerd depended on this story and others like it to convince the Anglo-American religious world that the Crossweeksung awakening, and the Great Awakening in general, was truly God's work. His 1746 journal was very much an apologia for moderate evangelicalism.[80] Thus, several years before Brainerd's own religious autobiography was used for the same purpose by Jonathan Edwards, Brainerd himself had upheld some of his Indian converts as models of sinners saved by grace and living in faith. In fact, he thought they were such good models that no criticism of either their conversions or the evangelistic means employed to achieve them would be possible.[81] That these anonymous Indians should have been ignored by succeeding generations of white Christians, who preferred to cite David Brainerd as their model of true religion, comes, in one sense, as no surprise, given the might of later racism and the Indians' receding place in white Americans' consciousness. At the same time, it is surprising that later evangelicals failed to employ these native converts in the way that Brainerd and Edwards had, as striking evidence of the gospel's power to change lives. More surprising yet is the way these Indians were long ignored by students of colonial religion, including Brainerd scholars, a historical oversight that, until very recently, long awaited correction.

A Transformed Life

The denouement of Brainerd's life took eleven months to play out. Housebound in Elizabethtown, New Jersey, and Northampton, Massachusetts, for most of that time, the twenty-nine-year-old missionary fought losing battles with physical affliction and emotional depression. As difficult as the previous four years of ministry had been at times, nothing seemed worse to him than his idle passing of days in 1747. Strong yearnings for death returned, mixed once again with present feelings of uselessness.[82]

Yet Brainerd's final year was not altogether dark. His physical strength ebbed and flowed, occasionally affording him enough "clearness of thought and composure of mind" to talk and write about those things he considered most vital to the colonial church.[83] High on his list was promoting Indian missions. Norman Pettit may be right that Brainerd's original desire was to be a scholar; but once he became a missionary, there is no denying that evangelizing Indians and watching God's kingdom descend among them became central concerns.[84] The fortunes of his congregation in Cranbury, now left in the hands of his brother and fellow missionary John, especially "lay much on his heart" during the last two weeks of his life. Edwards wrote that when Brainerd spoke of his people, "it was with peculiar tenderness; so that his speech would be presently interrupted and drowned with tears."[85]

Those tears should not be discounted as simply signs of a dying man's agony. Brainerd had defended the healthy emotionalism of the Cranbury Indians, whose spiritual crises and releases had often included much weeping. Following their bent, he had privileged a compassionate God over a stern one in his preaching to them. Perhaps that compassionate God is who Brainerd now contemplated meeting face to face as he was called to give an account of himself.

Ever since he had left Yale, Indians had been making important differences in Brainerd's life. Those "differences" varied depending on the character of the Native Americans he encountered and on the relationship he experienced with them. Brainerd no doubt felt closest to the Christian Indians in New Jersey, but his repeated trips to the Pennsylvania interior reflect how powerfully he was drawn to the far larger groups of unevangelized natives living there.[86] Both types of Indians influenced him, and their impact on his emotional and spiritual health, sense of calling and ministerial worthiness, preaching style and content, understanding of missionary success, hopes for the coming of Christ's millennial kingdom, and vision of true religion should be acknowledged in any telling of his story. Such a comment may no longer seem arresting. Yet until recently, all versions of his life rehearsed since the 1750s had minimized or eliminated the natives' role and had principally portrayed Brainerd as a model of true virtue, example of sacrificial missionary service, definer of missionary success, and defender of the moderate Awakening against rational Arminianism and religious enthusiasm. In his otherwise excellent introduction to Edwards's *Life of David Brainerd,* for example, Norman Pettit failed to include any Indians in his discussions of Brainerd's adversaries, friends, associates, and confidants. Brainerd was placed solely in the contexts of white New England religion, as though he had spent his abbreviated career as a pastor in New Haven rather than as a missionary to at least four different groups of Indians.[87]

Perhaps interpreters of Brainerd had overlooked native influence in part because of Brainerd's own imperviousness to it.[88] His recurrent self-absorption sealed him off from others, especially alien Indians. So, too, did a missionary strategy that often featured preaching at natives he barely knew rather than becoming one of them and, in the process, earning the right to be heard. Likewise, his notion of evangelistic success provided personal solace but shifted attention back to his own soul, and away from those of his charges. How willful or deliberate Brainerd was in shielding himself from any Indian impress is difficult to say. But in the end, what emerges as most striking in his story is that in spite of whatever conscious or unconscious efforts were made to avoid the native touch, he nevertheless felt it and was changed by it.

To leave Indians out, therefore, will not do. With Native Americans absent or barely visible, the picture of Brainerd's life in particular and of early American religion in general is incomplete and even distorted. Nor is it enough simply to recall how, when, and why this missionary impacted the lives of natives. That portrait is still too partial, still too one-dimensional. Only by painting the reciprocal exchanges among Indians and Brainerd do we create an image that comes closer to the reality of their eighteenth-century worlds. Only by recovering the significant, and at times dramatic, ways encounters with Native Americans colored the religious experience and thought of Euro-Americans do we do justice to the full story of early American religious history.

5

Martyrs, Healers, and Statesmen

DAVID BRAINERD WAS UNUSUAL BUT NOT UNIQUE. ASPECTS OF HIS MISSIONary sojourns find parallels before and after him in the long history of religious encounters in early America. Specifically, his close working relationship with Delaware interpreter Moses Tatamy and desire to mold him into a particular kind of Christianized, Anglicized Indian assistant both echoes and foreshadows the experiences of other groups of European newcomers in their endeavors to spread the gospel to native peoples. They, too, relied heavily upon the talents of native assistants. Though now virtually forgotten, hundreds, perhaps thousands, of Native American Christian preachers, teachers, *dogiques,* interpreters, catechists, and deacons carried on the work of the church within early America in the sixteenth, seventeenth, and eighteenth centuries.[1] Past studies of native assistants have devoted much attention to the ways in which Europeans sought to control or limit the authority Christian Indians could exercise. Often this was achieved through denying natives any chance at ordination. The resulting frustrations over their lack of equal status divided native converts from their white brethren and in the long run very likely curtailed the effectiveness of the church overall.[2] Certainly this was an important part of the story of religious leadership and religious power in colonial America. However, it was hardly the whole story. European Christians who crossed the Atlantic were themselves often uncertain about what kind of pastoral or priestly leadership would be required or desired in the dramatically new settings of colonial cities and towns, let alone in the wilds of the backcountry. What kind of men (and for some groups, women) would make the best missionaries? What qualities of mind and character were most essential? What talents and skills would ensure evangelistic success? What biblical or historical models of leadership were most relevant? How should colonial leaders relate to their spiritual charges? Who could train and equip ministers and missionaries most effectively? All these questions and more came into play as European Christians sought to transplant their faith to North America and pass it on to the indigenous peoples.

Answers were formulated on the basis of what the Europeans brought with them but also arose in the midst of the give and take of their interactions with one another and Native Americans. As they performed their Christianizing work, Protestant and Catholic newcomers turned invariably to Indian converts for help. Naturally, they attempted to inculcate within any native assistants the particular styles and convictions of their brand of Christianity, including their notions about religious leadership. As a result, Christian Indian *dogiques* and deacons, not surprisingly, were indoctrinated in, and usually did their duties according to, the designs of those European believers who had introduced them to the new faith. What *is* surprising is that colonial sources reveal that they also carried on their duties according to the vibrant traditions and styles of religious and political leadership natives had long practiced within their own Indian cultures. In the process, native assistants showed colonists ways of leading that were sometimes too powerful to ignore. When that happened, Indians had opportunities to shape colonial Americans' attitudes and actions regarding what constituted authentic, faithful Christian leadership. Over the course of colonial history, leadership models clearly varied across the spectrum of Protestant and Catholic communities that took hold within the expanse of early America. One only has to think of the Puritans' faithful shepherd, the Quakers' traveling preacher, and the Methodists' itinerant evangelist. What did not vary as much was the possibility that within European-Native American religious interaction, individual Indians through the force of their own example and the power of their own traditions might affect what those models were.

Etienne Totiri, Johannes Wassamapah, and Good Peter (Gwedelhes Agwelondongwas) were three such Indians. Totiri ministered alongside French Jesuits in the 1640s at his home Huron village of Teanaostaiaé (St. Joseph II) as well as among neighboring Neutrals. A Mahican, Wassamapah co-labored with German Moravians in Shekomeko, New York and Bethlehem, Pennsylvania in the 1740s. Oneida chief Good Peter operated primarily within the orbit of the Congregationalist/Presbyterian missionary efforts among his people in central New York from the 1750s into the 1790s. Though widely separated by time, space, culture, language, and political circumstance, the individual stories of these three men will remind us that Europeans were not alone in promoting or defining the Christian message in early America, or in leading those who claimed the name of Christ. Natives could be key players, too. And not just for their peoples. Their witness in word and deed was simply too compelling for the Euro-American Christians around them to ignore, dismiss, or fully control. In the end, their own thinking about and practice of Christian leadership was different for having known these men.

A HURON MARTYR

French Jesuits began their work along the banks of Georgian Bay in Huronia in 1634 and likely made their first visit to Teanaostaiaé the following year. Impressed by the prospects of evangelistic success there, missionaries including Father Jean de Brébeuf and Father Charles Garnier made stops at the village in each of the next several years before deciding in 1638 to establish a more permanent mission presence. They moved the mission of St. Joseph from Ihonatiria to Teanaostaiaé (St. Joseph II) and used it as one of four main bases from which to itinerate among outlying Huron settlements. During these first few years, Hurons at Teanaostaiaé vacillated in their welcome of the priests, sometimes seemingly eager to have them, other times driving them from the village when they seemed to be the cause of local epidemics.[3]

Amid this mixed reception, Jesuits managed to baptize several dozen children and adults, most of whom died within the year.[4] Slowly but surely, however, between 1639 and 1641 some healthy adults began to receive religious instruction, were baptized, and formed the nucleus of a fledgling Huron Christian enclave within what was by then the largest Huron village. Among them was Christine Totiri. Later memorialized as one who "from the moment of her conversion . . . had always progressed in the practice of the highest virtues of Christianity," she was the first of many in her extended family to align with the newcomers' message.[5] By 1641, her sons, daughter-in-law, and grandchildren were all a part of the Christian fold—none more so than Etienne Totiri.[6] Following his mother's example, Totiri exemplified such an array of Christian virtues in leading the believers of his village that he amazed the Jesuit fathers and antagonized the much larger traditionalist majority in St. Joseph.

At least that is how he is presented in the *Jesuit Relations*. These annual reports were written by missionaries in the field and provided a chance not only to inform superiors and coworkers of their many activities, but, once edited and printed, to publicize their work among the religious order's patrons and friends in France. Crafted with those audiences in mind, the *Relations* gave Jesuits a prime opportunity for self-presentation and a literary means to construct the Amerindians they encountered in ways that served Jesuit purposes. Nuns, monks, priests, and pious laity on both sides of the Atlantic came to know the missionaries and their native charges primarily through its pages.[7]

The Jesuit preoccupation with martyrdom, though only one theme in a more complex self-image, stands out in the reports of the mid-seventeenth century. At one level, this is perfectly understandable given the very real physical dangers they faced and the grim fate that befell eight of their number in the Iroquois-Huron wars of the 1640s. But as Allan Greer has recently suggested, Jesuits were already inclined to think of themselves in these terms when they arrived in New France. Missionary work elsewhere sparked by the prior century's Catholic Reformation had renewed popular interest in and practical possibilities for sacrificial death in the cause of Christ. Jesuits in particular seemed to have relished the thought that their service might culminate in such a spiritually heroic act, so much so that members of other orders eventually accused them of a "martyrdom complex." Hearkening back to an era in church history when saint and martyr had been synonymous notions, members of the Society of Jesus gravitated toward a view of religious leadership that championed a willingness to die for the sake of the gospel as the highest mark of Christian sanctity. Once Father Isaac Jogues was slain in 1646, writers of the *Relations* were more than ready to compose saints' "Lives" of him and later martyrs that showed the exemplary piety of the Jesuit fathers.[8] Even before that, however, their letters spoke expectantly of the prospect that within their New World context, some would be called upon to pay the ultimate price.[9] Gabriel Lalemant, on the eve of his arrival in New France, poured out his desire to Christ himself: "it is necessary that your blood, shed no less for these barbarians than for us, be efficaciously applied to them; I wish to cooperate therein with your grace, and to sacrifice myself for them . . . your kingdom should be extended to all nations; I desire to spend my blood and my life in order to extend it to these."[10]

According to Greer, within the colonial genre of religious biography or hagiography (built into the *Relations* and other New France writings), Amerindians only very gradually became something more than supplementary figures in the story of heroic Christian witness in New France. Hence, it was not until the early eighteenth century that accounts made several natives, including Catherine Tekakwitha, the primary object of attention as full-fledged saints or martyrs.[11] Yet right from the start of the *Relations*, certain Hurons had made a strong enough impression upon the missionary fathers to force themselves more fully into the center of the narrative being constructed. Greer mentions Joseph Chihwatenha as one such native.[12] Another was Etienne Totiri. He first appears in the *Relation* of 1642–43 in a report on the work at St. Joseph. There, in the words of Father Charles Garnier, he emerges initially as a model of Christian hospitality. With no place to hold Mass and already facing persecution, the village's small Christian minority and their missionary overseers had reason to despair in the winter of 1641–42. But in stepped Etienne Totiri, offering one end of his longhouse for the construction of a chapel. Appropriately, services began being held there on the feast day of Saint Joseph. Totiri's act of generosity filled a practical need, encouraged the believers, and gave tangible proof of his identification with the Christian cause.[13]

Garnier elaborated further on Totiri's hospitality and its results in a private letter to his brother, dated May 22, 1642. He reported that the Christians were attending Mass in the chapel every day as well as confession every Saturday. The two resident French priests were ready to serve them, but they themselves had been shown "a thousand courtesies" by Totiri, whose sacrifice of part of his cabin had deprived him of critical storage space for corn and wood. When the priests compared his generosity to that of French aristocrats who had given up their wealth to build chapels, Totiri and his mother responded by offering them another gift, her beaver robe. The Jesuits graciously declined, explaining that it was not their intent to solicit more.[14] Aware of how costly such a gift would be in the midst of a Georgian Bay winter, Garnier was clearly moved emotionally and perhaps even spiritually by these acts of kindness.

If Totiri's material sacrifices could touch the newcomers (and by extension their readers), all the more so when it came to his bold declaration that he was willing to die for his faith. Within a few lines of being introduced to Totiri, readers learned that following the construction of the chapel, persecution of the village's Christians intensified. Totiri was especially targeted because he was "the most fervent in the Faith" and had been willing to give up part of his longhouse. Despite grave threats, Totiri and his family remained steadfast in their religious devotion. When told to leave the village, he responded that he was willing to follow the lead of the priests because he was now "more attached to them than to my Country and to all my relatives, because they bring us the promise of eternal happiness." According to the *Relation*, Totiri went on to declare his readiness for the martyr's mantle:

> I fear not death, since GOD has enlightened my mind, and has shown me things more important than this bodily life, against which alone any design can be harbored. Let them kill my mother, my wife, my children, and my brothers; after them, the blow that is to give me happiness will fall on me! My Soul is not attached to my body,—a single instant can separate them; but faith shall never be ravished on me.[15]

The *Relation* of 1642–43 made several additional references to Totiri, each one enlarging the portrait of his religious leadership and pointing ultimately to the assertion that here was a martyr-in-waiting. Garnier noted that when he and the other fathers were absent, Totiri gathered the Christians together for worship and catechetical instruction. The priests were apparently confident enough in his familiarity with the liturgy and grasp of basic doctrine to encourage such religious exercises to go on under his oversight. In addition, they reported that amid the all-too-present reality of disease and death, Totiri visited the sick and evangelized the dying. Although his efforts to convert an elderly woman were to no avail, this "good Christian" still learned an important spiritual lesson—"the gift of Faith is not a present from earth . . . [for] GOD alone can touch the heart." Most dramatically, the *Relation* relayed a story of how Totiri responded to the ranting of a demoniac and the resulting accusations of the village against its Christian inhabitants. One of St. Joseph's leaders, Astiskoua, had been filled by a demon as he was about to enter the church for baptism on Easter Sunday. He burst from the scene, ran to nearby villages, began destroying property in his wake, and shouted that he must "kill all the French, as they alone were ruining the whole country." When he returned to St. Joseph, others restrained him, but his violent outbursts left many in the community calling for the expulsion if not the execution of the French. As tensions mounted and a mob was about to let loose its fury, Totiri boldly exclaimed that if the French were to be killed, he should be also, for he was as guilty of being a Christian as they were, and it was that which was a "crime" in the eyes of his fellow Hurons. Astiskoua then managed to escape and proceeded to leave a trail of destruction in his wake as he went about the village targeting the cabins of Christians. Finally, he sought out Etienne himself for a spiritual showdown. Astiskoua exclaimed, "It is on thee that I wish to avenge myself; I must burn thee." In the face of such a challenge, Totiri might have been expected to resort to some form of self-defense or to invoke the superior power of the Christian Trinitarian God to drive out the demon or at least to protect him. Instead, in Garnier's words, Totiri "commended himself to GOD, resigned himself to his holy will, and, being resolved to endure everything, he held out to the possessed man both his arms, clasped together and quite naked, to be burned." Then, in a climatic moment, Totiri enjoined him to take "courage" and " 'burn me, if thou wilt.' " Upon hearing those words, "the Madman stopped," went away, and turned his wrath elsewhere.[16]

For *Relation* readers, here was a lesson too plain to miss—the kind of spiritual leadership that would have real power in Huron country would be the sacrificial servant ready to be bruised, afflicted, and martyred. And if a recent Huron convert such as Totiri could incarnate that truth, could any less be expected of the Jesuit fathers or their supporters?

In finishing this story, Garnier made sure that there was an important role for the Jesuit fathers to play. He assured his superiors that under the tumultuous circumstances, "the little Flock of Faithful ones needed their Pastor" (i.e., him) to calm them down and to minister as best he and the other fathers could to Astiskoua himself. For their trouble, they received from him only verbal and physical abuse. But in the end, Astiskoua's story had a happy ending, for his possession ceased and he reiterated his earlier desire to enter the Christian community through baptism.[17]

Overall, if this account fashioned the priests in a good light, it was no less laudatory of Totiri's spiritual courage or the willingness of his fellow native believers to "endure everything for the love of God," inspired as they were by "the hope of Paradise."[18] Such a picture of the work in St. Joseph made clear the need for the Jesuits but affirmed the capability of the Amerindians not only to embrace the faith but to exhibit precisely the kind of Christian virtues, and especially the willingness to be martyred, that the missionaries wished for themselves and their charges. Within the hagiographic genre that characterized much of what was contained in the *Relations*, Totiri was made to fit neatly into Jesuit hopes and aspirations. His story was too good (too good to be true?) not to be shared with supporters on both sides of the Atlantic.

Over the next several years, Totiri became something of a common figure in the annual reports sent back to Paris. As before, each new episode written about him added breadth and depth to the collective image being formed of this native assistant. The rest of 1642 and 1643 found Totiri once again enduring significant trials for the sake of the gospel. That spring, he and several other Huron traders had made their way to Quebec and on their return linked up with Father Isaac Jogues and his associates. Somewhere near Three Rivers, a group of Iroquois attacked their party and captured Jogues. Totiri managed to escape but in the process lost almost all his trade goods. Once more, association with the Jesuits had exacted a material price for him.[19] He continued his trading activities that fall and into the winter of 1643. His travels included time spent among the Neutrals, a neighboring Indian people situated between lakes Erie and Ontario. According to the *Relation* of 1643–1644, Totiri and several other Christian Hurons "performed the duty of Apostles" while carrying on their business there. The Neutrals' fascination with the rosaries worn around the Hurons' necks opened a door for an extended conversation about the mysteries of the Christian faith. Totiri proved willing and able to jump into the deep end of the theological pool as he shared his Christian beliefs. For example, he discussed with them the character of God, describing him as creator and sustainer of all things, as invisible, and as omnipresent. What the Neutrals thought of all of that is unclear, but their attention was piqued when Totiri provided graphic detail of the hellish fate that awaited those who failed to love his god. The Jesuit writer was persuaded that these evangelistic efforts met "perhaps with more success for the present than we ourselves [the Jesuits] could have had."[20]

Totiri finally returned to St. Joseph in the spring or summer of 1643, only to be greeted with the word that his mother had died the previous summer. Though he was heartbroken, his reception of the news became another occasion to affirm his faith and to exercise spiritual leadership in the community. He rejoiced that "she had died a good Christian" and prayed publicly to God to "hasten our death, if it please you, for thereby you will hasten our happiness." When others came to console him, he did the consoling, encouraging them to change their tears into joy for the sake of showing their unbelieving neighbors that "we have Faith and the hope of Paradise in our hearts."[21]

Eight months later, Totiri had another opportunity to offer spiritual wisdom regarding his mother's death. Only then did his brother, Paul Okatakwan, casually pass on to him and in turn, to the Jesuit fathers, the story that in her waning moments, Christine had claimed to have a vision of the Virgin Mary accompanied by young Frenchmen. She delighted in the sweet words being spoken to her by the Virgin. At the time, Paul tried to persuade her that she was just imagining it, but Christine insisted the vision was real and then passed away. Upon hearing the story, Totiri showed none of Paul's hesitation in accepting the vision as true and even offered a partial interpretation: "those young Frenchmen of such rare beauty were Angels from Heaven, who accompanied the most blessed Virgin."[22]

That the Jesuits wrote approvingly of Christine's vision and Totiri's interpretation reflects their own growing comfort level in the mid-seventeenth century with visions and dreams as means through which the Holy Spirit could reveal his will to believers. Mysticism was an increasingly important stream within French Catholicism, as suggested by the fact that someone like Marie de l'Incarnation was emerging at this same moment.[23] Within New France, Jean de Brébeuf had a series of mystical experiences in the 1630s and 1640s that included visions.[24] Yet missionaries were still not quite prepared for the central place dreams and visions occupied within the cultures of the Iroquois and Hurons.[25] The Europeans reacted with combinations of wonder and scorn, fascination and dread. The postconversion dreams of Native

Americans posed an especially tricky phenomenon for priests to evaluate. Were such experiences pagan carryovers, or did they represent a genuine message from God? Jerome Lalemant, Jesuit writer of the *Relation* of 1643–44 regarding St. Joseph, wondered aloud whether he should even include an account of a dream Totiri had upon three occasions. Having expressed his hesitation, the father went ahead and used the native's own words, which described seeing a cross in the sky dripping with the crucified Christ's blood. A crowd of people moved toward the cross from the West, attracted by the "loving looks" of the savior. Totiri then heard a voice insisting he pray; so he did and found himself filled with an overwhelming fear and love. Lalemant noted that he would have dismissed the dream "were it not that the impressions that it has left in his [Totiri's] heart are supernatural." Totiri now spoke of little besides his Christian faith. For his part, Lalemant tried to make sense of the dream—perhaps it was a prophecy of the future conversion of the Neutrals, to which Totiri had already contributed.[26]

Other parts of Lalemant's report that year reinforced the portrait of Totiri as peripatetic preacher, teacher, and evangelist, and now added a new image, dedicated Christian husband and father. In the former roles, his speaking skill, highly valued by Hurons and Frenchmen alike, allowed his words, under God's inspiration, to penetrate "into the very depths of their hearts" and made his listeners "feel a portion of what he himself feels." In the new role, Totiri was presented as head of an extended family that was unsurpassed in its piety. His wife, Madeleine, described as inferior to him neither "in intelligence" nor "in virtue," devoted herself to instructing other women in the faith with a verve that matched her husband's. Their three-year-old daughter could already recite catechism answers and set prayers, so used was she to hearing them spoken. Here was a family and a household where, thanks to the leadership of Totiri, Christian truth was proclaimed and Christian virtue practiced.[27]

That family, along with the other believers in St. Joseph, found their faith continually tested by the hostility of their neighbors. On a regular basis they were told either to leave the village or, if they stayed, to keep their beliefs to themselves and not participate in Huron councils or feasts. Some even suggested forcing the Christians to renounce their faith. Increasingly ostracized, ridiculed, and threatened by the traditionalist majority, the small band of Christians wondered how best to defuse the situation. At a council of their own, they met to discuss their options and came to the conclusion that the matter was in God's hands and that they must be prepared to endure suffering for his sake. As the one to whom the rest looked for leadership, Totiri had the last word: "let us dread nothing but sin."[28]

Describing such stalwart faith in the face of persecution prompted the *Relation* writer in 1643 to launch into a meditation on the glorious future that might await some of these Huron converts. With perhaps Etienne Totiri in mind, Jerome Lalemant boldly told his readers, "I know not how these storms [the persecution] will end; but I am not without hope of seeing, in a few years, martyrs for the Faith in these countries, and perhaps we [the Jesuit fathers] shall not be the first. The fervor of some one of these good Neophytes will deserve that favor from Heaven." Modern sensibilities being what they are, it seems shocking that the prospect of martyrs would arouse Lalemant's *hope* rather than his *fear*. But these lines underscore once again the Jesuit championing of the martyr's way. For French readers at the time, the more shocking claim was likely his proposal that a Native American Christian might be worthy of such a blessing and honor. Lalemant took pains to elaborate on the point to persuade his audience. He explained that he knew some Amerindians "whom God seems to be preparing for that grace, who disregard their lives, and look upon such a death as a reward for what they do and wish to do for the advancement of the Faith." If God could do such a work within "the heart of a barbarian," surely Jesuits and other European Christians should be ready and willing to follow his lead whatever the cost.[29]

Tensions between traditionalists and Christians in Teanaostaiaé remained strong over the next several years. During celebration of the Ononharoia, the main Huron winter festival, in 1645–46, fighting erupted, leaving several Christians beaten and one man wounded by a hatchet blow. Anthropologist Bruce Trigger has suggested that the purpose of physical and verbal attacks on Christians was apparently not to kill or expel them but rather to pressure them into participation in traditional rites and customs.[30] By and large, these efforts proved futile, an indication of the change in converts' values. However, they did make the Christians inclined to keep their faith largely private, at least until 1645. Then it was once again Etienne Totiri who trod new ground and, in the process, showed Jesuit and Huron alike an awe-inspiring leadership. According to Father Paul Ragueneau, author of the *Relation* of 1645–46, Totiri was the first Christian Huron to take his faith into the proverbial public square. The occasion was the execution of a native (probably Iroquois) captive at Taenhatentaron (St. Ignace). A large, agitated crowd gathered to watch him burn and to hurl insults. Amid their shouts and the cries of the victim, Totiri suddenly began to preach. Grabbing their attention with his own fiery presence, Totiri used the vivid image at hand—the burning victim—to illustrate the fate that awaited those who failed to love and obey the true God. His graphic and prolonged depiction of the horrors of hell silenced the mob. Perhaps then in quieter tones he told them that all was not lost for God had provided a remedy. If they would "adore that great God who has created both the heavens and the earth, and tremble at the sight of his awful judgments," then their eternity would be free of flames.[31]

Totiri's words stirred his listeners, some to wonder at his zeal, others to denounce his strange message. But he was not done yet. Now his actions would speak as loudly as his words. Having earlier assured the crowd that he was not there to try to release the prisoner, Totiri approached the "half roasted" man, assured him that he would do him no further harm, and spoke of a loving God who wished to bless his soul in heaven. Revived a bit by what he heard, the captive recalled a similar execution scene in which he had watched and listened to a group of Huron prisoners tell one another of the joys of heaven that lay ahead. Could such tales be true? Totiri provided further instruction and soon the man began to plead for baptism. Hearing his request, the crowd reacted angrily, insisting that eternal punishment in whoever's afterlife was his appropriate destiny. Totiri thought otherwise, though, and began to search wildly for water to administer the rite. Showing no concern for himself, he endured "a thousand insults and numerous blows" while securing the water and sprinkling the prisoner. Thanks to Totiri's heroic deed, the man expired confident of his future happiness in heaven. When other Christians congratulated him on his brave acts, Totiri averred that the Lord, not he, was responsible for what had happened and had empowered him through the taking of the Eucharist that morning.[32]

The *Relation* of 1645–46 recounted one final story of Totiri's extraordinary leadership. With more of their number succumbing to disease, the Christians of St. Joseph decided to enhance their cemetery by adding a cross. But rather than just erecting it there, they chose to organize a processional through the village so that they could very publicly display the cross as the great symbol of their faith. Those who marched received the usual verbal attacks from their hostile neighbors. Within days or weeks, the cross itself came under literal attack from local children, who threw stones and refuse upon it. That was more than Totiri could tolerate, for both his Huron and Christian sensibilities were aroused. When evening arrived that day and most of the villagers were within earshot, Totiri seized the moment. He climbed onto the roof of one of the longhouses and let out an enormous yell like one warning of an approaching enemy. Alarmed Huron men and women came running, weapons in hand. Totiri's booming voice pounced upon them, declaring that the enemy lay within, not outside, the village. The Christian cemetery had been desecrated, a clear violation of one of the Hu-

rons' own cherished traditional beliefs. How could they let this dis-
respect of sacred things and sacred space happen? Better that they destroy his home, beat his body, or even kill him. All those things Totiri
would "endure . . . with love." But for them to attack something consecrated to God was another matter. They best be aware that it was "a
terrible thing to take God as an enemy."[33]

Totiri's message had its desired effect. Thereafter traditionalist parents
kept their offspring from doing any more damage, perhaps not wanting
to give the despised rabble-rousing preacher any more ammunition.
Such an outcome might have struck faithful readers of the Jesuit *Relations* as predictable, at least those who had grown familiar with Totiri's
accomplishments over the previous five years. The stories relayed about
him would have left them imagining that there was little this native
assistant could not or would not do. A quick review of the roles in which
the *Relations* had cast him underscores the point: generous donor, hospitable host, powerful preacher, effective teacher, wise interpreter of
dreams, bold evangelist, pious husband and father, dependable *dogique*,
persecuted Christian, courageous witness, potential martyr. The fathers'
reports left no doubt as to who was the native leader of the flock in St.
Joseph. Totiri's exploits fleshed out in vivid detail the costs of discipleship
for Huron converts in New France and gave the missionaries a ready
example of the type of leaders they would hope to train.

But in Totiri the Jesuits also gave a portrait of what kind of Christian
leadership was required of those Europeans who would serve in Huronia. He embodied most, if not all, of the leadership qualities to which
they themselves aspired. As they depicted him for their readers, including potential recruits, the high value the Jesuits placed upon such Christian duties as attending Mass, learning Catholic doctrine, participating
in the sacraments, and spreading the gospel shone through in the model
Totiri set for all those around him. More especially, his willingness to
suffer cheerfully for Christ in the face of persecution, even to the point
of losing his life, made Totiri the kind of sacrificial servant the Jesuits
wanted themselves to be. Their bent toward martyrdom surfaced repeatedly as they framed his story. And as the likelihood of his meeting
that fate grew stronger in the mid-1640s, so, too, did Jesuit admiration
and envy for this Huron headman.

Why did the Jesuits represent Totiri in such a positive light? Clearly,
much of the answer lies in their desire to illustrate the transforming
power of the gospel and the success of their missionary efforts. He and a
handful of other Native American converts provided the best evidence
that the fathers' work was not in vain. The indigenous people of New
France could understand and practice Christianity well if taught prop-

erly. They could even become examples worthy enough for Europeans, Jesuits included, to follow.[34]

These motives, while important, may not be the whole story, however. Taken alone, they leave the impression that the *Relations'* authors were solely responsible for the shape natives took within their reports. Totiri and other Amerindians are treated as mere inventions of the fathers' will. What if, instead, Totiri was allowed some agency of his own? What if it were supposed that whether the Jesuits knew it or not, the force of Totiri's character was sufficient to affect what they wrote about him? And what if we imagined that in the course of their encounter with Totiri, he came to influence the missionaries' own thinking about being a minister in New France?[35] Whatever is thought of Jesuit ideals or of Totiri's out of the ordinary behavior, such possibilities may not be as farfetched as they initially seem. What explains, for example, the consistency with which Totiri was presented across multiple years and by multiple authors? Was it simply a matter of later writers copying what earlier ones had said? Was it orchestrated in some conscious fashion or a mere coincidence? Or did Totiri's actual personality and deeds lend themselves to the positive portrayal they always received? More tellingly, why is it that so much of what Totiri purportedly said and did reflects core Huron values and traditions? Now on the one hand, it seems clear that his embrace of Christianity forced him to break with a host of Huron beliefs and customs. Hence, his ongoing struggle with the traditionalists. Yet, on the other hand, the actions attributed to him conform at many points with what scholars know of Huron ways, perhaps especially in regard to the exercise of power. Bruce Trigger has argued that, "the ideal Huron chief was a wise and brave man who understood his followers and won their support by means of his generosity, persuasiveness, and balanced judgment."[36] That description is more than apt for the Totiri we meet in the *Relations*. For example, his willingness to convert part of his longhouse into a chapel for the community's use, as well as his other material sacrifices, was indicative of the Huron view of leadership as something that "involved repeatedly securing the consent of followers" through being "unstintingly generous." Moreover, the speaking skill that he exemplified on more than one occasion was cultivated in the context of a culture that made oratorical abilities one of the prime qualifications for becoming and remaining a chief. The very word for chief in the Huron language, *yarihwa,* meant "he is of great voice." Admittedly, some of Totiri's public discourses did not conform to the Hurons' preference for "quiet persuasiveness," but they did demonstrate another crucial Huron value—courage (more about that below).[37] Totiri's interest in dreams and efforts to interpret them properly constituted another clear carryover from what was expected of Huron leaders. Although he did not go so far as to be a would-be shaman (a medicine man whose powers included the ability to interpret dreams accurately), Totiri paid the kind of attention to his own dreams or visions and those of his mother that was customary in his culture. Even the presence of Jesus, Mary, and angels in their dreams was not wholly new; Hurons traditionally believed that Iouskeha and Aataentsik were two of several supernatural beings who took on human appearance in dreams and visions.[38]

Perhaps more than anything else, Totiri exemplified the bravery expected of Huron men in general and those in authority in particular. "The ideal [Huron] man," Trigger explains, "was a brave warrior who was self-reliant, intolerant of restraint, and indifferent to the pain that others might try to inflict on him."[39] Totiri's independent spirit accorded well with what Huron society prescribed, even if it brought him into conflict with many of his neighbors. And his willingness to test his own courage over and over again was precisely what Huron men were supposed to do. Finally, his readiness to endure pain and death at the hands of his rivals with a stiff upper lip showed how well he had imbibed the messages conveyed to all Huron boys about what it meant to be a man. Totiri's stoicism in the face of personal danger amazed the Jesuits. They took it as a measure of his deep Christian faith. But it was also or alternatively a sign of how deeply engrained Huron values were within his heart and mind.

If Totiri embodied the qualities of the ideal Huron warrior, Jesuits may have been eager to learn from him. John Steckley has argued that the Jesuits sought to build upon elements of Huron culture in the presentation of the gospel. More specifically he sees them borrowing the cultural image of the warrior and using that model to explain the power and character of Christian supernatural entities. Within that scheme, "Christian spirit figures such as God, Jesus, the Devil and his demons" were depicted as "ultimate warriors." To the extent that Steckley is right, Jesuits may have drawn upon and welcomed what Totiri could teach them about this Huron ideal. His life as they knew it displayed those traits that they in turn could use to make plain to other natives the even greater power and goodness of Jesus, the supreme warrior.[40]

What all of this suggests is the possibility, perhaps even the likelihood, that however constructed the figure of Totiri might be in the Jesuit *Relations*, its construction was shaped not only by the missionaries and the audiences they served but also by Totiri himself and the Huron culture he brought with him, and the willingness of Jesuits to borrow from and be influenced by that culture. I would argue that this was especially true in relation to concepts of leadership. The members of the

Society of Jesus arrived in New France with a set of ideals about what spiritual leadership would entail. Prominent among those ideals was martyrdom. During the 1640s and prior to the violent deaths of Jogues and other Jesuits, Totiri's acts, rooted in traditional Huron ways but now adapted for Christian ends, gave the missionaries a fuller and sharper view of how to lead a body of Christians in Huron country. More specifically, his life made plain the costs of following Christ in a hostile environment. Not surprisingly, martyrdom remained a key element in the Jesuit vision during those years. No doubt that was due in part to the strength of their preexisting notions carried from Europe. But there is good reason to think that it was also due to the powerful witness of Amerindians such as Totiri. His life reinforced and refined their thinking. In him and through him, Jesuits found and created a ready example of the kind of leader they hoped they could be. In this way, the Totiri of the Jesuit *Relations* was both reflector and shaper of what Jesuits told themselves and their public about religious leadership.

The *Relations* are frustratingly silent about what became of Etienne Totiri after 1646. Thereafter, in general, missionary reports became increasingly focused on political matters and said little about individual believers. One possibility is that he abandoned the new faith and missionary writers were too disappointed or embarrassed to report his apostasy. This seems unlikely for a variety of reasons, including the fact that in the face of the threat of Iroquois attack in 1647–48, many more Hurons were moving toward than away from the Church. More likely is the prospect that Totiri himself was one of the many victims of that attack when it finally came in July 1648. As the Iroquois laid waste to Teanaostaiaé, they killed and captured Christian and non-Christian Hurons alike.[41] If Totiri met his end there, it was because he was a Huron, not because he was a Christian. In that regard, he would not have been a Christian martyr in any traditional sense. Yet one wonders, if his fate had been known by one of the Jesuits familiar with him, might his story have been completed in a way to fulfill his martyr's destiny? On the other hand, perhaps in 1648 the Jesuits already had all the martyrs they could handle.

A MAHICAN HEALER

A century later and a few hundred miles to the southeast, another group of European Christians, this one from Germany, was beginning a new missionary work among the Mahicans of New York and Connecticut. Members of the Unitas Fratrum—the Moravians—believed that salvation was possible for any human being and therefore it was incumbent upon them to bring the good news of Christ to people around the globe. Following that call, Moravians set off from their Herrnhut headquarters in Saxony in the 1730s to Africa, South America, Russia, Greenland, and the British mainland colonies of North America. A short-lived settlement in Georgia was followed by a decision in 1740 to find a more permanent location in Pennsylvania, a quest that soon led them to found Bethlehem.[42] That same year Moravian missionary Christian Heinrich Rauch met two Mahicans, whom he called Tschoop and Schawash, in New York City, and there began a relationship that opened the door to Moravian evangelism along the Hudson River.

Tschoop, or Job as the English called him, was the Mahican sachem Wassamapah (later he was baptized with the name Johannes), who was in New York representing fellow Mahicans in a dispute over land rights in Shekomeko, a community located east of the Hudson River in Dutchess County. As part of a small remnant of Mahicans living there or across the border in Connecticut, he and Schawash may have been looking for any allies they could muster. Whether that fact or some other reason prompted them to accept Rauch's offer to come to Shekomeko is hard to say. What is clear is that he arrived in their town within a month and began to share a distinctively Moravian version of the Christian message.[43]

At the time, Moravians were placing an especially strong emphasis upon the physical suffering and sacrifice of Jesus. Count Nicolaus von Zinzendorf, the Moravians' patron and spiritual leader, popularized a "Blood and Wounds" theology that in the 1740s captured the imagination and hearts of most of his Moravian brethren and shaped the missionary message and methods Rauch and others used in evangelizing Indians. Christ's death on the cross and its consequences for human salvation was the core of the gospel in Zinzendorf's view and needed to be the starting point, not the culminating claim, of missionary evangelism. Sinners needed to know the lengths to which the Savior (whom Moravians called the *Heiland*) had gone to save their souls. The *Heiland*'s bloody body, and particularly his side wound, came to be portrayed in graphic detail in sermons, hymns, and religious paintings. Moravian believers were clearly drawn to this theology and vocabulary, for it injected a deeply emotional and even sensual element into their faith. That they internalized its message is evident in their short spiritual autobiographies. One Moravian immigrant, Margarethe Edmonds, ended her memoir by writing, "I hope that my dear Savior will keep me in Him and in His wounds and in His dear Congregation, and always wash me in His costly blood until I receive the grace to see Him face to face and to kiss His pierced feet."[44]

Historian Jane Merritt has recently argued that it was precisely this Moravian stress upon the "power inherent in the body and blood of Christ" that "most attracted Indians" to what Moravians were saying.[45] That certainly seems to have been true for Wassamapah. Before telling his story, though, it is worth pausing for a moment and considering how this theology may have also helped to shape what Moravians wanted in their community leaders. As a Christian movement, Moravianism went back to the early fifteenth century. But the group had reconstituted itself only in the 1720s and therefore had had little time to develop firm ideas about what their leadership should be like. In the process of defining their "Blood and Wounds" theology, however, Zinzendorf and others presented a powerful portrait of Jesus that provided Moravian missionaries, and more broadly, Moravian leaders (both male and female) with someone to emulate. The *Heiland* was the sacrificial servant who in life identified with the hurts of others and in death humbled himself even to the point of crucifixion, all for the sake of sinners. Brokenness, woundedness, humility, sacrifice, perseverance in the face of suffering and torture—these were the qualities that Jesus exemplified and to which Moravian followers were called.[46] They are strikingly reminiscent of what modern Catholic theologian Henri Nouwen has labeled the "wounded healer" image of Christ and Christian leadership. Nouwen's phrase seems apt to capture what Moravians hoped their missionary and lay leaders would embody. As he explains it, a minister, following the example of Jesus, "is called not only to care for his own wounds and the wounds of others, but also to make his wounds into a major source of his healing power." When a minister comes to understand and accept her own pain, whether physical or emotional, then she is in a better place to see her wounds as a help to herself and others, not because she can take away the pain but because she can make plain how she shares in the pain and in the corresponding hope for liberation. Her message as a wounded healer then becomes, "The master [the savior] is coming— not tomorrow, but today, not next year, but this year, not after all misery is passed, but in the middle of it, not in another place but right here where we are standing."[47]

It would be stretching the point to suggest that mid-eighteenth-century Moravians framed their ministerial or missionary task precisely in Nouwen's terms. Yet there seems to be at least a family resemblance to what he says in the way they spoke about and went about their work. Wassamapah's conversion and subsequent pastoral work illustrates the point and suggests as well the role early native converts played in further defining Moravian notions of Christian leadership. August Spangenberg, a key Moravian missionary and theologian from the 1740s on, met Wassamapah within a couple of years of the Mahican's coming to faith and heard him explain how previously he had been a very wicked man. Earlier efforts by ministers of other denominations had been rebuffed by him and other Mahicans. But there was something dramatically different in the message and approach of Christian Rauch when he arrived in August 1740. Rather than insulting his intelligence and culture, or preaching a list of moral dos and don'ts, Rauch had simply laid out the gospel story of Christ's life, suffering, death, and resurrection, pronounced Christ's willingness to save him from his misery-filled life, and then shockingly, "lay down on a board in my hut, and fell asleep, being fatigued with his journey." Wassamapah was left to wonder, "What manner of man is this? There he lies and sleeps so sweetly. I might kill him immediately, and throw him out into the forest;—who would care for it?" Wassamapah was clearly amazed at Rauch's actions, but he was even more preoccupied with what he had just heard: "I could not get rid of his words. They continually recurred to me; and though I went to sleep, yet I dreamed of the blood which Christ had shed for us."[48]

This was to be the first in a series of moments, both while awake and while asleep, in which Wassamapah was grabbed by the blood of Jesus. In a letter he sent to Zinzendorf in December 1741, he recalled, "my first feeling in my heart was from his blood and when I heard that he was also the Saviour of the heathen and that I yet did owe him my heart, I felt a drawing towards him in my heart." Whenever he heard that the Lamb of God had shed his blood for sinners, he thought, "there must be something in it, for my heart got every Time warm'd by it." As his contemplation of the lamb's sacrifice intensified, Wassamapah "did often dream of it" and was afterward eager to tell others how in his dream "a teacher did stand before me and did preach to me of the blood of our Saviour."[49]

Wassamapah's testimony reinforces what recent historians have suggested about the compelling appeal of Christ's bloody torment for many Indians as well as the centrality of dreams and visions to Native American spirituality. For Mahican and other native males, Christ's stoic endurance of great physical abuse at the hands of his enemies may have resonated with their cultural ideal of the "ultimate warrior captive," the one who could maintain his strength of character amid the vilest of tortures.[50] The manner in which Christ shed his blood, then, bespoke his spiritual power. Being told of such power in a dream only convinced Wassamapah all the more that he should pay attention to the message Rauch proclaimed. He, like virtually all the other Native Americans the Moravians would encounter, believed that dreams were a vital medium to the spirit world, a bridge of sorts between humans and supernatural powers.[51] If he was at all typical, Wassamapah would have devoted considerable energy to interpreting his dreams. In that way, he would have been not only like fellow Mahicans but also like his European colonial neighbors, who similarly analyzed dreams (and much else) for their spiritual content. Dreams and the act of dreaming had different cultural meanings for Indians and Euro-Americans, but both people groups were prepared to believe that dreams could offer important spiritual assistance of one kind or another. And among colonial Christian bodies, few were more open to the spiritual potency of dreams and visions than the Moravians. Their Pietist leanings disposed them toward belief in a God who spoke through a variety of means. Christians naturally had to discern whether such messages came from Christ or the devil.[52] That task was pretty straightforward, however, when it came to judging dreams like Wassamapah's.

The common ground of sorts that Mahicans and Moravians found in the power of blood and the revelations of dreams and visions drew them together and began a series of religious exchanges that shaped both communities in the formative decade of the 1740s. In those years, Moravians were just beginning to establish a foothold on this side of the Atlantic, a fledgling religious movement at best, especially in upper New York. Meanwhile, politically weak and economically vulnerable Hudson River Mahicans struggled to hold on to their most valuable asset (at least in the eyes of neighboring whites), their land, while living on the periphery of both colonial New York and their own nation, whose center had moved to Stockbridge, Massachusetts, in 1740. Moravians and Mahicans alike were in a marginal position.[53] Both were anxious, at least unconsciously, to draw strength from the other. Early converts such as Wassamapah became immediate links between the two communities. This might have happened anyway, but the fact that Wassamapah and several other converts were influential chiefs made it more likely. Soon they assumed major responsibilities within the emerging Mahican Moravian community.[54] Over the next several years until his death in 1746, Wassamapah, or Johannes, as he came to be known to fellow Moravians (native and white) after his baptism, did it all—he translated, preached, counseled, and evangelized; he led worship, wrote hymns, and discussed theology; he offered political advice and provided political representation; and he taught missionary methods and shared in Holy Communion.[55]

Moravian diaries and letters allow glimpses of Johannes at work.[56] As various German Moravians, often couples, moved in and out of Shekomeko between 1740 and 1744, he and a handful of other native men and women helped hold the small but growing congregation together. That became even more dramatically the case in December 1744, when the white Moravians were driven out of the Hudson Valley by religious and political opponents. Thereafter Johannes functioned as perhaps their lead preacher as well as their principal political and legal agent.[57] Into all these tasks, he brought the habits and skills of a seasoned Mahican leader, and none more so than his speaking ability. For example, in February 1743, Johannes arrived in Potatick, Connecticut, sent there by his congregation to evangelize neighboring Indians. Moravian missionary Martin Mack witnessed the event with a good deal of amazement:

> The Indians came together & John Preached to them they were all full of wonder at him, & said, they never had heard the like in all their Lives! It is true, heres a fine Preacher, & indeed every one has not his Method. E.G. He paints the Bad Heart out: & to that end he takes a little board, & draws A Heart thereon with a Coal, & all round it spikes, pricks, & thorns, & then says Schineo (behold) So is a Heart when Satan Dwells in it, & from within comes all Wickedness; but that gave the Indians a far greater Impression, than all the Studied & contrived Speeches of the Learned could have done.[58]

Johannes's oratorical gifts became widely known (and later memorialized in Moravian histories) and made him a logical choice to represent the causes of Mahicans, Moravians, and Christ in an array of settings. As he went about this and other work, he came to embody for German Moravians much of the best of what they were hoping for in evangelized Native Americans, and even for themselves. From their point of view, "few of his countrymen could vie with him in point of Indian oratory. His discourses were full of animation, and his words penetrated like fire into the hearts of his countrymen." Moreover, his preaching emphasized the blood of Christ, for "whether at home, or on a journey, he could not forbear speaking of salvation purchased for us by the suffering of Jesus, never hesitating a moment whether his hearers were Christians or Heathens."[59] Spangenberg was reported to have described Johannes as having "the countenance of a Luther," a man of strong conviction and admirable courage in the face of many foes.[60] Yet he was also a man of great humility. When Johannes wrote to the Moravians in Bethlehem asking their blessing upon the establishment of a formal Mahican congregation in Shekomeko, he rehearsed his sinful past, insisting that he had been as "cold as Ice & Dead as a stone." Yet "the blood of our happy maker hath melted me & made me burn." Now he preached to others, believing that "it may be they may become better in one hour than I in two years." Johannes summed up his heart's desire: "If he [Christ] will make use of me I will most gladly be used."[61]

Such humility paralleled what German Moravians expected of their leaders, for when motivated by the love of God, "nothing was too difficult, no obstacle was too big, and no sacrifice too great."[62] Zinzendorf had told all Moravian missionaries a decade earlier (1732) that they should "humble themselves below the people they ministered to."[63] Similarly, Johannes's willingness to take on any task the *Heiland* required (and his record of service indicates that his actions matched his words) looks very much like the "jack-of-all trades" model of missionary life carried out by Christian Heinrich Rauch, Gottlieb Büttner, Martin Mack, and others in Shekomeko in the 1740s. Alongside a variety of spiritual duties, they were to support themselves through a "normal" livelihood. In this case, that meant aiding the Mahicans in their farming and sharing in their relative poverty.[64] The missionaries were also repeatedly called upon to function as political agents, a role Johannes knew all too well.

Capping off Johannes's exemplary record was the fact that he did it amidst much physical and emotional pain. Johannes's choice to live as a Moravian Christian entailed giving up his prior pattern of persistent drunkenness (perhaps alcoholism). Whenever he told the story of his coming to faith, he made a point of highlighting this behavioral change, an indication perhaps of how difficult a transition it was. Local whites and non-Christian Indians only made it more difficult. Their participation in the area liquor trade as suppliers and consumers, respectively, made both groups hostile to any person or group who stood against their enterprise.[65] For Johannes, opposition to his new drinking habits was matched by disdain for his new beliefs. Right after his conversion, he had to look no further than his own household for staunch foes to his new theology. As he put it, "my nearest friends were my enemies—my Wife, my Children and the greatest enemy was the mother of my Wife, who said I was not so good as a Dog, if I would no more believe in her God."[66] Whatever his motives for adopting Christianity, when he did so, Johannes entered a religious wilderness and found himself largely alone. Like the Moravian missionaries sent to evangelize them, Mahican converts, and especially the first ones, felt alien in their world, regardless of how familiar or unfamiliar their surroundings. Time and the growth of a more substantial Mahican Moravian community ameliorated some of this type of pain. But Johannes had enough physical ailments to make the concept of sharing in the sufferings and wounds of Christ all too real. In January 1742, due to lameness in at least one of his legs, he was unable to travel to Pennsylvania with three other natives to become the first baptized Mahican Moravians in Shekomeko (he was baptized in April in Shekomeko). Though that affliction stayed with him the rest of his life, his extensive travel to perform political and religious duties suggests he grew accustomed to enduring that pain. Later that year, he was flat on his back with some kind of illness but nevertheless managed to participate in a meeting with Zinzendorf and another competing, and rather contentious, clergyman. In 1744 he burned himself badly but within three days attended a "Labourers Conference," a meeting of Moravian missionaries and native assistants, where he translated, "tho' very unwell." In 1746, after his move to Bethlehem, Johannes succumbed to smallpox along with many of the other transplanted Mahicans from Shekomeko.[67]

To the extent that Johannes's Christian devotion and work after 1740 mirrors what German Moravians prescribed for themselves, it is possible to argue that they remade him in their own image, particularly in later pious accounts that clearly constructed him as an ideal Mahican convert.[68] Johannes's postconversion life of service to the church and his people conforms strikingly well to what I have labeled the Moravians' "wounded healer" model of Christian leadership. But amid the fluid environment of the Moravians' first missionary foray in the middle colonies, it is also possible to argue that Johannes and other Mahicans reshaped these European Christians in their image. Two recent historians of the Moravian experience in eighteenth-century America suggest forms this influence may have taken. Karl-Wilhelm Westmeier believes that Count Zinzendorf's mission strategy for North America was profoundly affected by his encounter with Mahicans. Zinzendorf spent a week at Shekomeko in late August 1742 consulting with the first four baptized Mahicans, including Johannes. As a result of those discussions, Zinzendorf laid out a set of ideas by the end of that week that became key guidelines for future Moravian mission work among Native Americans. Among the recommendations Johannes and the others helped Zinzendorf to formulate were "the universal validity of the Gospel which must be shared with Native Americans and white people alike," the need for "pastoral care of new converts," "the position and offices of Native church workers," and "the way of life of the missionaries." The last point included a strong emphasis on the white missionaries' need to immerse themselves in the Native American culture. To that end, "in Shekomeko," Westmeier says, "the [white] Moravians learned the art of boiling maple sugar, to appreciate Wampum, use bark canoes, and hunt the Native American way. At times the missionaries lived in wigwams and the Shekomeko chapel was always a typical bark structure." They also worked hard at learning to understand and speak Mahican. In all these ways, they consciously sought to be recipients of Mahican culture.[69]

Jane Merritt has recently suggested that Moravian missionaries were also *unconscious* recipients and practitioners of Native American ways. Though her research focuses more on Pennsylvania, her claims apply equally well to Shekomeko. As she explains it,

> As missionaries established social alliances with Indians and struggled for their souls, they had to make sense of Indian religious practices. In understanding, even trying to eradicate, older customs, the Moravians unavoidably participated in the religious lives of natives. During the 1740s and 1750s, missionaries listened to, recorded, and interpreted dreams, blessed hunters and their lodges, dispensed magical medicines, performed rituals over the dead and dying, and offered personal spiritual power through the blood of Christ. As they incorporated native idioms and rituals into their attempts to bring Indians into a common Christian faith, Moravian missionaries, perhaps unwittingly, acted more and more like shamans, their native counterparts. Although each borrowed language and concepts from the other, in many ways Indians absorbed Moravians, rather than vice versa.[70]

To the extent that these processes went on in Shekomeko, Johannes would have been at the heart of them. His positions of importance within the existing Mahican community and within the nascent Christian congregation made him a pivotal figure in the religious and cultural exchanges that dominated Moravian-Indian relations. From him, the German newcomers could have learned how best to communicate, literally and figuratively, with other Mahicans and neighboring Indians. Rauch, Büttner, Mack, Zinzendorf, Spangenberg, and others took careful note of his preaching style, political astuteness, and linguistic dexterity. Through his words and actions, Johannes showed them what it meant to provide leadership within a native community. As he matured in his new faith, he also came to show them what it meant to provide leadership within a Christian community.

The lessons learned at Shekomeko, the Moravians' first extended encounter with Native Americans, were not lost on them, and for at least the next generation, perhaps two, Moravian ideas on how best to spread the gospel to native peoples and on what sort of Christian leadership was required in colonial America owed much to what had happened there.[71] This occurred despite the fact that circumstances forced the white missionaries and later the Mahican congregation to leave the area within a few years of getting started. White settlers wanted their land, competing English ministers wanted them for their own congregations, and other Indians wanted them to move for the sake of one or another political or military alliance.[72] Under such pressures, Johannes and other Christian Mahican leaders convinced most of their people that a move to join other Moravians in Bethlehem offered the best hope of living as they wished. But this was not an easy choice, and as of June 1746, Johannes's own wife, Martha, remained in Shekomeko. He implored her and the others still there to be "inclosed in the Wounds" and to remember that "we have cost the Savior his Blood."[73] Little did Johannes know that living in Pennsylvania in the summer of 1746 would cost him his own blood. Two months later, perhaps weakened by the stress of their move, he and dozens of other natives were dead from smallpox. After a tearful funeral, Johannes was buried in the Moravian cemetery in Bethlehem.[74] His placement there, at the heart of the Moravian movement in America, is a fitting reminder of the central role this early Mahican convert played in teaching Moravians of all kinds what they wanted in the wounded healers who led them.

An Oneida Statesman

About the time Johannes was persuading handfuls of other Mahicans to join the Moravian fold, Congregational missionary John Sergeant visited the Oneida village of Oquaga along the east branch of the Susquehanna River in south central New York.[75] Arriving in 1744, Sergeant initiated a set of contacts between English Congregationalists and Presbyterians and the Oneidas that would last well into the next century. Like most religious exchanges within Indian country in early America, Sergeant's visit produced no immediate dramatic results. Nor did it seem to matter much in the grand scheme of colonial life. But the principals involved here, or at least the people groups of whom they were a part, were not so marginal within eighteenth-century America as Mahicans and Moravians. The Oneidas were one of the still powerful Six Nations of the Iroquois Confederacy, and New England Congregationalists, heirs of the Puritans, continued to wield considerable political and religious influence. Over the course of the next half-century, members of both groups would play key roles in the tumultuous events that rocked colonial America and birthed a new nation.

Among the Oneidas, few men became more prominent in those decades than the warrior Gwedelhes Agwelondongwas [Agorondajats] or as he became known to the English, Good Peter.[76] Good Peter was a member of the Eel Clan; his leadership extended from at least the era of the Seven Years' War in the mid-1750s through to the time of his death in 1792. Distinguished far more by his diplomatic skill and Christian character than by his military prowess, he served as an important link between the Oneidas and first the British, then the patriots, and finally the United States and New York state governments. He also served as an important link between his people and the various missionaries who came amongst the Oneidas from mid-century on. Of them, Samuel Kirkland was by far the most important and enduring. After two years of ministering to the Senecas in western New York, Kirkland began his work with the Oneidas in 1766 at the age of twenty-four. He spent most of the next forty years, essentially the rest of his life, in that work, which often involved as much politicking as it did preaching or teaching. He became a key figure in the Oneidas' decision to support the Revolution and in their later negotiations with the new national and state governments. For him, as for Good Peter, service to his people and his god meant merging political and religious duties.[77]

Kirkland met Good Peter in November 1764. What began then as a cordial exchange developed over the years into a very close friendship, especially in the era following the War for Independence. During the second half of the 1780s and the 1790s, the Oneidas struggled to reconstitute themselves after the devastation of the war. Despite their being on the winning side, the Revolution had cost the Oneidas dearly, in part because the great majority of Iroquois had supported the British. Now the Oneidas faced an even more formidable foe—the onslaught of westward-moving white settlers who were eager to grab a piece of their land. White land hunger found support within the federal government and even more so within the New York state government. The Oneidas came under great pressure to sell or lease portions of their homelands and did so in a series of deals, despite the warnings of Good Peter. In 1792, he looked back on the prior eight years with much dismay, for the land deals had brought nothing but trouble. The Oneidas were left territorially shrunk, economically impoverished, politically emasculated, and internally divided.[78] Amid that turmoil, Samuel Kirkland's missionary efforts foundered as well. His support for certain land sales and decision to purchase significant land for himself, after pledging never to do so back in the 1770s, aroused strong opposition to him among some Oneidas and other whites. Although he remained on good terms most of the time with Good Peter, Kirkland had to contend with a growing "pagan party" within the Oneidas, which rejected his Christianizing and civilizing efforts and wished to retain native ways and to revive traditional Iroquoian religious rituals.[79]

Under such circumstances, it might have appeared that Oneida and Congregational/Presbyterian fortunes were headed in the same downward direction. But while overall these Indians did continue to struggle, eventually leaving their territory in New York in the 1830s and 1840s for Wisconsin and Canada, the white religionists capitalized on the new opportunities afforded by westward migration.[80] Stirred by the early fires of the Second Great Awakening, Congregationalists and Presbyterians embarked on an ambitious home missionary enterprise and sealed their close ties in the 1801 Plan of Union. Concerned (at least initially) with evangelizing both resident Indians and migrating whites, missionaries, pastors, and teachers carried their evangelical Calvinist faith into America's interior, particularly western New York and the Western Reserve (Ohio). Although eventually numerically outpaced by Baptists and Methodists, Congregational ministers were key players in the religious milieu of hundreds of new communities being formed on the western frontier in the early republic. As they performed their tasks, they often found themselves playing dual political and religious roles reminiscent of what Samuel Kirkland performed in the preceding decades. Jeffersonian opponents at the time derided Congregationalists as "priest-politicians" intent on advancing the cause of the Federalist Party more than the cause of Christ. Several generations of historians have perpetuated that caricature and left a false impression of what the typical Congregational missionary was about in the era from 1790 to 1820. A recent revisionist study by James Rohrer provides a helpful corrective. He argues that these ministers quite consciously avoided involvement in party politics and public controversy. Such entanglements were increasingly frowned upon amid the voluntaristic spirit that was taking over America in the post-Revolutionary era. Still, they had to rely upon "political sagacity" to do their work effectively and were well aware that "their efforts to promote orthodoxy [Edwardsean Calvinism] on the frontier had political implications." One crucial political lesson to be learned was that in the new republic, authority of any kind would be based less "upon education, status, or ordination" and more on "the ability to inspire and maintain popular confidence." Within their very fluid environments, ministers came to realize that the power to persuade would grow ever more important in their quest to win or retain the loyalties of their constituents. Their message might continue to uphold "traditional orthodox values," but "they recognized the need to adjust to changing circumstances . . . [regarding the] means to advance these values." Traditionalism and innovation were both required for success.[81] As those Congregational ministerial efforts were getting under way in the 1790s, the model someone like Samuel Kirkland provided of a savvy missionary long accustomed to gaining influence primarily through the power of his words in a context far beyond the reach of New England's standing order, and carefully attuned to the social, religious, and political winds of the day, traveled west and shaped the kind of Christian leadership these Calvinists hoped to exercise within the early republic.[82]

At the same time, another strain of Congregational, and more broadly, evangelical Protestant, thought about missionary leadership in the new nation drew even more directly from Kirkland's example. As R. Pierce Beaver explained in the 1960s, when it came to missions to Indians, the United States government and many American Christians were happy to accept the idea that a partnership between church and state was appropriate. Missionaries with government aid were to play a central role in the Christianizing and civilizing project outlined most tangibly by Secretary of War Henry Knox in the late 1780s.[83] Dissatisfied with the levels of violence between whites and Indians in the west and opposed to dealing with natives strictly through naked force, Knox proposed a policy of saving the Indians through cultural conversion.[84] To achieve this end, "missionaries of excellent moral character, should be appointed to reside in their nations, who should be well supplied with all the implements of husbandry, and the necessary stock for a farm."[85] Knox's confidence in missionaries to play such a role stemmed in part from his wide use of them already as diplomatic agents. On numerous occasions during his term as secretary of war through 1794, Knox relied on missionaries to exert influence on their native charges to opt for peace rather than war. Few if any missionaries were more central to the execution of that strategy than Samuel Kirkland. Perhaps his most important assignment came in 1792, when he was asked to select and lead several dozen Iroquois leaders to Philadelphia for talks with the federal government aimed at dissuading the Six Nations from joining with hostile tribes in the Old Northwest.[86] The relative success of that mission makes it not surprising that Knox turned to Kirkland again the next year and indicated his intent to make the Congregationalist's plan for an agricultural academy among the Oneidas the first tangible experiment in his civilizing project.[87] The Knox-Kirkland partnership sent the message to like-minded religionists that under the right circumstances, missionary leaders could draw effectively upon the powers of both church and state to enhance the spread of the gospel to Native Americans and to ensure the social well being of those under their care.

Twin impulses, then, about the type of religious leadership needed for Congregationalism to prosper, especially in relation to America's emerging political and social realities, may be seen as being carried west by its ministers in the 1790s and beyond. On the one hand, they were prepared to accept the idea that in a democratic America, their following would depend on their ability to persuade. Moral suasion rather than state coercion would be the order of the day. On the other hand, they believed that in appropriate situations, skillful missionary statesmen could partner with government for their mutual benefit. However much these dual impulses had the potential for being in tension with one another, in each case the life and ministry of Samuel Kirkland served as a propelling force and a compelling example.[88]

Yet the chain of influence did not start or end there, for whatever lessons about Christian leadership Kirkland came to embody, he himself had learned largely from Good Peter. By the time Kirkland entered Oneida territory in the 1760s, Good Peter was already well established as an important go-between for his people with English political and religious officials. As mentioned earlier, his contact with white missionaries likely began as early as the 1740s in Oquaga, the southernmost Oneida town in central New York. Just when he responded favorably to the Christian message is difficult to discern, but he may have been among a group of Oneidas and Tuscaroras from Oquaga who visited Jonathan Edwards's Stockbridge mission for schooling and religious instruction in the early 1750s. Shortly after that, one of Edwards's assistants, Gideon Hawley, moved to Oquaga as a missionary under the auspices of the New England Company. Hawley arrived in June 1753 and remained there until hostilities related to the Seven Years' War prompted him to leave in 1756.[89] As in Stockbridge, Hawley's efforts concentrated upon trying to make native residents literate in English and acquainted with the rudiments of Christian belief.[90] There is good reason to think that in those years Good Peter and Hawley worked closely together, for when Hawley left, he turned over the role of "schoolmaster" to a "Peter," and in subsequent years Good Peter was one of a number of Oneidas pleading for Hawley's return or the provision of a suitable substitute.[91] After a brief return visit in 1761, Hawley told Eleazar Wheelock that "were Isaac [Dekayenensere, another Oneida leader] or Peter ordained, they would be contented without an English missionary."[92] Because that did not happen, Oneida requests continued to be directed to Sir William Johnson, superintendent of Indian affairs for the British government and the most powerful colonial official within Iroquoia. During the war, Johnson and Good Peter established a mutually beneficial relationship, enough so that Johnson referred to him in 1757 as "a great Friend of mine." Good Peter supplied him with military intelligence.[93] In return, the Oneida warrior did not hesitate to ask for help in meeting the critical needs of his people for food, ammunition, a resumption of trade, the removal of English forts (by the end of the war), the protection of their lands, and a resident Christian minister.[94]

Good Peter's success in gaining the respect and admiration of Johnson and others continued in the 1760s. Johnson wrote a travel pass for Peter and his wife in February 1765 that described him as a "very faithfull and Pious Indian" who had been "of much Service for some years past among his countrymen & others, giving them all the insight he could in Principles of Religion."[95] The couple was on its way to Lebanon, Connecticut, to see Eleazar Wheelock in hopes of securing a minister/schoolmaster for their community. Wheelock ran a school that trained whites to evangelize natives (Kirkland had been his first white student) and taught natives English Christian ways. From Wheelock's perspective, Good Peter's arrival could not have been more providential, for in that very hour not only were two ministerial candidates being examined, one of them already designated as a missionary to the Oneidas, but to top it off, an Indian interpreter arrived just then, too.[96] The whole serendipitous encounter endeared Good Peter to Wheelock and secured for Oquaga and other Oneida communities a renewed interest in supplying them with a consistent missionary presence.

Samuel Kirkland was part of that missionary presence from 1766 on, but he had already begun taking lessons from Good Peter two years earlier. As the novice pastor headed west to the Senecas, he spent four days with the Oneida leader, ostensibly to deliver Joseph Wooley, a schoolteacher, to the village. Kirkland's journal entries for those days reveal much about Good Peter's character and the kind of Iroquoian leadership he would exhibit to him for the next thirty years. Kirkland noted first that he had reached "the residence of *Good Peter*, commonly so called, from his religious character." His arrival was "welcomed by *Good Peter* with the greatest cordiality," and he and the others were glad for the presence of Mr. Wooley who they promised to care for and "to adopt . . . into their *tribe*." The conversation then turned to Kirkland's larger mission to the Senecas. Good Peter counseled that "it was too soon; that their minds were not yet calmed, after the tumults and troubles of the late war [Pontiac's War, 1763–64]." Yet "he knew some very influential characters among them who were great friends to Sir William [Johnson] and had always been friendly to the Americans." Peter went on to tell Kirkland their names, though "he considered it as a bold if not hazardous enterprise." Still, if Kirkland's "heart was bent upon it God was almighty and every where present. He could preserve one there as well as any where else & from his very heart he wished God the Father & his son Jesus Christ" to be with Kirkland and protect him as he spread the gospel. As the men parted two days later, they "took an affectionate leave." Wooley was overcome with emotion in the moment. Kirkland "tried to console him. So also did Good Peter."[97]

If Kirkland were paying attention, there was much to pick up about functioning well within Iroquoia from that first encounter with Good Peter. For one thing, it was important to make for yourself a good name. Among the Six Nations, as among other eastern woodland Indians, names were a means of identifying a person's essential character. "Good Peter" was hardly the name affixed to Agwelondongwas by his Oneida brethren. But the English who put this appellation upon him acted in the spirit of the native custom. In that simple designation, they conveyed the righteous and upright character of this one who deserved respect and a listening ear. Good Peter's warm reception of Kirkland's party bespoke another longstanding Iroquois trait, an emphasis on generosity as an essential mark of a good leader. Usually gifts were exchanged as a means of conveying friendship and hospitality. Though Kirkland did not mention receiving specific "gifts" from the Oneida headman, his "gift" of Joseph Wooley was reciprocated with provisions of lodging and food, a healthy supply of political advice, and the promise to make Wooley fully one of their own. The Iroquois were long accustomed to incorporating newcomers into their ranks, so the promise to adopt Wooley was more than a polite offer. They were also long accustomed to offering the type of wise counsel that Good Peter passed along. In a style consistent with the Six Nations' consensual approach to decision making and overriding desire for peace, Good Peter apprised Kirkland of the risks involved in his mission to the Senecas and highlighted ways he might be more effective. The missionary would need to cultivate personal contacts with established allies if he hoped to gain a hearing among the politically alienated Senecas. Such advice to forge kinship-like ties to Iroquois "brothers" who in turn had close links to a "father" like Sir William Johnson echoed traditional Iroquois diplomatic wisdom. So, too, did Peter's willingness in the end to let Kirkland make up his own mind about going west. It bespoke on the one hand, the Oneidas' aversion to compulsion and on the other, their conviction that in all human affairs, the power to persuade was paramount. Even Peter's assurances that divine sovereignty would overrule in Kirkland's case due to the Almighty's omnipresence and omnipotence might be seen as something more than his recently learned Calvinism. Oneidas had long believed that great spiritual power permeated all of Iroquoia and could dramatically affect human fortunes for good or ill. Acting in accord with the spirits' will had always been as important for them as for any disciple of Christ.[98]

When Kirkland left Oquaga on that cold November day, his final image of Good Peter was of him consoling Joseph Wooley. That act of care and compassion was simply one more instance of Peter behaving according to Iroquoian chiefly virtues, in this case good will and selflessness.[99] In the years to come, Kirkland would have numerous additional opportunities to observe and be mentored by this impressive Oneida leader. For example, an incident in 1773 made Kirkland more aware of

Peter's most treasured ability and his thoroughly Iroquoian soul. In March of that year Kirkland, now living at the Oneida village at Kanowalohale, paid a visit to Oquaga and its resident missionary, Aaron Crosby. Crosby quickly made him aware of a longstanding dispute between Good Peter and Isaac, another Oneida headman, whom Kirkland described as "a speaker among the Indians who frequently officiates in their religious meetings but [is] vain and conceited." Kirkland took it upon himself to mediate the conflict. A range of religious and political factors may have given rise to the disagreement, but by the time Kirkland intervened another issue had emerged, Isaac's objection to Good Peter's speaking in public.[100] Likely feeling jealous and threatened, Isaac had good reason to worry that if Peter had more occasions to display his rhetorical talents, which were known to be considerable, his own influence within the community would suffer, for nothing was more highly valued among Iroquois leaders than skillful oratory. As Daniel Richter has explained, "The greatest Iroquois orators were far more than mouthpieces [for councils]. In an oral culture they were the repositories of ancient wisdom, the masters of diplomatic protocol, and the purveyors of the powerful words of Condolence and Peace. The few who possessed the skill and talent wielded enormous influence."[101] In a late night meeting, Kirkland managed to persuade Isaac to make some concessions. He then went immediately to Peter and reported the good news. His Oneida friend "was quite overcome with the unexpected revolution, and broke out in a kind of Rapture with a peculiar emphasis: 'rasatste ne Raweneiyoh,' God is mighty."[102] To Kirkland, Peter's joy at the achievement of compromise and the prospect of renewed harmony no doubt signaled the Indian's appropriate desire for Christian brotherhood. To other Oneidas, it was the natural response of a leader, who akin to his forefathers and foremothers, cared deeply about peace and unity.

In the next two decades, Good Peter repeatedly called upon his remarkable speechmaking gifts to secure a modicum of peace and unity for the Oneidas as a whole. But his best efforts were no match for the divisive and destructive effects of the Revolutionary War, white westward expansion, Oneida land sales, and unenforced federal treaties. Under those pressures and further disagreements over whether or how to embrace Christianity, Oneidas became factionalized and weaker.[103] Good Peter did succeed, however, in gaining for himself great respect as a speechmaker, and with that came at least a certain access to power and the potential for influence that Richter has suggested. When he died in 1792, a pained Kirkland regretfully noted in his journal that "the whole Confederacy will feel the loss of *Good Peter*. His equal is no where to be found among all the Indian Nations."[104]

By that point, Kirkland and Peter had grown accustomed to working shoulder-to-shoulder. Between September 1785 and September 1792, they collaborated closely, though they did not always agree, on the political, diplomatic, economic, and religious affairs of the Oneidas.[105] The prior decade had been difficult for both men. During the war, Kirkland had had to give up most of his normal missionary activities, had spent much of his time in service to Congress and the Continental Army, and had his home and church destroyed.[106] Now in 1785 he sought to reestablish his ministry. Good Peter had endured even greater hardships. First, he witnessed the ripping apart of the League of the Iroquois as the Revolution took hold. Then mid-war, he was called upon by the American forces to serve as an emissary to British Colonel Guy Johnson and his Iroquois allies. Not only did that diplomatic mission fail, but Peter and three other native representatives (one Oneida, two Mohawks) were harshly imprisoned for five months and then kept captive for another three years. Peter was even forced to function as a spokesperson for his Six Nations enemies. United States commissioners were still demanding his release at the announcement of the Treaty of Fort Stanwix in October 1784, a full year after the Treaty of Paris had ended the Revolutionary War.[107] Finally back in Oneida territory in 1785, Good Peter welcomed the chance to reunite with Kirkland.

For the next seven years, Good Peter served as a catechist, psalm song leader, preacher, interpreter, religious discussant, and personal confidant with and to Kirkland. As such, he was considered Kirkland's "native assistant." But such a label hardly conveys the nature of their relationship. Fortunately, sources from the period are comparatively rich in providing a picture of Good Peter's activities and own perspective. Kirkland recorded snippets of their conversations along with chunks of Peter's sermons. Scribes for the Commissioners of Indian Affairs and other government bodies took down many of Peter's speeches, and Peter himself narrated a memoir of sorts, tracing the Oneidas' complex land deals. From these materials emerges a figure of substantial skill, wisdom, and integrity. Perhaps most important for Kirkland and for the Congregationalist/Presbyterian missionary enterprise that would follow in his wake was Good Peter's joint and unequivocal dedication to the interests of his own people and the interests of the Christian gospel as he understood them. He saw no contradiction or tension between the two (certainly other Oneidas, including his own son, did) and championed both causes with similar skills and passion. As he had since at least the 1760s, Peter encouraged other natives to embrace Christianity and many other aspects of English colonial culture. In that postwar era, Oneidas engaged with and responded to Christianity in a range of ways, belying a simple division of them into "Christian" and "pagan" parties. Peter was certainly among those most committed to the Christian way, yet he was no pawn of the church or of the white political structures. He and other like-minded Oneidas "took selected aspects of Christianity and reinterpreted them to render them congruent with preexisting beliefs and practices."[108] Meanwhile, his acute sense of justice made him a vocal opponent of many of the agreements that other Oneidas came to accept to their long-term detriment. He battled with the force of his personality, presence, and tongue for positions religious, political, and economic that were of his own making.[109] Over the course of his career, and perhaps especially in his final years, his leadership engendered near universal respect and admiration, if not universal agreement.

As Kirkland tried to rekindle his ministry among the Oneidas, it took him little time to become aware again of how great an asset Good Peter could be. Paramount was the native's ability to communicate effectively in many different settings and with many different audiences. Within weeks of putting together a preaching circuit in various Oneida villages, Kirkland reported to his wife Jerusha that "Good Peter gave an exhortation last sabbath Evening after Lecture that exceeded almost any declaration I ever heard."[110] That pattern, of Peter following Kirkland's sermon with one of his own, became a common mode of operation for the two men. In February 1787, for instance, Kirkland noted that he preached for about two hours and was about to dismiss the crowd "when Good Peter rose & begged to say a few words. He spoke for half an hour like an apollus & with the energy of a son [of] Thunder. Could I do justice to his harangue, I would attempt to committing it to paper, but I feel myself altogether unequal to it." Kirkland managed to jot down a few lines from the Oneida's address, but his sense of inadequacy about conveying the thrust of what Good Peter said was well placed.[111] Too much of what the Indian communicated lay in the manner of his delivery for the white missionary to capture it on a page. At best, Kirkland could simply say that when Good Peter addressed others on the "nature of the Christian religion," he "spoke with a noble eloquence & good judgment." His orations left Kirkland and no doubt many others feeling humbled and inspired: "I could not but feel a pleasure, while he was speaking, to think that his exhortations far outdid my sermons. I have often thought that if I could speak with as much fluency as he that I would preach everyday of my life."[112]

Much the same sense of awe is generated in the attempts to record Good Peter's diplomatic addresses. Minute takers for the Commissioners of Indian Affairs permitted themselves the editorial liberty to describe his speeches as "elegant," or as delivered "in the most lively and pathetic Stile."[113] That may have been their way of acknowledging the difficulty of recommunicating the full effect of what he said in his native tongue. Simply copying down or translating his words, not to mention the challenge of conveying Oneida thoughts in English, was insufficient for denoting what happened when Good Peter spoke.[114] Nevertheless, the proceedings they kept indicate vital aspects of Peter's Iroquoian oratorical style. Perhaps most important, they show him as a master of all the diplomatic protocols that had been practiced by his ancestors within the Confederacy. He knew the long history of the Covenant Chain and drew upon it to plead the case of the Oneidas and the other members of the Six Nations. Negotiations did not always end with the result Peter wanted. But whites and Indians alike went away from having heard him persuaded that what he had spoken was said in good faith and with the best interests of his people at heart.[115]

In an era when persuasive speech was becoming the most valuable tool in the marketplace of religious and political ideas, Kirkland and the stream of missionaries who followed after him could hardly have had a better teacher than Good Peter. What made the Oneida leader that much *more* valuable to Kirkland was that he combined his public speaking talents with equally adept private counseling skills. Through their extensive contact, the two came to be on familiar, perhaps even intimate, terms. Years after Peter's death, Kirkland recalled fondly if also painfully a late-night conversation the two had had regarding the unpardonable sin. The native was distraught that his son had transgressed to such a point that he would never "obtain true repentance & forgiveness from God." Seeing that "Good Peter in this free conversation appeared to be so deeply affected," Kirkland "soon directed the subject of conversation to relieve his mind."[116] If in this case it was the white missionary who served as the compassionate and wise friend, in most other instances it was the Indian who played that role. On numerous occasions, Good Peter found ways of being an advocate for Kirkland's personal and familial interests.[117] On a grander scale, he provided crucial advice on mission strategy, political alliance, and diplomatic posturing. This may be seen especially well in what Peter taught Kirkland about how to relate to other Iroquois nations. In late 1787, encouraged by his missionary benefactors, Kirkland proposed an evangelistic trip to the Senecas. Much as he had done twenty-three years earlier, Good Peter warned against it. The Senecas had never been open to Christianity, and the antagonism engendered by the divisions of the Revolution had only intensified their attachment to traditional beliefs. Members of mission boards were to be commended for their concern, "But they do not know the prejudices of Indians, & the obstacles in the way of opening their [Seneca] eyes to see the true light." Peter made the point even blunter to Kirkland: "I know more of their dispositions & manners than you do—I resided among them."[118]

It would be easy to chalk up Good Peter's opposition to the proposed trip as nothing more than a product of his leftover wartime bitterness against the Senecas as well as his fear of losing Kirkland if it were not for what happened four years later. In his own timing and in his own way during the first four months of 1792, the Oneida headman found opportunity to nudge some key members of the Seneca nation toward the religious and political path he hoped they would go. Kirkland was there to observe:

> Much praise is due to Good Peter. . . . He improved every opportunity, with admirable address, to remove the prejudices, that subsisted in the minds of some of the Senekas against the Christian religion. The Farmers Brother (so called) one of the first characters in the whole Seneka nation, told me . . . that he should soon make a public declaration of his Faith in the doctrines of Christianity let his nation say what they would of him. With this sachem, Good Peter took unwearied pain.

Kirkland went on to claim that through Good Peter's influence, "the manners & sentiments of the Senekas, Onondagas & Cayugas gradually assimilated to those of the Oneidas."[119] All this took place amid the complicated diplomatic mission assigned to Kirkland and Good Peter to bring a host of Iroquois leaders to Philadelphia for meetings with the federal government. As the entourage gathered, slowly made its way to the capital city, and there engaged in several weeks of negotiations, the lifelong missionary was often overwhelmed by the task. But at every turn, his Oneida colleague was there to instruct him on what to do. Kirkland was usually smart enough to follow his advice and repeatedly acknowledged his debt. In January Peter counseled the missionary on the nuances of approaching their traditional Iroquois foe, Joseph Brant, after which Kirkland wrote Henry Knox that "I can have no better Indian councellor than good Peter. They [the other Iroquois headmen] stand in fear of him—he is very prudent, & friendly."[120] In February, "Good Peter harranged me two hours with Great engenuity & address upon the condition & character [of] these two different nations, Viz, Onandagers & Cayogas." Peter wanted to make sure that his white friend did nothing to offend Iroquois brothers with whom the minister was less familiar. Kirkland took the message to heart and "thanked him for his advice & unreserved freedom with which he had spoken to me upon the Subject."[121] A few days later, Kirkland once again confided that "I am favored with one of the ablest Indian *councellors* in good Peter—without his aid, I should feel myself much more embarrassed."[122] By the time their joint mission was complete in May, Kirkland could speak of the Oneida chief only in superlatives: "as a councellor & speaker, there is not his equal in the whole five nations."[123]

A counselor and a speaker—these were the twin roles in which Good Peter excelled and in which he mentored Samuel Kirkland. Into both he brought the traditional wisdom and customs of the Oneidas along with his comparatively newfound Christian convictions. Such a combination of traditionalism and innovation sounds much like what James Rohrer has found Congregational ministers on the frontier embracing in the following quarter century. Even more to the point, Good Peter's ability to persuade, inspire, and instruct within highly sensitive and fluid religious and political contexts, in combination with his admirable moral character, gave him great influence over whites and Indians alike, the very influence that westward-moving Calvinists wanted to emulate and exercise in the early republic.[124]

No wonder Kirkland kept on lamenting Good Peter's passing long after the headman's death in 1792. There were simply no other leaders like him. "Alas! What would I give for the influence and eloquence of good Peter," Kirkland wrote in 1799.[125] He tried to find a substitute in another elderly Oneida chief, Skenandon. Their friendship became well known, prompting one historian of the Oneidas a century ago to write that "it was thought that Kirkland at times was as much influenced by his Indian friend as the latter was by him. Their friendship was one of those fine things that work together creating the nobler episodes of history. The grand warrior, a superb type of manhood, and the white hero were in all ways co-laborers through life."[126] Such words, shorn of their romanticism, might in retrospect be better applied to the bond built between Kirkland and the one labeled Good Peter.

THE POWER OF EXAMPLE

What's in a name? The English were not the only Europeans who occasionally did well at affixing names to their native brethren that, in keeping with Indian custom, befit the character of the person. Or at least they fit what European Christians hoped natives would become through their influence. When French Jesuits gave Totiri the Christian name of "Etienne," they placed upon him the mantle of Stephen, Christianity's first martyr. Their choice of names seems hardly coincidental, for in Stephen's willingness to proclaim the gospel of Christ in the face of persecution, even to the point of risking his own life, they found the model of religious leadership they wished to cultivate in their Huron converts and within their own order's ranks. When German Moravians baptized Wassamapah as Johannes, they invoked the name of the beloved disciple, John, the one to whom Jesus entrusted his own mother from the agony of the cross, the one known to be closest to the savior. John clung to Jesus even as Moravians in the 1740s wanted Mahicans and themselves to cling to the *Heiland.* So, too, when English Congregationalists started calling Agwelondongwas Good Peter, they hearkened back to the apostle whose powerful preaching and forceful leadership had guided the New Testament church in its first decades amid the mighty Roman Empire. Peter was the rock, a stalwart amongst the fledgling band of believers whose only power lay in the force of the gospel message they proclaimed and lived out. Might this latter-day Peter be the same for his Oneida people?

Surely the Congregationalists who came into contact with Oneidas in the second half of the eighteenth century hoped so, even as earlier Jesuits and Moravians had harbored their own hopes for Indian converts such as Totiri and Wassamapah. All European Christian groups sought to mold natives they evangelized into exemplars of the type of religious leadership and spiritual commitment they were in the process of championing for themselves. As Presbyterian David Brainerd sought to make Moses Tatamy his ideal Anglicized Christian assistant, so Jesuits, Moravians, and Congregationalists worked to construct Native American leaders in their own images. In New France, Jesuits came to believe that nothing less than Christian martyrs were called for if the gospel was going to go forward. For Moravians, the faith would be spread and led by wounded healers, humble persons whose own pain had found healing in the wounds of Christ. Among late-eighteenth-century Congregationalists, missionary statesmen were required, men who could negotiate well within the complicated and rapidly changing religious and political worlds of a newly independent nation.

In the cases of Totiri, Johannes, and Good Peter, each of these Euro-American Christian bodies succeeded in inventing the kind of religious leader they desired. But the story was never one of mere native conformity to European dictates. Instead, amid the reciprocal flow of influence that so often characterized the encounters of the spirit in early America, Native American Christian leaders, through the power of their own personalities and gifts, and through the force of their own Indian leadership traditions, could help to define and refine what Euro-Americans wanted in their religious leaders. This was especially true when European Christian bodies were just finding a place in North America. In that formative stage, groups such as the Jesuits in the 1640s and the Moravians in the 1740s were malleable enough to be shaped by those they evangelized and nurtured. Toward the end of the eighteenth century, Congregationalists were in a similar position as they embarked on a missionary project that took them away from the established order in New England and challenged them to reinvent themselves in a democratic America.

Within these cultural moments, Etienne Totiri, Johannes, and Good Peter had opportunity to show white Christians what effective Jesuit, Moravian, and Congregationalist leadership might look like. While each man had particular gifts born out of and well suited to the specific cultural traditions of his people, three common characteristics of their leadership stand out. First, all three men demonstrated superb speaking skills. Totiri's fiery rhetoric, Johannes's graphic illustrations (literally), and Good Peter's diplomatic parlance all kept their audiences in rapt attention and communicated the Christian message in equally persuasive, though quite different, ways. Each testified in his own style to the power of the gospel and to the value placed upon great oratory within Native American oral cultures. Second, all three natives exhibited unusual courage. Faced with a myriad of problems and confronted by strong political and religious foes, they held firm to the new faith they had embraced, endured physical and verbal abuse, functioned as power brokers within the larger, often hostile, imperial geopolitical world, and risked their places of significance within their own native communities. Finally, all three showed intense concern for the well-being of their own peoples. Their embrace of Christianity was never simply a quest for individual gain. Instead, it was intimately tied to their communally based desires for political peace, economic viability, physical health, social justice, and spiritual well-being. Plenty of their fellow natives rejected the paths they proposed. But few could question the passion and sincerity with which Totiri, Johannes, and Good Peter made their cases. In the end, the leadership they provided for their bands of Hurons, Mahicans, and Oneidas testified to the dynamism of their personalities, flowed from the strength of their native traditions, and transformed the groups of Euro-American Christians with whom they interacted.

6

Encountering Death

The White People now live very close to us and are growing ever numerous and we think your living here has a tendency to prevent Trouble and difficulties between us & them—we think it is likely that when they know you are gone they will be more severe toward us, and perhaps you may hear of Trouble in this way before you arrive at Home and some of us may [even] Loose our lives by them.[1]

THE ONEIDA BRETHREN OF GOOD PETER WHO SPOKE THOSE WORDS IN JANUary 1800 knew all too well that the new century portended more of the troubles and difficulties they had seen in the last. The final quarter of the eighteenth century, since the beginning of the American Revolution, had been especially trying, despite their support for the winning side. Now the unrelenting advance of unlimited numbers of white settlers threatened their peace and perhaps their very lives. And their situation was about to grow worse, with the imminent departure of those with whom these Oneida spoke, a small group of Quaker missionaries who had lived and worked with them during the prior four years. According to this set of native leaders, the Friends' presence had a quelling influence on other whites; their withdrawal would likely mean more violence and very soon. A handful of Quakers seemingly stood in the gap between Indian survival and Indian death.[2]

It may seem curious that any body of Native Americans would link their fate to a few pacifists from Philadelphia, but Quakers and Indians had a long history together, a history in which the fates of both peoples had become interwoven. If those Oneida thought that their immediate future depended on what Quakers did, so, too, did Friends tie their future to what became of Indians. In that respect, the spiritual descendants of George Fox were little different from most of their neighbors in the early republic. Americans were eager to seize the opportunities afforded by the new nation. Like their colonial forebears, they hoped that Native Americans would not stand in their way, but if they did, they were prepared to take whatever steps might be necessary to clear them away. Indians had, of course, been in retreat, or so it seemed to whites, for the past two centuries, and not just geographically. Their populations had plummeted in the wake of the European arrival. As historian Francis Jennings has hauntingly put it, "The American land" that European newcomers entered in the centuries after Columbus "was more like a widow than a virgin. Europeans did not find a wilderness here; rather, however involuntarily, they made one."[3] As early American history unfolded, money, time, and numbers were all on the side of the Euro-Americans, so much so that by the beginning of the nineteenth century, it was not hard to imagine a nation void of its original inhabitants. After all, Indians could die in droves for only so long.

Historical demographers continue to debate the precise numbers and overall scope of Indian population decline, but the pattern is clear: wherever natives had contact with Europeans and their microbes in North America, the results were disastrous.[4] Alien diseases, though hardly the only killer of indigenous peoples, dealt death blows to Native Americans from the Atlantic to the Pacific in large enough numbers to repeatedly catch the attention of the new arrivals. Europeans listened and watched with combinations of curiosity, bewilderment, horror, grief, and delight as Indians told or displayed the story of their people's misery and affliction. Accounts of lands "emptied" and of villages that were no more became common fare when natives spoke with traders and missionaries or when colonists conversed with one another about the fate of the first Americans. Encountering Indians in early America meant encountering death.

Much has been made traditionally of Euro-American fears that contact with Native Americans might result in the colonists' demise. But for the large majority of settlers in the colonial era, the more prevalent and striking reality was the ubiquity of *Indian* death. Native mortality was a critical ingredient in all the ways in which Indians and Europeans interacted, and the religious encounter was no exception. In death as in life, Indians exerted an important shaping influence over European colonial religion. From the time the conquering Spanish spoke of the Aztecs lying dead in heaps and wondered what that meant for Catholic evangelism, Europeans wrestled with the religious implications or significance of Indian death. Sometimes that reflection took a practical turn, as when missionaries offered physical and spiritual aid during epidemics or decided to invest their energies among groups whose losses were not so severe. Of course, nothing was a greater practical necessity to colonists as a whole than ensuring that native death, whether from disease, war, slavery or some other cause, did not spread to them, so most were prompted to arm themselves with guns and prayers. Concerns over their own mortality naturally turned settler thoughts heavenward. What did God have in mind for them in the hereafter? But they also wondered what the divine was up to in the here and now. What were they to make of declining native populations? Was God doing them a favor by emptying the land of its heathen inhabitants? Were they in any way responsible for what was happening to Indians? Were Indian deaths to be lamented or celebrated or both?

How Euro-American Christians came to answer those questions and how those answers impacted their religious faiths and identities are issues worth investigating. On one level it may seem odd for a study of "encounters of the spirit" to take up a topic such as death and depopulation. Yet the argument of this book throughout has been that all dimensions of cross-cultural encounters in early America, from war to trade to treaties, could affect the religious beliefs and practices of Europeans and Indians alike. No part of the contact between these human communities should be presumed to be void of religious significance. Detailing the contours of all those many other stories largely awaits the energies and inquiries of future scholars. For now, though, the focus will be upon death—Indian death—and what it meant for European colonial religion.

To suppose that the deaths of one's family, friends, and foes might have had some spiritual import for natives and colonists in early America hardly takes a leap of faith. After all, Indian and European worldviews typically understood death as an event that linked this life to the next and was full of spiritual content. But did Euro-Americans care enough about the deaths of Indians in general to ascribe religious meanings to them? Did they read the phenomenon of native mortality in theological terms? As suggested above in the case of the early Spanish, they certainly could, and colonial records testify that many later Euro-American Christians certainly did. Religious interpretations stood alongside or mixed with scientific, political, socioeconomic, and racial explanations of why Indian numbers were declining and what that meant for the future of the continent. As they sought to make sense of native death, colonists often linked their own earthly and sometimes even their heavenly destinies to the fate of Native Americans. In the process, the passing of Indians came to color colonial religious hopes, fears, ambitions, and prejudices.

To see how and why that could happen, this chapter will trace the relationships between one body of colonial Christians, the Society of

Friends, and their native and European neighbors, first in New England and then in the middle colonies of Pennsylvania and New Jersey. As noted above, like most European newcomers, Quakers found their lives and their faith entwined with Indians from the early days of their arrival in the New World in the mid-seventeenth century. That pattern continued over the next one hundred years and beyond, into the American Revolution and the era of the early republic. Their work among the Oneida of central New York in the late 1790s was only their latest encounter with Native American peoples for whom the prospect of death, through whatever means, was all too real. Amid those encounters, the perspectives Friends developed on Indians and Indian death arose out of their distinctive experiences and religious traditions, and reveal especially well the power natives, dead or alive, could exercise over colonial hearts, minds, and souls.

NATIVE DEATH AND DIVINE PROVIDENCE

By the time Quakers entered Massachusetts in the 1650s, plenty of Indians were already dead. Along the Atlantic coast, New England's natives were among the first to suffer. Interaction with European fishermen and traders exposed them to a range of diseases they were immunologically ill prepared to combat. Between 1616 and 1618, a plague hit that reduced the size of coastal tribes by 70 to 90 percent. Fifteen years later in 1633, a smallpox epidemic dealt another harsh blow to native communities. About the same time, Huron and Iroquois (especially Mohawks) living in New York and New France contracted Old World diseases, and for the next several decades "the death of the Indian [was] one major theme of Jesuit writings." Similarly, in the 1630s the Lenni Lenape of Pennsylvania began to feel the effects of their new neighbors, Dutch and Swedish settlers. Over the course of the next half century, they endured three or more smallpox epidemics that substantially shrank their numbers. The arrival of far more colonists after 1682, now from England, Scotland, Ireland, and the German states, only exacerbated their problems. Gabriel Thomas's *Historical and Geographical Account of Pensilvania and of West-New-Jersey*, published in 1698, observed that "the Indians themselves say, that two of them die to every one Christian that comes in here." According to historian Thomas Sugrue, that may be "as accurate a statement as any expressing the tremendous depopulation of Pennsylvania's Indians in the seventeenth century." Robert Beverley's history of Virginia, printed in 1705, put it even more bluntly for his colony: "The *Indians* of *Virginia* are almost wasted." Tidewater peoples had been fighting a losing battle with English diseases since before John Smith's arrival in Jamestown. Further south, some native groups had lost hundreds of their peoples in the sixteenth century amid Spanish incursions into their territories. Far more groups experienced cataclysmic drops in population between the 1680s and the 1730s when thousands of European settlers moved in. Epidemic disease once again did most of the damage, but warfare, Indian slavery, and forced migration took their tolls as well.[5] A half century later and thousands of miles west, the presence of a few hundred Spanish friars, soldiers, settlers, and government officials, along with their microbes, plants, and animals, was all that was needed for many of Alta California's native peoples to begin to suffer catastrophic losses.[6]

Thomas and Beverley were just two of the many Euro-Americans who took note of natives' prodigious population decline. Newcomers were amazed at the speed with which large numbers of Indians were dying. They, like the natives themselves, endeavored to gain perspective on why this was happening and what it meant for the future of their people. One popular explanation among scientifically inclined Europeans focused on the bodies of Native Americans, according to a recent study by Joyce Chaplin. She perceptively analyzes how the Indians' large population losses of the early seventeenth century prompted the English to reach increasingly dismal conclusions about the physical suitability of the Indians for the American environment. At a time when England's own population was growing rapidly, and was taken by some to be "a sign of England's new prosperity and power," the natives' demographic crisis revealed the comparative weakness of Indian bodies.[7] That finding tragically set the English on a course toward racism:

> [English] explanations eventually posited that the native peoples were less resistant than the English to disease and that their susceptibility was natural to their bodies; further, by the late seventeenth century, the English emphasized that their own physical type thrived and persisted in its original form, despite exposure to an American milieu for more than a generation. By applying discourse on nature to native American attrition and English vigor, colonists defined a new idiom, one which argued that the significant human variation in North America was not due to external environment but instead lay deeper within the bodies of its European and Indian peoples.[8]

From the view that Indians were biologically inferior, the English did not have to travel very much further to the conclusion that natives were bound for extinction.

Nor did they have to take responsibility for introducing the diseases that were killing so many Native Americans. If indigenous peoples were constitutionally susceptible to epidemic disease, the problem was inherent to them, not a result of the English arrival. Indian claims to the contrary were refuted or ignored, despite the lack of English certainty about how diseases spread.[9] Moreover, whether or not medical theory could provide all the definitive answers, many Englishmen were content to say that God alone was responsible for sending disease. In fact, providential explanations of Indian death were at least as commonplace as scientific ones in seventeenth-century America. For people accustomed to ascribing major events (and many minor ones) to the divine hand, it was natural to see God's will at work in native mortality.

That will often seemed mysterious and even inscrutable. Some colonists were content to say simply that "it pleased the Lord" for this or that to have occurred. So William Bradford wrote of the pestilence that "swept away many of the Indians from all the places near adjoining." Others spoke more confidently of a God who was definitely acting on their behalf when it came to Indian death. John Smith saw providence intervening at many turns in the early history of Virginia when lives literally hung in the balance. In 1622, "if God had not put it into the heart of an Indian" to warn whites of an imminent Indian attack, far more than the 347 settlers who were killed might have lost their lives. More generally, the colony's history demonstrated that "God had laid this Country open for us, and slaine the most part of the inhabitants by civill warres and a mortal disease." John Winthrop was similarly confident that God was opening a space for migrating Puritans in Massachusetts and beyond. In 1634, amid a new epidemic, he wrote that "[as] for the natives, they are near all dead of the small pox, so the Lord hath cleared out title to what we possess." There was no doubt in his mind that "for the natives in these parts, God's hand hath so pursued them as for 300 miles space the greatest part of them are swept away by the smallpox." A decade later, other New England Puritans echoed Winthrop's sentiments when rehearsing for their English brethren "remarkable passages of his [God's] providence to our Plantation." First on their list of God's good works was "sweeping away great multitudes of the Natives by the small Pox a little before we went thither, that he might make room for us there." The writers of *New Englands First Fruits* also thanked God for the peace that had prevailed in the colony, apart from their war with the Pequots. In that conflict, "Gods hand from heaven was so manifested" that a small colonial army had routed the Pequots "to the great terrour and amazement of all the Indians to this day: so that the name of the Pequits (as of *Amaleck*) is blotted out from under heaven there being not one that is, or, (at least) dare call himselfe a

Pequit."[10] Divine providence, in such a view, was prepared to go so far as to exterminate native peoples if it suited its pleasure and plan.

At least some New Englanders were willing to go that far, and then baptize their efforts after the fact with claims of divine blessing. Amid the hostilities of the Pequot War, many Puritans were inclined to entertain self-images as the New Israel, and to cast their Indian enemies as one or another of the tribes who stood in the way of their possession of the Promised Land. The Old Testament, and particularly the books of Deuteronomy, Joshua, and Judges, provided plenty of examples of righteous violence, and Puritans were willing to use those scriptures to justify their own, even when it involved tracking down and slaughtering Pequot women and children. As with the ancient Hebrews, when a foe was "blotted out from under heaven," Puritans read it as a result of divine action and a sign of their own unique covenantal relationship with God.[11]

Whether slain by disease or the proverbial sword, then, dead Indians signaled providential blessings for many Puritans and other colonial Americans in the mid-seventeenth century. Whatever the cause, Indian losses were settler gains and an indication of God's approval of English actions, including their possession of native land. Missionaries such as the Mayhews and John Eliot would not have agreed, but on this topic as with much else their voices were on the margins of New England opinion. That a text, *New Englands First Fruits,* aimed ostensibly at arousing interest in evangelizing Indians, could rejoice at the "sweeping away" of natives, shows how colonists could "take spiritual comfort from indigenous death even as they express[ed] their desires to save Indians' souls."[12] Destroying Indians or "saving" them (converting them) seem to point in opposite directions, but for Puritans either outcome demonstrated God's favor upon the New Englanders.

NATIVES AND FRIENDS IN NEW ENGLAND

That *Puritans* needed saving and a new perspective on the workings of the divine was a heretical suggestion from the Puritans' point of view. But that is precisely what the first Friends to arrive in English America began saying in 1656. They set about trying to convince their new neighbors of the reality of the "Light within" and met immediate opposition from the Massachusetts government. Quickly outlawed, Quakerism became a despised and persecuted sect. For four years, the colony tried to squash the fledgling movement through executions. When that did not work, they tried banishing foreign Quakers from their midst. Despite those efforts, a few dozen colonists became Friends and concentrated themselves in Salem. By the late 1660s, the tacit responsibility for controlling and combating them passed from the provincial government to the colony's Congregational ministers. Combative is precisely what the early New England Quakers proved to be, as they kept up a war of words with the religious establishment, particularly down to about 1680.[13]

Among the verbal barbs Puritan pastors threw at Quakers was the claim that they were alien to the colony and a threat to the orthodox community. Friends were lumped with all those other groups who in the minds of Puritans stood outside, and over against, their efforts to maintain a godly society—Catholics, witches, and Indians. In particularly trying circumstances, any or all of those outsiders, including Quakers, could be painted as nothing less than agents of Satan. King Philip's War in 1675–76 and the witchcraft crisis of the early 1690s were two such occasions.[14] In both cases, Friends became linked to Indians in ways that would shape Quaker consciousness and identity for the rest of early American history.

By the mid-1670s, Friends had had two decades in which to establish relations with Native Americans in southern New England and wherever else Quakers traveled. Quaker sources from that era consistently represented Indians in positive terms, highlighting their friendship and hospitality and often holding up natives as, in the words of Josiah Coale, "more sober and Christian-like toward us than the Christians so-called."[15] Such attitudes may have been especially present among Friends in colonies where they and Indians were clearly outsiders, and less the case in a place, such as Rhode Island, where Friends came to exert political control.[16] As shown by Coale's words quoted above, Friends were fond of complimenting Indians at the expense of Puritan clergy and magistrates, whose persecution of Quakers in Massachusetts, Plymouth, and Connecticut was depicted as the antithesis of Christian hospitality. Writing on the eve of King Philip's War, George Fox left little to the imagination when he told the Massachusetts government that "these your monstrous laws [against Quakers] . . . make your name to stink, and the Heathen to blaspheme the name of Christianity by your wilful cruelty." In Fox's view, attacks on Quakers alienated Friends and Indians alike.[17] For their part, natives "sometimes compared the Puritans unfavorably to Quakers . . . [and] may have wondered whether the Quakers were really English" given the fierce opposition to them in most of New England. Both Friends and Indians, then, found it convenient to use the other's behavior not only as a basis for friendship but as a rhetorical weapon in their battles with Puritans.[18] They both countered Puritan efforts to portray them as beyond the pale.

When Native American–Puritan battles turned into literal war in 1675, Quaker principles and loyalties were tested even more severely, as Friends were pulled in multiple directions. On one level, they could sympathize with Indian grievances against the English and continue their critiques of Puritan rule. For several years prior, some Quakers had been predicting that God would punish New England for its persecution of Friends. Now that judgment had arrived in the form of King Philip, the Wampanoags, and their Indian allies. Massachusetts Quakers did not waste the opportunity to link the colony's sufferings to their own and to attribute God's wrath to the sorry treatment they had received for twenty years. George Fox recorded their views in his journal, noting that "the sober people [of New England] said, 'the judgments of God came upon them for persecuting the Quakers.' "[19] Not surprisingly, Puritan leaders would hear nothing of it, and claimed on the contrary that the colony's leniency toward Quakers was one of the sins for which it was now paying. Allowing Quakers to live there and spread their heresies must be one of the reasons God was so upset with them.[20] Thus, both Quakers and Puritans saw the war as God's judgment on sin, but whose sin was responsible was a matter of dispute.[21]

If that theological question absorbed the attention of some Quakers and drew them toward Indians, more typically the war pressed very practical issues and choices onto the shoulders of New England Friends that in some cases pushed them apart from natives. Individual Quakers faced a host of moral quandaries in the war as they tried to sort out their duties to friends and enemies. That required that they first of all determine who was who, and whether neutrality was a possibility. Those issues were even more acute for the Friends who led Rhode Island's government. What were their responsibilities as magistrates toward their own citizens and the English residents of other colonies? What measures were appropriate to take defensively and offensively? How were they to treat Indian peoples with whom they had traditionally been on good terms? As Meredith Baldwin Weddle has argued in her recent study of seventeenth-century Quaker pacifism, King Philip's War confronted "Quakers with the practical need to define the parameters of their peace testimony—to test their principles and underlying foundation for those principles and to choose how they would respond to violence." In Rhode Island, "Quaker peace principles would, for the first time anywhere in the world, be juxtaposed with the inherent demands of political office." She finds that in the years leading up to the war, the Quaker government matched other colonial governments in their military preparedness, but did act upon their "peace testimony" in passing legislation that allowed for exemptions from military service on the basis of conscience. Once Rhode Island was in the war, pacifism played little if any role in affecting its political decisions, apart from maintaining the exemption for "conscientious objectors." Even if political officials had had personal reservations about the use of force, Quaker notions at the time about magistrates' obligations to fight against evil would have trumped them.[22] In fact, some of the colony's Quaker leaders served in the military.[23] Such decisions make clear that Quaker pacifism was not a fixed doctrine but instead a set of principles in the process of being defined in practice by individuals in specific circumstances. And there was plenty of possibility for disagreement, as evidenced by the group of Rhode Island Quakers who critiqued their government's actions as inconsistent with Friends' peace testimony. In "A Testimony From Us (in Scorn Called Quakers, But Are) the Children of Light," they condemned any Quakers who had "encouraged" war "by Word or Practice." No doubt they had in mind a number of the actions of the Rhode Island government that had clearly furthered military activity. Quakers who failed in this way "wound[ed] their own Souls . . . & pierce[d] in themselves affresh the Righteous Life."[24]

In the aftermath of the war, other New England governments criticized Rhode Island and its Quaker officials for doing too little during the conflict on behalf of their neighbors, and for that matter, on behalf of their own citizens. It is easy to imagine those officials feeling as though they were damned if they did, and damned if they didn't. That was only one of the ill feelings and bitter tastes that the war left in Quakers. For a peace-loving people, however they worked out their peace testimony in practice, the carnage of the conflict on both sides was appalling. The per capita losses for Indians and the English were astonishingly high, higher in fact than in any other later American war. If those deaths were the most distressing outcome of the conflict, Friends could still identify other casualties that were almost as bad. For example, signs of a less acrimonious relationship with Massachusetts Puritans that appeared in the early 1670s were now reversed. In general, relations with other colonies and colonists became more strained, seemingly regardless of what stance Quakers took. Certainly those Friends who refused military service were often resented by other colonists, and attacks on them of one sort or another continued in the postwar era. Even worse, the stability of the Quaker community itself had been undermined or at least severely tested by the different perspectives Friends had reached on how to act in the war. Though apparently no disciplinary actions were taken by Quakers toward fellow Friends for their choices in the war, the diversity of their actions no doubt pushed Quaker forbearance to its limit.[25]

Then, too, their record of mutual friendship with southern New England Indians had been dramatically broken. Quaker John Easton, Rhode Island's deputy governor, sought diplomatic solutions to the conflict for several months after the war began. When his efforts came to naught, the colony joined with its New England neighbors in the fight. Native groups such as the Narragansetts found all of this perplexing since up to 1675, they had retained good relations with Rhode Island's Quaker government and were aware of its antagonistic relationship with Puritans. Why would Rhode Islanders abandon them and side with Plymouth and Massachusetts? However natives answered that question, they had little choice but to see Friends in a new light. Thereafter, whether part of a colony's political leadership or plain citizens, and regardless of their level of support or cooperation with the war effort, Quakers in Rhode Island and elsewhere were deemed part of the English and therefore part of the enemy by Philip's forces.[26]

New England Friends were disappointed by this souring of their friendship with Native Americans. That disappointment was part of their broader dismay with all the troubles King Philip's War had wrought. In its wake, Quakers sought to reconstruct positive ties to Indians and to show Englishmen and Native Americans alike how Friends were different. That began by offering interpretations of the war that would dissent from the self-serving histories of the war that appeared shortly after its conclusion. Keen on self-justification, other New Englanders wrote and read accounts that demonized natives and defended the righteousness of colonial actions against Indian sinners. Then and later, Quakers disagreed, and laid blame for the war primarily on Puritan policies.[27] Massachusetts Quaker Edward Wharton and Rhode Islander John Easton in 1675 wrote some of the earliest accounts of the conflict. They both cited persecution of Friends (and God's concomitant judgment) and Indian grievances, respectively, as the main causes of the war.[28]

In subsequent years, Quakers averred that in contrast to the disasters Puritans had precipitated, the war had not in fact spoiled the special relationship between Friends and natives. During the next generation, "a myth developed among Quakers that the early New England Quakers were immune from Indian violence because the Indians knew about and admired their nonviolence and therefore did not feel threatened by them."[29] Based on a number of reports from King Philip's War itself, Quakers told themselves that if they depended solely on God for protection, even to the point of remaining in their homes rather than seeking shelter in a garrison or town, Indians would honor their peaceableness and not harm them. Traveling Quaker preacher Thomas Chalkley made that point emphatically in his 1704 journal amid a new round of New England violence, the Mohawk raids on western settlers: "About this

Time the *Indians* were very barbarous in the Destruction of the *English* Inhabitants scalping some, and knocking out the Brains of others (Men, Women, and Children) by which the Country was greatly alarmed, both Night and Day; but the Great Lord of all was pleased wonderfully to preserve our Friends, especially those who kept faithful to their peaceable Principle." Chalkley rehearsed several stories illustrating his point, including that of one Quaker farmer who was told by a group of Indians "That they had no Quarrel with the Quakers, for they were a quiet, peaceable People, and hurt nobody, and that therefore none should hurt them. But they said, That the Presbyterians in these Parts had taken away their Lands, and some of their Lives, and would now, if they could, destroy all the *Indians*." Having provided that rationale for Indian actions, Chalkley went on to underscore the ferocity of native attacks and to contrast the behavior of other New Englanders, who "went to their Worship armed," with that of Friends, who held large meetings and attended "without either Sword or Gun, having their Trust and Confidence in God."[30]

Meredith Baldwin Weddle has suggested that the myth of Quaker immunity to Indian violence served to make more precise the dictates of Quaker peace testimony.[31] The myth also confirmed for them how different and better their way with Indians was for all concerned. Other colonists too often sowed seeds of aggression and injustice toward natives, and consequently reaped a harvest of harm. Animosities and hostilities were so intense as to portend total mutual destruction. Friends stood apart from that cycle of violence—or at least they told themselves that they did—and instead reaped a harvest of harmony with native peoples eager to live peaceably with settlers of their sort.

Quakers were not the only ones who saw their relationship with southern New England Indians as out of the ordinary. Puritan critics in the 1680s and '90s, in the context of the witchcraft crisis and King William's War, once again latched Friends and natives together as dangerous threats to colonial well-being. Both were accused of practicing witchcraft and condemned as mortal enemies.[32] Cotton Mather leveled particularly harsh attacks in 1689 and again in 1699. The latter work, *Decennium Luctuosum,* recounted the past decade of war with Indians and depicted Quakers as scavenging upon the souls of colonists in communities that had lately been "devoured by the Salvages." The two diabolical forces worked hand-in-hand, the one attacking the body, the other the soul.[33] Mather's vitriolic prose was in part designed to respond to the charges of Thomas Maule, a contentious Quaker from Salem, whose 1695 pamphlet, *Truth held forth and maintained according to the testimony of the holy prophets,* recited a long list of Puritan wrongs. Maule was perhaps the last New England Friend to wage public attacks on the Puritan establishment, and he went down swinging. Noteworthy here is his twin emphasis on Puritan abuses of Native Americans and Quakers. If for Mather those two groups were Satan's handymen, for Maule they were co-victims of Puritan wickedness. Not much needed to be said to his readers about how Friends had suffered under Puritan rule. As for Indians, he excoriated the first-generation Puritans for destroying native lives instead of saving them. Rather than treating them according to the Golden Rule and turning them to Christ, they had instead "turn[ed] them in to the Grave, where there is no Repentance." That was "a strang turning indeed, by a People that pretended so much to Gods Truth." By the 1690s, Puritans were being judged for their "unrighteous dealings" with natives over several generations: "the Lord hath suffered to reward the Inhabitants [of New England] with a double measure of Blood, Fire, and Sword." Maule went so far as to equate Puritan behavior with Spanish treatment of natives in New Spain; for him, Puritans were guilty of their own Black Legend in New England. He didn't even have kind words for the Puritans' praying Indians. They were great dissemblers and they were "no more to be credited [or trusted] than they that never prayed in their life."[34]

Maule may have painted Puritans in darker colors than most Friends, while the myth of Quaker protection from Indian violence may have portrayed Friends in brighter hues than the historical record warranted. But the resulting black-and-white picture that emerged in Quaker minds of how Quakers interacted with Indians versus the ways other colonists treated them was too plain to miss. By the early 1700s, war with natives had become endemic in New England. For the better part of three decades, violent conflict had been present as often as not. The imperial government, the region's rulers, and most settlers had grown increasingly fond of the idea of eliminating Indians altogether. They continued to be attracted to the notion that native death was a clear marker of divine blessing upon colonial aims and actions. Friends found little in all of that to agree with. King Philip's War had been a great trial for them and taken a heavy toll. Renewed hostilities in the 1690s tested them once again. From the Quaker point of view, natives and colonists killing one another was a product of human injustices, evoking divine judgment, not divine approval. Indians, like Quakers, were often the victims of Puritan prejudices and misdeeds. Natives were not indiscriminate brutes but instead careful observers of colonial behavior, so if Friends kept up their peaceable ways, they could ensure their own protection. But what about the protection of the Indians themselves and other colonists? Wasn't peace rather than war God's intent for all people? Couldn't some means be found of preserving friendship with Native Americans that would prevent suffering on all sides?

A HOLY EXPERIMENT WITH INDIANS

It did not take Quakers in early America until the eighteenth century to pose those types of questions. Instead, the opportunities to oversee the planting of new English colonies in the 1670s and 1680s put Friends in the position not only to ask those questions but to chart their own answers. Quakers came to those responsibilities with the experiences of other colonies in mind, and none more so than New England's fate in King Philip's War. As Friends founded West Jersey in 1676 and Pennsylvania a few years later, they assumed their tasks cognizant of the sorry chain of events that had befallen the northern colonies (and perhaps also Virginia in Bacon's Rebellion, also fought in 1676). George Fox exhorted Jersey Quakers in 1676 to "honour the Lord in all your undertakings . . . so that you may answer the light, and the truth, in all people, both by your godly lives and conversations." As Friends observed what was happening in New England, so others would be watching them: "For many eyes of other governments or colonies will be upon you; yea, the Indians, to see how you order your lives and conversations." Fox repeated the same exhortation in an epistle six years later, reminding New Jersey Friends that "the eyes of other nations will be upon you" and of their consequent need to "exceed them [other colonies] in truth, in righteousness, in holiness, justice and equity, and in the wisdom of God." Because Quakers had been outspoken critics of governments that failed to live up to those standards, they must now use their political power to "exceed" others in doing that which was "just and right." To fail in this "will bring both the judgment of God upon you, and the judgment of truth that you and we profess."[35]

George Fox's voice was hardly the only one newly arrived Quakers were listening to in West Jersey and Pennsylvania. Yet his words and the vision they implied of colonial societies living in peace and holiness under Quaker rule is not far from what William Penn himself laid out in a 1681 letter to Quaker James Harrison. Penn expressed gratitude to God for the land grant he had received and imagined that "an holy experiment," unthinkable in England, might be possible in his new colony. His duty was to "serve his [God's] truth & people; that an example may be Sett up to the nations."[36] J. William Frost has persuasively argued that Penn, at least initially, envisioned his "holy experiment" in specifically spiritual, even eschatological, terms. It was to be a place where God did the experimenting and "where the rule of the Lord . . . [was] so pervasive that it may usher in the end of time." Frost finds that at least some other Friends in England shared Penn's vision for Pennsylvania, a vision that included a desire to treat with Native Americans in what they considered truly Christian ways.[37]

The Lenapes and other native peoples of New Jersey and Pennsylvania had already had many decades of contact with European immigrants by the time English Friends arrived. They established the typical sets of economic and cultural exchanges with Swedish and Dutch settlers, and compared to the bloody violence that beset native-newcomer relations in most other parts of North America in the seventeenth century, the Delaware Valley remained quiescent. Still, many Lenapes died from disease, relations were often tense, and Euro-Americans such as Governor Johan Printz of New Sweden envisioned a time when the landscape would be free of Indians altogether.[38] No wonder an idealistic William Penn, and perhaps local natives as well, thought there was room for improvement. Penn's writings from the early 1680s, when his Christian utopianism was at its height, embody his hopes and aspirations for the colony's relations with Indians. In promoting Pennsylvania privately and publicly, he repeatedly denounced other Christian colonists and colonies for their ill treatment of natives. As he told his friend Robert Boyle, Indians were "the worse for those they should have been the better for."[39] The remedy was simple: "Don't abuse them, but let them have Justice, and you win them." Penn urged fellow Friends, as Fox had done, to live on a higher moral plane than their neighbors, whether European or native. Indians deserved to be treated with the same dignity and fairness as any other human beings.[40] In 1685, he happily reported that a "great friendship" had been struck up with area Indians in the first years of the colony, thanks to common submission to a fair and equitable justice system. He told his English readers that in Pennsylvania, "We [colonists] leave not the least indignity to them [natives] unrebukt, nor wrong unsatisfied. Justice gains and aws them."[41]

Other Jersey and Pennsylvania Friends similarly attested that they and local Indians were living in harmony.[42] Yet within a few more years, practical realities prompted Penn's utopian hopes to recede, and the meaning of the holy experiment began to evolve toward what later historians have highlighted as the distinctive features of early Pennsylvania—its political, economic, and religious freedoms, and its pacifism. Despite those changes, however, Indians and how they were treated remained a core element in how Penn and other Quakers defined the colony's identity and their own. Even if Pennsylvania lost its millennial significance, it was still a unique place, in part because of what it was attempting to do in relation to natives.[43] Influenced by the Friends' experience in New England before and during King Philip's War, what he knew of prior European relations with Indians in the Delaware Valley, the admonitions of George Fox and other Quaker leaders, and Friends' convictions about the moral and spiritual worth of native lives, Penn set out to chart a different course and establish a different model of how immigrants and natives might coexist. That goal itself coexisted in practice, sometimes antithetically, with Penn's material and political hopes for the colony, but it persisted for the rest of his life. How well he succeeded in achieving it remains a matter of debate. Thomas Sugrue reminds us that regardless of Penn's intentions, "In the very process of settlement, Penn and his colonists unleashed forces which, even in the absence of coercion and violence, transformed the region's environment, decimated the native population, and pushed natives westward." James O'Neil Spady agrees, pointing out that Penn's colonial policies created unprecedented disruptions for the Lenapes by bringing in thousands of new settlers within a very few years in the 1680s. Moreover, Sugrue says, "By selling land to prospective colonists before treating with the Lenape, Penn displayed an astonishing indifference to Indian rights to the land."[44] Such criticisms counter the longstanding praise Penn has received from historians for his Indian policies and argue that however unwittingly, Quakers made their own significant contributions to Indian death and displacement.

Wherever the truth lies in that debate, at the time eighteenth-century Pennsylvanians, and especially Quakers, believed that Penn had succeeded marvelously, even heroically, in establishing peaceful and equitable relations with the Lenapes. And plenty of Indians thought so too, or were at least willing to employ it as a useful past. Penn's dealings with natives in the first years of the colony took on mythic status in the era following his death. In 1771, those dealings became immortalized iconographically in Benjamin West's painting, *William Penn's Treaty with the Indians*. The historicity of the event that this work depicts remains uncertain, but there is no doubt about the fact that by the time West put brush to canvas, Penn's legacy, and by implication the Quakers' legacy, with natives had been long celebrated. It served as a very usable past for peoples with a range of agendas. For example, after 1700, Delawares, Susquehannocks, and Iroquois became fond of recalling the special understanding Penn had demonstrated in treating with them whenever they were meeting with Pennsylvania officials to discuss grievances they had with the colony.[45] Part of their rhetorical efforts at moral suasion to gain diplomatic concessions, the native appeal to a harmonious past also typically included a plea that the "Friendship that has long subsisted" would persist so that colonists' "Children and our Children may ever continue as they have hitherto been, one Body, one Heart, and one Blood to all Generations."[46] Diplomatic go-betweens or negotiators, some of them native, some Euro-American, also made regular references to Penn's positive example as they sought to smooth out rough places in intercultural relations. For all involved, "Penn cast a long shadow." Pennsylvania governors similarly invoked the founding myth of friendship and benevolence at councils with Indians, but they seemed more reluctant to make promises about the future or to show as much interest in Indians as Penn had.[47] Already by the 1720s and 1730s, they were pursuing policies toward natives that would soon be seen by many Quakers (and Indians) as a repudiation of Penn's achievement.

Individual Quakers and groups of Friends also hearkened back to the colony's founding moments when advising one another about how to relate to Indians. For them, those years "became a golden age of harmony against which future disruptions could be tested."[48] So Pennsylvania minister Thomas Chalkley encouraged a number of Quaker settlers in Virginia in the late 1730s to be sure to purchase their lands fairly and legally from local natives, and in that way to follow the "Example of our worthy and honourable late Proprietor, *William Penn;* who, by his wise and religious Care, in that Relation, hath settled a lasting Peace and Commerce with the Natives, and, through his prudent Management therein, hath been instrumental to plant in Peace, one of the most flourishing Provinces in the World." Chalkley warned that the consequences of defrauding Indians would be high indeed, the very lives of their wives and children.[49] In retrospect, his words may be seen as prophetic for his own colony, for the infamous Walking Purchase had been completed the year before and would ultimately wreak native violence upon Pennsylvanian homes.

Fraudulent land deals were only one of the ill practices against Native Americans that conscientious Friends decried and for which they employed William Penn as a righteous model. Another was selling liquor to Indians. Some Friends throughout the colony's history had failed to adhere to the Society's prohibitions against that practice, and so the Philadelphia Yearly Meeting in 1722 determined that it was necessary to speak to the issue again. Its published epistle condemned any Quaker participation in the liquor trade and reminded its readers that their forebears had done the same in the 1680s once it became clear that natives were suffering from their access to rum and other strong drink. For Quakers then or now to exploit natives through liquor dishonored Quaker moral testimony. It also repaid Indians and God himself ill for good, for when the first Friends had arrived in Penn's Woods, "it pleased Almighty God by his over-ruling Providence, to influence the Native

Indians so as to make them very helpful and serviceable to those early Settlers, before they could raise Stocks or Provisions to sustain themselves and Families."[50] To treat Indians with anything less than a reciprocal hospitality, then, was to do them a disservice and to ignore God's provision for his people.

The Yearly Meeting's letter reveals that for Quakers, the founding myth included more than Penn's benevolent ways with natives. Antecedent to his actions were the work of divine providence and the cooperation of the Lenapes. God had paved the way for Quaker settlers to survive, and natives had been his instrument. Together Friends and natives could be mutually beneficial under the guiding light of a sovereign providence. If Pennsylvania was a "Holy Experiment," God, Indians, and Quakers all had crucial roles to play in its success.

Such views of how providence, Euro-Americans, and Native Americans fit into Pennsylvania's beginnings stand in marked contrast with how colonists elsewhere, and perhaps especially in New England, conceived of their provinces' foundings. Their "creation" myths, as described above, similarly emphasized the workings of providence in relation to local Indians as preparatory steps for colonial survival and success. But more often than not, rather than seeing their god influencing natives to be friendly and helpful, they pictured him killing indigenous peoples by the thousands to open space for their arrival and the planting of Christianity. Early proponents of those myths were echoed in the eighteenth century by new historians of the region. Harvard graduate and Baptist minister John Callender published a history of Rhode Island in 1739 that gave full expression to the "sweeping away" image of the hand of providence. Callender graphically recounted how prior to the English arrival in Plymouth, "*Indians* had been dreadfully wasted away by devouring Sickness . . . so that the Living sufficed not to bury the Dead, and the Ground was covered with their Bones in many Places." That turn of events had "wonderfully made Room for the *English* at *Plymouth* and *Massachusetts*." There was no doubt in Callender's mind that such wonder-inspiring developments were the work of the "*wonderful and unsearchable Providence of God.*" He admitted that the ways of divine providence were often inscrutable, but in the case of the "*driving out of the Natives, and planting Colonies of Europeans,*" one would have to be "willfully blind" not to see "*that the Hand of the Lord hath wrought this.*" All of the New World, not just New England, displayed this pattern as God worked his will out among the nations. The Lord had "consumed *the Natives*" for their sins, and "their detestable Vices" had "drawn on those mortal Sicknesses, which [had] wasted away all within the English Pale."[51]

Callender's history gave Euro-Americans a picture of themselves as the benefactors of a righteous God determined to effectuate his plan in colonial America. Indian death and depopulation were critical steps in the outworking of his design. Their demise was just punishment from the divine judge and a necessary precursor to a refilling of the land with Europeans.

Not all commentators on native mortality in the first half of the eighteenth century gave so much credit to divine action. In some minds, Indian behavior itself was reason enough for their decline. Poor diet, poor health care, poverty, and intemperance were just some of the reasons cited by Congregationalist missionary John Sergeant and others for the erosion of native populations. Other missionaries thought it less a matter of Indian self-destruction than a product of Euro-American oppression. As mentioned in chapter 3, Society for the Propagation of the Gospel minister Francis Le Jau blasted Indian slave traders in South Carolina for their ill use of natives. When an epidemic hit the colony in 1711, he interpreted it as God's punishment on settlers for their mistreatment of Indians and Africans. For Massachusetts pastor Solomon Stoddard, the colonists' failure lay in their paucity of efforts to convert natives. The result had been divine judgment in the form of the many wars between New England's Indians and the English, and the loss of many lives.[52] Stoddard's grandson, Jonathan Edwards, while living among Indians in Stockbridge, compiled his own list of ways colonists had contributed to native decline, including the "killing of multitudes of them, and easily diminishing their numbers with strong drink."[53]

However much these Euro-American observers differed in their explanations of the prevalence of Indian death, they concurred in saying or implying that Native Americans were a dying race. The popular nineteenth-century literary trope of the vanishing Indian had not yet quite appeared, but colonial sentiment was moving in that direction as native disappearance in the long run seemed more and more inevitable.[54] Even experienced colonial negotiators such as Conrad Weiser "embraced the idea that getting along with Indians was only a necessary step on the road to a brighter future, a time when those Indians would follow the forest into oblivion."[55]

It is hard to say what middle-colony Friends thought of those sentiments since on the matter of Indian death as a whole, they were comparatively quiet in the generation after William Penn. Perhaps their silence was a measure of their obliviousness to the native de-peopling of Pennsylvania through death and out-migration. More likely, in the absence of war, it was a by-product of their residual faith that Penn's holy experiment in Euro-Indian relations remained viable and could continue to be mutually beneficial. Even if conflict and death had been the norm elsewhere when Europeans and natives met, the Pennsylvania experience continued to be a noteworthy exception. Maintaining belief in that myth required Friends to affix their eyes on live Indians, not dead ones.

HATING NATIVES AND HATING QUAKERS

That belief would be tested as never before in the 1750s and 1760s. The hostilities that commenced on the Pennsylvania frontier in 1754–55 initiated a decade of profound change for Friends and Indians alike. Though tensions and antagonisms had almost always existed just below the surface in Pennsylvania-native relations and sporadically boiled over into isolated violence, nothing like the bloody conflict that came to be called in Europe the Seven Years' War had ever been seen in the colony. On the eve of the war, Krista Camenzind has recently argued, "Euro-Pennsylvanians and their Native neighbors clung to the ideal of . . . William Penn's 'holy experiment,' which they credited with the preceding seven decades of peace."[56] Their peace, however achieved, was sufficiently real and long to allow Quakers to believe that they had accomplished something unique among the colonies. It gave Friends "a fundamental aspect of their identity as a people in the province."[57] And it allowed them to perpetuate the myth developed among New England Friends, and described earlier, that Quaker pacifism ensured their safety from native attacks. As one 1720s Quaker pamphlet explained, where men used violence against Indians to gain their desires, as in New England, they "must fight to defend what they do." In contrast, in Pennsylvania, "The Quakers have hurt no Man, and no Man offers to hurt them." By the Quakers' treating natives well, Friends and Indians visited freely in one another's homes, and any Quaker could "travel safely and singly thro' all the [Indian] Nations of *North America*, who will be ready to receive and assist him."[58]

The French and Indian War dealt severe blows to all those Quaker beliefs, not to mention peace itself, and it left Friends having to face hard questions. What had gone wrong in their holy experiment? Who or what was to blame? Why was God no longer blessing them with peace? Were their own sins responsible for precipitating divine anger and judgment? Were they to continue in positions of political authority, even if that meant sacrificing their peace testimony? Those issues confronted Friends at a time when some of their leaders were already pushing for important changes within the Quaker community. Beginning in the late 1740s, minister John Churchman and a few other influential

Friends initiated calls for internal reforms within Quakerism that would revitalize its ethical and spiritual commitments and practice. Not surprisingly, the reformers looked to the biblical past for inspiration as well as for models of behavior. But they also once again idealized the early years of Pennsylvania and used them to prod fellow Quakers toward renewal.[59]

That past took on even greater significance as reformers considered how best to respond to the tragedy of war. The knowledge that professional armies were doing battle within Pennsylvania's borders was bad enough, but the news of what was happening between settlers and Indians was far more shocking. Native raids killed well over a thousand colonists in Virginia and Pennsylvania between 1754 and 1758. Panic-stricken farmers fled eastward, fearful for their lives, hateful toward any Indians, and resentful of a provincial government associated with Quakerism (and its pacifism) that in their minds supplied too little protection. Ironically, it was the judgment that the government's actions were not pacifist enough that led a group of Quaker legislators to withdraw voluntarily from the Assembly in 1756, urged on by a range of Friends including visiting English preachers Catharine Payton and Mary Peisley.[60] The Assembly's decision to go along with the governor's proclamations that declared war upon the Delawares and offered rewards for Delaware scalps, male and female, staggered most Friends inside and outside the government. Few actions could have stood more starkly against Penn's peaceable legacy. Quaker appeals to counter the proclamations reminded officials once more of the colony's early history, citing the roles of divine providence and cooperative Indians in placing Pennsylvania on a firm footing:

> The Settlement of this Province was founded on the Principles of Truth, Equity, and Mercy, and the Blessing of Divine Providence attended the early Care of the first Founders to impress these Principles on the Minds of the Native Inhabitants, so that when their Numbers were great and their Strength vastly Superior, they received our Ancestors with Gladness, relieved their Wants with open Hearts, granted them peaceable Possession of the Land, and for a long Course of Time gave constant and frequent Proofs of a cordial Friendship, all which we humbly ascribe to the infinite Wisdom and Goodness of God.[61]

To repay God's original favor with licensed barbarism against native peoples who had long been considered friends was foolish and dangerous policy.

Friends historians have interpreted the decision of the four Quaker assemblymen to give up their legislative seats as the beginning of the end of direct Quaker involvement in Pennsylvania's government. A longstanding element of the holy experiment—Quaker political rule and service—was to be abandoned over the next twenty years. But even as that was happening, many Friends were not inclined to give up on the experiment in intercultural relations. As Jack Marietta notes, "the original peace between William Penn and the Delawares remained for them an icon without a crack in it."[62] Peace and harmony were worth trying to restore, and reforming Quakers eagerly took up the task, now from positions outside public office. Pennsylvania Friends in 1756 founded the "Friendly Association for Regaining and Preserving Peace with the Indians by Pacific Measures," an essentially philanthropic organization whose mission was to foster peace and to address the factors that had precipitated war in the first place. Led by Israel Pemberton and other socially and politically prominent Quakers, the Friendly Association gave them an instrument through which to exert informal influence over colonial affairs and to distribute charity to the Delaware.[63]

Friends, whether part of the Association or not, generally believed that Indians deserved justice and were naturally inclined toward peace and friendship with colonists. Native Americans, like all human beings, were made in God's image and were part of his family, and therefore entitled to respect and Christian treatment. George Fox had made those points in the 1670s, and Quakers eighty years later, but now in the midst of war, were prepared to echo them.[64] So John Churchman, one of the most prominent of the reforming Quakers, after listening to several remarkable Indian speeches at a treaty in 1757, concluded that "the Lord was in them [the Indians] by his good Spirit." The Inner Light was surely at work. What clearer evidence could one want that "all colours were equal to him [God], who gave life and being to all mankind; we should therefore be careful to examine deeper than the outward appearance . . . if we desire to be preserved from error in judgment."[65] Such affirmations of racial equality would be harder, not easier, to come by in the years to come, as Quaker views became even more marginalized.

For now, though, Churchman and other Association members remained optimistic. They managed to arrange for and attend a series of councils at Easton, Pennsylvania, with native leaders and government representatives. They were confident that a return to the colony's pacifist policies was possible if mistakes and injustices were acknowledged and amended. To that end, as they spoke with disaffected Indians, they repeatedly criticized the Walking Purchase of 1737 and other injurious actions of the colony's proprietors that in their view had precipitated righteous anger among Indians, positions they also communicated in separate correspondence with Lieutenant Governor William Denny and the Provincial Council.[66] Israel Pemberton and other Friends were heartened by the warmth with which some native headmen spoke of the colony's early years and of the possibility of the Friendly Association's helping to restore the revered peace and friendship of William Penn's day. One of the Iroquois diplomats, Oneida sachem Scarouyady, told Pemberton, "Your Fathers declar'd that they had nothing but Love & Good will in their Hearts to all Men." He continued, "We thought the People of that Profession had been all dead and bury'd in the Bushes or in the Ashes but We are very glad there are some of the Same Men living."[67]

According to some recent scholars, the Association succeeded in paving the way toward the end of the war in Pennsylvania in 1758 by aiding in the negotiation of the Treaty of Easton. That agreement calmed the Pennsylvania frontier temporarily, in part because it promised no further westward migration and settlement by whites. The Association kept up its advocacy work into the 1760s, pleading with proprietors Thomas Penn and Richard Penn "to guard against the fatal Consequences of losing the Friendship of the Indians, which your honourable Father & our Ancestors had obtain'd in the first Settlement of this Province." It also contributed about £5,000 to the relief of various Indian peoples within the colony.[68] Other "successes" of the Society of Friends during the war were noted in Quaker journals. Traveling ministers Daniel Stanton and William Reckitt both described how amid all the frontier violence and bloodshed, few Quakers had been "ill used" by Indians. Echoing once more the myth of Quaker protection from native attacks, they explained the continued well-being of most Friends as the result of Indian love for William Penn, the Quaker reputation for nonviolence, and the willingness of Quaker families to rely solely on God's protection for their survival.[69] The Yearly Meeting of 1758 made similar claims, expressing its gratitude "for the peculiar favor extended and continued to our Friends and Brethren in profession, none of whom have as we have yet heard been Slain nor carried into Captivity."[70] During his travels to western Pennsylvania in 1758–59, Quaker trader James Kenny "saw himself as representing a Quaker legacy of peace" and similarly discovered that in spite of the war's animosities, many natives still held a special regard for Friends. Prominent Quaker minister John Woolman's visit to several Indian communities in 1763 convinced him that reconciliation with natives was possible if all parties pursued economic justice and pacifism. Native circumstances as a result of the prior decade reinforced his conviction, shared with other radical pacifists, that war itself, and not just Quaker participation in it, had to be vigorously opposed.[71]

If Quakers, and especially reforming ones, were disposed to read those types of events as successes, most other Pennsylvanians were not. Friends had experienced plenty of internal division and turmoil during the war, as they split over a range of issues such as whether to remain in government, the other demands of their peace testimony, and calls for stricter discipline. Moreover, their consciences were strained from wrestling with the guilt of their own sins that in their minds had brought down God's wrath upon them in the form of war.[72] But none of the loathing aroused in their internecine battles or self-condemnation could compare to the intense hatred now directed toward them by fellow colonists and even the British government. Amid the Seven Years' War, Friends in Pennsylvania came to be disparaged and despised to an unprecedented degree. In the years preceding the conflict, the colony's proprietors and their supporters had already been rallying opposition to continued Quaker political control. Their case became easier to make during the war, when any failure on the government's part to act on behalf of its citizens was laid at the feet of Quakers and blamed on their pacifism. Despite the resignation of some Quaker legislators from the Assembly, that body was still identified in the public mind with the Society of Friends. Complaints against its policies, especially from devastated western settlers, who were overwhelmingly non-Quaker, became attacks on the Society itself. The same logic shaped public perceptions of the work of the Friendly Association. Though it was a private organization initiated by a relatively small number of Quakers and not an official arm of any Quaker ecclesiastical body, the Association's efforts were ascribed to all Friends. That meant that when government officials criticized the Association for meddling in the colony's diplomatic and military affairs, Friends in general became suspect for their political designs. Even more troublesome was the Association's benevolence toward the Delaware. In the minds of most colonists, handing out aid to Indian peoples who had been wreaking havoc on the Pennsylvania frontier for the past three years was ludicrous if not treasonous. It did not matter which Indians were receiving that aid; they were all bad, even the Christian ones. At least that was the perspective of thousands of Euro-Pennsylvanian frontiersmen as they struggled to recover from the displacement and carnage of war. Under their circumstances, it also certainly did not matter which Quakers were handing out that aid; they were all guilty of caring more about the enemy than about their fellow settlers. Quaker patronage toward Native Americans showed their true colors. If they wished to befriend murderous Indians, they deserved the same hatred natives did.[73]

Members of the Friendly Association hardly anticipated that their philanthropic actions would provoke such ire, but the exigencies of war had a way of producing all kinds of unintended consequences. Those Quakers with a strong historical memory might have been reminded of the troubles Friends had encountered during and after King Philip's War. Then and now, their peace testimony cut against the grain, inflicting self-wounds as well as venomous attacks from others. So, too, had their record of friendship with Indians. What might otherwise have been seen as a positive, in times of crisis became a liability as colonists were inclined to lash out at the Indian other and all those associated with them. As a result, in the early 1760s, there were more and more Pennsylvanians who thought that "the Quakers loved the Indians too much." Their "defense of the Indians," according to Krista Camenzind, "actually fueled the fires of Indian hatred and hastened the end of Penn's legacy of intercultural tolerance and peace."[74]

Hating Indians and hating Quakers marched hand in hand, then, by the end of the French and Indian War. They literally marched together in early 1764 in the form of the Paxton Boys as they proceeded toward an assault on Philadelphia. By that point, the Pennsylvania frontier had once again become a battle zone with the advent of Pontiac's War the previous spring. Natives attacked a string of British forts in the west and then carried the fight eastward across the Allegheny Mountains into Pennsylvania settlements. Delaware warriors were among the raiding Indian parties, the same native people whom the Friendly Association had wooed with gifts. These Quaker "friends" were killing colonists. And the Quaker-dominated Assembly was refusing to send aid to embattled settlers. What plainer evidence could there be that natives and Friends were a twin threat to Pennsylvanians' survival?

The frontier crowd that became known as the Paxton Boys had been looking for a chance to exact some revenge. Their fury was not a new phenomenon. It had been growing for at least a decade amid the trials of the Seven Years' War and had been latent for a long time before that. With the resumption of hostilities and new threats to settler welfare, a burning racial hatred flowed through their veins, one that marked any and all Indians, including neighboring friendly ones, as potential targets for evening the score.[75] The Paxton Boys eventually found their prey in the band of Conestoga Indians living near Lancaster. They descended upon their settlement on December 14, 1763, burned it, and killed six Conestogas. Two weeks later, a larger group of men, now numbering about one hundred, came back and brutally slaughtered the other fourteen Conestogas in Lancaster, where they had been temporarily protected by town officials. The Paxton Boys proudly announced that their next assignment was to kill the Moravian Indians who had recently fled to Philadelphia seeking the colony's protection.

Shocked and more than a bit terrified by news of the massacre, provincial officials took seriously the Paxton Boys' threat and sought to quiet the storm by removing the Native American Moravians to New York for everyone's safety. But New York's governor, and most likely many of its citizens, would not hear of it, so back came the Indians to Philadelphia in late January 1764. As the enraged frontiersmen approached, the city readied itself for a bloody contest. Even one to two hundred young Quaker men took up arms, apparently having determined that the prospect of more innocent native lives being butchered by a riotous gang was sufficiently horrific to suspend their pacifism. In the end, the Paxtonites' advance was headed off diplomatically by a group of colonial leaders, including Benjamin Franklin, who met them at neighboring Germantown. They were assured that the colonial government would consider their grievances, and to that end, Matthew Smith and James Gibson wrote up *A Declaration and Remonstrance* that gave officials a detailed list of their complaints.[76] All the reasons why the colony needed to be vigilant against Indians, who "Experience has taught us . . . are all Perfidious," were enumerated. The petition also made clear the Paxton Boys' hatred of the Society of Friends, who had "abetted our *Indian* Enemies" and usurped provincial political authority.[77]

Smith and Gibson's accusations proved to be the first volleys in a war of words that pounded back and forth between Pennsylvanians for the rest of 1764. Even as the Paxton Boys went home to their farms, their actions and their cause became the focus of a quantitatively unprecedented pamphlet war, as no fewer than sixty-three publications appeared. The debate turned into a contest between Paxtonian defenders and Quakers. Though many of the writers on the Quaker side were not themselves Friends, in the public mind it was Quakerism as much as the Paxton Boys that was on trial. With skilled sarcastic wit, Quaker attackers employed language and image, in the form of political cartoons, to castigate Friends as power-hungry hypocrites willing to do anything and to sacrifice anyone for their own gain.[78] And chief among their sins was their far too cozy relationship with Indians. "That Quakers have been partial, and shewn more real Affection for Enemy Savages than for their fellow Subjects, of certain Denominations," wrote David Dove, "is so well known in this Province, and has on the present Occasion been so fully demonstrated to the World, that I should deem it Loss of Time to say any more on so recent and glaring a Fact!"[79] That unholy alliance is what explained the Quaker-led Assembly's refusal to provide adequate frontier defenses and what accounted for their philanthropy to natives when at the same time they refused to help western settlers. It was also why their pretenses to pacifism so quickly went by the boards when Indian and Quaker lives were threatened in Philadelphia. Pamphleteers were not entirely sure why natives and Friends were so close, they just knew that "In many things change but the Name, / Quakers and Indians are the same."[80] Perhaps it was because Quakers wanted natives to kill as many of their political opponents in the west as possible. Or maybe "the Affection which some Principals of that Sect have shewn to Indians, and the great Care they are now taking of them can possibly be owing to the Charms of their Squaws, [or] to any particular Advantages that may arise from their Trade."[81]

However farfetched those speculations were, in the public climate of the mid-1760s, "Quakers could be made to appear more unrepresentative, more inconsistant [sic], and more insincere than the Paxtonians who opposed them."[82] Friends' defenders utilized some of the same literary devices as their foes and even conjured up conspiracy theories to explain the sinister forces arrayed against them. Overall, according to one recent scholar, the Quaker side was not quite as effective in making its case, not the least because of the difficulty of explaining away the embarrassing actions of those dozens of Friends who had grabbed weapons at the crisis moment back in February.[83] What Quakers did not try to explain away was their legacy of friendship with neighboring Indians. That bond, they claimed, had always been undertaken for the sake of mutual benefit, and the colony's long history of peace testified to its prudence. Charges that they had shown "gross partiality to Indians" at the expense of western settlers or that they abetted hostile Indians were simply not true. Euro-Americans and Native Americans had both received Quaker charity, and no Friend had betrayed the English cause in the war. In fact, no group had worked harder to win Indians to the English side than Quakers.[84]

Friends' refusal to disown their actions in either the distant or the recent past toward natives could be interpreted as the natural self-justifying response of a group under vicious literary attack. After all, everything from their honesty to their pacifism and loyalty was being ridiculed in the press. And at the same moment their traditional dominant place within provincial politics was going the way of the flesh. Who could blame them for a little self-justification? On the other hand, the tide of provincial opinion toward Indians in general was swinging so decisively in the direction of violent opposition, it is a wonder that Friends did not jump on the bandwagon for the sake of self-preservation. In the decade that stretched from the beginning of the French and

Indian War through the Paxton Boys controversy, Pennsylvania and Pennsylvanians in thought and action moved toward the mainstream of colonial American experience. Over was the long peace that had set the province apart from other major British colonies. Over as well was the psychic appeal of a founding myth that envisioned a Pennsylvania that could be shared by natives and newcomers. Now it was clear that however laudable those early efforts at diplomacy had been, they were no longer relevant. In the public mind, events had shown that the Quaker way could not work; pacifism had cost hundreds of colonist lives. No Indian could be trusted. It was them or us, their lives or ours. Pennsylvania's future, America's future hung in the balance. Whose vision would win out?

Quakers in Pennsylvania had always imagined that the choice would not be necessary, that a common vision or at least peaceful coexistence was possible. In retrospect, we can identify ways in which Friends contributed to the subversion of their own dream. To their credit, they caught on to some of these, such as engaging in dishonest land dealings and selling liquor. But their awareness of those practices in the 1750s and 1760s, as earlier, did not persuade them that they should give up on the holy experiment in intercultural relations. Nor did the gruesome deaths of hundreds of colonists and Indians. If anything, the tragedies of war and the horrors of Christian Indians' being massacred by colonial farmers showed Quakers just how much Pennsylvania needed to get back to Penn's original design.

By the mid-1760s, most of their neighbors disagreed and were moving closer to the belief that Indian extinction was a necessary corollary to Euro-American expansion and success. Quakers were reluctant to accept that premise. As Friend Charles Read put it, "There are People so sanguine that, without considering, would wish the whole Race of Indians extinct, but they shew their Ignorance of the real Interest of the Nation."[85] For Read and other Quakers, to welcome Indian death and destruction would mean condoning the attitudes and actions of those they had long condemned, going back to their battles with Puritans a century earlier. They had staked their reputation and their identity on carving out a just and peaceable way with natives. To admit or to conclude that that was not possible, or even worse, to suppose that their original vision was fundamentally flawed, was too painful a proposition to entertain. Better to be a minority voice crying out in the wilderness against colonial aggression than a partner, even a silent one, to Indian extermination. The former was at least a role their Quaker brothers and sisters had been used to playing elsewhere. The latter would have meant seeing Indian death as a blessing and, consequently, the Quaker holy experiment as a failure. Few Friends were willing to accept that judgment on Indians or themselves.

KEEPING INDIANS ALIVE

Dying Indians remained a reality and an image with which Quakers wrestled off and on during the closing decades of the eighteenth century and into the nineteenth century. That Pennsylvania Friends paid any attention at all to natives in this era is itself worth noting. They certainly had enough other things to worry about amid colonial resistance to Britain, the War for Independence, and the construction of the new republic. Meanwhile, by the eve of the Revolution, there may have been fewer Indians in Pennsylvania than in any other British colony, a chilling testament that the province's "long peace" had not precluded the same, or worse, outcomes on the survival of native communities as more hostile policies elsewhere in the colonies.[86] Natives were more and more out of sight for most Quakers and may have been equally out of mind much of the time. Yet that is not the whole story. During the American Revolution, some Quaker leaders, and in particular Anthony Benezet, continued to speak out on behalf of reviving or preserving the Friends' holy experiment with Indians. Then in the next decade, Friends more broadly joined the emerging national conversation on the future of Native Americans. Persuaded that the matter once again warranted Quaker care, they sought to find a means of keeping Indians and their own self-image as faithful bearers of Penn's legacy alive.

Quaker trials during the revolutionary era were too voluminous and are too well known to warrant repeating here. Suffice it to say that their efforts at practical neutrality and their principled opposition to war brought mostly scorn and abuse upon them from all sides but especially from local patriots who labeled anyone who was not an active supporter of their cause a Loyalist. Though painful, Friends' sufferings provided an opportunity for reflection and renewal according to Quaker reformers. They saw this time of testing as a providential impetus for the majority of Friends to get serious about living out their faith. Calls went out for Friends to embrace a simpler and more ascetic lifestyle. More controversial proposals entailed refusals to pay taxes, to take oaths or affirmations, or to accept Continental currency. Most controversial of all were efforts to abolish slavery, not only among Quakers but within Pennsylvania as a whole and beyond.[87]

Few if any Quakers, or Americans for that matter, were more outspoken on these issues, including abolitionism, than Anthony Benezet. For at least the last thirty years of his life (he died in 1784), Benezet was a vigorous antislavery advocate. The Revolutionary War seemed to re-double his energies for seeing slavery end. His and other Quakers' iden-tification with African Americans, slave and free, may have been due to their shared sense of outsider status, which the war made more acute. The same may have also been true for Quakers with Indians. Because Quakers were perceived as closet Tories and since most Native Ameri-cans sided with the British, the war pushed both groups further to the margins of mainstream American society.[88] Empathizing with the plight of natives and concerned for their future, as he had been since the 1750s when he was a member of the Friendly Association, Benezet led other Friends to the conviction that something more needed to be done on behalf of Indians.

Between 1780 and 1784, Benezet published three pamphlets that to one degree or another addressed the issue of Indian survival from a distinctively Quaker perspective. The first, *A short account of the people called Quakers,* was intended to give the general public in America and elsewhere a brief description and history of Friends in the English colo-nies. It focused primarily on Pennsylvania and offered an interpretation of the colony's past that championed the principle of liberty of con-science. Thanks to that freedom, the province had welcomed persons of all persuasions. Yet many of the newcomers had proved to be of "dif-ferent dispositions from the first settlers" and were concerned only to "amass wealth and aggrandize themselves." Tellingly, Benezet identi-fied the principal result of their greed as the end of peace with natives. "The friendly disposition of the Indians," which had been "conspicuous for a long course of years, in favour of the inhabitants" and had given Pennsylvania "an uninterrupted peace of more than sixty years," had been ruined by colonial materialism. Thereafter Pennsylvania had be-come just like all the other colonies, suffering "severely from the incur-sions of the natives." Some settlers' pursuit of raw self-interest had "very much reversed the system of happiness so long and successfully pursued" by colonists and Indians alike. Fear, violence, and death now stood much too often in its place.[89]

Benezet's version of Pennsylvania's past may be read as a classic Quaker call to plain living. The values Euro-Americans had chosen to live by had had profound consequences for all the peoples who inhab-ited the region. Violence was the product of injustice, and injustice was the fruit of selfish desires. What did it profit a man to gain the whole world but lose his soul and his life? Far better to recall what had made for happiness and peace for so long in the colony.

Benezet was ready and willing to help readers in that task two years later in his pamphlet *The plainness and innocent simplicity of the Christian religion. With its salutary effects, compared to the corrupting nature and dreadful effects of war.* As his title implied, Benezet wished to promote pacifism as a biblical and rational alternative to any resort to war, which for him was always ill-advised. Pennsylvania provided a prime example of what and what not to do. Contrary to the claims of politicians who said that war, or the threat of it, was the only effective means of defense against potential oppressors, this colony's history showed the only sure source of protection in this world—divine favor. God was happy to cooperate and bless peoples and rulers who were committed to a "spirit of peace and good order." In Pennsylvania that had meant that "so long as the government continued chiefly in the hands of a people principled against war, . . . they experienced the protecting hand of providence, and enjoyed an uninterrupted tranquillity for more than sixty years." Peace had been maintained with all neighboring Indians, whereas Canada and other colonies "who pursued different measures, suffered dreadfully from their Indian neighbours." In almost prophet-like fashion, Benezet laid out a call to the barely born nation to heed the lessons of history, repent from the sins of the past and present, and return to the divinely blessed ways of founding father William Penn in relation to Indians.[90]

Most patriots were not inclined to pay much attention to William Penn in the revolutionary era.[91] Nor were they disposed to think very well of most Native Americans. That became distressingly clear to Benezet as he read fellow Pennsylvanian Hugh Henry Brackenridge's epilogue to *Narratives of a late expedition against the Indians,* a 1783 pamphlet detailing the fighting between patriots and Indians on the Pennsylvania and Ohio frontiers. The bloody conflict had left Brackenridge in no mood to take prisoners, literally or figuratively. His opening line made clear his opinion of Native Americans: "I subjoin some observations with regard to the animals, vulgarly called Indians." Questioning natives' humanity, he went on to insist that Indians had forfeited any legitimate claim to territory by failing to improve the land through tilling it and therefore "ought to be driven from it." Moreover, their ill-treatment of war prisoners was sufficiently egregious to "justify [their] extirmination." In fact, even if Indians reformed "from these practices, they ought not to live: These nations are so degenerate from the life of man, so devoid of every sentiment of generosity, so prone to every vicious excess of passion, so faithless, and so incapable of all civilization, that it is dangerous to the good order of the world that they should exist in it." Brackenridge proceeded to invoke a series of biblical precedents, including the destruction of Sodom and Gomorrah as "a sufficient order to exterminate the whole brood." He denied that schooling or any other means of trying to civilize Indians would make any difference in their character. The best policy the new nation could adopt, he wrote, would be to push all of them beyond "the Ohio and Missisippi waters" and eventually drive them "to the cold snows of the north west, where darkness reigns six months in the year" and where "their practices shall be obscured, and the tribes gradually abolished."[92]

Brackenridge's vituperation on Indian character was a direct cause of Benezet's decision to write *Some Observations on the situation, disposition, and character of the Indian Natives of this continent.* As he explained in a letter to fellow Friend George Dillwyn, "the prevailing prejudice in the back settlements against all Indians as expressed in Brackenrige's publication, . . . so strongly incentive to the utter extirpitation of Indians, appears to call for the most weighty consideration . . . [and] a duty to endeavor to remove [those attitudes] by giving the necessary information to many otherwise well-disposed who are under inconsiderate and mistaken prejudices." Convinced that the future of both Euro-Americans and Native Americans hung in the balance, Benezet worried that few persons had been in a position like he had to experience "the fidelity and candour of Indians" and hoped to convey that view especially to "sensible, generous minded youth."[93] The announced object of his pamphlet, printed in 1784, the same year as his death, was to "obviate some mistakes which have been embraced, respecting the Natives of this land." Implicitly countering Brackenridge and explicitly echoing long-standing Quaker claims that Indians were fully human and fully rational beings capable of "receiving the refining influence of our holy religion," he told readers that his was a balanced perspective, neither championing white superiority nor overestimating Indian virtue, even when it came to "their affectionate reception of our Ancestors on their first settlement of Pennsylvania." If Benezet was careful not to overstate the Quakers' founding myth, he still took pains to emphasize the friendly and just relations that prevailed with natives in early Pennsylvania and New Jersey, and even on some occasions in New England, thanks to the benevolence of persons on both sides. Contrary to the claims of some Americans that Indians were "naturally ferocious, treacherous, and ungrateful," the historical record showed that particularly in the early stages of colonization, natives "generally manifested themselves to be kind, hospitable and generous to the Europeans, so long as they were treated with justice and humanity." Unfortunately, thereafter, "unjust and cruel treatment from European Aggressors" had predictably provoked natives to "fury and vengeance." Equally tragic, colonial Christians with few exceptions had missed opportunities to acquaint Indians with the gospel and instead incited "the poor Natives, when it has suited their political purpose, to violence amongst themselves, and to become parties in the wars they have waged one against another." More and more, Euro-Americans had a "disposition to misrepresent and blacken the Indians, in order to justify, or palliate the practice of unjust and cruel measures towards them."[94] A horrific case in point was the recent massacre of Moravian Indians at Gnadenhutten in the Ohio country. Benezet devoted a dozen pages to rehearsing their history and defending their innocence. His words became ever more passionate, finally crescendoing in an outcry against genocide:

> In vindication of this barbarous transaction [the killing of the Moravian Indians], endeavours have been used, to make us believe, that the whole race of Indians are a people prone to every vice, and destitute of every virtue; and without a capacity for improvement. What is this but blasphemously to arraign the wisdom of our Creator, and insinuate, that the existence He has given them, is incompatible with his moral government of the world. But this must be admitted to make way for the proposal of endeavouring the universal extirpation of Indians from the face of the earth. Such, alas! is the manner in which too many of the pretended followers, of the meek and suffering Saviour of the world, would fulfil the prophecy concerning him, *"That he shall have the Heathens for his inheritance, and the uttermost Parts of the earth for his possession."*[95]

Here was Benezet's ultimate fear laid bare. Euro-American racism toward Indians had grown to the point, as indicated by Brackenridge's pamphlet and by the actions of patriot soldiers, that it would condone, promote, and even carry out native eradication and then have the gall to portray its deadly work as the fulfillment of biblical prophecy. What could be more antithetical to the true spirit of Christ? To harbor such prejudices on the basis of "the colour of our skins" or "outward circumstances or profession" to the point of being "zealous for the extirpation of all Indians" was to be in "a state of alienation from God, and reprobate concerning a true faith in the Lord Jesus Christ, which works only by love."[96]

Benezet was at a loss to say anything new in the rest of his pamphlet. He simply reiterated earlier positive claims about Indian character and then returned once more to reviewing the lessons of colonial history. As usual, most of New England's past demonstrated the ill effects of treating natives poorly. Meanwhile, the early years of Pennsylvania and New Jersey served as a helpful model, if not a golden age, when Indian numbers were "so great, that they might have easily destroyed the settlers" but instead chose to be "nursing fathers" to them. Now that the tables (and numbers) were reversed, Benezet clearly hoped that the new nation would learn from and embrace the Quaker legacy with Native Americans. Not to do so portended a violent and deadly future for the early republic, and one inimical to Christ's kingdom.[97]

Anthony Benezet was out front of most other Friends in publicly voicing his concerns about the fate of American Indians in the 1780s. On this issue, as with others, he was an extraordinary advocate for racial equity and justice. Yet much of what he affirmed derived from a long-established Quaker memory of having charted a distinctive path with Native Americans. In their minds, the Quaker holy experiment with Indians had worked, and the last few decades of violent conflict with natives only made that more clear. The growing number of Americans determined to see more native deaths had to be opposed in some fashion. Too much was at stake to be silent about those being silenced. The cause of Christ hung in the balance. So, too, did Indian lives and Quaker identity.

Leading Quaker bodies heeded Benezet's call in the late eighteenth century and settled on a strategy to aid Native American survival in step with the ideals and realities of the times. As briefly mentioned in the opening of this chapter, these Friends initiated efforts to facilitate Indian adoption of Euro-American agricultural and settlement patterns. The New York, Philadelphia, and Baltimore Yearly Meetings all oversaw small-scale missionary projects in the late 1790s and early 1800s in which Friends were sent to live among Oneidas, Senecas, and Ohio Indians (Miamis, Potawatomis, and others) for the purposes of teaching them farming techniques, supplying them tangible aid, and persuading them to give up their hunting lifestyles.[98] A range of motives lay behind Quaker actions. Some hoped that their close contact with natives on temporal matters might gradually draw Indians to see the light of Christian faith.[99] More immediately, though, the chief concern was to alleviate some of the economic deprivation and demographic demise Quakers believed many if not all native peoples were experiencing. As they had done in the past, Friends often attended, usually at the natives' request, treaty councils held in Philadelphia and elsewhere in the 1790s. What they heard and saw on those occasions shaped their humanitarian impulse. So William Savery, after listening to representatives of the Six Nations at Canandaigua, New York, in 1794, noted in his journal that the Quakers' "minds were seriously turned to consider the present state of these six nations; and a lively prospect presented, that a mode could be adopted by which Friends and other humane people might be made useful to them in a greater degree than has ever yet been effected." Unprecedented benevolence was necessary "for the cause of humanity and justice" and "for the sake of this poor declining people."[100] To that end, he and the other five Quaker representatives returned to Philadelphia and appealed for help to the Friends' Meeting for Sufferings, and through it to the Yearly Meeting. The latter body responded by establishing a standing committee on Indian affairs, which in turn decided on the policy of sending missionaries to instruct natives "in husbandry, and useful trades." Given the condition of "those distressed inhabitants of the wilderness," the extraordinary kindness with which Native Americans had treated the first Quakers in Pennsylvania, traditional Quaker commitments to universal brotherhood and justice, and the greater likelihood of peace if Indian communities were economically stable, the Indian Committee set out to make a difference.[101]

In retrospect, their efforts, and those of the other yearly meetings, proved to be very modest in scope and even more modest in effect. In most cases, it took several years before anything concrete was done, and when it was, it involved only handfuls of Friends and tools reaching Indians. Moreover, Quakers often erred in their judgments about the current economic conditions, lifestyles, and needs of those they served. Prone to see all natives as poor, they failed to see the differences in the circumstances faced by some Indian groups versus others. Prone as well to attribute native poverty to their dependence on the hunt, Friends failed to understand the character of Indian agriculture, the sexual division of labor within native societies, and even the purposes of hunting for native peoples. Quakers embraced the then popular theory that hunting societies were bound to decline demographically when confronted by agricultural and commercial societies. Benjamin Franklin and a range of Enlightenment thinkers in Europe had advanced the notion that human communities might pass through four developmental stages—hunting, pasturage, agriculture, and commerce—and that those on the lower end of the developmental ladder would ultimately not survive the spread of civilization. With that view in mind, Quakers could not help but conclude that Indians were doomed to extinction, and sooner rather than later, unless they rapidly changed their mode of subsistence. United States federal officials seemingly agreed and announced policies under presidents Washington and Jefferson to assist Native Americans in making the transition to becoming property-owning yeoman farmers.[102] Quakers were happy to get on board with that kind of program, and government officials, in turn, were pleased to lend their encouragement to the Friends' missionary initiatives.[103] In the end, though, neither group achieved the successes they hoped for.

All that being said, it would be a mistake to underestimate the significance of Quaker concern for Indians at the turn of the nineteenth century. Friends were by no means unique in all their perspectives on natives, as indicated by their ready acceptance of their age's latest cultural and demographic theories. They were as susceptible as other Euro-Americans to misinterpret and misunderstand Native Americans and to believe in the cultural superiority of the white man's ways. Yet their embrace of the assimilationist program stemmed from a longstanding concern for Indian survival. Quaker historians debate whether their humanitarian efforts were designed to gain Friends the respect of others or to set them apart as a distinct body.[104] Either way, Friends generally wanted to stand in the way of those many Americans who seemed to have no qualms about speeding up the process of native depopulation through displacing and even eliminating any Indians who got in their way. In an early republic where persuading Indians to acculturate appeared as the humanitarian alternative to aggressive conquest and native extirpation, Quakers saw no choice but to embrace the former plan. The resultant missionary actions were small and tentative because they were new and experimental, not because they did not matter to Friends. They in fact may be seen as one more attempt to perpetuate the Quakers' holy experiment with Native Americans. Teaching Indian men how to use a plough and Indian women how to spin became new means toward that old end, and keeping Indians alive remained an important measure of Quaker success.

NATIVE DEATH AND QUAKER IDENTITY

As the nineteenth century began, the future of Native Americans living east of the Mississippi River was uncertain. Indians remained central to life in America in the early republic, but even many of them sensed that U.S. expansion would soon bring a time when they would be marginalized to an unprecedented degree.[105] The Lewis and Clark expedition of 1803–1806 portended a day when natives west of the Mississippi would experience a similar fate. In retrospect, we know that many Indian peoples proved remarkably resilient in the face of shrinking lands and shrinking populations. Yet from the standpoint of many Euro-Americans at the time, the disappearance of natives was an expected outcome. Divine providence may have surprised early waves of settlers along the Atlantic seaboard by emptying the land of many of its Indians, but their successors two centuries later had come to expect it. In their minds, whether providence was still the cause or instead some combination of human factors deserved the credit, the destinies of the new nation and the nations of native peoples pointed in opposite directions. One was bound for glory, the others bound for the grave.

Such attitudes in the early republic built upon the experiences of earlier colonial Americans. For generations, Europeans in America had found ways to read Indian deaths in positive terms—positive terms about Euro-Americans that is. The blessing of God, the sign of their physical and cultural superiority, the product of a proper cultivation of the earth, the result of their military skill and training—all these were lessons to be learned from witnessing native attrition. Even the passing of Christian Indians became cause for a certain kind of celebration and publicity, for these were "good deaths," the fruit of divinely blessed Euro-American evangelistic efforts.[106] Though missionary authors intended those accounts to illustrate Indian Christianization, not the prospect of native extinction, some colonial readers were no doubt happy to welcome the passing of any natives. It should be said that many newcomers expressed sympathy when they saw native communities suffering. But the primary effect that encountering dying and dead Indians had upon European colonial religion was an intensification of religious pride and arrogance. Colonists did not have to belong to a Christian body that saw themselves as divinely chosen to have a strong sense of God's special favor upon them when they took stock of colonial gains and native losses. In fact, few colonial developments did more to bolster their sense of divine favor than native depopulation. The more Indians vanished, the more confident average Euro-Americans became that their nation and their Christian faith were right and true and good.[107]

Quakers were not the only colonial Christians to dissent from such views and to derive a contrary message about the meaning of Indian death. Nor were they free of self-righteousness or spiritual pride. But they do provide an especially clear example of the power that native mortality could exercise over colonial American religion, and they illustrate that that power did not lead all colonists to the same conclusions. For the 150 years surveyed in this chapter, Friends rarely rejoiced over native deaths or found in them good news about themselves. Instead, out of their encounters with Native Americans and their broader colonial experience, the preservation of Indian lives, if not Indian cultures, emerged as a marker for Quakers of how well and how much Friends were influencing the colonial world around them. Or to put it another way, from the Quaker point of view, most native mortality signaled how far colonial America was from living according to the Christian ideals Friends promoted and perhaps also how far Friends themselves were from living out those ideals.

How and why Quakers had come to judge their own success by the yardstick of Native American fortunes should now be clearer. From the beginning of Friends' experiences in North America, they became linked to Indians in their own minds. That was partially because others linked them together, usually as objects of disdain and animosity. Quakers and Indians shared an outsider status, especially in times of colonial crisis. But there were other reasons as well for Friends' sense of connection to natives. In seventeenth-century New England, Quakers chose to interpret the region's conflicts with Indians as the fruit of unjust policies toward natives and Friends. Quakers and Indians were co-victims of Puritan oppression. When the Wampanoags and their allies responded with violence, Friends were exempt from native hostilities because of their peaceableness, at least according to the Quaker myth that developed. Yet the war was still a very troubling experience for Friends. It had tried their consciences, shown that violence and warfare in early America would most often be directed toward Native Americans, and represented at some level a failure of Christian peacekeeping and justice. At roughly the same time, and with the conflicts of New England in mind, other Friends embarked on new colonial experiments in New Jersey and Pennsylvania that, at the urging of George Fox and others, consciously sought to steer a different course with local natives. Persuaded within a short time that providence had smiled upon their efforts by providing kind and cooperative Indian neighbors, whose full humanity and readiness for Christianity Friends happily affirmed, Quakers in those colonies developed a heroic view of their founding fathers and founding moments that celebrated both sides' commitment to peaceful, just relations. Friends and natives repeatedly invoked that myth across the eighteenth century to call all parties back to the holy experiment William Penn and his native partners had begun. When conscientious Friends saw Indian lands and, even worse, Indian lives violated, they lamented the departure from Penn's hopes and plans such acts represented. In their minds, Native American losses usually needed to be interpreted as Quaker losses, and never more so than in the violence of the Seven Years' War and the subsequent Paxton Boys raids. Under those circumstances, defending Indians brought down on Friends new levels of rebuke but in the process resolidified their attachment to natives and their sense that their fates were intertwined. Quaker Anthony Benezet reasserted that point in the 1780s in the face of some of the most extreme calls for Indian elimination, and other Friends followed suit in the next two decades. Their efforts to preserve Indian lives were a continuation of what had become a critical part of what it meant to be a Friend in America.

Like other Euro-Americans, then, but perhaps even more so, members of the Society of Friends throughout early America were shaped by their encounter with the prospect and reality of native death. Dying and dead natives evoked Quaker grief and stirred what Friends considered righteous anger and actions when those deaths were in their eyes the needless fruit of war or greed or bad theology. They also pricked Friends' moral consciences and forced them to work out more precisely the meaning and bounds of their peace testimony. Concerns over the integrity of that peace testimony contributed to the wide-ranging internal efforts at reform that touched most aspects of Quaker practice in the mid to late eighteenth century. As they sought to figure out how to live faithfully as Friends, few Quakers grasped the sad irony that their own presence in what had in recent memory been Indian country, however benevolently intended, contributed to native attrition in one way or another. Instead, they typically responded to the passing of Native Americans with laments that other colonists, including on occasion disobedient Friends, had sown seeds of discord and reaped harvests of destruction in their dealings with Indians. In the face of such circumstances, Quakers assigned themselves the task of marking out a different way with natives. As they charted that course, Friends developed sanguine views of themselves as the protectors of Indians, a myth of innocence as powerful as the one other colonial Christians embraced about themselves as they saw their numbers increasing and Indian numbers decreasing. That was perhaps the most significant way Indian death affected Quakers' religious experiences, sensibilities, and self-identities because it pushed them toward a vision of themselves and their mission in America that was larger and more mythical than it might otherwise have been, and more connected to Indians than most early Quakers would have anticipated or many later Quakers realized. Friends' ability to realize that vision was always limited, constrained by their own and others' choices. But what had started in the colonial era continued into the early republic as Quakers tied their own success to the life and death of Indians.

Epilogue

In September 1772, recently ordained and commissioned Presbyterian pastor David McClure arrived in northeastern Ohio hoping to minister to the Delaware Indians living along the Muskingum River. His journey westward had included a stop at Brotherton, New Jersey, where he met with John Brainerd and the remnants of the Christian Indian congregation begun by Brainerd's older brother a quarter century earlier. McClure would return there the following summer and spend several days with a discouraged Brainerd, who was distressed by the "little success of his labours" amid a flock that, beset by alcohol abuse and dismal prospects for the future, shrank yearly. The new missionary could only call Brainerd's charges "a poor race of beings."[1] McClure's trek west in 1772 also included a visit to the Moravian village of Kuskuskies in western Pennsylvania. There he observed a well-ordered community of Delaware living and worshiping with several German Moravian missionary families. McClure attended morning and evening prayer with them in a log church adorned with religious paintings of the life of Christ. The services, all in the Delaware language, consisted of short sermons preceded by "devout hymns." "In singing," McClure noted, "they all, young & old bore a part, & the devotion was solemn & impressive. . . . Their hymns are prayers addressed to Jesus Christ, the lamb of God, who died for the sins of men, & exhortations & resolutions to abstain from sin . . . & to live in love & the practice of good works, as he has given us example." Already moved by the holy sounds he heard, McClure waited on his interpreter, Joseph Peepy, to help him make sense of the texts. Peepy was a well-known translator and one sought out by missionaries, for he himself was a Delaware Christian convert, brought to faith under the tutelage of the Brainerds. Before the two men traveled on to their principal destination, McClure marveled at the Germans' success:

> The Moravians appear to have adopted the best mode of Christianizing the Indians. They go among them without noise or parade, & by their friendly behaviour conciliate their good will. They join them in the chace, & freely distribute to the helpless & gradually instill into the minds of individuals, the principles of religion. They then invite those who are disposed to hearken to them, to retire to some convenient place, at a distance from the wild Indians, & assist them to build a village, & teach them to plant & sow, & to carry on some coarse manufactures.[2]

Finally at New Comer's Town (Kighalampegha), the largest Delaware settlement on the Muskingum, McClure readied himself for his new ministry. He was barely unpacked, however, when he discovered that his stay was to be short-lived. The town's Delaware council decided that it would be best for all concerned if McClure returned home, and told him so within two weeks of his arrival. In that time, area natives had already been communicating the same message to the missionary in less formal ways. For much of the fortnight, for example, a good portion of the community, which had close to a hundred families, indulged in a "drunken frolic," hardly the sort of welcome McClure was hoping for. He did manage to preach on consecutive Sundays, as well as on several weekdays, to Indian audiences. But he found most of his listeners disinterested or confused by what he said or didn't say. Under those circumstances, he was thankful for the pious efforts of Peepy, who followed up his sermons with emotional appeals of his own: "My Interpreter, who appeared deeply impressed at the melancholy condition of his countrymen, conversed with great freedom, fluency & feeling on their spiritual state. With tears flowing from his eyes, he told them many solemn truths, and made an affectionate and serious application of the discourse to them."[3]

Delaware resistance to McClure was expressed perhaps most tellingly in a series of objections raised by the speaker of the council. First he wondered why the "Almighty *Monetho*" (Manitou), who was the creator of all things and father of all peoples, would send the Bible to whites and not to Indians. He argued that in lieu of the Bible, "the Great Monetho has given us knowledge here, (pointing to his forehead) & when we are at a loss what to do, we must *think*." McClure privately described this contention as a "deistical objection, founded in the pride of erring reason, and more than I expected from an uncultivated heathen." Publicly, he responded by trying to make a case that within God's sovereignty the good news had been progressively revealed to many different people groups and that it was now the task of the English to bring the knowledge of the Bible to Indians. Seemingly unimpressed, the speaker moved quickly onto a second objection, "if we take your religion, we must leave off war, and become as women, and then we shall be easily subdued by our enemies." Very likely echoing arguments some Delaware had previously made against Moravian and Quaker pacifists of both races, he and others clearly worried about the political consequences of their religious choices. So, too, did they worry about their land if they allowed McClure to stay. He might attract more white settlers to Ohio, a prospect they looked dimly upon. As the speaker put it, "the white people, with whom we are acquainted, are worse, or more wicked than we are, and we think it better to be such as we are than such as they are." Likely feeling a bit exasperated at this point in the exchange, McClure gave his interpreter a few ideas on how to respond to that objection and then turned the conversation over to Peepy.[4]

No doubt having heard such arguments from fellow natives before, Peepy began by making it clear that not all whites were true Christians, especially not the traders these Indians were used to doing business with at Fort Pitt and other trading posts. To find real Christians, they would have to "go to Philadelphia. There you will see good people, who love the word of the Great God, and mind it." Whether Peepy intended those comments to indict the Christian character of all the colonists who had settled the Pennsylvania backcountry in recent decades is hard to say, though the unpleasant memories of the Paxton Boys and other frontier violence makes that inference at least plausible. What is clear in what he said is that he was as concerned about native losses as any of the Delaware brethren who stood before him. As he continued his speech, he recalled with them, in typical native fashion, happier days, and then lamented the current situation:

> We remember . . . that our fathers told us, how numerous the Indians were in their days, & in the days of their fathers. Great towns of Indians were all along the sea shore, and on the Rivers, and now, if you travel through that country, you will scarcely see an Indian; but you will see great and flourishing towns of white people, who possess the land of our fathers. And we are cut off, and fall back upon these distant rivers, and are reduced to a small number. The white people increase, and we Indians decrease.

Having identified himself as one of them and as a sharer in their plight, Peepy, perhaps repeating sentiments he had heard from McClure or other whites, went on boldly to offer an explanation for their turn of fortune: "The white people worship the true God, and please him, and God blesses and prospers them. We and our fathers worshiped Devils, or them that are no Gods, and therefore God frowns upon us." If they continued ignorant of the true God when they now had "an opportunity to know God and worship him," he would cut them off and "give this good country to a people that shall serve him." The Delawares' fate would be like that of "a great many powerful Indian nations" who had already been extinguished. Even the very memory of them as a people was at risk: "And if it shall be asked what has become of the Indians that lived here? none will be able to tell." According to McClure, "good Joseph['s] . . . lengthy prophetic" speech "took hold" of his audience. "Kings, Councillors & warriors . . . hung down their heads and made no reply."[5]

As with so many other moments in the encounters of the spirit in early America, it is impossible to know with certainty just what was passing through the hearts and minds of the Delaware that day, including Peepy's. Perhaps many were overcome with sadness as he spoke of the enormous transformations of their worlds within the past few generations. Perhaps others were dismayed that one of their own would place the blame for their declining lands and numbers on their long-standing sacred beliefs. Perhaps a few wondered whether Peepy might somehow be right and that appropriation of Christianity, for whatever reasons, might someday be necessary for their survival. Native peoples had been wrestling with those types of religious questions and emotions for several centuries by this point. In this case, the community determined that "it was necessary that the friendship between King George and them, should be made more firm and strong, before they could receive the english so much into favor, as to take their religion." So two days after Peepy's appeal, McClure heard the council's decision and concluded that "the prospect of being instrumental of much good to these poor & perishing heathen, was no more."[6]

McClure soon left town, but not before telling the Delaware that "they would have no more good fortune if they did not accept the Gospel. God would send judgment upon [their] city and eradicate them from the face of the earth." At least that is what he was reported to have said, according to Moravian missionary David Zeisberger, who had heard it from Joseph Peepy. Peepy visited Zeisberger and the nearby Moravian community of Schönbrunn shortly after McClure's departure and apparently rehearsed for them the Presbyterian's ill-advised tactics. As Zeisberger recorded their conversation in his diary, Peepy told them that McClure "talked very carelessly. For example, he supposedly said often that the Indians had so much beautiful and good land, but it was lying in waste and they did not use it because they were lazy people who did not want to work and resented the White people using it. In a few years all the land would be taken away from them. The White people would establish cities and towns there and drive the Indians away or even destroy them." Peepy concluded that McClure said these and "other such things, so it is no wonder that they [the Delaware] sent him away." Zeisberger and his Moravian colleagues no doubt concurred.[7]

Memorable neither for their success nor their duration, David McClure's brief sojourns with various Delaware Indian communities in 1772–73 nevertheless show many of the themes and dimensions of the religious encounters of early America this book has tried to illumine. Indigenized worship music, competing evangelistic strategies, rigorous theological exchanges, disillusioned missionary dispositions, creative native assistants, transformed religious identities, perishing Indian populations—all these and much more were a part of the encounters of the spirit that occurred as Native American and European peoples interacted across the wide expanses of early American history and geography. Amid a bewildering myriad of contacts, Indian lives and cultures were invariably changed by what the newcomers brought. But so, too, were the lives, cultures, and religions of the Europeans. As they met natives, a reciprocal flow of influence moved from one to the other, leaving marks upon Euro-Americans that for too long have remained hidden or covered over. Nowhere has that veil been thicker than in depictions of colonial Christianity. Often presented as a world little changed by its interaction with America's native inhabitants, it should be seen instead as a world regularly made new by the crucible of intercultural contact.

The contingencies of life within early America were such that the shapes and sizes, and the depth and duration, of Indian effects upon the newcomers' religion fit no neat patterns. Sweeping generalizations may someday emerge or reemerge about the Indian impact on European colonial religion, but for the moment we still do not know enough about the religious encounters of those centuries to make many wide-ranging claims. We can say that few if any parts of natives' and Europeans' religions were immune to being influenced by the other. Preceding chapters and the work of a host of other scholars have pointed up ways in which native rituals and belief systems were altered through contact with Europeans. Far more attention here has been placed on showing how colonists' worship practices and rites, forms of spirituality, styles of speech, types of leadership, theological convictions, missionary approaches, religious emotions, and self and group identities could be reshaped by encountering Native Americans. That list may not exhaust all the dimensions of religion, but it is wide enough to raise the suspicion that the native touch likely reached whatever corners remain. It is also possible to say that that touch reached all the corners of the Euro-American population. From New France to New Spain, from the Carolinas to the Ohio country, from Boston to Philadelphia, wherever new-comers called home in early America, their worlds including their religious worlds were affected by Indians' presence and power. Moreover, that proved true for colonists whether they themselves were part of the strong or weak, rich or poor, devout or profane, clergy or laity, male or female, young or old. It is easy to imagine that those on the margins of Euro-American society and Christianity were most susceptible and perhaps most open to native influence. And yet in many of the case studies examined here, figures close to the core of the colonial church were among those whose faiths were in some important way altered by encountering Indians. Even David Brainerd fits that description, for if he began as a marginal character in the colonial church, his legacy moved him near the center and kept him there for generations to come. Within the give and take of New World religious encounters, greater direct contact with Native Americans upped the odds that settlers of whatever variety would be impacted significantly by Indians. As they met and developed relationships with individual Nahuas, Hurons, Wampa-noags, Cherokees, Delawares, Oneidas, and hosts of other native peoples, particular English, Dutch, French, German, Spanish, and other European migrants entered into religious exchanges, often without knowing it. Consciously or not, their religious lives were changed as a result. That said, it was also the case that there were plenty of colonists who knew few or no Indians by name and nevertheless had the same experience. The histories of Puritans, Quakers, and French and Spanish Catholics recounted here have made it clear that face-to-face meetings, let alone personal relationships, were not required for natives to play large roles in shaping colonial religion. Sometimes those effects persisted for multiple generations. More often they were limited to portions of the lifetimes of those personally involved. Either way, they point to the value of recovering or retelling the stories of particular moments and peoples. Those stories may have some larger and longer significances, but they are valuable to know in and of themselves as a critical part of early American religious history.

That history, of course, was linked to events that circled the globe in the early modern era. The beaches and forests and villages of North America were hardly the only places where encounters of the spirit were taking place amongst peoples of vastly different cultural and religious backgrounds. Take, for example, the German Pietists sent by the king of Denmark to establish the first Protestant outreach in south India at the beginning of the eighteenth century, or the much better known cases of Italian Jesuits in China and Dutch Calvinist settlers in southern Africa a century earlier. Their experiences were among the innumerable moments of contact that occurred with increasing frequency as the comparatively isolated worlds of Asia, Africa, Europe, and the Americas penetrated one another in unprecedented ways in the three centuries after Columbus. Religious encounters were part and parcel of the cultural interchanges that transformed millions of lives on those five continents, and forever changed our world. Peoples' faiths were an essential element of what they carried into and out of those exchanges. Only rarely, and perhaps never, did those faiths come out exactly as they went in. Meeting the other, the cultural and religious stranger, in whatever way, was simply too formative an experience to leave behind no signs of its having taken place. The Europeans who came to North America were not exempt from that rule. Their encounters of the spirit with Native Americans changed all involved. And so in the swirl of early modern history, and the tumult of early American history, the religious beliefs and practices of countless men and women were shaped and reshaped amid the reciprocal streams of influence that flowed between natives and newcomers.

Notes

INTRODUCTION

1. Daniel Defoe, *Robinson Crusoe* and *A Journal of the Plague Year* (New York: Random House, 1948), 232, 243–44.

2. The novel's original title was *Life and Strange and Surprizing Adventures of Robinson Crusoe.*

3. Gary B. Nash, "The Concept of Inevitability in the History of European-Indian Relations," in *Inequality in Early America,* ed. Carla Gardina Pestana and Sharon V. Salinger (Hanover, N.H.: University Press of New England, 1999), 267–80, traces this historiography from the colonial era through the 1950s, with special attention to American history textbooks.

4. This revisionist model of interpretation is best represented by Francis P. Jennings, *The Invasion of America: Indians, Colonialism, and the Cant of Conquest* (Chapel Hill: University of North Carolina Press, 1975).

5. While many recent works embody this changing perspective, one eloquent articulation of it is in the prologue to Daniel K. Richter, *Facing East from Indian Country: A Native History of Early America* (Cambridge, Mass.: Harvard University Press, 2001), 1–10.

6. On the notion of natives encountering new worlds in the wake of the European arrival, see James H. Merrell, *The Indians' New World: Catawbas and Their Neighbors from European Contact through the Era of Removal* (Chapel Hill: University of North Carolina Press, 1989). On the need to bring Indians into the center of early American histories, see James H. Merrell, "Some Thoughts on Colonial Historians and American Indians," *William and Mary Quarterly,* 3rd ser., 46 (1989): 94–119, and Daniel K. Richter, "Whose Indian History?" *William and Mary Quarterly,* 3rd ser., 50 (1993): 379–93.

7. James Axtell makes a similar point in "The Indian Impact on English Colonial Culture," in his *The European and the Indian: Essays in the Ethnohistory of Colonial America* (New York: Oxford University Press, 1981), 272–75. Recent works that do suggest ways in which Euro-Americans' religion was influenced by the encounter with Indians include Natalie Zemon Davis, *Women on the Margins: Three Seventeenth-Century Lives* (Cambridge, Mass.: Harvard University Press, 1995), 63–139 (on Marie de l'Incarnation); Richard Cogley, *John Eliot's Mission to the Indians before King Philip's War* (Cambridge, Mass.: Harvard University Press, 1999); Gerald R. McDermott, "Jonathan Edwards and American Indians:

The Devil Sucks Their Blood," *New England Quarterly* 72 (1999): 539–57; Erik R. Seeman, "Reading Indians' Deathbed Scenes: Ethnohistorical and Representational Approaches," *Journal of American History* 88 (2001): 17–47; and Russell Bourne, *Gods of War, Gods of Peace: How the Meeting of Native and Colonial Religions Shaped Early America* (New York: Harcourt, 2002).

8. James Axtell, *The Invasion Within: The Contest of Cultures in Colonial North America* (New York: Oxford University Press, 1985).

9. Kenneth M. Morrison, *The Solidarity of Kin: Ethnohistory, Religious Studies, and the Algonkian-French Religious Encounter* (Albany: State University of New York Press, 2002), 3.

10. Among writings too voluminous to cite here, representative works include Neal Salisbury, " 'I Loved the Place of My Dwelling': Puritan Missionaries and Native Americans in Seventeenth-Century Southern New England," in Pestana and Salinger, *Inequality in Early America,* 111–33; James P. Ronda, " 'We Are Well As We Are': An Indian Critique of Seventeenth-Century Christian Missions," *William and Mary Quarterly,* 3rd. ser., 34 (1977): 66–82; Daniel K. Richter, " 'Some of Them . . . Would Always Have a Minister with Them': Mohawk Protestantism, 1683–1719," *American Indian Quarterly* 16 (1992): 471–84; Gregory Evans Dowd, *A Spirited Resistance: The North American Indian Struggle for Unity, 1745–1815* (Baltimore: Johns Hopkins University Press, 1992); Jane T. Merritt, *At the Crossroads: Indians and Empires on a Mid-Atlantic Frontier, 1700–1763* (Chapel Hill: University of North Carolina Press, 2003); and Joel W. Martin, *Sacred Revolt: The Muskogees' Struggle for a New World* (Boston: Beacon Press, 1991).

11. Salisbury, " 'I Loved the Place of My Dwelling,' " 112.

12. James H. Merrell, " 'The Customes of Our Countrey': Indians and Colonists in Early America," in *Strangers within the Realm: Cultural Margins of the First British Empire,* ed. Bernard Bailyn and Philip D. Morgan (Chapel Hill: University of North Carolina Press, 1991), 146–52; Axtell, *Invasion Within,* 242–43; Stafford Poole, "Some Observations on Mission Methods and Native Reactions in Sixteenth-Century New Spain," *Americas* 50 (1994): 338.

13. Richard White, *The Middle Ground: Indians, Empires, and Republics in the Great Lakes Region, 1650–1815* (Cambridge: Cambridge University Press, 1991), xi.

14. Michael D. McNally, "The Practice of Native American Christianity," *Church History* 69 (2000): 834–59; Joel W. Martin, *The Land Looks After Us: A History of Native American Religion* (Oxford: Oxford University Press, 2001).

15. On African-American slave Christianity, see Sylvia Frey and Betty Wood, *Come Shouting to Zion: African American Protestantism in the American South and British Caribbean to 1830* (Chapel Hill: University of North Carolina Press, 1998), and Albert J. Raboteau, *Slave Religion: The "Invisible Institution" in the Antebellum South* (New York: Oxford University Press, 1978). On Native American Christianity, see David J. Silverman, "Indians, Missionaries, and Religious Translation: Creating Wampanoag Christianity in Seventeenth-Century Martha's Vineyard," *William and Mary Quarterly,* 3rd ser., 62 (2005): 147–74; Salisbury, "I Loved the Place of My Dwelling," 113–28; Hilary E. Wyss, *Writing Indians: Literacy, Christianity, and Native Community in Early America* (Amherst: University of Massachusetts Press, 2000), 15. For another example of Christianity being indigenized, see Lamin Sanneh, *West African Christianity: The Religious Impact* (Maryknoll, N.Y.: Orbis Books, 1983).

16. David D. Hall, *Worlds of Wonder, Days of Judgment: Popular Religious Belief in*

Early New England (New York: Alfred A. Knopf, 1989); Jon Butler, *Awash in a Sea of Faith: Christianizing the American People* (Cambridge, Mass.: Harvard University Press, 1990); Richard Godbeer, *The Devil's Dominion: Magic and Religion in Early New England* (Cambridge: Cambridge University Press, 1992). Among works on early modern religion in Europe, the classic account is Keith Thomas, *Religion and the Decline of Magic* (New York: Scribner, 1971).

17. Colin G. Calloway, *New Worlds for All: Indians, Europeans, and the Remaking of Early America* (Baltimore: Johns Hopkins University Press, 1997), 26–33.

18. Daniel A. Scalberg, "The French-Amerindian Religious Encounter in Seventeenth and Early Eighteenth-Century New France," *French Colonial History* 1 (2002): 101–12.

19. Axtell, *Invasion Within*, 302–27. Other recent works on "white Indians" include June Namias, *White Captives: Gender and Ethnicity on the American Frontier* (Chapel Hill: University of North Carolina Press, 1993), and Matthew C. Ward, "Redeeming the Captives: Pennsylvania Captives among the Ohio Indians, 1755–1765," *Pennsylvania Magazine of History and Biography* 125 (2001): 161–89.

20. Axtell, *Invasion Within*, 286.

21. Charles L. Cohen, "The Colonization of British North America as an Episode in the History of Christianity," *Church History* 72 (2003): 553–68, presents a strong case for placing early American history, and especially early American religious history, in the larger context of the history of Christianity around the globe.

22. The December 2003 issue of *Church History* was dedicated to the theme of "The Missionary Impulse in United States History." Its articles speak well to the issue of reciprocal cultural and religious influence, especially Grant Wacker, "Introduction," *Church History* 72 (2003): 699–702, and Rachel Wheeler, " 'Friends to Your Souls': Jonathan Edwards' Indian Pastorate and the Doctrine of Original Sin," *Church History* 72 (2003): 736–65.

23. Lamin Sanneh, *Translating the Message: The Missionary Impact on Culture* (Maryknoll, N.Y.: Orbis Books, 1989), 167–90 (quote on 172).

24. John L. Comaroff and Jean Comaroff, *Of Revelation and Revolution: The Dialectics of Modernity on a South African Frontier,* 2 vols. (Chicago: University of Chicago Press, 1991–97), 2:23.

25. Fernando Cervantes, "Epilogue: The Middle Ground," in *Spiritual Encounters: Interactions between Christianity and Native Religions in Colonial America,* ed. Nicholas Griffiths and Fernando Cervantes (Lincoln: University of Nebraska Press, 1999), 276.

26. Nicholas Griffiths, "Introduction," in ibid., 1–2.

27. David Murray, "Spreading the Word: Missionaries, Conversion and Circulation in the Northeast," in ibid., 43–64 (quote on 58).

28. Griffiths, "Introduction," 7–8.

29. Sandra M. Gustafson, *Eloquence Is Power: Oratory and Performance in Early America* (Chapel Hill: University of North Carolina Press, 2000); Wyss, *Writing Indians;* Laura M. Stevens, *The Poor Indians: British Missionaries, Native Americans, and Colonial Sensibility* (Philadelphia: University of Pennsylvania Press, 2004); Kristina Bross, *Dry Bones and Indian Sermons: Praying Indians in Colonial America* (Ithaca, N.Y.: Cornell University Press, 2004); Joshua David Bellin, *The Demon of the Continent: Indians and the Shaping of American Literature* (Philadelphia: University of Pennsylvania Press, 2001).

30. Bellin, *Demon of the Continent,* quotes on 9, 10, 73, 75.

31. Butler, *Awash in a Sea of Faith;* Patricia Bonomi, *Under the Cope of Heaven: Religion, Society, and Politics in Colonial America,* updated ed. (New York: Oxford University Press, 2003); Mark A. Noll, *A History of Christianity in the United States and Canada* (Grand Rapids, Mich.: Eerdmans, 1992). Bonomi's book is an updated edition of her original 1986 work and now contains much more coverage of Native Americans, including a helpful discussion of recent scholarship in her new preface, xi–xiv.

32. Leigh Eric Schmidt, "Practices of Exchange: From Market Culture to Gift Economy in the Interpretation of American Religion," in *Lived Religion in America: Toward a History of Practice,* ed. David D. Hall (Princeton: Princeton University Press, 1997), 73.

33. Robert Orsi, "Everyday Miracles: The Study of Lived Religion," in Hall, *Lived Religion in America,* 7.

34. Bourne, *Gods of War, Gods of Peace,* xiii–xiv.

35. Catherine L. Albanese, "Exchanging Selves, Exchanging Souls: Contact, Combination, and American Religious History," in *Retelling U.S. Religious History,* ed. Thomas A. Tweed (Berkeley and Los Angeles: University of California Press, 1997), 200–226.

1. THE SOUNDS OF WORSHIP

1. *The Mission,* prod. Fernando Ghia and David Puttnam, dir. Roland Joffé, Goldcrest, 1986. This is not to suggest that music was not an important element in the encounters of other European peoples and Native Americans. For example, French Jesuits in seventeenth-century New France and German Moravians in eighteenth-century New York, Pennsylvania, and North Carolina used song extensively in the building of Christian communities among native peoples. For an excellent account of the role of music within the missions of Alta California, see James Sandos, *Converting California: Indians and Franciscans in the Missions* (New Haven: Yale University Press, 2004), 128–53.

2. The classic account of this process, originally published in 1933, is Robert Ricard, *The Spiritual Conquest of Mexico: An Essay on the Apostolate and Evangelizing Methods of the Mendicant Orders in New Spain, 1523–1572,* trans. Lesley Byrd Simpson (Berkeley and Los Angeles: University of California Press, 1966).

3. Gauvin Alexander Bailey, *Art on the Jesuit Missions in Asia and Latin America, 1542–1773* (Toronto: University of Toronto Press, 1999), 150–51.

4. James Schofield Saeger, "*The Mission* and Historical Missions: Film and the Writing of History," in *Based on a True Story: Latin American History at the Movies,* ed. Donald F. Stevens (Wilmington, Del.: Scholarly Resources, 1997), 63–84. Saeger finds the film's suggestion that the Guaraní were attracted to the Jesuit missions through music "bizarre" and argues instead that these natives welcomed the Jesuits for the iron implements they provided (67). In my view, Saeger underestimates the power of music and the visual arts in the encounter between missionaries and native peoples.

5. Ricard, *Spiritual Conquest,* is the most prominent example of this perspective.

6. James Lockhart, *The Nahuas after the Conquest: A Social and Cultural History of the Indians of Central Mexico, Sixteenth through Eighteenth Centuries* (Stanford, Calif.: Stanford University Press, 1992), 4–5. For broader examples and assess-

ments of shifts in scholarly assessments of the religious encounter in Mexico and Spanish America in general, see Erick Langer and Robert H. Jackson, eds., *The New Latin American Mission History* (Lincoln: University of Nebraska Press, 1995), and Susan Deeds, "Pushing the Borders of Latin American Mission History," *Latin American Research Review* 39 (2004): 211–20.

7. Louise M. Burkhart, *The Slippery Earth: Nahua-Christian Moral Dialogue in Sixteenth-Century Mexico* (Tucson: University of Arizona Press, 1989), portrays the encounter of the Nahua and Spanish as a dialogue. Stafford Poole, "Some Observations on Mission Methods," 337–49, suggests that the topic of evangelization and natives' responses in New Spain "is a subject of tortuous complexity" (quote on 337).

8. Lockhart, *Nahuas after the Conquest*, 4.

9. Charles E. Dibble, "The Nahuatlization of Christianity," in *Sixteenth-Century Mexico: The Work of Sahagún*, ed. Munro S. Edmonson (Albuquerque: University of New Mexico Press, 1974), 225–33; Bailey, *Art on the Jesuit Missions*, 10, 35–39.

10. Frances F. Berdan and Patricia Rieff Anawalt, eds., *The Essential Codex Mendoza* (Berkeley and Los Angeles: University of California Press, 1997), 166–67.

11. Robert Stevenson, *Music in Mexico: A Historical Survey* (New York: Thomas Y. Crowell, 1952), 18.

12. Lockhart, *Nahuas after the Conquest*, 203; Diego Durán, *History of the Indies of New Spain*, trans. Doris Heyden (Norman: University of Oklahoma Press, 1994), 259, 283–87, 317, 321, 327, 368, 435.

13. As quoted in Stevenson, *Music in Mexico*, 20.

14. Ibid., 18–19. John Bierhorst, trans. and ed., *Cantares Mexicanos: Songs of the Aztecs* (Stanford, Calif.: Stanford University Press, 1985), 97–98, identifies some native singers by name, based on their being mentioned in the texts of these native songs.

15. Stevenson, *Music in Mexico*, 18.

16. Bernardino de Sahagún, *Florentine Codex: General History of the Things of New Spain*, trans. Arthur J. O. Anderson and Charles E. Dibble, 13 vols. (Santa Fe, N.M.: School of American Research, and Salt Lake City: University of Utah, 1950–82), 9:56.

17. Book Two of Sahagún's history focuses on Aztec ceremonies and provides many descriptions of the ritual roles of song and dance in native life. For samples see Sahagún, *Florentine Codex*, 3:13–17, 22, 27–28, 34, 53–54, 87–88, 140–41.

18. Toribio de Benevente o Motolinía, *Memoriales o Libro de Los Cosas de la Nueva España y de Los naturals de Ella*, ed. Edmundo O'Gorman (Mexico: Universidad Nacional Autónoma de Mexico, 1971), 384. I am indebted to my colleague Leonor Elías for assistance in translating this passage and others.

19. Durán, *History of the Indies of New Spain*, 319–22.

20. Robert Stevenson, "The Music of Colonial Spanish America," in *The Cambridge History of Latin America*, ed. Leslie Bethell, 8 vols. (Cambridge: Cambridge University Press, 1984) 2:71.

21. Stevenson, *Music in Mexico*, 51–52.

22. Ibid.; Bernal Díaz del Castillo, *The True History of the Conquest of Mexico*, trans. Maurice Keatinge (1800; reprint, Ann Arbor: University Microfilms, 1966).

23. See for example Motolinía's enthusiastic reports in Frances Borgin Steck, trans. and ed., *Motolinía's History of the Indians of New Spain* (Washington, D.C.: Academy of American Franciscan History, 1951), 105, 296–97.

24. As quoted in Ricard, *Spiritual Conquest,* 168.

25. Lockhart, *Nahuas after the Conquest,* 203.

26. James Lockhart and Enrique Otte, trans. and eds., *Letters and Peoples of the Spanish Indies, Sixteenth Century* (Cambridge: Cambridge University Press, 1976), 213.

27. As quoted in Stevenson, *Music in Mexico,* 54.

28. Charles Gibson, *The Aztecs under Spanish Rule: A History of the Indians of the Valley of Mexico, 1519–1810* (Stanford, Calif.: Stanford University Press, 1964), 101–103.

29. Stafford Poole, "Iberian Catholicism Comes to the Americas," in Charles H. Lippy, Robert Choquette, and Stafford Poole, *Christianity Comes to the Americas* (New York: Paragon House, 1992), 39.

30. Lockhart, *Nahuas after the Conquest,* 210–18.

31. Serge Gruzinski, *The Conquest of Mexico: The Incorporation of Indian Societies into the Western World, 16th–18th Centuries,* trans. Eileen Corrigan (Cambridge: Polity Press, 1993), 66.

32. Stevenson, *Music in Mexico,* 80; Gibson, *Aztecs under Spanish Rule,* 140–41.

33. Gruzinski, *Conquest of Mexico,* 57.

34. As quoted in Stevenson, *Music in Mexico,* 63–64.

35. Ibid., 65.

36. Ibid., 63; Gibson, *Aztecs under Spanish Rule,* 121.

37. Gruzinski, *Conquest of Mexico,* 65–66.

38. Gibson, *Aztecs under Spanish Rule,* 117–21.

39. Ricard, *Spiritual Conquest,* 178.

40. Sandos, *Converting California,* 141–42, identifies many of these same motives amongst the Indian musicians and singers in the Alta California missions.

41. Robert Stevenson, *Music in Aztec and Inca Territory* (Berkeley and Los Angeles: University of California Press, 1968), 9.

42. McNally, "Practice of Native American Christianity," 834–59.

43. Stevenson, *Music in Aztec and Inca Territory,* 179.

44. Stevenson, *Music in Mexico,* 91.

45. Gruzinski, *Conquest of Mexico,* 57.

46. Overall, at least four categories of music seem to have been present in Mexico during the first few decades after the conquest: native music and dancing that were part of traditional celebrations (these traditional rites clearly continued after the conquest, but to what extent is difficult to know); Nahua melodies with altered, Christian texts; Spanish music with Nahuatl texts; Spanish music with Latin and Spanish texts. Some of the last group eventually included works written by mestizos and Nahuas. To what extent the "Spanish music" written and performed in sixteenth-century Mexico came to be influenced by natives in any of its dimensions (melodies, rhythms, instrumentation, etc.) is very difficult to determine. I am indebted to my Westmont colleague Grey Brothers and to Craig Russell, both musicologists, for assistance on this point.

47. As quoted in Stevenson, *Music in Mexico,* 64.

48. Ibid., 18, 53.

49. Gibson, *Aztecs under Spanish Rule,* 121–23.

50. Stevenson, *Music in Mexico,* 59–66 (quotes on 59, 60, and 65).

51. Ibid., 66.

52. Gabriel Saldívar, *Historia de la Música en Mexico: Epocas Precortesiana y Colonial* (Mexico: Editorial "Cultura," 1934), 90–94; Gruzinski, *Conquest of Mexico,* 66.

53. For discussions of the role of the immigrant Spanish population in different regions of sixteenth-century Mexico, see James Lockhart, "Capital and Province, Spaniard and Indian: The Example of Late Sixteenth-Century Toluca," in *Provinces of Early Mexico: Variants of Spanish American Regional Evolution*, ed. Ida Altman and James Lockhart (Los Angeles: UCLA Latin American Center Publications, 1976), 99–123, and David M. Szewczyk, "New Elements in the Society of Tlaxcala, 1519–1618," in Altman and Lockhart, *Provinces of Early Mexico*, 137–53.

54. Stanley G. Payne, *Spanish Catholicism: An Historical Overview* (Madison: University of Wisconsin Press, 1984), 49–50.

55. Henry Kamen, *The Phoenix and the Flame: Catalonia and the Counter Reformation* (New Haven: Yale University Press, 1993), 110, 129–30.

56. Payne, *Spanish Catholicism*, 49–50; Kamen, *Phoenix and the Flame*, 113–14. These changes occurred over a long period of time in the sixteenth and seventeenth centuries and certainly did not affect the Catholic Church in all parts of Spain.

57. Joseph A. Baird, Jr., *The Churches of Mexico* (Berkeley and Los Angeles: University of California Press, 1962), 21–26.

58. As quoted in Ricard, *Spiritual Conquest*, 169.

59. Stevenson, *Music in Mexico*, 58.

60. Ricard, *Spiritual Conquest*, 176.

61. James Lockhart, *Of Things of the Indies: Essays Old and New in Early Latin American History* (Stanford, Calif.: Stanford University Press, 1999), 115, suggests that the Spanish Catholic presence gave Nahuas "new ways of besting the neighboring altepetl [a sociopolitical unit of city-state size] . . . in superlative churches, elaborate accoutrements, and resplendent processions."

62. As quoted in Ricard, *Spiritual Conquest*, 168. While such statements reflect Spanish attitudes about native abilities, they may also reflect the friars' experience in Spain itself, where the laity and much of the clergy showed little interest in the Catholic Church's "internal things."

63. Gibson, *Aztecs under Spanish Rule*, 100.

64. Linda A. Curcio-Nagy, "Faith and Morals in Colonial Mexico," in *The Oxford History of Mexico*, ed. Michael C. Meyer and William H. Beezley (New York: Oxford University Press, 2000), 155–56. She points out that dependence on a "visual approach turned out to be unexpectedly problematic, because its success depended upon how the natives interpreted the images, which could be different from how they were intended to be by the friars" (155).

65. Kamen, *Phoenix and the Flame*, 117–19; Sara T. Nalle, *God in La Mancha: Religious Reform and People of Cuenca, 1500–1650* (Baltimore: Johns Hopkins University Press, 1992), 26–29. This is not to say that lay Spaniards did not have a lively and active religious life. William A. Christian, Jr., *Local Religion in Sixteenth Century Spain* (Princeton: Princeton University Press, 1981), details the many sides of lay and clerical religiosity in central Spain in the mid-sixteenth century.

66. Kamen, *Phoenix and the Flame*, 82–84; Nalle, *God in La Mancha*, xiii, 26–31. What was seen as the persistence of folk beliefs (magic) among both Spanish clergy and laity was one of the issues addressed in the reform efforts generated by the Council of Trent. Lockhart, *Of Things of the Indies*, 113, argues that the first generation of friars "wanted an austere religion with emphasis on morality rather than on saints and pomp." He suggests that the Spanish laity and secular clergy pushed for more of the latter, although even the friars "took it for granted that any consecrated church should have a particular patron saint." Spanish

newcomers came from a homeland where it was customary for local communities to put their own stamp on Catholic worship and devotion. I see the friars of two minds on how elaborate to make worship, almost from the very start of mission work in Mexico.

67. Ricard, *Spiritual Conquest*, 168; Curcio-Nagy, "Faith and Morals," 156; Pauline Moffitt Watts, "Languages of Gesture in Sixteenth-Century Mexico: Some Antecedents and Transmutations," in *Reframing the Renaissance: Visual Culture in Europe and Latin America 1450–1650*, ed. Claire Farago (New Haven: Yale University Press, 1995), 140–51. Watts argues that "the Franciscans relied upon languages of images and gestures, unfolded in ritual theatres which served at once to initiate the Indians into the Christian cosmos and to mute the phobic reactions of the missionaries themselves to the indigenous religions they confronted" (141).

68. As quoted in Stevenson, *Music in Mexico*, 88–90.

69. It would be a mistake to assume that all the Spanish who came to Mexico wanted to bring with them the *same* Catholicism. Many members of the mendicant orders took a dim view of the Iberian popular Catholicism embraced and practiced by lay immigrants. Regular clergy-colonist tensions resulted. Curcio-Nagy, "Faith and Morals," 153, 155.

70. Gruzinski, *Conquest of Mexico*, 118–20.

71. Bailey, *Art on the Jesuit Missions*, 20.

72. Gibson, *Aztecs under Spanish Rule*, 118–20; Bailey, *Art on the Jesuit Missions*, 20–21.

73. Serge Gruzinski, *Painting the Conquest: The Mexican Indians and the European Renaissance*, trans. Deke Dusinberre (Paris: Flammarion, 1992), 158.

74. Ibid., 150–69; Gruzinski, *Conquest of Mexico*, 22–23, 186–88; Bailey, *Art on the Jesuit Missions*, 12–13, 17–18, 20, 36–38; Jeanette Favrot Peterson, "Synthesis and Survival: The Native Presence in Sixteenth-Century Murals of New Spain," in *Native Artists and Patrons in Colonial Latin America*, Emily Umberger and Tom Cummins (Tempe: Arizona State University Press, 1995), 14–31. Burkhart, *Slippery Earth*, 184–93, argues more broadly for a partnership between friars and Indians in sixteenth-century Mexico, the result of which was "the creation of their own society, different from European society and from that of the colonists and mestizos around them" (184).

75. From early on, the Spanish set out to train a group of native craftsmen who could construct European material goods. Such craftsmen contributed to the smorgasbord of material objects that filled some rural parish churches: "fabrics and chasubles from Rouen, Castile and Holland, chalices and candelabra forged in local silver, crosses, shields and blazons made of tropical bird feathers showing Christ with crucifixion wounds, Michoacán flutes, Italian trumpets, pious images painted on morocco leather, et cetera." Gruzinski, *Painting the Conquest*, 150.

76. Gibson, *Aztecs under Spanish Rule*, 103, provides a table listing existing *doctrinas* in 1570. All had between one and five resident friars. Curcio-Nagy, "Faith and Morals," 156, emphasizes the itinerant nature of friar work, especially in the early years. She argues that the friars generally traveled in pairs.

77. From a stylistic point of view, music historians suggest that there is little evidence that Spanish music within Mexico was itself influenced by indigenous styles. European music and native music may have coexisted within certain church services when Nahuatl hymns (Christian texts with native melodies)

were used alongside European chant and polyphony. The musical partnership I describe, then, has to do with the people involved and their relationships, and less with the music itself.

78. Curcio-Nagy, "Faith and Morals," 156–57.

79. As quoted in Stevenson, *Music in Mexico,* 61.

80. Gruzinski, *Painting the Conquest,* 158, suggests that such hidden native musical expressions "reacquired openly anti-Spanish and pagan content" but also incorporated European instruments and musical styles that "lent indigenous celebrations a hybrid, rearranged tenor."

81. Louise M. Burkhart, "Pious Performances: Christian Pageantry and Native Identity in Early Colonial Mexico," in *Native Traditions in the Postconquest World,* ed. Elizabeth Hill Boone and Tom Cummins (Washington, D.C.: Dumbarton Oaks Research Library and Collection, 1998), 374; Watts, "Languages of Gesture in Sixteenth-Century Mexico," 149.

82. Joaquín García Icazbalceta, *Don Fray Juan de Zumárraga,* 4 vols. (1881; reprint, Mexico: Porrua, 1947), 3:156–57. Bierhorst, *Cantares Mexicanos,* 108–109, gives a somewhat different reading of this order.

83. Burkhart, "Pious Performances," 362–63, 374–75; Stevenson, *Music in Mexico,* 64; Watts, "Languages of Gesture in Sixteenth-Century Mexico," 150, suggests that such synodical efforts at regulation occupied "a world apart from the precariously balanced frontiers of histories, actions, and meanings spliced together by monks and Nahuas through their shared ritual drama."

84. Stevenson, *Music in Aztec and Inca Territory,* 109; Diego Durán, *The Book of the Gods and Rites and the Ancient Calendar,* ed. Fernando Horcasitas and Doris Heyden (Norman: University of Oklahoma Press, 1971), 299–300.

85. Bierhorst, *Cantares Mexicanos,* 110–11; Stevenson, *Music in Aztec and Inca Territory,* 124.

86. Burkhart, *Slippery Earth,* 11–12, 20–45 passim, provides the most thoroughgoing discussion of the dialogue that ensued between Spanish and Nahua over religion and the challenges of translation. Her study focuses on catechistic texts translated into Nahuatl, used to instruct natives in the Christian faith. Also see Curcio-Nagy, "Faith and Morals," 157–59. Lockhart, *Of Things of the Indies,* 98–119, discusses the broader issue of Spaniards and Nahua misreading practices or ideas of the other. He calls this process "Double Mistaken Identity, in which each side of the cultural exchange presumes that a given form or concept is functioning in the way familiar within its own tradition and is unaware of or unimpressed by the other side's interpretation" (99).

87. Sanneh, *Translating the Message,* provides a positive assessment of the role of translation in the spread and growth of Christianity around the world since the first century. Comaroff and Comaroff, *Of Revelation and Revolution,* 2:78–118, emphasize the tensions Western missionaries experienced as they wrestled with how much native agency to permit and ways to control it. They often welcomed native assistants to the work of evangelism and translation, but worried about African apostasy. From the Comaroffs' perspective, those doubts "with which missionaries constantly vexed themselves, were a product not of the actions of the Africans but of the imaginings of the Europeans" (80).

88. Bierhorst, *Cantares Mexicanos,* 3–4, 12, 16–17, 33–38, 86–88.

89. Gruzinski, *Painting the Conquest,* 158.

90. Louise Burkhart, *Holy Wednesday: A Nahua Drama from Early Colonial Mexico* (Philadelphia: University of Pennsylvania Press, 1996), 4–5.

91. Lockhart, *Of Things of the Indies,* 118, argues that by the last third of the sixteenth century, friars knew that Nahua practice and understanding of Christianity included pagan elements, but the Europeans were inclined to accept "the compromise."

92. Curcio-Nagy, "Faith and Morals," 152; Poole, "Iberian Catholicism Comes to the Americas," 40–41.

93. The quote is from Ricard, *Spiritual Conquest,* 178.

94. Stevenson, *Music in Aztec and Inca Territory,* 163–64, describes the positive interpretation of Indian music making given in Diego Valadés's *Rhetorica Christiana,* published in 1579. Valadés was a Franciscan born in Mexico, probably to a Spanish father and Indian mother. For a provocative view of Valadés's work, see Pauline Moffitt Watts, "Hieroglyphs of Conversion: Alien Discourses in Diego Valadés's *Rhetorica Christiana,*" *Memorie Domenicane* 22 (1991): 405–33. Burkhart, "Pious Performances," 369–71, takes a dimmer view than mine of how the friars read Nahua Christian practice, including their bent toward religious ceremony and ritual display.

95. As quoted in Stevenson, *Music in Mexico,* 57.

96. Ricard, *Spiritual Conquest,* 96–104; *Motolinía's History of the Indians of New Spain,* 105, provides one missionary's testimony to the eagerness with which natives took up Christianity. To what degree natives had in fact taken hold of the new faith remains debatable. Ricard's choice to echo the friars' contentions that Indians had quickly embraced Christianity in a meaningful way is challenged in J. Jorge Klor de Alva, "Spiritual Conflict and Accommodation in New Spain: Toward a Typology of Aztec Responses to Christianity," in *The Inca and Aztec States, 1400–1800: Anthropology and History,* ed. George A. Collier, Renato I. Rosaldo, and John D. Wirth (New York: Academic Press, 1982), 345–66.

97. A. D. Wright, *Catholicism and Spanish Society under the Reign of Philip II, 1555–1598, and Philip III, 1598–1621* (Lewiston, N.Y.: Edwin Mellen Press, 1991), 113–59, provides a discussion of the issues facing the regular clergy in sixteenth-century Spain.

98. Klor de Alva, "Spiritual Conflict and Accommodation in New Spain," 345–66.

99. As quoted in Stevenson, *Music in Mexico,* 89–90.

100. As quoted in ibid., 61.

101. Poole, "Iberian Catholicism Comes to the Americas," 33. The notion of the "missionary as missionized" in New Spain is treated at length in Burkhart, *Slippery Earth,* 16–45.

102. Curcio-Nagy, "Faith and Morals," 162–63, points to another kind of native influence upon Europeans' religion—the embrace of native healing arts into the popular religion of the average colonist.

103. Poole, "Iberian Catholicism Comes to the Americas," 43–44.

104. Bailey, *Art on the Jesuit Missions,* 14. As Bailey explains it, the *Patronato* was based on an authority given to kings early in the sixteenth century and officially made law by Philip II. It provided that in their colonial possessions the "rulers of Spain and Portugal were empowered to appoint bishops, to license churchmen and control their movements, to intervene in matters of religion and spiritual jurisdiction, to collect tithes, and even to approve the construction of religious buildings, a power which the Spanish kings did not even enjoy in most of Spain until the eighteenth century" (14).

105. Doris Heyden, "Translator's Introduction," in Durán, *History of the Indies of New Spain,* xxxii.

106. Bailey, *Art on the Jesuit Missions*, 18.

107. Burkhart, *Slippery Earth*, 18.

108. Lockhart, *Nahuas after the Conquest*, 203.

109. As quoted in Edith Buckland Webb, *Indian Life at the Old Missions* (Los Angeles: Warren F. Lewis, 1952), 245–46.

110. Sandos, *Converting California*, 148, speaks to the reciprocal impact of music making: "By joining the choir, Indians had chosen to learn the new music and to learn enough Spanish to cooperate with the priest in their joint venture. Although Indians learned from the priest, they also shared their talents with him. Reciprocity, rather than simple dominance, characterized these clerical events."

2. A LANGUAGE OF IMITATION

1. Alexander Young, ed., *Chronicles of the First Planters of the Colony of Massachusetts Bay from 1623 to 1636* (Boston: Little and Brown, 1846), 133–34.

2. Ibid., 149; Salisbury, " 'I Loved the Place of My Dwelling,' " 114. By that point, the New England Company had become the Massachusetts Bay Company following the issuing of a charter under royal seal in early March.

3. Cotton Mather, *The Triumphs of the Reformed Religion: The Life of the Reverend John Eliot* (Boston: Benjamin Harris and John Allen, 1691), 85. Cogley, *John Eliot's Mission to the Indians*, 5–6, suggests that the Craddock-Endecott approach to missions (what Cogley calls the "affective model") was especially important in the years preceding Eliot's more formal missionary labors, which began in 1646.

4. Helpful introductions to the experiences of each of these peoples in the colonial era are provided in Robert S. Grumet, *Historic Contact: Indian People and Colonists in Today's Northeastern United States in the Sixteenth through Eighteenth Centuries*, Contributions to Public Archeology (Norman: University of Oklahoma Press, 1995), 55–193.

5. Scholarly interest in the words with which Indians and Puritans spoke to and about one another continues to grow. Samples of that scholarship may be found in Henry W. Bowden and James P. Ronda, "Introduction," in *John Eliot's Indian Dialogues: A Study in Cultural Interaction*, ed. Henry W. Bowden and James P. Ronda (Westport, Conn.: Greenwood Press, 1980), 3–45; Robert James Naeher, "Dialogue in the Wilderness: John Eliot and Indian Exploration of Puritanism as a Source of Meaning, Comfort, and Ethnic Survival," *New England Quarterly* 62 (1989): 346–68; and Jill Lepore, *The Name of War: King Philip's War and the Origins of American Identity* (New York: Alfred A. Knopf, 1998). Many of the other secondary sources cited in this chapter also reflect this strong interest in the languages of the New England encounter.

6. Lepore, *Name of War*, xiv.

7. My summary of this scholarship is based on Roy Harvey Pearce, " 'The Ruines of Mankind': The Indian and the Puritan Mind," *Journal of the History of Ideas* 13 (1952): 200–217; Richard Slotkin, *Regeneration through Violence: The Mythology of the American Frontier* (Middletown, Conn.: Wesleyan University Press, 1973), 54–56, 77–93, 97–115; G. E. Thomas, "Puritans, Indians, and the Concept of Race," *New England Quarterly* 48 (1975): 3–27; Charles Segal and David Stineback, eds., *Puritans, Indians, and Manifest Destiny* (New York: Putnam, 1977); Richard Slotkin and James K. Folsom, *So Dreadfull A Judgment: Puritan*

Responses to King Philip's War, 1676–1677 (Middletown, Conn.: Wesleyan University Press, 1978), 35–37, 61–75, 265–66; Axtell, *The European and the Indian*, 302–309; William S. Simmons, "Cultural Bias in the New England Puritans' Perceptions of Indians," *William and Mary Quarterly,* 3rd ser., 38 (1981): 56–72; Dane Morrison, *A Praying People: Massachusett Acculturation and the Failure of the Puritan Mission, 1600–1690* (New York: Peter Lang, 1995); Alfred A. Cave, *The Pequot War* (Amherst: University of Massachusetts Press, 1996); and Calloway, *New Worlds for All.* Further discussion of this historiography may be found in Richard Pointer, "Selves and Others in Early New England: Refashioning American Puritan Studies," in *History and the Christian Historian,* ed. Ronald A. Wells (Grand Rapids, Mich.: Eerdmans, 1998), 149–55.

8. The quotes in this paragraph are taken from Calloway, *New Worlds for All,* 7, 196–97. More radical claims for a certain type of Puritan "Indianization" are put forward in John Canup, *Out of the Wilderness; The Emergence of an American Identity in Colonial New England* (Middletown, Conn.: Wesleyan University Press, 1990).

9. A recent work that moves in something of the same direction with respect to how the cultivation of praying Indians affected Puritan identity is Kristina Bross, *Dry Bones.*

10. My discussion of Guy's encounter with the Beothuck in Newfoundland is based on Stephen Greenblatt, *Marvelous Possessions: The Wonder of the New World* (Chicago: University of Chicago Press, 1991), 91–93, 99–102.

11. Ibid., 105–109; James Axtell, *Beyond 1492: Encounters in Colonial North America* (New York: Oxford University Press, 1992), 102–103. Axtell explains that the natives similarly saw the newcomers as childlike; to accommodate them, Indians "devised simplified pidgin languages." Such tongues might be called "imitation languages" and be seen as a stage between imitating speech and a language of imitation.

12. The earliest account of Squanto's role is provided in *Journall of the English Plantation at Plimoth* (1622; reprint, Ann Arbor, Mich.: University Microfilms, Inc., 1966), 35–36. Also see Neal Salisbury, "Squanto: Last of the Patuxets," in *Struggle and Survival in Colonial America,* ed. David G. Sweet and Gary B. Nash (Berkeley and Los Angeles: University of California Press, 1981), 228–46.

13. I am following Kathleen J. Bragdon in using the term "Ninnimissinuok" to refer to the Native American peoples of southern New England. Kathleen J. Bragdon, *Native Peoples of Southern New England, 1500–1650* (Norman: University of Oklahoma Press, 1996), xi.

14. Lepore, *Name of War,* 29.

15. There is a substantial literature on Puritan views of Indians. For a more positive assessment than those presented by the works in note 7, see Karen Ordahl Kupperman, *Settling with the Indians: The Meeting of English and Indian Cultures in America, 1580–1640* (Totowa, N.J.: Rowman and Littlefield, 1980).

16. William Wood, *New England's Prospect,* ed. Alden T. Vaughan (1634; reprint, Amherst: University of Massachusetts Press, 1993), 81, 96–97. Roger Williams, *A Key into the Language of America,* 5th ed. (London: Gregory Dexter, 1643), 19, similarly noted a native friend's ability to "make a good Drum in imitation of the *English.*"

17. Puritans were certainly not alone in their bent toward imitation. Historians of early America have long noted a strong mimetic impulse among many colonists as they sought to pattern life in the New World after what was custom-

ary or fashionable in the Old. What perhaps set Puritan imitation apart from other colonial varieties was its intense biblical primitivism. At a more purely literary level, some Puritans may have been drawn to a language of imitation through familiarity with uses of imitation in Renaissance literature. For one discussion of the latter see G. W. Pigman III, "Versions of Imitation in the Renaissance," *Renaissance Quarterly* 33 (1980): 1–32.

18. Perry Miller's seminal statement on the Puritan mission is in "Errand into the Wilderness," in Perry Miller, *Errand into the Wilderness* (Cambridge, Mass.: Belknap Press of Harvard University Press, 1956), 1–15. Alternative interpretations of that mission have been offered in Andrew Delbanco, "The Puritan Errand Re-Viewed," *Journal of American Studies* 18 (1984): 343–60, and Theodore Dwight Bozeman, "The Puritans' 'Errand into the Wilderness' Reconsidered," *New England Quarterly* 59 (1986): 231–51.

19. Theodore Dwight Bozeman, *To Live Ancient Lives: The Primitivist Dimension in Puritanism* (Chapel Hill: University of North Carolina Press, 1988), 4–19.

20. Williams, *Key into the Language of America,* 139.

21. John F. Moffitt and Santiago Sebastian, *O Brave New People: The European Invention of the American Indian* (Albuquerque: University of New Mexico Press, 1996).

22. E. Brooks Holifield, *Theology in America: Christian Thought from the Age of the Puritans to the Civil War* (New Haven: Yale University Press, 2003), 29–30. Also see E. Brooks Holifield, *Era of Persuasion: American Thought and Culture, 1521–1680* (Boston: Twayne, 1989), 243–48.

23. My discussion of Indian concepts of time is based on Anthony Giddens, *Central Problems in Social Theory: Action, Structure, and Contradiction in Social Analysis* (Berkeley and Los Angeles: University of California Press, 1979), 219–22, and Bragdon, *Native Peoples,* 246.

24. Paul A. Robinson, "Lost Opportunities: Miantonimi and the English in Seventeenth-Century Narragansett Country," in *Northeastern Indian Lives, 1632–1816,* ed. Robert S. Grumet (Amherst: University of Massachusetts Press, 1996), 25–26.

25. Bragdon, *Native Peoples,* 246.

26. Bross, *Dry Bones,* explores the figure of the praying Indian as an Indian sermon within missionary literature.

27. Silverman, "Indians, Missionaries, and Religious Translation," 147–74 (quote on 154–55).

28. Thomas Shepard, *The Clear Sun-shine of the Gospel Breaking Forth upon the Indians in New-England,* in Michael P. Clark, ed., *The Eliot Tracts* (Westport, Conn.: Praeger, 2003), 124.

29. Wyss, *Writing Indians,* 21.

30. Bozeman, *To Live Ancient Lives,* 139, 153, 268.

31. Morrison, *Praying People,* 76–87; Harold W. Van Lonkhuyzen, "A Reappraisal of Praying Indians: Acculturation, Conversion, and Identity at Natick, Massachusetts, 1646–1730," *New England Quarterly* 63 (1990): 396–428. Daniel Mandell, " 'Standing by His Father': Thomas Waban of Natick, circa 1630–1722," in Grumet, *Northeastern Indian Lives,* 170–71, argues that praying Indians in Natick and elsewhere made substantial cultural changes in the second half of the seventeenth century, but those changes were still "moderated by the persistence of aboriginal ideas and customs." The result was something of a cultural "middle ground."

32. Cogley, *John Eliot's Mission to the Indians*, 241–42.

33. Wyss, *Writing Indians*, 22.

34. Edmund S. Morgan, *Visible Saints* (Ithaca, N.Y.: Cornell University Press, 1963), 64–80, gives the classic account of the Puritan morphology of conversion.

35. Charles L. Cohen, "Conversion among Puritans and Amerindians: A Theological and Cultural Perspective," in *Puritanism: Transatlantic Perspectives on a Seventeenth-Century Anglo-American Faith*, ed. Francis J. Bremer (Boston: Massachusetts Historical Society, 1993), 248–54. Cohen makes the important point that despite the close parallels with English confessions in 1659, Indian narratives still were distinctive in a number of ways, thanks to the natives' own "socio-psychological backgrounds" (255) that shaped their appropriation of Christianity. Eliot recorded the Indian narratives offered on these three occasions in tracts printed in London between 1653 and 1660: John Eliot and Thomas Mayhew, Jr., *Tears of Repentance: Or, a further Narrative of the Progress of the Gospel Amongst the Indians in New England*, in Clark, *The Eliot Tracts*, 249–95; John Eliot, *A Late and Further Manifestation of the Progress of the Gospel Amongst the Indians in New-England*, in Clark, *The Eliot Tracts*, 297–320; [John Eliot], *A further Account of the progress of the Gospel Amongst the Indians In New England*, in Clark, *The Eliot Tracts*, 358–96.

36. Richter, *Facing East from Indian Country*, 110–29 (quotes on 117, 118, and 125).

37. Wyss, *Writing Indians*, 23. Wyss discusses Eliot's linguistic challenges in relation to his efforts to render the Massachusett language in written form.

38. Ibid., 22. Bross, *Dry Bones*, 27–34, discusses how New England Puritan representations of praying Indians in the mid-1600s, through assigning a vital role for themselves and their supporters in London in God's millennial plans, shaped Puritan identity in both locations.

39. *New Englands First Fruits*, in Clark, *The Eliot Tracts*, 59.

40. J. William T. Youngs, Jr., "The Indian Saints of Early New England," *Early American Literature* 16 (1981/82): 243–48.

41. Eliot and Mayhew, *Tears of Repentance*, 259–60.

42. Youngs, "Indian Saints," 247.

43. Bross, *Dry Bones*, 104.

44. Henry Whitfield, ed., *Strength Out of Weaknesse, or a Glorious Manifestation of the Further Progresse of the Gospel among the Indians in New England*, in Clark, *The Eliot Tracts*, 226.

45. John Eliot, *The Dying Speeches of Several Indians* (Cambridge, n.d. [1685?]); Matthew Mayhew, *A Brief Narrative of the Success which the Gospel hath had, among the Indians* (Boston: Bartholomew Green, 1694); James P. Ronda, "Generations of Faith: The Christian Indians of Martha's Vineyard," *William and Mary Quarterly*, 3rd ser., 38 (1981): 369–94, discusses the profiles of 176 Indian converts provided in Experience Mayhew's tract *Indian Converts*, published in London in 1727. Other discussions of Mayhew's tract may be found in Wyss, *Writing Indians*, 52–80, and Seeman, "Reading Indians' Deathbed Scenes," 17–47.

46. Bross, *Dry Bones*, 189.

47. Here I take exception to the depiction of Puritan views of Indians as almost entirely negative found in works such as Pearce, " 'The Ruines of Mankind' "; Thomas, "Puritans, Indians, and the Concept of Race"; Simmons, "Cultural Bias in the New England Puritans' Perceptions of Indians"; and Cave, *Pequot War*, 13–48.

48. Henry W. Bowden and James P. Ronda, "Introduction," in *Indian Dialogues*, 36.

49. That these were *Indian* converts made a difference to Puritan authors speculating about the eschatological significance of New World mission work.

50. Lepore, *Name of War*, 156–58.

51. Ibid., 138–41.

52. Slotkin and Folsom, *So Dreadfull A Judgment*, 61–63.

53. Bozeman, *To Live Ancient Lives*, 154.

54. Puritan excitement over early Indian missions as well as Puritan speculation over Indian origins may be sampled in [Thomas Shepard?], *The Day-Breaking, if not the Sun-Rising of the Gospell with the Indians in New England*, in Clark, *The Eliot Tracts*, 79–100; Shepard, *Clear Sun-shine of the Gospel*, 101–39; Henry Whitfield, *The Light Appearing more and more towards the perfect Day*, in Clark, *The Eliot Tracts*, 169–209; and Whitfield, *Strength Out of Weaknesse*, 211–47.

55. Lepore, *Name of War*, 10.

56. Alden T. Vaughan and Edward W. Clark, "Cups of Common Calamity: Puritan Captivity Narratives as Literature and History," in *Puritans among the Indians: Accounts of Captivity and Redemption, 1676–1724*, ed. Alden T. Vaughan and Edward W. Clark (Cambridge, Mass.: Harvard University Press, 1981), 4–6.

57. Calloway, *New Worlds for All*, 7. Not all Puritans shared these worries. According to Cogley, *John Eliot's Mission to the Indians*, 248, Eliot never "used pagan natives as symbols of what 'Indianizing' colonists might or had become—lazy and lustful degenerates who lived beyond the pale of civilized institutions. In fact, Eliot betrayed no fear that he might be corrupted by the native 'heart of darkness.'"

58. Lepore, *Name of War*, 5–8, 11, 88–89, 112–13, 129–31, 175 (quote on 6). Lepore emphasizes the colonists' special disdain for the Indians' "skulking way of war" (112–13), but it is interesting to note that John Eliot wrote rather approvingly of the English learning it in a letter to Robert Boyle in 1677: "Now we are glad to learn the skulking way of war. And what God's end is, in teaching us such a way of discipline, I know not." "Letters of Rev. John Eliot of Roxbury, to Hon. Robert Boyle," Massachusetts Historical Society, *Collections* 1st ser., 3 (1794): 178.

59. Vaughan and Clark, "Cups of Common Calamity," 17.

60. Increase Mather, "An Earnest Exhortation," in Slotkin and Folsom, *So Dreadfull A Judgment*, 174–75.

61. [Shepard], *Day-Breaking*, 86.

62. Examples include Wyss, *Writing Indians*; Bross, *Dry Bones*; and Silverman, "Indians, Missionaries, and Religious Translation."

63. Naeher, "Dialogue in the Wilderness," 346–47.

64. [Shepard], *Day-Breaking*, 99.

65. For two examples from after the 1670s, see "Letters of Eliot to Boyle," 183–84, and [Increase Mather, Cotton Mather, and Nehemiah Walter], *A Letter, about the present state of Christianity, among the Christianized Indians of New-England* (Boston: Timothy Green, 1705), 6–9.

66. Greenblatt, *Marvelous Possessions*, 105.

67. [Shepard], *Day-Breaking*, 88.

68. Whitfield, *Strength Out of Weaknesse*, 230.

69. Bross, *Dry Bones*, 111.

70. Whitfield, *Strength Out of Weakenesse*, 242.

71. Eliot and Mayhew, *Tears of Repentance*, 266.

72. Jane Kamensky, *Governing the Tongue: The Politics of Speech in Early New England* (New York: Oxford University Press, 1997), 51.

73. Salisbury, " 'I Loved the Place of My Dwelling," 113; Richter, *Facing East*, 125, 126, 128–29; Silverman, "Indians, Missionaries, and Religious Translation," 161–62, 160, 146, 173.

74. Silverman, "Indians, Missionaries, and Religious Translation," 174.

75. Lamin Sanneh, "Vincent Donovan's Discovery of Post-Western Christianity," in Vincent J. Donovan, *Christianity Rediscovered* (Maryknoll, N.Y.: Orbis, [2003]), 152.

76. Len Travers, "The Missionary Journal of John Cotton, Jr., 1666–1678," *Proceedings of the Massachusetts Historical Society* 109 (1997): 55.

77. [Shepard], *Day-Breaking*, 85–86, 89–90.

78. *Indian Dialogues*, 107–108.

79. Ibid., 120–44; Lepore, *Name of War*, 68, 219.

80. Eliot told Richard Baxter that the "instructive dialogs" were "p[art]'ly historical." F. W. Powicke, ed., *Some Unpublished Correspondence of the Reverend Richard Baxter and the Reverend John Eliot, the Apostle of the American Indians, 1656–1682* (Manchester: Manchester University Press, 1931), 62.

81. Scholars' studies of the *Dialogues* may be found in Bowden and Ronda, "Introduction"; Bross, *Dry Bones*, 112–45; David Murray, *Forked Tongue: Speech, Writing and Representation in North American Indian Texts* (Bloomington: Indiana University Press, 1991); and Thomas Scanlan, *Colonial Writing and the New World, 1583–1671: Allegories of Desire* (Cambridge: Cambridge University Press, 1999).

82. Indians used many "languages" and arguments to express their rejection of Christianity. For an overview of that opposition, see Ronda, " 'We Are Well As We Are,' " 66–82.

83. *Indian Dialogues*, 71, 73, 134–35.

84. Ibid., 71.

85. Bozeman, *To Live Ancient Lives*, 137.

86. *Indian Dialogues*, 134. Eliot could have based Philip's challenge upon the confession he had heard Natick convert Poquanum make two decades earlier: "When the Indians first prayed to God, I did not think there was a God, or that the Bible was Gods Book, but that wise men made it." Eliot and Mayhew, *Tears of Repentance*, 290.

87. *Indian Dialogues*, 71, 141.

88. Ibid., 135–41.

89. Mather, *Triumphs of the Reformed Religion*, 124–35 (quote on 128). James Axtell, *After Columbus: Essays in the Ethnohistory of Colonial America* (New York: Oxford University Press, 1988), 114, argues that contrary to Protestant accusations at the time and the skepticism of some modern scholars, Jesuit missionaries were as demanding as the Puritans in holding "Indians to a high standard for baptism and church admission."

90. [Shepard]. *Day-Breaking*, 93.

91. Both of these definitions were in use in the seventeenth century. *Oxford English Dictionary*, 2nd ed., s.v. "affect."

92. Williams, *Key into the Language*, 137–38.

93. As quoted in Margery Ruth Johnson, "The Mayhew Mission to the Indians, 1643–1806" (Ph.D. diss., Clark University, 1966), 78. Williams made this point in his tract *Christenings Make Not Christians*, published in London in 1645.

94. Increase Mather, *A Brief History of the War with the Indians in New-England* (Boston: John Foster, 1676), 13.

95. As quoted in Lepore, *Name of War,* 105.

96. Harald E. L. Prins, "Chief Rawandagan, Alias Robin Hood: Native 'Lord of Misrule' in the Maine Wilderness," in Grumet, *Northeastern Indian Lives,* 102–105, offers the intriguing suggestion that non-Puritan English settlers in Maine may have staged "comical burlesques" (103) that would have satirized both the local Abenaki people and standard English targets like the Puritans.

97. Bross, *Dry Bones,* 110.

98. Eliot, *Late and Further Manifestation,* 305.

99. Salisbury, " 'I Loved the Place of My Dwelling,' " 125; Wyss, *Writing Indians,* 34–36; Michael P. Clark, "Introduction," in Clark, *The Eliot Tracts,* 23.

100. Eric S. Johnson, "Uncas and the Politics of Contact," in Grumet, *Northeastern Indian Lives,* 37; Kamensky, *Governing the Tongue,* 52–55.

101. Axtell, *After Columbus,* 116–18, provides a helpful analysis of Indian syncretism, arguing that too often syncretism has been a "red herring dragged across the discussion of the quality of native conversions" (117).

102. Discussions of the Puritan self are legion. The places to begin remain Perry Miller, *The New England Mind: The Seventeenth Century,* 2nd ed. (Cambridge, Mass.: Harvard University Press, 1954), Perry Miller, *The New England Mind: From Colony to Province* (Cambridge, Mass.: Harvard University Press, 1953), and Sacvan Bercovitch, *The Puritan Origins of the American Self* (New Haven: Yale University Press, 1975).

103. David Lyle Jeffrey, *People of the Book: Christian Identity and Literary Culture* (Grand Rapids, Mich.: Eerdmans, 1996), 276–81.

104. Axtell, *Invasion Within,* 131–78.

105. Bross, *Dry Bones,* 27.

106. Axtell, *After Columbus,* 106.

107. Lepore, *Name of War,* 104–105. Lepore's concern is with demonstrating how the encounter with Indians endangered the colonists' cultural identity as English. My point here is that the encounter could also endanger the colonists' religious identity as Puritans. While closely related, the two identities were not identical.

108. Ibid., 8–10, 175. Lepore argues that the English sought to alleviate such fears by writing accounts of the war that fashioned the colonists as just and *English* in their actions.

3. A SCENE OF NEW IDEAS

1. Samuel Kirkland, *The Journals of Samuel Kirkland,* ed. Walter Pilkington (Clinton, N.Y.: Hamilton College, 1980), 53–58, 87n1.

2. Recent scholarship has made clear that growing European consciousness of the "other" in the early modern era transformed intellectual and popular minds alike. Karen Ordahl Kupperman, ed., *America in European Consciousness, 1493–1750* (Chapel Hill: University of North Carolina Press, 1995); Stuart B. Schwartz, ed., *Implicit Understandings: Observing, Reporting, and Reflecting on the Encounters between Europeans and Other Peoples in the Early Modern Era* (Cambridge: Cambridge University Press, 1994); Anthony Pagden, *European Encounters with the New World* (New Haven: Yale University Press, 1993); J. H. Elliott, *The Old World*

and the New (Cambridge: Cambridge University Press, 1992); Fredi Chiappelli, ed., *First Images of America: The Impact of the New World on the Old,* 2 vols. (Berkeley and Los Angeles: University of California Press, 1976); Donald F. Lach and Edwin J. Van Kley, *Asia in the Making of Europe,* 3 vols. (Chicago: University of Chicago Press, 1965–92); Eve Kornfeld, "Encountering the 'Other': American Intellectuals and Indians in the 1790s," *William and Mary Quarterly,* 3rd ser., 52 (1995): 287–314.

3. This subject has been studied more effectively by students of African-European interaction. The following studies offer rich portraits of how African values, customs, social structures, and convictions touched and sometimes changed the religious and moral understanding of white settlers: Mechal Sobel, *The World They Made Together: Black and White Values in Eighteenth-Century Virginia* (Princeton: Princeton University Press, 1987); Martha Saxton, *Being Good: Women's Moral Values in Early America* (New York: Hill and Wang, 2003); William D. Piersen, *Black Yankees: The Development of an Afro-American Subculture in Eighteenth-Century New England* (Amherst: University of Massachusetts Press, 1988); William D. Piersen, "Black Arts and Black Magic: Yankee Accommodations to African Religion," in *Wonders of the Invisible World: 1600–1900,* ed. Peter Benes (Boston: Boston University Scholarly Publications, 1995), 34–43; David W. Wills, "The Central Themes of American Religious History: Pluralism, Puritanism and the Encounter of Black and White," *Religion and Intellectual Life* 5 (1987): 30–41. Among studies detailing Indian influence, Russell Bourne, *Gods of War,* may be the most ambitious. He asserts that the collective encounter of Indians and Europeans in North America is best understood as "a confrontation of two historic and still evolving religious systems, with immense consequences for the different cultures" (xiii).

4. Axtell, *Invasion Within,* 286. Calloway, *New Worlds for All,* 90, 154–55, echoes Axtell, arguing that the tolerant nature of Indian religions meant that there was little if any pressure exerted by Indians upon Europeans to alter their faiths.

5. Axtell, *Invasion Within,* 302–27, offers the classic discussion of the "white Indians." Also see Alden Vaughan and Daniel Richter, "Crossing the Cultural Divide: Indians and New Englanders, 1605–1763," American Antiquarian Society, *Proceedings* 90 (1980): 23–99. Richard White, *The Middle Ground,* 327–39, presents another perspective on religious hybridity among Euro-Americans.

6. Holifield, *Theology in America,* 1; Mark A. Noll, *America's God: From Jonathan Edwards to Abraham Lincoln* (New York: Oxford University Press, 2002), 6.

7. I am borrowing this phrase primarily from Timothy L. Smith's essay on "Religion and Ethnicity in America," *American Historical Review* 83 (1978): 1175–81. Smith argues that the process of migration "was often a theologizing experience" for nineteenth- and twentieth-century immigrants. My contention is that in the colonial era, intercultural contacts could and did provoke theologizing.

8. Orsi, "Everyday Miracles," 9.

9. Rachel Wheeler, " 'Friends to Your Souls,' " 736–65, makes precisely this argument with respect to the influence of Edwards's social context in Stockbridge. She argues that as he ministered to and interacted with his native congregation, he maintained his same Calvinist doctrine but adjusted his preaching style, and particularly his doctrinal applications, "to the specific pastoral needs of his congregation" (756). Moreover, "his experience among the Stockbridge

Indians was arguably what led Edwards to argue for human equality forged in universal depravity" in his treatise on *Original Sin* (761). Overall, surprisingly little attention has been given to the social contexts out of which Christian theology came in the seventeenth and eighteenth centuries in colonial America. Noll, *America's God,* fills much of the gap for the eighteenth century. For the prior century, Frank Hugh Foster, *A Genetic History of New England Theology* (1907; reprint, New York: Russell and Russell, 1963), 3–4, emphasizes that practical religious necessities gave rise to colonial theologizing, but does not extend his argument to the broader social context. More discussion is provided in Holifield, *Era of Persuasion,* 6–17, 35–132.

10. For an excellent analysis of the interactions of whites with one community of native Christians, see Silverman, "Indians, Missionaries, and Religious Translation," 141–74. Silverman makes extensive use of John Cotton, Jr.'s journal, which recorded hundreds of questions asked of him by his native parishioners. See Travers, "The Missionary Journal of John Cotton, Jr., 1666–1678," 52–101.

11. White, *Middle Ground,* 328–32, discusses the efforts of whites and natives to find shared meanings and interpretations of certain actions. More work needs to be done on the religious character of Indian diplomatic ceremonies and war rituals, including analyses of whether Europeans who participated in them saw their religious implications.

12. Merrell, *Indians' New World,* viii.

13. Muir, *Ritual in Early Modern Europe,* 191, 204–207 (quote on 191).

14. On Protestant privileging of mind over body, see ibid., 185–98, 207; on Native American religions' emphasis on practice, see McNally, "The Practice of Native American Christianity," 834–59; on Catholic missionary efforts to understand native religions, see Axtell, *Invasion Within,* 93–104; on Jesuit awareness of Indian fascination with books and literacy, see James Axtell, "The Power of Print in the Eastern Woodlands," in Axtell, *After Columbus,* 88–90; on Jesuit borrowing of essential Huron ideas for their presentation of the gospel, see John Steckley, "The Warrior and the Lineage: Jesuit Use of Iroquoian Images to Communicate Christianity," *Ethnohistory* 39 (1992): 478–509.

15. Merrell, *Indians' New World,* 165; James Axtell, ed., *The Indian Peoples of Eastern America: A Documentary History of the Sexes* (New York: Oxford University Press, 1981), xviii–xxi, 183; Helen C. Rountree, "Powhatan Priests and English Rectors: World Views and Congregations in Conflict," *American Indian Quarterly* 16 (1992): 485–500. While in Stockbridge, Massachusetts, Jonathan Edwards testified to the difficulty of getting local Indians to reveal their inner beliefs: "the thoughts of their hearts, and the ideas and knowledge they have in their minds, are things invisible." Jonathan Edwards, *Original Sin,* ed. Clyde Holbrook, vol. 3 of *The Works of Jonathan Edwards* (New Haven: Yale University Press, 1970), 160.

16. Peter H. Wood has rightfully warned against overlooking the chronological breadth and extreme diversity of interchanges between Europeans and Indians, and has recommended more examinations of particular encounters rather than efforts to offer "all-encompassing generalizations of contact." Much of this volume reflects my concurrence with Wood's general sentiment. But I believe the broader scope of this chapter can play a useful role in advancing scholarship. See Peter H. Wood, "North America in the Era of Captain Cook: Three Glimpses of Indian-European Contact in the Age of the American Revolution," in Schwartz, *Implicit Understandings,* 484–501 (quote on 501).

17. Olive Patricia Dickason, *The Myth of the Savage and the Beginnings of French Colonialism in the Americas* (Edmonton: University of Alberta Press, 1984), 29–59 (quote on 33).

18. Cornelius J. Jaenen, *Friend and Foe: Aspects of French-Amerindian Cultural Conflict in the Sixteenth and Seventeenth Centuries* (Toronto: McClelland and Stewart, 1976), 17–22; Cornelius J. Jaenen, " 'Les Sauvages Ameriquains': Persistence into the 18th Century of Traditional French Concepts and Constructs for Comprehending Amerindians," *Ethnohistory* 29 (1982): 45–52; Alden T. Vaughan, "Early English Paradigms for New World Natives," American Antiquarian Society, *Proceedings* 102, pt. 1 (1992): 33–67; Don Cameron Allen, *The Legend of Noah: Renaissance Rationalism in Art, Science, and Letters* (Urbana: University of Illinois Press, 1963), 120–28.

19. Pierre de Charlevoix, *History and General Description of New France*, trans. John G. Shea, 6 vols. (New York: Francis P. Harper, 1900), 5:1–64. Numerous and diverse colonial religious figures found the idea of Indians as Jews intriguing. Axtell, *Indian Peoples of Eastern America*, 183, suggests that many of Charlevoix's "contemporaries believed [the theory] well into the eighteenth century." Vaughan, "Early English Paradigms," 62–65, argues that the English on both sides of the Atlantic generally lost interest in the theory after 1660, although there were prominent later proponents such as Indian trader and administrator James Adair.

20. Robert Johnson, *The New Life of Virginea*, in *Tracts and Other Papers relating Principally to the Origin, Settlement, and Progress of the Colonies in North America*, ed. Peter Force, 4 vols. (1836–46; reprint, Gloucester, Mass.: Peter Smith, 1963), 1:7–8 (tract 7). Alfred A. Cave, "Canaanites in a Promised Land: The American Indian and the Providential Theory of Empire," *American Indian Quarterly* 12 (1988): 284–85, discusses Johnson and Strachey's ideas. The last quote of the paragraph is as quoted from Strachey in Cave.

21. Cave, "Canaanites in a Promised Land," 286–87.

22. Richard Cogley, "John Eliot and the Origins of the American Indians," *Early American Literature* 21 (1986/1987): 210–25. Cogley believes that Eliot lost confidence in the Lost Tribes theory by the late 1650s.

23. One classic discussion of the negative view of the Indians' nature is Roy Harvey Pearce, "The 'Ruines of Mankind,' " 200–17. Dutchman Adrian Van der Donck noted the belief about Indian childbirth in his description of New Netherland. Axtell, *Indian Peoples of Eastern America*, 21–22.

24. Williams, *Key into the Language of America*, 53.

25. Edwards, *Original Sin*, 151, 183. Gerald R. McDermott, *Jonathan Edwards Confronts the Gods: Christian Theology, Enlightenment Religion, and Non-Christian Faiths* (New York and Oxford: Oxford University Press, 2000), 194–206, discusses Edwards's views on Native American religion, Indian spiritual and moral capacities, and his native congregation in Stockbridge.

26. Wheeler, " 'Friends to Your Souls,' " 761–65.

27. Jaenen, *Friend and Foe*, 48–50, discusses the role of Catholic apocalyptical views in shaping Indian evangelism. Among many works that treat English colonial views on this topic, see J. A. DeJong, *As the Waters Cover the Sea: Millennial Expectations in the Rise of Anglo-American Missions, 1640–1810* (Kampen, Neth.: J. H. Kok, 1970); Richard Cogley, "John Eliot and the Millennium," *Religion and American Culture* 1 (1991): 227–50; John S. Erwin, *The Millennialism of Cotton Mather: An Historical and Theological Analysis* (Lewiston, N.Y.: Edwin

Mellen Press, 1980), 175–85; W. Clark Gilpin, *The Millenarian Piety of Roger Williams* (Chicago: University of Chicago Press, 1979), 121–34. Edwards addressed the issue in *A History of the Work of Redemption*, ed. John F. Wilson, vol. 9 of *The Works of Jonathan Edwards* (New Haven: Yale University Press, 1989), 432–34, 472–73, and in some of his other *Apocalyptic Writings*, ed. Stephen J. Stein, vol. 5 of *The Works of Jonathan Edwards* (New Haven: Yale University Press, 1977), 47, 363–64.

28. Ruth H. Bloch, *Visionary Republic: Millennial Themes in American Thought, 1756–1800* (Cambridge: Cambridge University Press, 1985), 47–50. The millennial speculations of Old Light Jonathan Mayhew and New Light Jonathan Edwards both foresaw economic futures characterized by Anglo-American patterns.

29. Pagden, *European Encounters*, 17–21, recounts this incident based on Gonzalo Fernández de Oviedo's early history of America.

30. Axtell, *The European and the Indian*, 307–10. David S. Lovejoy, "Satanizing the American Indian," *New England Quarterly* 67 (1994): 603–21, emphasizes the Puritan tendency to see natives in devilish terms. Godbeer, *Devil's Dominion*, 189–93, highlights New Englanders' tendency to equate native religion with witchcraft and the Devil.

31. Timothy J. Shannon, *Atlantic Lives: A Comparative Approach to Early America* (New York: Pearson Longman, 2004), 43.

32. Allan Gallay, *The Indian Slave Trade: The Rise of the English Empire in the American South, 1670–1717* (New Haven: Yale University Press, 2002), 116–17; White, *Middle Ground*, 57.

33. Paul Du Ru, *Journal of Paul Du Ru: Missionary Priest to Louisiana*, trans. Ruth Lapham Butler (Chicago: Caxton Club, 1934), 26–29; Gallay, *Indian Slave Trade*, 120–22. A broader discussion of European reactions to Indian mourning practices may be found in Axtell, *European and Indian*, 110–28.

34. Gallay, *Indian Slave Trade*, 114–16 (quote on 116). Pierre Le Moyne, Sieur d'Iberville noted many times the de-population due to disease occurring among these tribes as he traveled through the regions at this same time. Pierre Le Moyne, Sieur d'Iberville, *Iberville's Gulf Journals*, trans. and ed. Richebourg Gaillard McWilliams (University: University of Alabama Press, 1981), 122, 128, 140–41.

35. As quoted in Gallay, *Indian Slave Trade*, 111–12.

36. John Demos, *The Unredeemed Captive: A Family Story from Early America* (New York: Alfred Knopf, 1994), 55–76. Among John Williams's several publications relating to his captivity, the best known was *The Redeemed Captive Returning to Zion* (Boston: B. Green, 1707). Another analysis of Williams's narrative is Evan Haefeli and Kevin Sweeney, "Revisiting *The Redeemed Captive*: New Perspectives on the 1704 Attack on Deerfield," *William and Mary Quarterly*, 3rd ser., 52 (1995): 3–46. These two authors provide a full account of the events of the 1704 conflict in Evan Haefeli and Kevin Sweeney, *Captors and Captives: The 1704 French and Indian Raid on Deerfield* (Amherst: University of Massachusetts Press, 2003).

37. Demos, *Unredeemed Captive*, 46–49, 77–252. The broader phenomenon of Indian captives and captivity narratives, according to Charles Hambrick-Stowe, prompted a redefinition of New England's collective pilgrimage within Puritan theology. Charles Hambrick-Stowe, *The Practice of Piety: Puritan Devotional Disciplines in Seventeenth-Century New England* (Chapel Hill: University of North Carolina Press, 1982), 256–65.

38. Rolena Adorno, "The Discursive Encounter of Spain and America: The Authority of Eyewitness Testimony in the Writing of History," *William and Mary Quarterly*, 3rd ser., 49 (1992): 210–28 (quote on 211).

39. Slotkin and Folsom, *So Dreadfull A Judgment*, 62–63, 66, 175–76. Peter N. Carroll, *Puritanism and the Wilderness: The Intellectual Significance of the New England Frontier, 1629–1700* (New York: Columbia University Press, 1969), 212–16, makes clear that Mather's view was shared by other Puritan leaders at the time. Similar arguments regarding divine providence's use of native hostility for its own ends were made during the Pequot War in the 1630s and later in the eighteenth century by the likes of Solomon Stoddard, Jonathan Edwards, and Samuel Hopkins. For samples, see Solomon Stoddard, *Question whether God is not Angry with the Country for doing so little towards the Conversion of the Indians* (Boston: B. Green, 1723), 6–11, and Samuel Hopkins, *An Address to the People of New-England* (Philadelphia: Franklin and Hall, 1757), 13. God could also use one Indian people to be the instrument of his judgment against another native group, according to one colonial resident of New Netherland. "Journal of New Netherland, 1647," in *Narratives of New Netherland, 1609–1664*, ed. J. Franklin Jameson, Original Narratives of Early American History (1909; reprint, New York: Barnes and Noble, 1959), 276–77.

40. Mather reached this conclusion a generation after the war. Increase Mather, *Ichabod, or, a Discourse Shewing what Cause there is to Fear that the Glory of the Lord, is Departing from New-England* (Boston: Timothy Green, 1702), 71–73.

41. Gallay, *Indian Slave Trade*, 329–30.

42. As quoted in ibid., 234–35, 237.

43. Francis Daniel Pastorius, "Circumstantial Geographical Description of Pennsylvania," in *Narratives of Early Pennsylvania, West New Jersey, and Delaware, 1630–1707*, ed. Albert Cook Myers, Original Narratives of Early American History (1912; reprint, New York: Barnes and Noble, 1959), 384–85, 401–402, 419–20, 437 (quotes on 384, 401–402).

44. John Lawson, *A New Voyage to Carolina*, ed. Hugh T. Lefler (Chapel Hill: University of North Carolina Press, 1967), 243.

45. Examples include explorer Amerigo Vespucci (Dickason, *Myth of the Savage*, 63), Recollect missionary Gabriel Sagard (Jaenen, *Friend and Foe*, 105), Jesuit priest Paul Le Jeune (Dickason, *Myth of the Savage*, 108), and Indian captive James Smith (James Smith, *An Account of the Remarkable Occurrences in the Life and Travels of Colonel James Smith, During his Captivity with the Indians* ([Philadelphia: J. Grigg, 1831], 57).

46. Samuel Cole Williams, ed., *Adair's History of the American Indians* (1930; reprint, Nashville: National Society of the Colonial Dames of America, 1953), xxxvii, 1–230 (quote on xxxvii).

47. Ibid., 229.

48. Ibid., 390.

49. Ibid., 390–91.

50. Ibid., 391.

51. Representative samples of religious denunciations of traders' ill influence on Indians may be found in Charles T. Gehrig and Robert S. Grumet, "Observations of the Indians from Jasper Danckaerts's Journal, 1679–1680," *William and Mary Quarterly*, 3rd ser., 44 (1987): 104–20; Frank J. Klingberg, "The Indian Frontier in South Carolina as Seen by the S. P. G. Missionary," *Journal of Southern History* 5 (1939): 482–83, 492–95; Gerald T. Goodwin, "Christianity, Civiliza-

tion, and the Savage: The Anglican Mission to the American Indian," *Historical Magazine of the Protestant Episcopal Church* 43 (1973): 100–101, 106–107; Cotton Mather, *A monitory and hortatory letter to those English, who debauch the Indians, by selling strong drink unto them* (Boston, 1700); John Heckewelder, *History, Manners, and Customs of the Indian Nations,* rev. ed. (1817; Philadelphia: Historical Society of Pennsylvania, 1876), 189, 328–44; Milo M. Quaife, ed., *John Long's Voyages and Travels in the Years 1768–1788* (Chicago: R. R. Donnelley, 1922), 41–44.

52. Lawson, *New Voyage to Carolina,* 211, 244–46 (quotes on 211, 244).

53. Gallay, *Indian Slave Trade,* 262–63.

54. Ibid., *passim.*

55. One sign that some people were interested in such questions was the brisk sales of Anglican bishop Thomas Wilson's manual on how settlers could be better Christian examples and witnesses to Indians. *The Knowledge and Practice of Christianity Made Easy to the Meanest Capacities, or An Essay towards an Instruction for the Indians* went through nine editions in the 1740s and 1750s.

56. Examples may be found in Patrick Frazier, *The Mohicans of Stockbridge* (Lincoln: University of Nebraska Press, 1992), 82–89, 160–71; Gerald R. Mc-Dermott, *One Holy and Happy Society: The Public Theology of Jonathan Edwards* (University Park, Pa.: Penn State University Press, 1992), 23–24, 164; Hopkins, *Address to the People of New-England,* 10; William Richardson, An account of my proceedings since I accepted the Indian Mission [October 2, 1758–March 17, 1759], January 30, 1759, Ms. diary, Wilberforce Eames Indian Collection, Indians Box 1, New York Public Library Manuscripts and Archives, New York.

57. Holifield, *Era of Persuasion,* preface, argues that persuasion was the chief mode of discourse in sixteenth- and seventeenth-century America, including exchanges between natives and colonists. In recent years, a number of scholars have questioned whether the term "conversion" should be used in reference to changes that occurred in Native Americans' religion as a result of contact with Christianity. These concerns may be sampled in David Sweet, "The Ibero-American Frontier Mission in Native American History," in Langer and Jackson, *The New Latin American Mission History,* 43–46; Morrison, *Solidarity of Kin,* 147–72; Neal Salisbury, "Embracing Ambiguity: Native Peoples and Christianity in Seventeenth-Century North America," *Ethnohistory* 50 (2003): 247–59. Much debate has also occurred over the genuineness of Indian conversions. For one argument in favor of seeing most of the conversions as bona fide, see Axtell, *After Columbus,* 100–21.

58. Shannon, *Atlantic Lives,* 44.

59. Richardson diary, December 29, 1758; January 13, 22, 1759.

60. The character and range of Indian-European religious dialogue defies easy summary. Beyond the other examples provided in this chapter, that dialogue may be sampled in Williams, *Key into the Language of America,* 56, 115, 131; Smith, *Account of Remarkable Occurrences,* 100–104; Henry Melchior Muhlenberg, *The Journals of Henry Melchior Muhlenberg,* trans. Theodore G. Tappert and John W. Doberstein, 3 vols. (Philadelphia: Evangelical Lutheran Ministerium of Pennsylvania and Muhlenberg Press, 1942–58), 2:437–38; James Kenney, "Journal of James Kenney, 1761–1763," ed. John W. Jordan, *Pennsylvania Magazine of History and Biography* 37 (1913): 168–73, 184, 191, 193; Colin G. Calloway, ed., *The World Turned Upside Down: Indian Voices from Early America* (Boston: St. Martin's Press, 1994), 44–49, 70–71; A. B. Hulbert and W. N. Schwarze, eds., "The Moravian Records; The Diaries of [David] Zeisberger Re-

lating to the First Missions in the Ohio Basin," *Ohio Archaelogical and Historical Quarterly* 21 (1912): 14–15, 22, 27–31. Insightful secondary analyses include Ronda, "'We Are Well As We Are,'" 66–82; Ronda, "Generations of Faith," 369–94; Naeher, "Dialogue in the Wilderness," 346–68; and White, *Middle Ground,* 323–39.

61. Richardson diary, December [*sic* January] 5, 1759, January 17, 24, 30, 1759, February 20, 1759.

62. Holifield, *Theology in America,* quotes on 4 and 5.

63. Ibid., 5, 31–34, 60–61, 69–70.

64. Luca Codignola, "The Holy See and the Conversion of the Indians in French and British North America, 1486–1760," in Kupperman, *America in European Consciousness,* 204–206.

65. "Father Juan Rogel to Father Jerónimo Ruiz del Portillo, April 25, 1568," in John H. Hann, trans. and ed., *Missions to the Calusa* (Gainesville: University of Florida Press, 1991), 236–38 (quote on 238).

66. Hann, ed., *Missions to the Calusa,* 228.

67. "Rogel to Ruiz del Portillo," 239, 241, 242 (quotes on 239 and 242).

68. Ibid., 241.

69. Ibid., quotes on 241, 237, 239, 243–44.

70. Ibid., 245–49 (quotes on 245 and 249).

71. Codignola, "Holy See and the Conversion of the Indians," 220, concludes that papal officials joined others in Europe in being disappointed with the results of Indian evangelism. He suggests (211–12) that as early as the 1660s, church officials responsible for New France shifted their focus from converting Indians to caring for French immigrants.

72. Stevens, *The Poor Indians,* 195–96; Codignola, "Holy See and the Conversion of the Indians," 205.

73. Axtell, *Invasion Within,* 53–59.

74. As quoted in Goodwin, "Christianity, Civilization, and the Savage," 106.

75. Representative sentiments are expressed in a thanksgiving sermon by East Apthorp, *The Felicity of the Times* (Boston: Green and Russell, 1763), 12–15. Axtell, *Invasion Within,* 133–34, explains that in claiming that Indians had to be made "men," the English employed three different meanings. Sometimes it meant that Indians "were the children of the human race," other times that they "were little better than animals," and most of the time that they were uneducated and uncultured.

76. Holifield, *Theology in America,* 5, 70–72 (quote on 5).

77. "Notes on the Iroquois and Delaware Indians," *Pennsylvania Magazine of History and Biography* 1 (1877): 163–67, 319–23 (quotes on 166). Weiser was certainly familiar with other elements of native religion that he found less enviable. He found that efforts to argue with such "superstitions" were usually met with Indian humor at his expense.

78. Quaife, *Long's Voyages and Travels,* 174–75.

79. Gregory A. Waselkov and Kathryn E. Holland Braund, eds., *William Bartram on the Southeastern Indians* (Lincoln and London: University of Nebraska Press, 1995), 35–36. See the editors' comments on the historicity of this story on pp. 200–201.

80. Ibid., 204–205.

81. Ibid., 46–47.

82. Ibid., 114, 197, 198.

83. Ibid., 58, 204.

84. Dowd, *Spirited Resistance,* 30–31, 41–44, 141–142, discusses native "separate" theology in the eighteenth and early nineteenth centuries. For one example of Euro-American–Native American dialogue on this issue, see Thomas Brainerd, *The Life of John Brainerd, The Brother of David Brainerd, and His Successor as Missionary to the Indians of New Jersey* (Philadelphia: Presbyterian Publication Committee, 1865), 232–35.

85. *London Chronicle,* "Extracts from the Account of the Captivity of William Henry," June 23–25, 25–28, 1768, in vol. 10 of Garland Library of Narratives of North American Indian Captivities (New York: Garland Publishing, 1977).

86. Alexander Henry, *Travels and Adventures in Canada and the Indian Territories* (1809; reprint, Ann Arbor, Mich.: University Microfilms, 1966), 167–73 (quotes on 172). Also see White, *Middle Ground,* 328–29.

87. Scalberg, "The French-Amerindian Religious Encounter 101–12 (quotes on 103, 107, and 107).

88. Axtell, *Invasion Within,* 325.

4. "Poor Indians" and the "Poor in Spirit"

1. Jonathan Edwards, *The Life of David Brainerd,* ed. Norman Pettit, vol. 7 of *The Works of Jonathan Edwards* (New Haven: Yale University Press, 1985), 331, 332. Edwards's *Life* is primarily his edited version of Brainerd's private diaries.

2. Merrell, "'The Customes of Our Countrey,'" 146–52; Axtell, *Invasion Within,* 242–43.

3. See Norman Pettit, "Editor's Introduction," to Edward's *Life of Brainerd,* 13. Indians found little place either in older popular accounts or in most scholarly assessments of Brainerd's significance published before 1990. For popular accounts, see Richard Ellsworth Day, *Flagellant on Horseback: The Life Story of David Brainerd* (Philadelphia: Judson Press, 1950); David Wynbeek, *David Brainerd, Beloved Yankee,* 2nd ed. (Grand Rapids, Mich.: Eerdmans, 1964); and Clyde S. Kilby, "David Brainerd," in *Heroic Colonial Christians,* ed. Russell T. Hitt (Philadelphia: Lippincott, 1966), 151–206. For scholarly assessments, see Joseph Conforti, "David Brainerd and the Nineteenth-Century Missionary Movement," *Journal of the Early Republic* 5 (1985): 309–29; Joseph Conforti, "Jonathan Edwards's Most Popular Work: 'The Life of David Brainerd' and Nineteenth-Century Evangelical Culture," *Church History* 54 (1985): 188–201; David L. Weddle, "The Melancholy Saint: Jonathan Edwards's Interpretation of David Brainerd as a Model of Evangelical Spirituality," *Harvard Theological Review* 81 (1988): 297–318; and Pettit's "Introduction," 1–71.

4. John Wesley, *An extract of the life of the late Rev. David Brainerd, missionary to the Indians,* 3rd ed. (London: G. Paramore, 1798).

5. Paul Harris, "David Brainerd and the Indians: Cultural Interaction and Protestant Missionary Ideology," *American Presbyterians* 72 (1994): 2; Stevens, *Poor Indians,* 5. Harris's article and my own essay on Brainerd, an earlier version of this chapter, Richard W. Pointer, "'Poor Indians and the Poor in Spirit': The Indian Impact on David Brainerd," *New England Quarterly* 67 (1994): 403–26, were among the first efforts to recapture the importance of Indians in Brainerd's life. A slightly earlier work that addressed Brainerd's interactions with

Native Americans was Richard A. S. Hall, *The Neglected Northampton Texts of Jonathan Edwards* (Lewiston, N.Y.: Edwin Mellen Press, 1990), 145–200.

6. Stevens, *Poor Indians*, 144.

7. Pettit, "Introduction," 25–32; Henry Warner Bowden, *American Indians and Christian Missions: Studies in Cultural Conflict* (Chicago: University of Chicago Press, 1981), 111–41; George M. Marsden, *Jonathan Edwards: A Life* (New Haven: Yale University Press, 2003), 323–24.

8. Merrell, "'Customes of Our Countrey,'" 152–56 (quote on 152); Ronda, "'We Are Well as We Are,'" 66–82; and Jennings, *Invasion of America*, 250–53.

9. Pettit, "Introduction," 33–36; Wynbeek, *Beloved Yankee*, 13–16.

10. Pettit, "Introduction," 26.

11. Brainerd's ill-fated career at Yale is explained by Norman Pettit, "Prelude to Mission: Brainerd's Expulsion from Yale," *New England Quarterly* 59 (1986): 28–50.

12. Edwards, *Life of Brainerd*, 188.

13. Ibid., 197; Weddle, "Melancholy Saint," 298–301; Pettit, "Introduction," 57; Wynbeek, *Beloved Yankee*, 55.

14. Edwards, *Life of Brainerd*, 193, 195.

15. As quoted in John Grigg, "The Lives of David Brainerd" (Ph.D. diss., University of Kansas, 2002), 115.

16. Edwards, *Life of Brainerd*, 199–200.

17. Wynbeek, *Beloved Yankee*, 54–55; Pettit, "Introduction," 57–59; Pettit, "Prelude to Mission," 47. Numerous commentators have suggested that Brainerd was particularly struck by the squalid living conditions of the Long Island Indians.

18. Axtell, *Invasion Within*, 329–33, bemoans the failure of European settlers to learn a greater measure of humility and tolerance from their interactions with Indians. Brainerd acknowledged his sense of inadequacy as a missionary on many occasions, but whether this stemmed more from his contact with natives or from his natural inclination toward self-condemnation is difficult to tell. Grigg, "Lives of Brainerd," 228–34, argues that it was the former. In either case, he was a man "poor in spirit."

19. Edwards, *Life of Brainerd*, 201; "Related Correspondence," in Edwards, *Life of Brainerd*, 588–89. See Frazier, *Mohicans of Stockbridge*, for a general account of these Indians, and also Lion G. Miles, "The Red Man Dispossessed: The Williams Family and the Alienation of Indian Land in Stockbridge, Massachusetts, 1736–1818," *New England Quarterly* 67 (1994): 46–47.

20. Pettit, "Introduction," 59–61; Margaret Connell Szasz, *Indian Education in the American Colonies, 1607–1783* (Albuquerque: University of New Mexico Press, 1988), 205–11; Samuel Hopkins, *Historical Memoirs, relating to the Housattunuk Indians* (Boston: S. Kneeland, 1753), 89–90; Axtell, *Invasion Within*, 197–204. Sergeant's missionary trip had been largely unsuccessful. First visiting the Susquehanna Indians, he carried a letter from the Stockbridge Indians extolling the truth of Christianity. After hearing the message, the Indians deliberated and then responded with the following (as told by Sergeant): "It is true, we have one Father above, and we are always in his Presence. The Indians have one Way of honouring and pleasing him, and the White People have another; both are acceptable in Him. I am glad to hear from my Brother, and to cultivate Friendship with him. He shall always find me here if he has any Message to send: But Christianity need not be the Bond of Union between us." Sergeant met with a

warmer welcome from natives along the Delaware River: thus his suggestion to Pemberton. See Hopkins, *Historical Memoirs,* 89–90.

21. Edwards, *Life of Brainerd,* 222, 228, 243–45; "Related Correspondence," 570–77; Szasz, *Indian Education,* 213–14. Some of Sergeant's methods had been publicly described in his *A Letter from the Rev. Mr. Sergeant of Stockbridge, to Dr. Colman of Boston* (Boston: Rogers and Fowle, 1743).

22. David Brainerd, *Mirabilia Dei inter Indicos, or the Rise and Progress of a Remarkable Work of Grace amongst a number of Indians* (Philadelphia: William Bradford, 1746), 79–80, 196–201. This is Brainerd's so-called public journal, covering the period from June 1745 to June 1746. The published version contained two parts (the second part was entitled *Divine Grace Displayed . . .*) and an extensive appendix. The Yale edition of *The Life of David Brainerd* interweaves parts of this public journal with Edwards' version of Brainerd's private diaries. Omitted are several critical passages, especially Brainerd's "general remarks" at the end of parts 1 and 2 (*Mirabilia Dei,* 65–80, 169–95) and the appendix (*Mirabilia Dei,* 196–248). See Pettit, "Introduction," 71–84, and "Related Correspondence," 561–62, on Brainerd texts and manuscripts.

23. Axtell, *European and the Indian,* 131–67, discusses how Indians served as teachers to the New English.

24. Edwards, *Life of Brainerd,* 204–208, 216–17, 221, 245; "Related Correspondence," 571–72; "Some Further Remains of the Rev. Mr. David Brainerd," in Edwards, *Life of Brainerd,* 484–86.

25. Edwards, *Life of Brainerd,* 207.

26. Brainerd's initial assessment of his circumstances in Kaunaumeek may be sampled in a letter to his brother John, dated 30 April 1743, in "Some Further Remains," 484–85. His change in attitude may be traced in Edwards, *Life of Brainerd,* 213–14, 216, 225, 228–29. His outcry against selfish ambition and worldly pleasures is evident in letters to John Brainerd, 27 December 1743, and Israel Brainerd, 21 January 1744, in "Some Further Remains," 486–88. One can only speculate about Brainerd's opinion of the relative opulence of John Sergeant's home in Stockbridge, where the missionary had married into the locally powerful Williams family.

27. Edwards, *Life of Brainerd,* 234. On his longing for death, see Edwards, *Life of Brainerd,* 201, 205, 215–17, 239; and on his millennial desires, 203, 205, 225–26, 228. DeJong, *As the Waters Cover the Sea,* 134–37, emphasizes Brainerd's interest in the expansion of the kingdom of God and argues that the "Indians, with whom he conversed daily, assumed a dominant place in his reflections on the kingdom" (quote on 135).

28. Edwards, *Life of Brainerd,* 202–203; "Some Further Remains," 485.

29. "Related Correspondence," 574–75.

30. Ibid., 575.

31. Ibid., 576; Wynbeek, *Beloved Yankee,* 86–87. Moravian A. G. Spangenberg's 1745 journal describes a similar native response to Brainerd at Shamokin, Pennsylvania, in June 1745. See William M. Beauchamp, ed., *Moravian Journals relating to Central New York, 1745–66* (Syracuse, N.Y.: Onondaga Historical Association, 1916), 7. Axtell, *Invasion Within,* 242–82, recounts the Shamokin incident and similar vignettes to illustrate the largely fruitless efforts of eighteenth-century English missionaries.

32. Edwards, *Life of Brainerd,* 249–51; "Related Correspondence," 577; C. A. Weslager, *The Delaware Indians: A History* (New Brunswick, N. J.: Rutgers Univer-

sity Press, 1972), 187–94; Francis P. Jennings, *The Ambiguous Iroquois Empire* (New York: Norton, 1990).

33. David Murray, "David Brainerd and the Gift of Christianity," *European Review of Native American Studies* 10 (1996): 23–24.

34. "Related Correspondence," 579; James H. Merrell, *Into the American Woods: Negotiators on the Pennsylvania Frontier* (New York: Norton, 1999), 86.

35. "Related Correspondence," 579–81.

36. Ibid., 577.

37. Edwards, *Life of Brainerd*, 251–60; "Related Correspondence," 577; Grigg, "Lives of Brainerd," 142; Stevens, *Poor Indians*, 141.

38. On Moravian missionary strategies, see Elma E. Gray, *Wilderness Christians: The Moravian Mission to the Delaware Indians* (1956; reprint, New York: Russell and Russell, 1973), 31–51; Earl P. Olmstead, *Blackcoats among the Delaware: David Zeisberger on the Ohio Frontier* (Kent, Ohio: Kent State University Press, 1991), 5–10, 35–36; Jane T. Merritt, *At the Crossroads*, 70–166. Among the contemporary accounts available of Moravian evangelism in Pennsylvania is "Br. Martin Mack's Journal from the 13th Sept. 1745 N. S. of his journey and visit in [?] Shomoko," in Records of the Moravian Mission among the Indians of North America, microfilm ed., reel 28, box 217, folder 12B, item 1, Archives of the Moravian Church, Bethlehem, Pennsylvania. I am indebted to James H. Merrell for this reference. On some of Brainerd's contacts with Moravians, see Richard A. Hasler, "David Zeisberger's 'Jersey Connection,'" *Transactions of the Moravian Historical Society* 30 (1998): 38–42.

39. Edwards, *Life of Brainerd*, 261–63, 265–66.

40. Edwards, *Life of Brainerd*, 252, 254–55, 259, 267–69; "Related Correspondence," 490.

41. Edwards, *Life of Brainerd*, 263; "Related Correspondence," 490.

42. Grigg, "Lives of Brainerd," 216–24.

43. Edwards, *Life of Brainerd*, 274–75, 278–79, 284. Herbert C. Kraft, *The Lenape: Archaeology, History, and Ethnography* (Newark: New Jersey Historical Society, 1986), 161–94, describes Delaware spirituality.

44. Edwards, *Life of Brainerd*, 285.

45. Conforti, "Brainerd and the Nineteenth-Century Missionary Movement," 320–22, and Conforti, "Edwards's Most Popular Work," 200.

46. Edwards, *Life of Brainerd*, 298–440; Wynbeek, *Beloved Yankee*, 145–235.

47. Merrell, "'Customes of Our Countrey,'" 146–52; Merrell, *Into the American Woods*, 88; Weslager, *Delaware Indians*, 261–63; Harris, "David Brainerd and the Indians," 7.

48. Brainerd, *Mirabilia Dei*, 241–42. Bowden, *Indians and Christian Missions*, 154, and Conforti, "Brainerd and the Nineteenth-Century Missionary Movement," 320, cite these remarks as representative of Brainerd's view of the Indians, but I think they reflect but one of many, sometimes incompatible, attitudes.

49. Merrell, "'Customes of Our Countrey,'" 131–37, 150–53. Brainerd tended to follow John Eliot and John Sergeant more than the Mayhew family approach with the Wampanoags on Martha's Vineyard on the issue of how swiftly and how fully Indians should be expected to give up their own ways and become "civilized."

50. Edwards, *Life of Brainerd*, 336, 358, 376–78, 390, 402–403, 414, 434, 435; Brainerd, *Mirabilia Dei*, 199–200, 240–42; Thomas Brainerd, *Life of John Brain-*

erd, 98–105. John Brainerd, *A Genuine Letter from Mr. John Brainerd . . . to his Friend in London* (London: J. Ward, 1753), 5–9, 14, indicates that the task of "civilizing" these Indians was still proceeding slowly six years later.

51. As quoted in Merrell, *Into the American Woods,* 89.

52. David Brainerd, Journal, 1745, microfilm copy, American Philosophical Society, Philadelphia, 1–2, 6. This is a manuscript copy of part one of the public journal, which appears to be in Brainerd's hand and which differs at numerous points from the printed version. On Tatamy's career in general, see William A. Hunter, "Moses (Tunda) Tatamy, Delaware Indian Diplomat," in *A Delaware Indian Symposium,* ed. Herbert C. Kraft (Harrisburg: Pennsylvania Historical and Museum Commission, 1974), 72–80.

53. Edwards, *Life of Brainerd,* 288. Brainerd did make progress in understanding and using the Delaware languages during 1745–46, while at the same time his listeners became more familiar with English. Nevertheless, Tatamy remained vital to Brainerd's ministry. Brainerd, *Mirabilia Dei,* 186, 196–201.

54. Grigg, "Lives of Brainerd," 153; Harris, "David Brainerd and the Indians," 6.

55. Brainerd, *Mirabilia Dei,* 13–14, 71–72, 226–27.

56. Ibid., 72.

57. Edwards, *Life of Brainerd,* 421. Brainerd had used a similar tactic a few months earlier in bringing six of his Indian converts from Crossweeksung to the Forks of the Delaware to speak to Indians there who had previously been hostile to Christianity. He hoped this would be "a means to convince them of the truth and importance of Christianity to see and hear some of their own nation discoursing of divine things." The strategy apparently worked, at least in persuading some of the Indians to pay closer attention. See Edwards, *Life of Brainerd,* 363.

58. Brainerd, *Mirabilia Dei,* 72.

59. Brainerd's aversion to recording Indian names contrasts with Moravian practice, as revealed in Moravian diaries. Brainerd may have been reluctant to record what he could not pronounce, but Indians were also reluctant to reveal their real names. See C. A. Weslager, "Delaware Indian Name Giving and Modern Practice," in Kraft, *Delaware Indian Symposium,* 135–45, and Weslager, *Delaware Indians,* 71–72.

60. Edwards, *Life of Brainerd,* 289–90, 338, 359; "Related Correspondence," 582–83; Brainerd, *Mirabilia Dei,* 77–78, 80, 238–39.

61. Edwards, *Life of Brainerd,* 307, 310, 312. At the end of part one of his public journal (*Mirabilia Dei,* 73), Brainerd noted that "God saw fit to improve and bless milder means for the effectual awakening of these Indians." See Pettit, "Introduction," 9–10, for a different interpretation of Brainerd's preaching methods.

62. John Grigg, "'A Principle of Spiritual Life': David Brainerd's Surviving Sermon," *New England Quarterly* 77 (2004): 281–82.

63. Harris, "David Brainerd and the Indians," 6.

64. Edwards, *Life of Brainerd,* 312–21, 342; Brainerd, *Mirabilia Dei,* 73–75.

65. Edwards, *Life of Brainerd,* 321–32. From the time the revival broke out, Brainerd made a point of noting his sermon texts in both his private diary and public journal. The texts he used both in Crossweeksung and in the Pennsylvania interior were Luke 14:16–23, Isaiah 53:3–6, Matthew 13, and Acts 2:36–39. Brainerd explained in his public journal (*Mirabilia Dei,* 73) that he noted his scriptural texts to counter any criticisms that those "awakened" were "only

frightened with a fearful noise of hell and damnation, and that there was no evidence that their concern was the effect of a divine influence."

66. Edwards, *Life of Brainerd*, 332–45. Marsden, *Jonathan Edwards*, 393, suggests that Edwards's interaction with his Indian congregation in Stockbridge, Massachusetts, confirmed what he had already learned from Brainerd on the virtues of preaching a milder gospel to natives.

67. Kraft, *Lenape*, 161–69, 176–79, 189, 193–94; Weslager, *Delaware Indians*, 55, 65–69, 107; Anthony F. C. Wallace, *King of the Delawares: Teedyuscung, 1700–1763* (Philadelphia: University of Pennsylvania Press, 1949), 14–17, 43–44. Robert Daiutolo, Jr., "The Early Quaker Perception of the Indian," *Quaker History* 72 (1983): 104–13, also describes the character of Delaware morality and religion in the context of explaining why Quakers had such a favorable view of them. Brainerd gives his own analysis of Indian religion in *Mirabilia Dei*, 212–25.

68. Brainerd, *Mirabilia Dei*, 232–34. Brainerd especially noted the difficulty he had convincing all Indians that they were sinners. One tactic he used was to emphasize the scriptural command to love God with all of one's heart, strength, and mind to reveal to natives their failure to obey God.

69. Ibid., 230–31.

70. Dowd, *Spirited Resistance*, 23–46.

71. Edwards, *Life of Brainerd*, 329–30.

72. Gustafson, *Eloquence Is Power*, 88–89.

73. Edwards, *Life of Brainerd*, 330; Marsden, *Jonathan Edwards*, 284–90.

74. Gustafson, *Eloquence Is Power*, 81–82, 84–85.

75. Based on his private diaries and public journal, Brainerd seems to have been less prone to periods of intense depression between August 1745 and October 1746 than at any other time from early 1742 (when he left Yale) to his death in October 1747. For examples of his growing affection for the Crossweeksung Indians, see Edwards, *Life of Brainerd*, 332–33, 349–51, 367–68, 380, 386–87, 422, 432–33, 436.

76. Edwards, *Life of Brainerd*, 350–51, 363, 390, 436; Brainerd, *Mirabilia Dei*, 137, commented on the effectiveness of this style of ministry: "I find particular and close Dealing with Souls in private, is often very successful."

77. Edwards, *Life of Brainerd*, 380.

78. On the Indian conjurer, see Edwards, *Life of Brainerd*, 308, 359, 391–95; on the woman in "great distress," 344, 346, 352–53, 362, 369–72, 373; on the "one who had been a vile drunkard," 362. For another account of an Indian spiritual pilgrimage, see Brainerd, *Mirabilia Dei*, 94–98.

79. Edwards, *Life of Brainerd*, 355–57.

80. Brainerd wished to present the revival in Crossweeksung as an amazing work of God's grace but one free of the "enthusiastic" excesses that had drawn sharp criticism from opponents of the Great Awakening. He repeatedly explained that while his Delaware converts showed strong, heartfelt emotions, they never exhibited "any mental disorders . . . such as visions, trances, [or] imaginations of being under prophetic inspiration." See *Mirabilia Dei*, 74–75, 187–88. On Brainerd's own rejection of religious enthusiasm, see Edwards, *Life of Brainerd*, 448–52, and Marsden, *Jonathan Edwards*, 234–35, 330–34.

81. Brainerd, *Mirabilia Dei*, 74–75. See Pettit, "Introduction," 5–6, 11–24, and Pettit, "Prelude to Mission," 46–50, on Edwards's use of Brainerd. Weddle, "Melancholy Saints," 297–318, finds that Edwards's use and interpretation of Brainerd was not altogether representative of who or what Brainerd was. Rich-

ard Hall, *Neglected Northampton Texts*, 145–200, offers a more thorough discussion of Edwards's use of Brainerd and argues that the missionary was Edwards's model of the good citizen in his ideal society. Marsden, *Jonathan Edwards*, 331, stresses Edwards's portrayal of Brainerd "as the exemplary New Light." Philip F. Gura, *Jonathan Edwards: America's Evangelical* (New York: Hill and Wang, 2005), 144–49, emphasizes Edwards's use of Brainerd as a living example of true religious affections and as a counter to seeping Arminianism.

82. Edwards, *Life of Brainerd*, 438–41, 448–50.

83. Ibid., 451.

84. Pettit, "Introduction," 37–51, 57. Brainerd devoted most of his energies during the last months of his life to promoting Indian missions any way he could. See Edwards, *Life of Brainerd*, 459–76, and "Some Further Remains," 496–99.

85. Edwards, *Life of Brainerd*, 471. Is it possible that Edwards's decision to take up the pastorate at the Indian congregation of Stockbridge, Massachusetts, four years later was influenced by his observation of Brainerd's love for his native congregants? Once he was in Stockbridge and in direct contact with Indians, Edwards's preaching style and message changed to adapt to them in ways not dissimilar to what Brainerd had done among the Delaware. Wheeler, " 'Friends to Your Souls,' " 748–61.

86. Even after Brainerd's success in Crossweeksung and his lack of success with inland Indians, he struggled over whether to settle down with his congregation of Christian Indians in Cranbury or to devote himself to itinerant evangelism among the far larger number of Indians on the frontier. Edwards, *Life of Brainerd*, 397, 400–402. Another missionary perspective on Brainerd's visits to the Pennsylvania interior is contained in "Br. Martin Mack's Journal." Moravian Mack contrasted the fruitlessness of Brainerd's strategy of periodic visits, during which he tried to gather the resident Indians to hear him preach, with the Moravian approach of living with the Delaware and patiently waiting for opportunities to speak to individual natives about "the Love of our Saviour."

87. Pettit, "Introduction," 42–71.

88. The ideas of this paragraph owe much to Michael Zuckerman's helpful reading of my original article.

5. Martyrs, Healers, and Statesmen

1. Although many studies of early America mention native assistants, few study them systematically. One large study that does is Jean F. Hankins, "Bringing the Good News: Protestant Missionaries to the Indians of New England and New York, 1700–1775" (Ph.D. diss., University of Connecticut, 1993). Also see Jean F. Hankins, "Solomon Briant and Joseph Johnson: Indian Teachers and Preachers in Colonial New England," *Connecticut History* 33 (1992): 38–60, and Keely McCarthy, "Conversion, Identity, and the Indian Missionary," *Early American Literature* 36 (2001): 353–69. According to Olive Patricia Dickason, Bishop de Saint-Vallier (1653–1727) defined *dogiques* as " 'masters of prayer and chant,' assisting in the work of evangelization and conducting prayers and certain portions of the services in the absence of missionaries." Dickason, *Myth of the Savage*, 264.

2. Though studying a different mission context, Comaroff and Comaroff, *Of*

Revelation and Revolution, 2:78–120, is perhaps the best work exploring white Christian efforts to control or limit "native agency" in propagating the gospel, and the range, in this case, of black African responses. The Comaroffs see these efforts as the product of white fears or doubts about whether a *black* Christian could be trusted with preaching, teaching, or translating the Christian message.

3. General works on mission activity in New France include Bruce G. Trigger, *The Children of Aataentsic: A History of the Huron People to 1660* (1876; reprint, Kingston: McGill-Queen's University Press, 1987); Bruce G. Trigger, *Natives and Newcomers: Canada's "Heroic Age" Reconsidered* (Kingston: McGill-Queen's University Press, 1985); Jaenen, *Friend and Foe;* John Webster Grant, *Moon of Wintertime: Missionaries and the Indians of Canada in Encounter since 1534* (Toronto: University of Toronto Press, 1984); Lucien Campeau, *La Mission des Jésuites chez les Hurons, 1634–1650* (Montreal: Les Editions Bellarmine, 1987); Carole Blackburn, *Harvest of Souls: The Jesuit Missions and Colonialism in North America, 1632–1650* (Kingston: McGill-Queen's University Press, 2000); Robert Choquette, "French Catholicism Comes to the Americas," in Charles H. Lippy, Robert Choquette, and Stafford Poole, *Christianity Comes to the Americas* (New York: Paragon House, 1992), 131–242. Hurons believed that witches were the cause of their illnesses and sometimes accused the Jesuits of being sorcerers. Other times they welcomed Christian baptism as a cure for their diseases. On Jesuit views of Huron and Iroquois religion, see Peter A. Goddard, "The Devil in New France: Jesuit Demonology, 1611–50," *Canadian Historical Review* 78 (1997): 40–62.

4. Confronting and seeking to baptize sick and dying children and adults remained a prominent feature of missionary life in New France throughout the seventeenth century. Allan Greer, *Mohawk Saint: Catherine Tekakwitha and the Jesuits* (New York: Oxford University Press, 2005), 5–7.

5. Reuben G. Thwaites, ed., *The Jesuit Relations and Allied Documents,* 73 vols. (1896–1901; reprint, New York: Pagent Book Company, 1959), 23:241. Her names are spelled variously as Christienne and Torihio.

6. Ibid., 21:287. His names are spelled variously as Estienne, and Totihri and Totiry. I have followed the spellings in Trigger, *Children of Aataentsic,* 698.

7. For a fine overview of the Relations, see Allan Greer, "Introduction," in Allan Greer, ed., *The Jesuit Relations: Natives and Missionaries in Seventeenth-Century North America* (New York: Bedford/St. Martin's Press, 2000), 1–19.

8. Allan Greer, "Colonial Saints: Gender, Race, and Hagiography in New France," *William and Mary Quarterly,* 3rd. ser., 57 (2000): 323–48. Blackburn, *Harvest of Souls,* 61–67, provides another discussion of the Jesuit preoccupation with martyrdom. Paul Perron, "Isaac Jogues: From Martyrdom to Sainthood," in *Colonial Saints: Discovering the Holy in the Americas,* ed. Allan Greer and Jodi Bilinkoff (New York: Routledge, 2003), 153–68, analyzes the narrative construction of Jogues' martyrdom in the Relations.

9. See, for example, *Jesuit Relations,* 15:59–67.

10. As quoted in Joseph P. Donnelly, S.J., *Jean de Brébeuf, 1593–1649* (Chicago: Loyola University Press, 1975), 268–69. On Brébeuf's readiness for martyrdom, see 134–38.

11. Greer, "Colonial Saints," 340–48. On Tekakwitha, see Greer, *Mohawk Saint.* I follow Greer's usage here in referring to her as Catherine, rather than Kateri as other scholars often do today.

12. Greer, "Colonial Saints," 342.

13. *Jesuit Relations,* 23:135.

14. Ibid., 21:285–87.

15. Ibid., 23:135–37, quotation on 137.

16. Ibid., 23:137–47; Trigger, *Children of Aataentsic,* 705–706.

17. *Jesuit Relations,* 23:147.

18. Ibid.

19. Ibid., 26:259; Trigger, *Children of Aataentsic,* 704–705.

20. *Jesuit Relations,* 27:21–23; Grant, *Moon of Wintertime,* 43–44.

21. *Jesuit Relations,* 26:261.

22. Ibid., 26:289–91.

23. Natalie Zemon Davis, *Women on the Margins,* 67–84; Jaenen, *Friend and Foe,* 70–71; Choquette, "French Catholicism," 168–69; Greer, *Mohawk Saint,* 72–77, 120–21.

24. Donnelly, *Jean de Brébeuf,* 132, 161–64, 181–82, 228.

25. For discussions of the Huron view of dreams, see Conrad E. Heidenreich, "Huron," in William G. Sturtevant, gen. ed., *Handbook of North American Indians,* Bruce G. Trigger, ed., *Northeast* (Washington, D.C.: Smithsonian Institution, 1978), 15:373–74; Bruce G. Trigger, *The Huron: Farmers of the North,* 2d ed. (Fort Worth: Harcourt Brace Jovanovich, 1990), 132–40; Robert Moss, "Missionaries and Magicians: The Jesuit Encounter with Native American Shamans on New England's Colonial Frontier," in *Wonders of the Invisible World: 1600–1900,* ed. Peter Benes (Boston: Boston University Scholarly Publications, 1992), 17–33; and Davis, *Women on the Margins,* 124–28.

26. *Jesuit Relations,* 26:263.

27. Ibid., 26:261–65; 21:287. For the Jesuit appreciation of the Hurons' speaking skill as well as the missionaries' reactions to the native languages they encountered in New France, see Peter A. Dorsey, "Going to School with Savages: Authorship and Authority among the Jesuits of New France," *William and Mary Quarterly,* 3rd. ser., 55 (1998): 408–14, Normand Doiron, "Rhetorique Jésuite de L'Eloquence Sauvage au XVII Siècle: Les *Relations* de Paul LeJeune (1632–1642)," *Dix-Septième Siècle* 43 (1991): 375–402, and Margaret J. Leahey, " 'Comment Peut un Muet Prescher L'Evangile?' Jesuit Missionaries and Native Languages of New France," *French Historical Studies* 19 (1995): 105–31. It is interesting to note the Jesuits' willingness to affirm a Christian who was Indian, lay, and married. In all those ways, Totiri was different from the missionaries, who were European, clerical, single, and celibate.

28. *Jesuit Relations,* 26:281–83; Trigger, *Natives and Newcomers,* 256–59. Daniel K. Richter, "Iroquois versus Iroquois: Jesuit Missions and Christianity in Village Politics, 1642–1686," *Ethnohistory* 32 (1985), 1–16, examines similar tensions aroused by Jesuit missions in Iroquoia.

29. *Jesuit Relations,* 26:283–85.

30. Trigger, *Children of Aataentsic,* 719–21.

31. *Jesuit Relations,* 29:263–65.

32. Ibid., 29:267–69.

33. Ibid., 29:275–77.

34. George R. Healy, "The French Jesuits and the Idea of the Noble Savage," *William and Mary Quarterly,* 3rd. ser., 15 (1958): 148–51, analyzes why the Jesuits depicted some Indians in a favorable light.

35. Greer, "Introduction," 17, suggests that "The *Relations* are far too interesting to be categorized as colonialist texts, pure and simple. . . . These writings, though undoubtedly the work of Europeans, were generally the product of

extensive consultation with Algonquians and Iroquoians. The native voice is by no means absent, even if it comes across in a garbled and distorted form." He further notes that "[t]he missionaries were, of course, there to teach the Indians, not learn from them, and yet it seems unlikely that the years of immersion in a different culture would leave their outlook unaltered." Greer has followed up his own proposal in *Mohawk Saint,* in which he details the influence of Catherine Tekakwitha on Jesuit missionary Claude Chauchetière: "as Chauchetière came to understand things in retrospect, the encounter with Catherine transformed him completely" (5). Other works that emphasize how the encounter with Native Americans shaped aspects of the religious experience and understanding of European Catholics in New France include Dorsey, "Going to School," 412–18, Davis, *Women on the Margins,* 93–139, and Jaenen, *Friend and Foe,* 78–79.

36. Trigger, *Huron,* 84. Also see Heidenreich, "Huron," 371–72.

37. Trigger, *Huron,* 81, 84, 97.

38. Ibid., 108–109.

39. Ibid., 97–98.

40. Steckley, "Warrior and the Lineage," 482–94.

41. Trigger, *Children of Aataentsic,* 738–39.

42. Beverly Prior Smaby, *The Transformation of Moravian Bethlehem: From Communal Mission to Family Economy* (Philadelphia: University of Pennsylvania Press, 1988), 3–9.

43. Accounts of the Moravian mission at Shekomeko are provided in George Loskiel, *The History of the Moravian Mission among the Indians of North America* (1794; London: T. Allman, 1838), 52–95; Sheldon Davis, *Shekomeko; or, the Moravians in Dutchess County* (Poughkeepsie, N.Y.: Osborne and Killey, 1858); Karl-Wilhelm Westmeier, *The Evacuation of Shekomeko and the Early Moravian Missions to Native North Americans* (Lewiston, N.Y.: Edwin Mellen Press, 1994); and Rachel Wheeler, "Women and Christian Practices in a Mahican Village," *Religion and American Culture* 13 (2003): 27–67.

44. Smaby, *Transformation of Moravian Bethlehem,* 7–9; David S. Schattschneider, "The Missionary Theologies of Zinzendorf and Spangenberg," *Transactions of the Moravian Historical Society* 22 (1975): 220–22; Hermann Wellenreuther and Carola Wessel, eds., "Introduction," in *The Moravian Mission Diaries of David Zeisberger, 1772–1781,* trans. Julie Tomberlin Weber (University Park: Pennsylvania State University Press, 2005), 51–58; Katherine M. Faull, "Introduction," in *Moravian Women's Memoirs: Their Related Lives, 1750–1820,* trans. and ed. Katherine M. Faull (Syracuse: Syracuse University Press, 1997), xxiii, xxxiii–iv (quote on xxiii).

45. Merritt, *At the Crossroads,* 112.

46. Schattschneider, "Missionary Theologies," 220; Smaby, *Transformation of Moravian Bethlehem,* 8–12; Albert H. Frank, "Spiritual Life in Schönbrunn Village," *Transactions of the Moravian Historical Society* 26 (1990): 28, 37n52; Wellenreuther and Wessel, "Introduction," 56–57.

47. Henri J. M. Nouwen, *The Wounded Healer: Ministry in Contemporary Society* (Garden City, N.Y.: Doubleday, 1972), 83–104, quotations on 84, 89, 97.

48. August Gottlieb Spangenberg, *An Account of the manner in which the Protestant Church of the Unitas Fratrum, or United Brethren, preach the Gospel, and carry on their Missions among the Heathen* (London: H. Trapp, 1788), 62–63. Wassamapah repeated this story often, and one version or another was reprinted in many later Moravian histories and religious tracts. For an example of the latter, see

Tschoop: The Converted Indian Chief (n.p.: American Sunday School Union, 1842). By 1870, the story appeared in poetic form in Edmund De Schweinitz, *The Life and Times of David Zeisberger: The Western Pioneer and Apostle of the Indians* (Philadelphia: J. B. Lippincott, 1870), 98–99.

49. Tschop to Zinzendorf, 19 December 1741, in English, Box 319, Folder 1, Item 2, Archives of the Moravian Church (MCA), Bethlehem, Pennsylvania.

50. Merritt, *At the Crossroads*, 112–13.

51. Westmeier, *Evacuation of Shekomeko*, 61, 65.

52. Merritt, *At the Crossroads*, 89–91, 102–10. Also see Jane T. Merritt, "Dreaming of the Savior's Blood: Moravians and the Indian Great Awakening in Pennsylvania," *William and Mary Quarterly*, 3rd ser., 54 (1997): 723–46; Wellenreuther and Wessel, "Introduction," 57–58.

53. Westmeier, *Evacuation of Shekomeko*, 65–340, details the marginal political and legal position of both the Moravians and the Mahicans. On the Mahicans, also see T. J. Brasser, "Mahican," in *Handbook of North American Indians*, 15:207–208.

54. Frank, "Spiritual Life," 35n22, explains the Moravians' use of native assistants: "Native Helpers were Indian converts who had proven themselves worthy of the position of trust and had been officially recognized by the congregation in a public meeting. Their duties included visiting from house to house, comfort and care of the sick, settling quarrels, enforcing all spiritual and civil ordinances of the congregation, assisting with worship and conducting some meetings for the Indian members, and occasional emissary duties in relationships with the Indian councils." Johannes Wassamapah performed all of these duties, and as one of the first native assistants among the Moravians, he likely played a large shaping role in defining the position for later natives and Moravian communities. More discussion of Indian Helpers may be found in Wellenreuther and Wessel, "Introduction," 61–65.

55. Wheeler, "Women and Christian Practice in a Mahican Village," 27–67, examines the lives of two baptized Mahican women in Shekomeko, Sarah and Rachel, and makes the case that the various Christian rituals that they engaged in, and that someone like Johannes often led, were understood in distinctively Mahican ways and played a crucial role in shaping the new identity that these converts were forming.

56. All of the following English-language materials illustrating Johannes's activities as a native assistant may be found in the Archives of the Moravian Church: Gottlob Büttner to Anton Seiffert, 17 October 1742, Box 111, Folder 7, Item 5, entries for 1 October and 11 October; Gottlob Büttner to Anton Seiffert, 28 November 1742, Box 111, Folder 7, Item 6, entries for 24 October, 30 October, 12 November, 13 November, 17 November, 21 November; Gottlob Büttner diary, 22 February–19 April 1743, Box 111, Folder 2, Item 3, entries for 25 February, 3 March, 13 March, 17 April; Gottlob Büttner diary, 9 April–1 August 1743, Box 111, Folder 2, Item 4, entry for 16 July; Gottlob Büttner diary, 10 August–31 December 1743, Box 111, Folder 2, Item 7, entries for 31 October, 8 December; Martin Mack journal, 22 February–11 March 1743, Box 111, Folder 3, Item 4, entries for 26, 27, 28 February; Martin Mack journal, 17 January to 23 February, 1744, Box 112, Folder 19, Item 1, entries for 5, 8 February; "Short Account of Martin Mack's Journey to Checomeco and Back Again to Bethlehem, 18 November–30 November 1745, Box 217, Folder 126, Item 2, entries for 22, 23 November; Christian Rauch journal, 16 March to 20 April 1744, Box 112, Folder 19, Item 3, entries for 1, 3, 7, 15 April.

57. Davis, *Shekomeko*, 41, states that by the end of 1743, there were 63 baptized Indians at Shekomeko and a "much greater number of constant and regular hearers." On the whites' departure from Shekomeko and the larger role of native preachers, see Westmeier, *Evacuation of Shekomeko*, 270–325, and Davis, *Shekomeko*, 41–47.

58. Martin Mack journal, 22 February–11 March 1743, entry for 27 February, MCA.

59. *Tschoop and Shabasch, Christian Indians of North America: A Narrative of Facts* (Dublin: M. Goodwin, 1824), 22.

60. De Schweinitz, *Life and Times of Zeisberger*, 116.

61. Johannes to Bethlehem Church, Box 319, Folder 1, Item 14, MCA.

62. Westmeier, *Evacuation of Shekomeko*, 78.

63. As quoted in ibid., 79n41.

64. Merritt, *At the Crossroads*, 102–104, makes clear that this Moravian integration into native life applied with equal force to women. Wellenreuther and Wessel, "Introduction," argue that "their sharing in almost all aspects the lifestyle of the Indian members of the congregation was one reason why the Moravians succeeded as missionaries" (66).

65. Westmeier, *Evacuation of Shekomeko*, 63.

66. Tschop to Zinzendorf, 19 December 1741, in English, Box 319, Folder 1, Item 2, MCA.

67. Loskiel, *Moravian Mission*, 55, 59–62; Martin Mack journal, 23 February–15 March 1744, Box 112, Folder 1, Item 2, entries for 26, 29 February and 1 March, MCA; "Names and Personal Notices of Christian Indians who lie buried at Bethlehem, Pennsylvania," in *Memorials of the Moravian Church*, ed. William C. Reichel, 2 vols. (Philadelphia: J. B. Lippincott, 1870), 1:147.

68. Examples of pious accounts include the pamphlets *Tschoop and Shabasch* and *Tschoop: The Converted Indian Chief;* Loskiel, *Moravian Mission;* De Schweinitz, *Life and Times of Zeisberger;* Reichel, *Memorials of the Moravian Church;* and W. N. Schwarze, "Memorial Address on the occasion of the Rededication of the Monument at Shekomeko," typescript, Box 113, MCA. Much of what they write about Johannes was based on earlier accounts provided in Spangenberg, *An Account of the Unitas Fratrum*, published in German in 1780 and in English translation in 1788.

69. Westmeier, *Evacuation of Shekomeko*, 49–51, 88–89. Zinzendorf's own account of his meetings with the four Mahicans is found in "Zinzendorf's Journey to the Mohican town of Shecomeco—August 10–August 31, 1742" in Reichel, *Memorials of the Moravian Church*, 1:55–57.

70. Merritt, *At the Crossroads*, 105–106.

71. Schattschneider, "Missionary Theologies," 213–33, explains the key ideas in the missionary strategies of Zinzendorf and Spangenburg as they were formulated in the 1730s and 1740s.

72. Merritt, *At the Crossroads*, 129–30.

73. Bethlehem Christian Indians to Shekomeko, 2 June 1746, Box 319, Folder 2, Item 1, MCA.

74. Bethlehem Church Register, vol. 1, 1742–1756, page 184, MCA; "Names and Personal Notices," 147.

75. This Oneida community had a number of names in the colonial era, including Onoquaga, but recent historians including Daniel Richter and Russell Bourne have chosen to refer to it as Oquaga. Daniel K. Richter, *The Ordeal of the*

Longhouse: The Peoples of the Iroquois League in the Era of European Civilization (Chapel Hill: University of North Carolina Press, 1992), 258–59; Bourne, *Gods of War, Gods of Peace,* 238–40.

76. This rendition of Good Peter's Oneida name is taken from Alan Taylor, *The Divided Ground: Indians, Settlers, and the Northern Borderland of the American Revolution* (New York: Alfred Knopf, 2006), 150. An alternative version, Agorondajats, may be found in Barbara Graymont, *The Iroquois in the American Revolution* (Syracuse: Syracuse University Press, 1972), 225. Franklin B. Hough, ed., *Proceedings of the Commissioners of Indian Affairs . . . in the State of New York,* 2 vols. (Albany: Joel Munsell, 1861) 1:490, lists his other European names as Domine Peter, Peter the Priest, and Peter the Minister, and other renditions of his Oneida name as Agwelentongwas or Agwelentonwas.

77. Bourne, *Gods of War,* 264–81, discusses Kirkland's changing role amid the revolutionary conflict. Karim Michel Tiro, "The People of the Standing Stone: The Oneida Indian Nation from Revolution through Removal, 1765–1840" (Ph.D. diss., University of Pennsylvania, 1999), 100–101, argues that Kirkland has often been given too much credit for convincing the Oneidas to support the patriot side. He suggests that the Oneidas made that choice on their own, although Kirkland and interpreter James Dean played key roles in helping "the Oneidas to see beyond the dismal example of the local militia and to understand that the rebels had a fair chance of success" (101). The two white men also functioned as important cultural go-betweens among the Oneidas and patriot forces.

78. Taylor, *Divided Ground,* 111–407, details this process closely in the 1780s and 1790s. Also see J. David Lehman, "The End of the Iroquois Mystique: The Oneida Land Cession Treaties of the 1780s," *William and Mary Quarterly,* 3d ser., 47 (1990): 522–47, and Laurence M. Hauptman, *Conspiracy of Interests: Iroquois Dispossession and the Rise of New York State* (Syracuse: Syracuse University Press, 1999). Good Peter's retrospective narrative on the fortunes of the Oneidas in the postwar era was conveyed to federal commissioner Timothy Pickering in Philadelphia in 1792 and may be found in "Good Peter's Narrative of Several transactions respecting Indian lands," Timothy Pickering Papers, Reel 60, Folios 121–134, Massachusetts Historical Society, Boston, Massachusetts.

79. Colin Calloway, "The Continuing Revolution in Indian Country," in *Native Americans and the Early Republic,* ed. Frederick E. Hoxie, Ronald Hoffman, and Peter J. Albert (Charlottesville: University Press of Virginia, 1999), 6; Pilkington, *The Journals of Samuel Kirkland,* 215–16, 231, 290, 297–98; Christine S. Patrick, "The Life and Times of Samuel Kirkland, 1741–1808: Missionary to the Oneida Indians, American Patriot, and Founder of Hamilton College" (Ph.D. diss., State University of New York at Buffalo, 1993), 395–97, 403, 416–22, 482–83; Taylor, *Divided Ground,* 208–14.

80. Tiro, "People of the Standing Stone," 200–51, discusses Oneida removal westward. Also see Laurence M. Hauptman and L. Gordon McLester III, eds., *The Oneida Indian Journey: From New York to Wisconsin, 1784–1860* (Madison: University of Wisconsin Press, 1999).

81. James R. Rohrer, *Keepers of the Covenant: Frontier Missions and the Decline of Congregationalism, 1774–1818* (New York: Oxford University Press, 1995), quotations on 35, 64, 42, and 101.

82. Amy DeRogatis, *Moral Geography: Maps, Missionaries, and the American Frontier* (New York: Columbia University Press, 2003), provides another inter-

pretation of Congregationalist missions activity. She emphasizes the role of David Brainerd as a model to home missionaries in the Western Reserve (61–89), a model that proved ill-suited to the realities missionaries ended up facing. She also finds (32–35) that the Connecticut Missionary Society gave up its efforts to evangelize Indians in the region after 1805 and concentrated exclusively on white settlers. Rohrer, *Keepers of the Covenant*, 109–11, also emphasizes the role of Brainerd as a model. Hankins, "Bringing the Good News," 297–307, compares the ministries of Brainerd and Kirkland.

83. R. Pierce Beaver, *Church, State, and the American Indians: Two and a Half Centuries of Partnership in Missions between Protestant Churches and Government* (St. Louis: Concordia, 1966), 63–66.

84. Reginald Horsman, "The Indian Policy of an 'Empire of Liberty,'" in Hoxie, Hoffman, and Albert, *Native Americans and the Early Republic*, 44–45; Fred Hood, *Reformed America: The Middle and Southern States, 1783–1837* (University: University of Alabama Press, 1980), 133–34; William G. McLoughlin, *Cherokees and Missionaries, 1789–1839* (New Haven: Yale University Press, 1984), 33–34. Knox was appointed secretary at war by the Confederation Congress in 1785 and then became secretary of war under Washington in 1789.

85. As quoted in Beaver, *Church, State, and the American Indians*, 64.

86. The Kirkland-Knox relationship may be followed in their correspondence. All of the following letters may be found in the Samuel Kirkland Papers, Hamilton College Archives (HCA), Hamilton, New York: Henry Knox to Samuel Kirkland, May 11, 1791; Samuel Kirkland to Henry Knox, January 5, 1792; Henry Knox to Samuel Kirkland, January 7, 1792; Samuel Kirkland to Henry Knox, January 27, 1792; Samuel Kirkland to Henry Knox, February 6, 1792; Samuel Kirkland to Henry Knox, February 13, 1792.

87. Beaver, *Church, State, and the American Indians*, 65–66.

88. Bourne, *Gods of War*, 230, offers high praise to Kirkland as an exemplary missionary statesman: "[Kirkland] not only went on to serve the church as the most effective of all white missionaries on the frontier but also served his nation, first as heroic frontier agent during the American Revolution and later as founder of Hamilton College in Clinton, New York." Similar sentiments are expressed in Axtell, *Invasion Within*, 370. Kirkland receives great attention and much criticism in Taylor, *Divided Ground*.

89. W. DeLoss Love, *Samson Occom and the Christian Indians of New England* (Boston: Pilgrim Press, 1899), 82–83. Love states that Good Peter was converted under Gideon Hawley. Taylor, *Divided Ground*, 150, places his conversion in 1748.

90. "Rev. Gideon Hawley's Journey to Oghquaga, Broome Co., 1753," in E. B. O'Callaghan, ed., *Documentary History of the State of New York*, 4 vols. (Albany: Weed, Parsons, 1849–51), 3:625–34. The New England Company had previously stationed Job Strong (1748–49) and Elihu Spencer (1748–49, 1750–51) in Oquaga.

91. William Johnson, *Papers of Sir William Johnson*, ed. Milton W. Hamilton et al., 14 vols. (Albany: University of the State of New York, 1921–65), 9:715–16; 3:872; 10:515–18. Love, *Samson Occom*, 83n4, claims that Good Peter itinerated among his people following Hawley's departure. After a five-year gap, the New England Company sent Amos Toppan to Oquaga in 1761. He was followed by Eli Forbes (1761–62). Then the Society in Scotland for Propagating Christian Knowledge sent a series of missionaries: Joseph Bowman (1762), Asaph Rice

(1762–63), Charles S. Smith (1763), and Titus Smith (1765). The New England Company then supplied Ebenezer Moseley (1765–72) and Aaron Crosby (1771–77). By the late 1760s, tensions developed between Anglican Johnson and the Congregational missionaries over the emerging political split with England. Those tensions carried into the American Revolution, with both sides competing for the loyalties, religious and political, of the Oneidas and other Iroquois nations.

92. As quoted in Hankins, "Bringing the Good News," 280.

93. *Papers of Johnson*, 9:613–14.

94. Ibid., 9:807–808, 10:97, 3:870–73.

95. Ibid., 4:648.

96. James Dow McCallum, ed., *The Letters of Eleazar Wheelock's Indians* (Hanover, N.H.: Dartmouth College, 1932), 80n2.

97. *Journals of Kirkland*, 3.

98. Richter, *Ordeal of the Longhouse*, 38–47, 24–25. According to Taylor, *Divided Ground*, 19–21, Kirkland first encountered Good Peter at a time when warrior chiefs within the Six Nations had recently become more powerful than sachems.

99. Richter, *Ordeal of the Longhouse*, 40–41.

100. *Journals of Kirkland*, 81.

101. Richter, *Ordeal of the Longhouse*, 46–47.

102. *Journals of Kirkland*, 81–82.

103. Tiro, "People of the Standing Stone," 147–99.

104. Ibid., 231. Several weeks later he expressed the same sentiment to Peter Thacher, secretary-treasurer of the Society in Scotland for the Propagation of Christian Knowledge, Kirkland's supporting mission agency: "The Oneidas have sustained an almost inexpressable [?] loss in the death of Good Peter—tho' the whole Confederacy have felt the shock. His equal is nowhere to be found in all the five nations." Samuel Kirkland to Peter Thacher, December 26, 1792, Samuel Kirkland Papers, HCA.

105. Taylor, *Divided Ground*, 218–19, notes that for a short time in 1788–89, the two men strongly disagreed over Good Peter's temporary support for the diplomatic and economic maneuverings of Peter Penet, a representative of sorts of the French government. Kirkland was especially disturbed by Good Peter's willingness to lend assistance to the Catholic priest who accompanied Penet.

106. Beaver, *Church, State, and American Indians*, 55–56; Bourne, *Gods of War*, 278–81, 289, 307; Frazier, *Mohicans of Stockbridge*, 205–206, 217–18, 227.

107. Graymont, *Iroquois in the American Revolution*, 224–29, 266, 278–79; Tiro, "People of the Standing Stone," 132–46.

108. Tiro, "People of the Standing Stone," 149. He suggests that the "Oneidas' expansion of the role of hymn-singing in Christian practice is the most striking example of how they modified Christianity to better accord with their traditional style of worship" (176).

109. Taylor, *Divided Ground*, 403–407, considers Good Peter to have been among the most creative Six Nations leaders in the postwar era.

110. Samuel Kirkland to Jerusha Kirkland, September 22, 1785, Samuel Kirkland Papers, HCA.

111. *Journals of Kirkland*, 130.

112. Journal of Samuel Kirkland, June 13 to October 1791, Society for Propagating the Gospel Records, Box 1, Folder 7, entry for October 2, Massachusetts Historical Society. Another possible key to Good Peter's power as a preacher was

his use of images that might have resonated well with his native listeners. Kirkland noted that on one occasion, Good Peter had exhorted his audience by proclaiming, "O! Sinners, look on the word of Jesus that is a glass in which you may see what you are" (*Journals of Kirkland,* 130). Karim Michel Tiro suggests that such an image might have connected with the widespread Indian association of "the reflective qualities of glass and still water . . . with mind, soul, and greatest being." Tiro, "People of the Standing Stone," 156–57. Also see Christopher L. Miller and George R. Hamell, "A New Perspective on Indian-White Contact: Cultural Symbols and Colonial Trade," *Journal of American History* 73 (1986): 311–28.

113. Hough, *Proceedings of the Commissioners of Indian Affairs,* 1:178, 218.

114. Daniel H. Usner, Jr., "Iroquois Livelihood and Jeffersonian Agrarianism: Reaching behind the Models and Metaphors," in Hoxie, Hoffman, and Albert, *Native Americans and the Early Republic,* 215, discusses the difficulty of white recorders capturing Iroquois meanings.

115. Good Peter's diplomatic speeches may be sampled in Hough, *Proceedings of the Commissioners of Indian Affairs,* 1:85–108, 176–79, 217–23, 226–29, 234–40, 274–80, 285–88, 291–94, 298–305, 312.

116. *Journals of Kirkland,* 356.

117. Ibid., 144, 159, 201.

118. Journal of Samuel Kirkland, June 1787–March 1788, Society for Propagating the Gospel Records, Box 1, Folder 6, entry for December 3, 1787, Massachusetts Historical Society; Patrick, "Life and Times of Kirkland," 403.

119. Samuel Kirkland to Peter Thacher, May 15, 1792, Samuel Kirkland Papers, HCA.

120. Samuel Kirkland to Henry Knox, January 27, 1792, Samuel Kirkland Papers, HCA; Bourne, *Gods of War,* 23–31, suggests that Kirkland and Brant had started off as good friends in the 1760s when they were both students at Wheelock's school in Connecticut. The Revolution split their loyalties and apparently their friendship.

121. *Journals of Kirkland,* 221.

122. Samuel Kirkland to Henry Knox, February 6, 1792, Samuel Kirkland Papers, HCA.

123. Samuel Kirkland to Peter Thacher, May 15, 1792, Samuel Kirkland Papers, HCA.

124. Rohrer, *Keepers of the Covenant,* 15–27, and DeRogatis, *Moral Geography,* 35–45, examine Congregationalist hopes for the west.

125. *Journals of Kirkland,* 305.

126. J. K. Bloomfield, *The Oneidas* (New York: Alden Brothers, 1907), 101.

6. Encountering Death

1. As quoted in Steven G. Gimber, "Kinship and Covenants in the Wilderness: Indians, Quakers, and Conversion to Christianity, 1675–1800" (Ph.D. diss., American University, 2000), 361.

2. Tiro, "People of the Standing Stone," 186–90, discusses the Quaker mission among the Oneida and suggests (190) that "Oneidas who lost their lives through violence generally did so at one anothers' [sic] hands, rather than at those of whites." Whites contributed indirectly to that violence through selling liquor to Indians, a practice Quakers condemned throughout the colonial era.

3. Jennings, *Invasion of America,* 30.

4. Particularly influential works on the Europeans' demographic impact on natives have included Wilbur R. Jacobs, "The Tip of the Iceberg: Pre-Columbian Indian Demography and Some Implications for Revisionism," *William and Mary Quarterly,* 3rd ser., 31 (1974): 123–32; Alfred Crosby, *The Columbian Exchange: Biological and Cultural Consequences of 1492* (Westport, Conn.: Greenwood, 1972); Henry F. Dobyns, *Their Number Became Thinned: Native American Population Dynamics in Eastern North America* (Knoxville: University of Tennessee Press, 1983); and Henry F. Dobyns et al., "Commentary on Native American Demography," *Ethnohistory* 36 (1989): 285–307.

5. On New England, Axtell, *Invasion Within,* 219–20; on New France, Greer, *Mohawk Saint,* 5–7 (quote on 5); Gabriel Thomas, "An Historical and Geographical Account of Pensilvania and of West-New-Jersey," in *Narratives of Early Pennsylvania, West New Jersey, and Delaware, 1630–1707,* ed. Albert Cook Myers, Original Narratives of Early American History (New York: Charles Scribner's Sons, 1912); Thomas J. Sugrue, "The Peopling and Depeopling of Early Pennsylvania: Indians and Colonists, 1680–1720," *Pennsylvania Magazine of History and Biography* 116 (1992): 13; Robert Beverley, *The History and Present State of Virginia* (1705), ed. Louis B. Wright (Chapel Hill: University of North Carolina Press, 1947), 232; on the colonial South, Peter H. Wood, "The Changing Population of the Colonial South: An Overview by Race and Region, 1685–1790," in *Powhatan's Mantle: Indians in the Colonial Southeast,* ed. Peter H. Wood, Gregory A. Waselkov, and M. Thomas Hatley (Lincoln: University of Nebraska Press, 1989), 89.

6. Steven W. Hackel, *Children of Coyote, Missionaries of Saint Francis: Indian-Spanish Relations in Colonial California, 1769–1850* (Chapel Hill: University of North Carolina Press, 2005), 65–123.

7. Joyce E. Chaplin, *Subject Matter: Technology, the Body, and Science on the Anglo-American Frontier, 1500–1676* (Cambridge, Mass.: Harvard University Press, 2001), 116–98 (quote on 132). For a discussion of early modern European views on death in general, see Philippe Ariès, *The Hour of Our Death,* trans. H. Weaver (Oxford: Oxford University Press, 1981).

8. Chaplin, *Subject Matter,* 158.

9. Ibid., 172–75.

10. William Bradford, *Of Plymouth Plantation, 1620–1647,* ed. Samuel Eliot Morison (New York: Alfred A. Knopf, 1953), 260; John Smith, "The General Historie of Virginia," in *Narrative of Early Virginia, 1606–1625,* ed. Lyon Gardiner Tyler, Original Narratives of Early American History (New York: Charles Scribner's Sons, 1907), 363; Smith as quoted in Chaplin, *Subject Matter,* 166; Winthrop as quoted in Francis J. Bremer, *John Winthrop: America's Forgotten Founding Father* (New York: Oxford University Press, 2003), 434, 191; *New Englands First Fruits,* in Clark, *The Eliot Tracts,* 74.

11. Stevens, *Poor Indians,* 164–69; Cave, *Pequot War.*

12. Stevens, *Poor Indians,* 167.

13. Carla Gardina Pestana, *Quakers and Baptists in Colonial Massachusetts* (Cambridge: Cambridge University Press, 1991), 2–39, 136, 145. On the long-term symbolic role within Quakerism of the early Quaker "martyrs" who were executed in Massachusetts, see Carla Gardina Pestana, "Martyred by the Saints: Quaker Executions in Seventeenth-Century Massachusetts," in Greer and Bilinkoff, *Colonial Saints,* 169–91.

14. Pestana, *Quakers and Baptists,* 145–50.

15. Quote from Josiah Coale in Steven W. Angell, " 'Learn of the Heathen':

Quakers and Indians in Southern New England, 1656–1676," *Quaker History* 92 (2003): 5.

16. Meredith Baldwin Weddle, *Walking in the Way of Peace: Quaker Pacifism in the Seventeenth Century* (New York: Oxford University Press, 2001), 117–18.

17. George Fox, *Cain against Abel, Representing New-England's Church-Hirarchy, In Opposition to Her Christian Protestant Dissenters* ([London?], 1675), 32.

18. Angell, " 'Learn of the Heathen,' " 2, 17.

19. George Fox, *A Journal or Historical Account of . . . George Fox* in *The Works of George Fox*, 8 vols. (1831; reprint, New York: AMS Press, 1975), 2:210.

20. Arthur J. Worrall, *Quakers in the Colonial Northeast* (Hanover, N.H.: University Press of New England, 1980), 38–39; Pestana, *Quakers and Baptists*, 151–55; Angell, " 'Learn of the Heathen,' " 13–14.

21. Weddle, *Walking in the Way of Peace*, 134; Lepore, *Name of War*, 102–103.

22. Weddle, *Walking in the Way of Peace*, 6, 120–28, 169–74 (quotes on 6).

23. Angell, " 'Learn of the Heathen,' " 15.

24. Weddle, *Walking in the Way of Peace*, 44, 183–96 (quotes on 188).

25. Ibid., 181, 201–11.

26. Angell, " 'Learn of the Heathen,' " 14–15.

27. Lepore, *Name of War*, 11–18, 102–103, 119.

28. Holifield, *Era of Persuasion*, 57.

29. Weddle, *Walking in the Way of Peace*, 215.

30. Thomas Chalkley, *A Collection of the Works of Thomas Chalkley: in two parts* (Philadelphia: B. Franklin and D. Hall, 1749), 39–40, 45. Rebecca Larson, *Daughters of Light: Quaker Women Preaching and Prophesying in the Colonies and Abroad, 1700–1775* (New York: Alfred A. Knopf, 1999), 116, confirms Chalkley's general point by describing how traveling Quaker female preachers moved unarmed about northern New England amid Queen Anne's War despite the threat of violence. They did so to prove "their reliance on God to protect them."

31. Weddle, *Walking in the Way of Peace*, 215–18.

32. Godbeer, *Devil's Dominion*, 194–203.

33. Cotton Mather, *Decennium Luctuosum. An History of Remarkable Occurrences, in the long war, which New-England hath had with the Indian salvages, from the year 1688* (Boston: B. Green and J. Allen, 1699), 162.

34. Thomas Maule, *Truth held forth and maintained according to the testimony of the holy prophets* ([New York]: William Bradford, 1695), 194–95, 213–14.

35. George Fox, *A Collection of Many Select and Christian Epistles, Letters and Testimonies . . . [of] George Fox* in *Works of George Fox*, 8:131, 195.

36. William Penn, *Papers of William Penn*, ed. Richard S. Dunn and Mary Maples Dunn, 5 vols. (Philadelphia: University of Pennsylvania Press, 1982), 2:108.

37. J. William Frost, "William Penn's Experiment in the Wilderness: Promise and Legend," *Pennsylvania Magazine of History and Biography* 107 (1983): 584–93 (quote on 584).

38. Michael Dean Mackintosh, "New Sweden, Natives, and Nature," in *Friends and Enemies in Penn's Woods: Indians, Colonists, and the Racial Construction of Pennsylvania* (University Park: Pennsylvania State University Press, 2004), 6, 14–17.

39. William Penn, "Letters of William Penn," *Pennsylvania Magazine of History and Biography* 6 (1882): 472–73.

40. "Letter from William Penn to the Committee of the Free Society of Traders, 1683," in Myers, *Narratives of Early Pennsylvania*, 236.

41. William Penn, "A Further Account of the Province of Pennsylvania," in Myers, *Narratives of Early Pennsylvania*, 276.

42. Stevens, *Poor Indians,* 186–89. English Quakers arranged for the publication of *A True Account of the Dying Words of Ockanickon, an Indian King* in 1682 and 1683 after receiving the testament from colonist John Cripps. The native's speech instructed his people to respect and live peaceably with their Quaker neighbors, and expressed his own desire to be buried among the Friends. Both printings included the signatures or marks of five natives and five Quakers as witnesses to the validity of this record of Ockanickon's speech. In Friends' minds, here was concrete evidence that the Quaker approach to living beside Indians was working. Two years later, Thomas Budd, one of the five Quaker witnesses, republished Ockanickon's dying words in his pamphlet *Good Order established in Pennsilvania and New Jersey in America.* In promoting settlement in the Quaker colonies, Budd reiterated the promising start Friends had made with the Delawares and the prospect of a future marked by mutual respect, friendship, and possibly even native conversion to Christianity. Nothing would do more to enhance the latter than Quakers' setting attractive examples through living just and peaceful lives.

43. Frost, "Penn's Experiment," 594–98.

44. Sugrue, "Peopling and Depeopling of Early Pennsylvania," 6, 17; James O'Neil Spady, "Colonialism and the Discursive Antecedents of *Penn's Treaty* with the Indians," in Pencak and Richter, eds., *Friends and Enemies,* 30–38. For a more positive assessment of Penn's policies, see Francis Jennings, "Brother Miquon: Good Lord!" in *The World of William Penn,* ed. Richard S. Dunn and Mary Maples Dunn (Philadelphia: University of Pennsylvania Press, 1986), 195–214.

45. Spady, "Colonialism and Antecedents of *Penn's Treaty,*" 39; Merrell, *Into the American Woods,* 119; James H. Merrell, "Afterword," in Pencak and Richter, *Friends and Enemies,* 267–68.

46. As quoted in Rayner W. Kelsey, *Friends and Indians, 1655–1917* (Philadelphia: Associated Executive Committee of Friends on Indian Affairs, 1917), 65.

47. Merrell, *Into the American Woods,* 122, 126; Spady, "Colonialism and Antecedents of *Penn's Treaty,*" 39.

48. Carla Gerona, "Imagining Peace in Quaker and Native American Dream Stories," in Pencak and Richter, *Friends and Enemies,* 50.

49. Chalkley, *Works of Chalkley,* 308–309. Gerona, "Imagining Peace," 50–52, recounts another passage from Chalkley in which he "recorded an Indian dream in his journal that illustrates the symbolic weight Penn's benevolence continued to carry among both Quakers and Indians following the Founder's return to England" (50). Larson, *Daughters of Light,* 224, notes that visiting English preacher Elizabeth Wilkinson sounded similar warnings about getting Indian permission to settle on their lands to Quakers in Virginia and the Carolinas in 1761.

50. *An epistle from our Yearly-Meeting in Burlington, for the Jerseys and Pennsylvania* (Philadelphia: [Andrew Bradford?], 1722), 4.

51. John Callender, *An historical discourse on the civil and religious affairs of the Colony of Rhode-Island and Providence Plantations in New-England in America* (Boston: S. Kneeland and T. Green, 1739), 69, 88–89, 91.

52. On Sergeant and Stoddard, Stevens, *Poor Indians,* 170–72, 180, 181; on Le Jau, Edgar Legare Pennington, "The Reverend Francis Le Jau's Work among Indians and Negro Slaves," *Journal of Southern History* 1 (1935): 457.

53. As quoted in Wheeler, " 'Friends to Your Souls,' " 746.

54. Stevens, *Poor Indians,* 161–62, 169–73.

55. Merrell, *Into the American Woods,* 37–38. Stevens, *Poor Indians,* 180, suggests that some colonial Christians held out hope that if more Indians were converted to their faith, natives could physically survive as a people.

56. Krista Camenzind, "From Holy Experiment to the Paxton Boys: Violence, Manhood, and Peace in Pennsylvania during the Seven Years' War" (Ph.D. diss., University of California, San Diego, 2002), 2.

57. Larson, *Daughters of Light*, 216.

58. *A Conference between a parish-priest, and a Quaker* (Philadelphia: Samuel Keimer, 1725), 33.

59. Jack D. Marietta, *The Reformation of American Quakerism, 1748–1783* (Philadelphia: University of Pennsylvania Press, 1984), 92–93.

60. *Minutes of the Provincial Council of Pennsylvania, From the Organization to the Termination of the Proprietary Government,* 10 vols. (Harrisburg, Pa.: Theo. Fenn, 1851–52), 7:292–93; Larson, *Daughters of Light,* 213–17.

61. *Minutes of the Provincial Council of Pennsylvania,* 7:85.

62. Marietta, *Reformation of American Quakerism,* 157.

63. Sydney V. James, *A People among Peoples: Quaker Benevolence in Eighteenth-Century America* (Cambridge, Mass.: Harvard University Press, 1963), 178–92; Camenzind, "Holy Experiment to the Paxton Boys," 161–204; Theodore Thayer, "The Friendly Association," *Pennsylvania Magazine of History and Biography* 67 (1943): 356–76.

64. Daiutolo, "Early Quaker Perception of the Indian," 103–19; Thomas Drake, "William Penn's Experiment in Race Relations," *Pennsylvania Magazine of History and Biography* 68 (1944): 377; Camenzind, "Holy Experiment to the Paxton Boys," 177, 189.

65. John Churchman, *An Account of the Gospel labours, and Christian experiences of a faithful minister of Christ, John Churchman* (Philadelphia: Joseph Crukshank, 1779), 185–86.

66. *Minutes of the Provincial Council of Pennsylvania,* 7:311–12, 638–46; Marietta, *Reformation of American Quakerism,* 188.

67. Camenzind, "Holy Experiment to the Paxton Boys," 187–88 (quote on 188). After a similar meeting in Philadelphia, visiting English preacher Catherine Payton was impressed by "the veneration the Indians retained for the memory of William Penn, and for his pacifist principles; and their great regard to Friends whom they stiled his children." As quoted in Larson, *Daughters of Light,* 223.

68. Francis P. Jennings, *Empire of Fortune: Crowns, Colonies, and Tribes in the Seven Years War in America* (New York: Norton, 1988), 339, 375; Fred Anderson, *Crucible of War: The Seven Years' War and the Fate of Empire in British North America, 1754–1766* (New York: Alfred A. Knopf, 2000), 269, 278–79; Israel Pemberton et al. to Thomas Penn and Richard Penn, 3rd mo. 20th day, 1760, [p.1], Friendly Association Manuscripts, Friends Historical Library, Swarthmore College, Swarthmore, Pennsylvania; Marietta, *Reformation of American Quakerism,* 189.

69. Daniel Stanton, *A journal of the life, travels, and Gospel labours, of a faithful minister of Jesus Christ, Daniel Stanton* (Philadelphia: Joseph Crukshank, 1772), 106–108; William Reckitt, *Some account of the life and Gospel labours of William Reckitt* (Philadelphia: Joseph Crukshank, 1783), 61–62.

70. As quoted in Jennings, "Brother Miquon," 207.

71. James Kenney, "James Kenney's 'Journal to Ye Westward,' 1758–59," ed. John W. Jordan, *Pennsylvania Magazine of History and Biography* 37 (1913): 419; Gerona, "Imagining Peace," 57; John Woolman, *The Journal and Major Essays of John Woolman,* ed. Phillips P. Moulton (New York: Oxford University Press, 1971), 117–38; Marietta, *Reformation of American Quakerism,* 173–74.

72. Marietta, *Reformation of American Quakerism,* 150–86; Gerona, "Imagining Peace," 53.

73. Critics of the Friendly Association included William Johnson. At the Easton treaty with Delawares in June 1762, he did not appreciate the role Israel Pemberton and other members of the Friendly Association played in seeking to defend native rights. Johnson accused them of "nursing Teedyuscung [the Delaware chief] & interfering where they have no right." [Friendly Association for Regaining and Preserving Peace with the Indians by Pacific Measures], Account of the Easton Treaty with Indians [1762], [pp. 11–13], Friendly Association Manuscripts; Camenzind, "Holy Experiment to the Paxton Boys," 217–32; Larson, *Daughters of Light*, 215, 223.

74. Camenzind, "Holy Experiment to the Paxton Boys," 224.

75. Krista Camenzind, "Violence, Race, and the Paxton Boys," in Pencak and Richter, *Friends and Enemies*, 204–20.

76. Narrative accounts of the Paxton Boys uprising may be found in John R. Dunbar, "Introduction," in *The Paxton Papers*, ed. John R. Dunbar (The Hague, Netherlands: Martinus Nijhoff, 1957), 3–55, and Brooke Hindle, "The March of the Paxton Boys," *William and Mary Quarterly*, 3rd ser., 2 (1946): 461–86.

77. *A Declaration and Remonstrance Of the distressed and bleeding Frontier Inhabitants*, in Dunbar, *Paxton Papers*, 108–109.

78. Alison Olson, "The Pamphlet War over the Paxton Boys," *Pennsylvania Magazine of History and Biography* 123 (1999): 31–55.

79. *The Quaker Unmasked; Or, Plain Truth*, in Dunbar, *Paxton Papers*, 210.

80. "The Cloven-Foot Discovered," in Dunbar, *Paxton Papers*, 86.

81. *The Quaker Unmasked*, 211. Similar attacks on the Quaker-Indian alliance may be found in "The Apology of the Paxton Volunteers," in Dunbar, *Paxton Papers*, 192, and *The Plain Dealer: Or, Remarks on Quaker Politicks in Pennsylvania* in Dunbar, *Paxton Papers*, 377.

82. Olson, "Pamphlet War," 54.

83. Ibid., 32, 50, 52.

84. *The Address of the People call'd Quakers*, in Dunbar, *Paxton Papers*, 136–37; *The Quaker Vindicated*, in Dunbar, *Paxton Papers*, 236.

85. *Copy of a Letter From Charles Read, Esq: To The Hon: John Ladd*, in Dunbar, *Paxton Papers*, 81.

86. Merrell, *Into the American Woods*, 302; Personal correspondence with Christopher Densmore, 13 February 2006.

87. Marietta, *Reformation of American Quakerism*, 222–71.

88. Ibid., 273.

89. Anthony Benezet, *A short account of the people called Quakers* (Philadelphia: Joseph Crukshank, [1780]), 9–10.

90. Anthony Benezet, *The plainness and innocent simplicity of the Christian religion. With its salutary effects, compared to the corrupting nature and dreadful effects of war* (Philadelphia: Joseph Crukshank, 1782), 21–23 (quotes on 23).

91. Frost, "Penn's Experiment,'" 579, contrasts Penn's reputation among French and American revolutionaries: "The French approved of Penn because he symbolized a new way of life. By contrast, the American revolutionaries disapproved of Penn because he symbolized an old way of life. For Americans Penn had come to represent peace, the rights of minorities (including Indians and, via his Quaker successors, Blacks), Quaker dominance, sectarian politics, absence of militia, ordered liberty, and union with England—the antithesis of everything the Pennsylvania radicals wanted in 1776."

92. H. H. Brackenridge, ed., *Narratives of a late expedition against the Indians; with an account of the barbarous execution of Col. Crawford; and the wonderful escape of*

Dr. Knight and John Slover from captivity, in 1782 (Philadelphia: Francis Bailey, 1783), 32–38 (quotes on 32, 36, 37, 38).

93. Anthony Benezet to George Dillwyn, 7 mo. 1783, Anthony Benezet Papers, Haverford College Library, Haverford, Pennsylvania.

94. [Anthony Benezet,] *Some Observations on the situation, disposition, and character of the Indian Natives of this continent* (Philadelphia: Joseph Crukshank, 1784), iii, iv, 8–9, 23.

95. Ibid., 35.

96. Ibid., 36, 37.

97. Ibid., 39–40, 46.

98. James, *People among Peoples,* 298–315.

99. Baltimore Yearly Meeting of the Religious Society of Friends, *A Brief Account of the Proceedings of the Committee . . . for promoting the improvement and civilization of the Indian natives* (Baltimore: Cole and Hewes, 1805), 48.

100. As quoted in Kelsey, *Friends and Indians,* 91–93 (quote on 91).

101. Gimber, "Kinship and Covenants," 314–15.

102. Daniel Richter, " 'Believing that many of the red people suffer much for the want of food': Hunting, Agriculture, and a Quaker Construction of Indianness in the Early Republic," *Journal of the Early Republic* 19 (1999): 601–28; Usner, "Iroquois Livelihood and Jeffersonian Agrarianism," 202–15; Benjamin Franklin, *The interest of Great Britain considered, with regard to her colonies . . . To which are added, observations concerning the increase of mankind* (Philadelphia: William Bradford, 1760), 39–45; Benjamin Franklin, *The Autobiography of Benjamin Franklin with Related Documents,* ed. Louis P. Masur, 2nd ed. (Boston: Bedford/St. Martin's, 2003), 128. In this passage in his autobiography, Franklin predicted that "if it be the Design of Providence to extirpate these Savages in order to make room for Cultivators of the Earth," rum would likely be the "appointed Means." Franklin claimed that strong drink had "already annihilated all the Tribes who formerly inhabited the Seacoast."

103. Kelsey, *Friends and Indians,* 94–95.

104. Those positions are represented in the works of James, *People among Peoples,* and Marietta, *Reformation of American Quakerism.*

105. The essays in Hoxie, Hoffman, and Albert, *Native Americans and the Early Republic,* make a strong case for the ongoing centrality of Indians within the new republic.

106. Seeman, "Reading Indians' Deathbed Scenes," 17–47; Stevens, *Poor Indians,* 160–62, 181–94; Bross, *Dry Bones and Indian Sermons,* 186–205.

107. Richard T. Hughes, *Myths America Lives By* (Urbana: University of Illinois Press, 2003), 28–43.

Epilogue

1. David McClure, *Diary of David McClure, Doctor of Divinity, 1748–1820,* ed. Franklin B. Dexter (New York: Knickerbocker Press, 1899), 19–30, 131–34 (quote on 133). Axtell, *Invasion Within,* 263–67, also profiles McClure's 1772 visit to the Ohio country. McClure had been educated at Eleazar Wheelock's Indian school in Connecticut as a boy, then gone to Yale. While a student there, he spent the summer of 1766 with Samuel Kirkland amongst the Oneida. Following his graduation, he taught at Wheelock's schools, first in Connecticut and

then at Dartmouth, where he was ordained in 1772. He and Levi Frisbie were commissioned by the Society in Scotland for Propagating Christian Knowledge to bring the gospel to the Ohio Indians.

2. McClure, *Diary of David McClure*, 50–52 (quotes on 50–51, 51).

3. Ibid., 61–79 (quote on 72). McClure's praise of Peepy contrasted with his earlier impression of him recorded just a few days prior to their arrival in New Comer's Town: "My Indian Interpreter, Joseph Pepee, appears to be a sincere christian, but the poor man is ignorant, his ideas contracted and his english broken" (59).

4. Ibid., 80–81.

5. Ibid., 81–82.

6. Ibid., 83.

7. Wellenreuther and Wessel, *Moravian Mission Diaries of David Zeisberger*, 107–108. In their "Introduction" to this volume (40–41), Wellenreuther and Wessel enumerate the reasons why a series of Protestant missionary attempts among the Indians of the Ohio region failed in the 1760s and 1770s. Only the Moravians would prove to have a modicum of success there beginning in 1772.

Bibliography

PRIMARY SOURCES

Manuscripts

American Philosophical Society, Philadelphia, Pennsylvania
David Brainerd Journal
Beinecke Library, Yale University, New Haven, Connecticut
Jonathan Edwards Papers
Billy Graham Center Archives, Wheaton College, Wheaton, Illinois
Society for the Propagation of the Gospel Records
Dartmouth College Library Special Collections, Hanover, New Hampshire
Samuel Kirkland Papers
Individual Manuscripts
Friends Historical Library, Swarthmore College, Swarthmore, Pennsylvania
Friendly Association Manuscripts
Hamilton College Archives, Hamilton, New York
Samuel Kirkland Papers
Haverford College Library, Haverford, Pennsylvania
Anthony Benezet Papers
Huntington Library, San Marino, California
Manuscript Collection
Massachusetts Historical Society, Boston, Massachusetts
Jeremy Belknap Papers
Timothy Pickering Papers
Society for Propagating the Gospel among Indians Records
Moravian Church Archives, Bethlehem, Pennsylvania
Records of the Moravian Mission among the Indians of North America
Newberry Library, Chicago, Illinois
Manuscript Collection
New-York Historical Society, New York, New York
Manuscript Collection
New York Public Library, New York, New York
Joseph Johnson Diary

Wilberforce Eames Indian Collection
New York State Library Manuscripts and Special Collections, Albany, New York
John Ogilvie Diary
Samuel Kirkland Diary

Published Primary Sources

Anderson, Arthur J. O., Frances Berdan, and James Lockhart, eds. *Beyond the Codices: The Nahua View of Colonial Mexico.* Berkeley and Los Angeles: University of California Press, 1976.

Apthorp, East. *The Felicity of the Times.* Boston: Green and Russell, 1763.

Axtell, James, ed. *The Indian Peoples of Eastern America: A Documentary History of the Sexes.* New York: Oxford University Press, 1981.

Baltimore Yearly Meeting of the Religious Society of Friends. *A Brief Account of the Proceedings of the Committee . . . for promoting the improvement and civilization of the Indian natives.* Baltimore: Cole and Hewes, 1805.

Beauchamp, William M., ed. *Moravian Journals relating to Central New York, 1745–66.* Syracuse: Onondaga Historical Association, 1916.

Benevente o Motolinía, Toribio de. *Memoriales o Libro de Los Cosas de la Nueva España y de Los naturals de Ella.* Ed. Edmundo O'Gorman. Mexico: Universidad Nacional Autónoma de Mexico, 1971.

Benezet, Anthony. *The plainness and innocent simplicity of the Christian religion. With its salutary effects, compared to the corrupting nature and dreadful effects of war.* Philadelphia: Joseph Crukshank, 1782.

——. *A short account of the people called Quakers.* Philadelphia: Joseph Crukshank, [1780].

[——]. *Some Observations on the situation, disposition, and character of the Indian Natives of this continent.* Philadelphia: Joseph Crukshank, 1784.

Berdan, Frances F., and Patricia Rieff Anawalt, eds. *The Essential Codex Mendoza.* Berkeley and Los Angeles: University of California Press, 1997.

Beverley, Robert. *The History and Present State of Virginia.* Ed. Louis B. Wright. Chapel Hill: University of North Carolina Press, 1947.

Bierhorst, John, trans. and ed. *Cantares Mexicanos: Songs of the Aztecs.* Stanford, Calif.: Stanford University Press, 1985.

Bowden, Henry, and James P. Ronda, eds. *John Eliot's Indian Dialogues: A Study in Cultural Interaction.* Westport, Conn.: Greenwood Press, 1980.

Brackenridge, H. H., ed. *Narratives of a late expedition against the Indians; with an account of the barbarous execution of Col. Crawford; and the wonderful escape of Dr. Knight and John Slover from captivity, in 1782.* Philadelphia: Francis Bailey, 1783.

Bradford, William. *Of Plymouth Plantation, 1620–1647.* Ed. Samuel Eliot Morison. New York: Alfred A. Knopf, 1953.

Brainerd, David. *Mirabilia Dei inter Indicos, or the Rise and Progress of a Remarkable Work of Grace amongst a number of Indians.* Philadelphia: William Bradford, 1746.

Brainerd, John. *A Genuine Letter from Mr. John Brainerd . . . to his Friend in London.* London: J. Ward, 1753.

Callender, John. *An historical discourse on the civil and religious affairs of the Colony of Rhode-Island and Providence Plantations in New-England in America.* Boston: S. Kneeland and T. Green, 1739.

Calloway, Colin G., ed. *Dawnland Encounters: Indians and Europeans in Northern New England*. Hanover, N.H.: University Press of New England, 1991.

——, ed. *The World Turned Upside Down: Indian Voices from Early America*. Boston: St. Martin's Press, 1994.

Chalkley, Thomas. *A Collection of the Works of Thomas Chalkley: in two parts*. Philadelphia: B. Franklin and D. Hall, 1749.

Charlevoix, Pierre de. *History and General Description of New France*. Trans. John G. Shea. 6 vols. New York: Francis P. Harper, 1900.

Churchman, John. *An Account of the Gospel labours, and Christian experiences of a faithful minister of Christ, John Churchman*. Philadelphia: Joseph Crukshank, 1779.

Clark, Michael P., ed. *The Eliot Tracts*. Westport, Conn.: Praeger, 2003.

A Conference between a parish-priest, and a Quaker. Philadelphia: Samuel Keimer, 1725.

Defoe, Daniel. *Robinson Crusoe* and *A Journal of the Plague Year*. New York: Random House, 1948.

Densmore, Christopher, ed. "Indian Religious Beliefs on Long Island: A Quaker Account." *New York History* 73 (1992): 431–41.

Díaz del Castillo, Bernal. *The True History of the Conquest of Mexico*. Trans. Maurice Keatinge. 1800. Reprint, Ann Arbor: University Microfilms, 1966.

Dickinson, Jonathan. *Jonathan Dickinson's Journal or, God's Protecting Providence*. Ed. Evangeline Walker Andrews and Charles McLean Andrews. New Haven: Yale University Press, 1945.

Dunbar, John R., ed. *The Paxton Papers*. The Hague: Martinus Nijhoff, 1957.

Durán, Diego. *The Book of the Gods and Rites and the Ancient Calendar*. Ed. Fernando Horcasitas and Doris Heyden. Norman: University of Oklahoma Press, 1971.

——. *History of the Indies of New Spain*. Trans. Doris Heyden. Norman: University of Oklahoma Press, 1994.

Du Ru, Paul. *Journal of Paul Du Ru: Missionary Priest to Louisiana*. Trans. Ruth Lapham Butler. Chicago: Caxton Club, 1934.

Edwards, Jonathan. *Apocalyptic Writings*. Ed. Stephen J. Stein. Vol. 5 of *The Works of Jonathan Edwards*. New Haven: Yale University Press, 1977.

——. *A History of the Work of Redemption*. Ed. John F. Wilson. Vol. 9 of *The Works of Jonathan Edwards*. New Haven: Yale University Press, 1989.

——. *The Life of David Brainerd*. Ed. Norman Pettit. Vol. 7 of *The Works of Jonathan Edwards*. New Haven: Yale University Press, 1985.

——. *Original Sin*. Ed. Clyde Holbrook. Vol. 3 of *The Works of Jonathan Edwards*. New Haven: Yale University Press, 1970.

Eliot, John. *The Dying Speeches of Several Indians*. Cambridge, n.d. [1685?].

——. "Letters of Rev. John Eliot of Roxbury, to Hon. Robert Boyle." Massachusetts Historical Society, *Collections*, 1st ser., 3 (1794): 177–88.

An epistle from our Yearly-Meeting in Burlington, for the Jerseys and Pennsylvania. Philadelphia: [Andrew Bradford?], 1722.

Faull, Katherine M., trans. and ed. *Moravian Women's Memoirs: Their Related Lives, 1750–1820*. Syracuse: Syracuse University Press, 1997.

Force, Peter, ed. *Tracts and Other Papers relating Principally to the Origin, Settlement, and Progress of the Colonies in North America*. 4 vols. 1836–46. Reprint, Gloucester, Mass.: Peter Smith, 1963.

Fox, George. *Cain against Abel, Representing New-England's Church-Hirarchy, In Opposition to Her Christian Protestant Dissenters*. [London?], 1675.

——. *The Works of George Fox.* 8 vols. 1831. Reprint, New York: AMS Press, 1975.

Franklin, Benjamin. *The Autobiography of Benjamin Franklin with Related Documents.* Ed. Louis P. Masur. 2nd ed. Boston: Bedford/St. Martin's, 2003.

——. *The interest of Great Britain considered, with regard to her colonies . . . To which are added, observations concerning the increase of mankind.* Philadelphia: William Bradford, 1760.

Gookin, Daniel. "Historical Collections of the Indians in New England." Massachusetts Historical Society, *Collections,* 1st ser., 1 (1792): 141–226.

Hann, John H., trans. and ed. *Missions to the Calusa.* Gainesville: University of Florida Press, 1991.

Heckewelder, John. *History, Manners, and Customs of the Indian Nations.* Rev. ed. 1817; Philadelphia: Historical Society of Pennsylvania, 1876.

Henry, Alexander. *Travels and Adventures in Canada and the Indian Territories.* 1809. Reprint, Ann Arbor, Mich.: University Microfilms, 1966.

Hopkins, Samuel. *An Address to the People of New-England.* Philadelphia: Franklin and Hall, 1757.

——. *Historical Memoirs, relating to the Housattunuk Indians.* Boston: S. Kneeland, 1753.

Hough, Franklin B., ed., *Proceedings of the Commissioners of Indian Affairs . . . in the State of New York.* 2 vols. Albany: Joel Munsell, 1861.

Hulbert, Archer B., and William N. Schwarze, eds. "The Moravian Records: The Diaries of [David] Zeisberger Relating to the First Missions in the Ohio Basin." *Ohio Archaeological and Historical Quarterly* 21 (1912): 1–115.

Iberville, Pierre Le Moyne, Sieur de. *Iberville's Gulf Journals.* Trans. and ed. Richebourg Gaillard McWilliams. University: University of Alabama, 1981.

Jameson, J. Franklin, ed. *Narratives of New Netherland, 1609–1664.* Original Narratives of Early American History. 1909. Reprint, New York: Barnes and Noble, 1959.

Johnson, William. *Papers of Sir William Johnson.* Ed. Milton W. Hamilton et al. 14 vols. Albany: University of the State of New York, 1921–65.

Jones, David. *A Journal of Two Visits made to some nations of Indians on the west side of the river Ohio in the Years 1772 and 1773.* 1774. Reprint, [New York]: Arno Press, 1971.

Journall of the English Plantation at Plimoth. 1622. Reprint, Ann Arbor, Mich.: University Microfilms, Inc., 1966.

Kenney, James. "James Kenney's 'Journal to Ye Westward,' 1758–59." Ed. John W. Jordan. *Pennsylvania Magazine of History and Biography* 37 (1913): 395–449.

——. "Journal of James Kenney, 1761–1763." Ed. John W. Jordan. *Pennsylvania Magazine of History and Biography* 37 (1913): 1–47, 152–201.

Kirkland, Samuel. *The Journals of Samuel Kirkland.* Ed. Walter Pilkington. Clinton, N.Y.: Hamilton College, 1980.

Klett, Guy S., ed. *Journals of Charles Beatty, 1762–1769.* University Park: Pennsylvania State University Press, 1962.

[Latrobe, Benjamin]. *A Succinct View of the Missions established among the Heathen by the Church of the Brethren, or Unitas Fratrum in a letter to a friend.* London: M. Lewis, 1771.

Lawson, John. *A New Voyage to Carolina.* Ed. Hugh T. Lefler. Chapel Hill: University of North Carolina Press, 1967.

Lockhart, James, ed., *We People Here: Nahuatl Accounts of the Conquest of Mexico.* Berkeley and Los Angeles: University of California Press, 1993.

Lockhart, James, and Enrique Otte, trans. and eds. *Letters and Peoples of the Spanish Indies, Sixteenth Century.* Cambridge: Cambridge University Press, 1976.

London Chronicle. "Extracts from the Account of the Captivity of William Henry." Vol. 10 of Garland Library of Narratives of North American Indian Captivities. New York: Garland Publishing, 1977.

Mather, Cotton. *Decennium Luctuosum. An History of Remarkable Occurrences, in the long war, which New-England hath had with the Indian salvages, from the year 1688.* Boston: B. Green and J. Allen, 1699.

[——]. *An Epistle to the Christian Indians, giving them a short account of what the English desire them to know and to do in order to their happiness.* Boston: Bartholomew Green, 1700.

——. *A monitory and hortatory letter to those English, who debauch the Indians, by selling strong drink unto them.* Boston, 1700.

——. *The Triumphs of the Reformed Religion: The Life of the Reverend John Eliot.* Boston: Benjamin Harris and John Allen, 1691.

Mather, Increase. *A Brief History of the War with the Indians in New-England.* Boston: John Foster, 1676.

——. *Ichabod, or, a Discourse Shewing what Cause there is to Fear that the Glory of the Lord, is Departing from New-England.* Boston: Timothy Green, 1702.

[Mather, Increase, Cotton Mather, and Nehemiah Walter]. *A Letter, about the present state of Christianity, among the Christianized Indians of New-England.* Boston: Timothy Green, 1705.

Maule, Thomas. *Truth held forth and maintained according to the testimony of the holy prophets.* [New York]: William Bradford, 1695.

Mayhew, Matthew. *A Brief Narrative of the Success which the Gospel hath had, among the Indians.* Boston: Bartholomew Green, 1694.

McCallum, James Dow, ed. *The Letters of Eleazar Wheelock's Indians.* Hanover, N.H.: Dartmouth College, 1932.

McClure, David. *Diary of David McClure, Doctor of Divinity, 1748–1820.* Ed. Franklin B. Dexter. New York: Knickerbocker Press, 1899.

Minutes of the Provincial Council of Pennsylvania, From the Organization to the Termination of the Proprietary Government. 10 vols. Harrisburg, Pa.: Theo. Fenn, 1851–52.

Muhlenberg, Henry Melchior. *The Journals of Henry Melchior Muhlenberg.* Trans. Theodore G. Tappert and John W. Doberstein. 3 vols. Philadelphia: Evangelical Lutheran Ministerium of Pennsylvania and Muhlenberg Press, 1942–58.

Myers, Albert Cook, ed. *Narratives of Early Pennsylvania, West New Jersey, and Delaware, 1630–1707.* Original Narratives of Early American History. 1912. Reprint, New York: Barnes and Noble, 1959.

"Notes on the Iroquois and Delaware Indians." *Pennsylvania Magazine of History and Biography* 1 (1877): 163–67, 319–23; 2 (1878): 407–10.

O'Callaghan, E. B., ed. *Documentary History of the State of New York.* 4 vols. Albany, N.Y.: Weed, Parsons, 1849–51.

[Penn, William.] "Letters of William Penn." *Pennsylvania Magazine of History and Biography* 6 (1882): 463–74.

——. *Papers of William Penn.* Ed. Richard S. Dunn and Mary Maples Dunn. 5 vols. Philadelphia: University of Pennsylvania Press, 1981–87.

Powicke, F. W., ed. *Some Unpublished Correspondence of the Reverend Richard Baxter and the Reverend John Eliot, the Apostle of the American Indians, 1656–1682.* Manchester: Manchester University Press, 1931.

Quaife, Milo M., ed. *John Long's Voyages and Travels in the Years 1768–1788*. Chicago: R. R. Donnelley, 1922.

———, ed. *The Western Country in the Seventeenth Century: The Memoirs of Antoine Lamothe Cadillac*. New York: Citadel Press, 1962.

Reckitt, William. *Some account of the life and Gospel labours of William Reckitt*. Philadelphia: Joseph Crukshank, 1783.

Reichel, William C., ed. *Memorials of the Moravian Church*. 2 vols. Philadelphia: J. B. Lippincott, 1870.

Sahagún, Bernardino de. *Florentine Codex: General History of the Things of New Spain*. Trans. Arthur J. O. Anderson and Charles E. Dibble. 13 vols. Santa Fe, N.M.: School of American Research, and Salt Lake City: University of Utah, 1950–82.

[Sergeant, John]. *A Letter from the Rev. Mr. Sergeant of Stockbridge, to Dr. Colman of Boston*. Boston: Rogers and Fowle, 1743.

Simmons, William S., and Cheryl L. Simmons, eds. *Old Light on Separate Ways: The Narragansett Diary of Joseph Fish, 1765–1776*. Hanover, N.H.: University Press of New England, 1982.

Smith, James. *An Account of the Remarkable Occurrences in the Life and Travels of Colonel James Smith, During his Captivity with the Indians*. Philadelphia: J. Grigg, 1831.

Smith, William. *A Discourse Concerning the Conversion of the Heathen Americans*. Philadelphia: Dunlap, 1760.

Spangenberg, August Gottlieb. *An Account of the manner in which the Protestant Church of the Unitas Fratrum, or United Brethren, preach the Gospel, and carry on their Missions among the Heathen*. London: H. Trapp, 1788.

Stanton, Daniel. *A journal of the life, travels, and Gospel labours, of a faithful minister of Jesus Christ, Daniel Stanton*. Philadelphia: Joseph Crukshank, 1772.

Steck, Frances Borgin, trans. and ed. *Motolinía's History of the Indians of New Spain*. Washington, D.C.: Academy of American Franciscan History, 1951.

Stoddard, Solomon. *Question whether God is not Angry with the Country for doing so little towards the Conversion of the Indians*. Boston: B. Green, 1723.

Thwaites, Reuben G., ed. *The Jesuit Relations and Allied Documents*. 73 vols. 1896–1901. Reprint, New York: Pagent Book Company, 1959.

Tyler, Lyon Gardiner, ed. *Narratives of Early Virginia, 1606–1625*. Original Narratives of Early American History. New York: Charles Scribner's Sons, 1907.

Vaughan, Alden T., and Edward W. Clark, eds. *Puritans among the Indians: Accounts of Captivity and Redemption, 1676–1724*. Cambridge, Mass.: Harvard University Press, 1981.

Waselkov, Gregory A., and Kathryn E. Holland Braund, eds. *William Bartram on the Southeastern Indians*. Lincoln: University of Nebraska Press, 1995.

Wellenreuther, Hermann, and Carola Wessel, eds. *The Moravian Mission Diaries of David Zeisberger, 1772–1781*. Trans. Julie Tomberlin Weber. University Park: Pennsylvania State University Press, 2005.

Wesley, John. *An extract of the life of the late Rev. David Brainerd, missionary to the Indians*. 3rd ed. London: G. Paramore, 1798.

Williams, John. *The Redeemed Captive Returning to Zion*. Boston: B. Green, 1707.

Williams, Roger. *A Key into the Language of America*. 5th ed. London: Gregory Dexter, 1643.

Williams, Samuel Cole, ed. *Adair's History of the American Indians*. 1930. Reprint, Nashville: National Society of the Colonial Dames of America, 1953.

Wilson, Thomas. *The Knowledge and Practice of Christianity Made Easy to the Meanest Capacities, or An Essay towards an Instruction for the Indians.* 10th ed. London: B. Dod, 1764.

Wood, William. *New England's Prospect.* 1634. Ed. Alden T. Vaughan. Reprint, Amherst: University of Massachusetts Press, 1993.

Woolman, John. *The Journal and Major Essays of John Woolman.* Ed. Phillips P. Moulton. New York: Oxford University Press, 1971.

Young, Alexander, ed. *Chronicles of the First Planters of the Colony of Massachusetts Bay from 1623 to 1636.* Boston: Little and Brown, 1846.

Secondary Sources

Adorno, Rolena. "The Discursive Encounter of Spain and America: The Authority of Eyewitness Testimony in the Writing of History." *William and Mary Quarterly,* 3rd ser., 49 (1992): 210–28.

Albanese, Catherine L. "Exchanging Selves, Exchanging Souls: Contact, Combination, and American Religious History." In *Retelling U.S. Religious History,* ed. Thomas A. Tweed, 200–226. Berkeley and Los Angeles: University of California Press, 1997.

Allen, Don Cameron. *The Legend of Noah: Renaissance Rationalism in Art, Science, and Letters.* Urbana: University of Illinois Press, 1963.

Altman, Ida, and James Lockhart, eds. *Provinces of Early Mexico: Variants of Spanish American Regional Evolution.* Los Angeles: UCLA Latin American Center Publications, 1976.

Anderson, Fred. *Crucible of War: The Seven Years' War and the Fate of Empire in British North America, 1754–1766.* New York: Alfred A. Knopf, 2000.

Angell, Steven W. " 'Learn of the Heathen': Quakers and Indians in Southern New England, 1656–1676." *Quaker History* 92 (2003): 1–21.

Ariès, Philippe. *The Hour of Our Death.* Trans. H. Weaver. Oxford: Oxford University Press, 1981.

Axtell, James. *After Columbus: Essays in the Ethnohistory of Colonial America.* New York: Oxford University Press, 1988.

———. *Beyond 1492: Encounters in Colonial North America.* New York: Oxford University Press, 1992.

———. *The European and the Indian: Essays in the Ethnohistory of Colonial America.* New York: Oxford University Press, 1981.

———. *The Indians' New South: Cultural Change in the Colonial Southeast.* Baton Rouge: Louisiana State University Press, 1997.

———. *The Invasion Within: The Contest of Cultures in Colonial North America.* New York: Oxford University Press, 1985.

Bailey, Gauvin Alexander. *Art on the Jesuit Missions in Asia and Latin America, 1542–1773.* Toronto: University of Toronto Press, 1999.

Baird, Joseph A., Jr. *The Churches of Mexico.* Berkeley and Los Angeles: University of California Press, 1962.

Beaver, R. Pierce. *Church, State, and the American Indians: Two and a Half Centuries of Partnership in Missions between Protestant Churches and Government.* St. Louis: Concordia, 1966.

Bellin, Joshua David. *The Demon of the Continent: Indians and the Shaping of American Literature.* Philadelphia: University of Pennsylvania Press, 2001.

Bercovitch, Sacvan. *The Puritan Origins of the American Self.* New Haven: Yale University Press, 1975.

Blackburn, Carole. *Harvest of Souls: The Jesuit Missions and Colonialism in North America, 1632–1650.* Kingston, Ontario: McGill-Queen's University Press, 2000.

Bloch, Ruth H. *Visionary Republic: Millennial Themes in American Thought, 1756–1800.* Cambridge: Cambridge University Press, 1985.

Bloomfield, J. K. *The Oneidas.* New York: Alden Brothers, 1907.

Bonomi, Patricia. *Under the Cope of Heaven: Religion, Society, and Politics in Colonial America.* Updated ed. New York: Oxford University Press, 2003.

Bourne, Russell. *Gods of War, Gods of Peace: How the Meeting of Native and Colonial Religions Shaped Early America.* New York: Harcourt, 2002.

Bowden, Henry W. *American Indians and Christian Missions: Studies in Cultural Conflict.* Chicago: University of Chicago Press, 1981.

Bowden, Henry W. and James P. Ronda. "Introduction." In *John Eliot's Indian Dialogues: A Study in Cultural Interaction,* ed. Henry W. Bowden and James P. Ronda, 3–45. Westport, Conn.: Greenwood Press, 1980.

Bozeman, Theodore Dwight. *To Live Ancient Lives: The Primitivist Dimension in Puritanism.* Chapel Hill: University of North Carolina Press, 1988.

——. "The Puritans' 'Errand into the Wilderness' Reconsidered." *New England Quarterly* 59 (1986): 231–51.

Bragdon, Kathleen J. *Native Peoples of Southern New England, 1500–1650.* Norman: University of Oklahoma Press, 1996.

Brasser, T. J. "Mahican." In *Northeast,* ed. Bruce G. Trigger, vol. 15 of *Handbook of North American Indians,* William G. Sturtevant, gen. ed., 198–212. Washington, D.C.: Smithsonian Institution, 1979.

Brainerd, Thomas. *The Life of John Brainerd, The Brother of David Brainerd, and His Successor as Missionary to the Indians of New Jersey.* Philadelphia: Presbyterian Publication Committee, 1865.

Bremer, Francis J. *John Winthrop: America's Forgotten Founding Father.* New York: Oxford University Press, 2003.

Brookes, George S. *Friend Anthony Benezet.* Philadelphia: University of Pennsylvania Press, 1937.

Bross, Kristina. *Dry Bones and Indian Sermons: Praying Indians in Colonial America.* Ithaca, N.Y.: Cornell University Press, 2004.

Burkhart, Louise. *Holy Wednesday: A Nahua Drama from Early Colonial Mexico.* Philadelphia: University of Pennsylvania Press, 1996.

——. "Pious Performances: Christian Pageantry and Native Identity in Early Colonial Mexico." In *Native Traditions in the Postconquest World,* ed. Elizabeth Hill Boone and Tom Cummins, 361–81. Washington, D.C.: Dumbarton Oaks Research Library and Collection, 1998.

——. *The Slippery Earth: Nahua-Christian Moral Dialogue in Sixteenth-Century Mexico.* Tucson: University of Arizona Press, 1989.

Butler, Jon. *Awash in a Sea of Faith: Christianizing the American People.* Cambridge, Mass.: Harvard University Press, 1990.

Calloway, Colin G. "The Continuing Revolution in Indian Country." In *Native Americans and the Early Republic,* ed. Frederick E. Hoxie, Ronald Hoffman, and Peter J. Albert, 3–33. Charlottesville: University Press of Virginia, 1999.

——. *New Worlds for All: Indians, Europeans, and the Remaking of Early America.* Baltimore: Johns Hopkins University Press, 1997.

Camenzind, Krista. "From Holy Experiment to the Paxton Boys: Violence, Manhood, and Peace in Pennsylvania during the Seven Years' War." Ph.D. diss., University of California, San Diego, 2002.

——. "Violence, Race, and the Paxton Boys." In *Friends and Enemies in Penn's Woods: Indians, Colonists, and the Racial Construction of Pennsylvania*, ed. William A. Pencak and Daniel K. Richter, 201–20. University Park: Pennsylvania State University Press, 2004.

Campeau, Lucien. *La Mission des Jésuites chez les Hurons, 1634–1650.* Montreal: Les Editions Bellarmine, 1987.

Campisi, Jack, and Lawrence M. Hauptman, eds. *The Oneida Experience: Two Perspectives.* Syracuse, N.Y.: Syracuse University Press, 1988.

Canup, John. *Out of the Wilderness: The Emergence of an American Identity in Colonial New England.* Middletown, Conn.: Wesleyan University Press, 1990.

Carroll, Peter N. *Puritanism and the Wilderness: The Intellectual Significance of the New England Frontier, 1629–1700.* New York: Columbia University Press, 1969.

Cave, Alfred A. "Canaanites in a Promised Land: The American Indian and the Providential Theory of Empire." *American Indian Quarterly* 12 (1988): 277–97.

——. *The Pequot War.* Amherst: University of Massachusetts Press, 1996.

Cervantes, Fernando. "Epilogue: The Middle Ground." In *Spiritual Encounters: Interactions between Christianity and Native Religions in Colonial America*, ed. Nicholas Griffiths and Fernando Cervantes, 276–85. Lincoln: University of Nebraska Press, 1999.

Chaplin, Joyce E. *Subject Matter: Technology, the Body, and Science on the Anglo-American Frontier, 1500–1676.* Cambridge, Mass.: Harvard University Press, 2001.

Chiappelli, Fredi, ed. *First Images of America: The Impact of the New World on the Old.* 2 vols. Berkeley and Los Angeles: University of California Press, 1976.

Choquette, Robert. "French Catholicism Comes to the Americas." In Charles H. Lippy, Robert Choquette, and Stafford Poole, *Christianity Comes to the Americas*, 131–242. New York: Paragon House, 1992.

Christian, William A., Jr. *Local Religion in Sixteenth Century Spain.* Princeton: Princeton University Press, 1981.

Cline, Sarah. "Native Peoples of Colonial Central Mexico." In *The Cambridge History of the Native Peoples of the Americas*, ed. Richard E. W. Adams and Murdo J. MacLeod. 3 vols. Vol. 2, 187–222. Cambridge: Cambridge University Press, 2000.

Codignola, Luca. "The Holy See and the Conversion of the Indians in French and British North America, 1486–1760." In *America in European Consciousness, 1493–1750*, ed. Karen Ordahl Kupperman, 195–242. Chapel Hill: University of North Carolina Press, 1995.

Cogley, Richard. "John Eliot and the Millennium." *Religion and American Culture* 1 (1991): 227–50.

——. "John Eliot and the Origins of the American Indians." *Early American Literature* 21 (1986/1987): 210–25.

——. "John Eliot in Recent Scholarship." *American Indian Culture and Research Journal* 14 (1990): 77–92.

——. *John Eliot's Mission to the Indians before King Philip's War.* Cambridge, Mass.: Harvard University Press, 1999.

Cohen, Charles L. "The Colonization of British North America as an Episode in the History of Christianity." *Church History* 72 (2003): 553–68.

——. "Conversion among Puritans and Amerindians: A Theological and Cultural Perspective." In *Puritanism: Transatlantic Perspectives on a Seventeenth-Century Anglo-American Faith,* ed. Francis J. Bremer, 233–56. Boston: Massachusetts Historical Society, 1993.

Comaroff, John L., and Jean Comaroff. *Of Revelation and Revolution: The Dialectics of Modernity on a South African Frontier.* 2 vols. Chicago: University of Chicago Press, 1991–97.

Conforti, Joseph. "David Brainerd and the Nineteenth-Century Missionary Movement." *Journal of the Early Republic* 5 (1985): 309–29.

——. "Jonathan Edwards's Most Popular Work: 'The Life of David Brainerd' and Nineteenth-Century Evangelical Culture." *Church History* 54 (1985): 188–201.

Crosby, Alfred. *The Columbian Exchange: Biological and Cultural Consequences of 1492.* Westport, Conn.: Greenwood, 1972.

Curcio-Nagy, Linda A. "Faith and Morals in Colonial Mexico." In *The Oxford History of Mexico,* ed. Michael C. Meyer and William H. Beezley, 151–82. New York: Oxford University Press, 2000.

Daiutolo, Robert, Jr. "The Early Quaker Perception of the Indian." *Quaker History* 72 (1983): 104–13.

Davis, Natalie Zemon. *Women on the Margins: Three Seventeenth-Century Lives.* Cambridge, Mass.: Harvard University Press, 1995.

Davis, Sheldon. *Shekomeko; or, the Moravians in Dutchess County.* Poughkeepsie, N.Y.: Osborne and Killey, 1858.

Day, Richard Ellsworth. *Flagellant on Horseback: The Life Story of David Brainerd.* Philadelphia: Judson Press, 1950.

Deeds, Susan. "Pushing the Borders of Latin American Mission History." *Latin American Research Review* 39 (2004): 211–20.

DeJong, J. A. *As the Waters Cover the Sea: Millennial Expectations in the Rise of Anglo-American Missions, 1640–1810.* Kampen, Neth.: J. H. Kok, 1970.

Delbanco, Andrew. "The Puritan Errand Re-Viewed." *Journal of American Studies* 18 (1984): 343–60.

Demos, John. *The Unredeemed Captive: A Family Story from Early America.* New York: Alfred Knopf, 1994.

Dennis, Matthew. *Cultivating a Landscape of Peace: Iroquois-European Encounters in Seventeenth-Century America.* Ithaca, N.Y.: Cornell University Press, 1993.

DeRogatis, Amy. *Moral Geography: Maps, Missionaries, and the American Frontier.* New York: Columbia University Press, 2003.

De Schweinitz, Edmund. *The Life and Times of David Zeisberger: The Western Pioneer and Apostle of the Indians.* Philadelphia: J. B. Lippincott, 1870.

Devens, Carol. *Countering Colonization: Native American Women and Great Lakes Missions, 1630–1900.* Berkeley and Los Angeles: University of California Press, 1992.

Dibble, Charles E. "The Nahuatlization of Christianity." In *Sixteenth-Century Mexico: The Work of Sahagún,* ed. Munro S. Edmonson, 225–33. Albuquerque: University of New Mexico Press, 1974.

Dickason, Olive Patricia. *The Myth of the Savage and the Beginnings of French Colonialism in the Americas.* Edmonton: University of Alberta Press, 1984.

Dobyns, Henry F. *Their Number Became Thinned: Native American Population Dy-*

namics in Eastern North America. Knoxville: University of Tennessee Press, 1983.

Dobyns, Henry F., et al. "Commentary on Native American Demography." *Ethnohistory* 36 (1989): 285–307.

Doiron, Normand. "Rhetorique Jésuite de L'Eloquence Sauvage au XVII Siècle: Les *Relations* de Paul LeJeune (1632–1642)." *Dix-Septième Siècle* 43 (1991): 375–402.

Donnelly, Joseph P., S.J. *Jean de Brébeuf, 1593–1649.* Chicago: Loyola University Press, 1975.

Dorsey, Peter A. "Going to School with Savages: Authorship and Authority among the Jesuits of New France." *William and Mary Quarterly,* 3d. ser., 55 (1998): 399–420.

Dowd, Gregory Evans. *A Spirited Resistance: The North American Indian Struggle for Unity, 1745–1815.* Baltimore: Johns Hopkins University Press, 1992.

Drake, Thomas. "William Penn's Experiment in Race Relations." *Pennsylvania Magazine of History and Biography* 68 (1944): 372–87.

Dunbar, John R. "Introduction." In *The Paxton Papers,* ed. John R. Dunbar, 3–55. The Hague: Martinus Nijhoff, 1957.

Elliott, J. H. *The Old World and the New.* Cambridge: Cambridge University Press, 1992.

Erwin, John S. *The Millennialism of Cotton Mather: An Historical and Theological Analysis.* Lewiston, N.Y.: Edwin Mellen Press, 1980.

Faull, Katherine M. "Introduction." In *Moravian Women's Memoirs: Their Related Lives, 1750–1820,* trans. and ed. Katherine M. Faull, xvii–xl. Syracuse: Syracuse University Press, 1997.

Foster, Frank Hugh. *A Genetic History of New England Theology.* 1907. Reprint, New York: Russell and Russell, 1963.

Frank, Albert H. "Spiritual Life in Schönbrunn Village." *Transactions of the Moravian Historical Society* 26 (1990): 20–38.

Frazier, Patrick. *The Mohicans of Stockbridge.* Lincoln: University of Nebraska Press, 1992.

Frey, Sylvia, and Betty Wood. *Come Shouting to Zion: African American Protestantism in the American South and British Caribbean to 1830.* Chapel Hill: University of North Carolina Press, 1998.

Frost, J. William. "William Penn's Experiment in the Wilderness: Promise and Legend." *Pennsylvania Magazine of History and Biography* 107 (1983): 584–93.

Gallay, Alan. *The Indian Slave Trade: The Rise of the English Empire in the American South, 1670–1717.* New Haven: Yale University Press, 2002.

Gannon, Michael V. *The Cross in the Sand: The Early Catholic Church in Florida, 1513–1870.* Gainesville: University of Florida Press, 1965.

Gehrig, Charles T., and Robert S. Grumet. "Observations of the Indians from Jasper Danckaerts's Journal, 1679–1680." *William and Mary Quarterly,* 3d ser., 44 (1987): 104–20.

Gerona, Carla. "Imagining Peace in Quaker and Native American Dream Stories." In *Friends and Enemies in Penn's Woods: Indians, Colonists, and the Racial Construction of Pennsylvania,* ed. William A. Pencak and Daniel K. Richter, 41–62. University Park: Pennsylvania State University Press, 2004.

Gibson, Charles. *The Aztecs under Spanish Rule: A History of the Indians of the Valley of Mexico, 1519–1810.* Stanford, Calif: Stanford University Press, 1964.

Giddens, Anthony. *Central Problems in Social Theory: Action, Structure, and Contra-*

diction in Social Analysis. Berkeley and Los Angeles: University of California Press, 1979.

Gilpin, W. Clark. *The Millenarian Piety of Roger Williams.* Chicago: University of Chicago Press, 1979.

Gimber, Steven G. "Kinship and Covenants in the Wilderness: Indians, Quakers, and Conversion to Christianity, 1675–1800." Ph.D. diss., American University, 2000.

Godbeer, Richard. *The Devil's Dominion: Magic and Religion in Early New England.* Cambridge: Cambridge University Press, 1992.

Goddard, Peter A. "The Devil in New France: Jesuit Demonology, 1611–50." *Canadian Historical Review* 78 (1997): 40–62.

Goodwin, Gerald T. "Christianity, Civilization, and the Savage: The Anglican Mission to the American Indian." *Historical Magazine of the Protestant Episcopal Church* 43 (1973): 93–110.

Grant, John Webster. *Moon of Wintertime: Missionaries and the Indians of Canada in Encounter since 1534.* Toronto: University of Toronto Press, 1984.

Gray, Elma E. *Wilderness Christians: The Moravian Mission to the Delaware Indians.* 1956. Reprint, New York: Russell and Russell, 1973.

Graymont, Barbara. *The Iroquois in the American Revolution.* Syracuse: Syracuse University Press, 1972.

Greenblatt, Stephen. *Marvelous Possessions: The Wonder of the New World.* Chicago: University of Chicago Press, 1991.

Greer, Allan. "Colonial Saints: Gender, Race, and Hagiography in New France." *William and Mary Quarterly,* 3d. ser., 57 (2000): 323–48.

——. "Introduction." In *The Jesuit Relations: Natives and Missionaries in Seventeenth-Century North America,* ed. Allan Greer, 1–19. New York: Bedford/St. Martin's Press, 2000.

——. *Mohawk Saint: Catherine Tekakwitha and the Jesuits.* New York: Oxford University Press, 2005.

Griffiths, Nicholas, and Fernando Cervantes, eds. *Spiritual Encounters: Interactions between Christianity and Native Religions in Colonial America.* Lincoln: University of Nebraska Press, 1999.

Grigg, John. "The Lives of David Brainerd." Ph.D. diss., University of Kansas, 2002.

——. " 'A Principle of Spiritual Life': David Brainerd's Surviving Sermon." *New England Quarterly* 77 (2004): 273–82.

Grumet, Robert S. *Historic Contact: Indian People and Colonists in Today's Northeastern United States in the Sixteenth through Eighteenth Centuries.* Contributions to Public Archeology. Norman: University of Oklahoma Press, 1995.

Gruzinski, Serge. *The Conquest of Mexico: The Incorporation of Indian Societies into the Western World, 16th–18th Centuries.* Trans. Eileen Corrigan. Cambridge: Polity Press, 1993.

——. *Painting the Conquest: The Mexican Indians and the European Renaissance.* Trans. Deke Dusinberre. Paris: Flammarion, 1992.

Gura, Philip F. *Jonathan Edwards: America's Evangelical.* New York: Hill and Wang, 2005.

Gustafson, Sandra M. *Eloquence Is Power: Oratory and Performance in Early America.* Chapel Hill: University of North Carolina Press, 2000.

Hackel, Steven W. *Children of Coyote, Missionaries of Saint Francis: Indian-Spanish Relations in Colonial California, 1769–1850.* Chapel Hill: University of North Carolina Press, 2005.

Haefeli, Evan, and Kevin Sweeney. *Captors and Captives: The 1704 French and Indian Raid on Deerfield.* Amherst: University of Massachusetts Press, 2003.

———. "Revisiting *The Redeemed Captive:* New Perspectives on the 1704 Attack on Deerfield." *William and Mary Quarterly,* 3d ser., 52 (1995): 3–46.

Hall, David D. *Worlds of Wonder, Days of Judgment: Popular Religious Belief in Early New England.* New York: Alfred A. Knopf, 1989.

Hall, Richard A. S. *The Neglected Northampton Texts of Jonathan Edwards.* Lewiston, N.Y.: Edwin Mellen Press, 1990.

Hambrick-Stowe, Charles. *The Practice of Piety: Puritan Devotional Disciplines in Seventeenth-Century New England.* Chapel Hill: University of North Carolina Press, 1982.

Hankins, Jean F. "Bringing the Good News: Protestant Missionaries to the Indians of New England and New York, 1700–1775." Ph.D. diss., University of Connecticut, 1993.

———. "Solomon Briant and Joseph Johnson: Indian Teachers and Preachers in Colonial New England." *Connecticut History* 33 (1992): 38–60.

Harris, Paul. "David Brainerd and the Indians: Cultural Interaction and Protestant Missionary Ideology." *American Presbyterians* 72 (1994): 1–9.

Hasler, Richard A. "David Zeisberger's 'Jersey Connection.'" *Transactions of the Moravian Historical Society* 30 (1998): 37–53.

Hauptman, Laurence M. *Conspiracy of Interests: Iroquois Dispossession and the Rise of New York State.* Syracuse: Syracuse University Press, 1999.

Hauptman, Laurence M., and L. Gordon McLester III, eds. *The Oneida Indian Journey: From New York to Wisconsin, 1784–1860.* Madison: University of Wisconsin Press, 1999.

Healy, George R. "The French Jesuits and the Idea of the Noble Savage." *William and Mary Quarterly,* 3d. ser., 15 (1958): 143–67.

Heidenreich, Conrad E. "Huron." In *Northeast,* ed. Bruce G. Trigger, vol. 15 of *Handbook of North American Indians,* William G. Sturtevant, gen. ed., 368–88. Washington, D.C.: Smithsonian Institution, 1979.

Hindle, Brooke. "The March of the Paxton Boys." *William and Mary Quarterly,* 3rd ser., 2 (1946): 461–86.

Holifield, E. Brooks. *Era of Persuasion: American Thought and Culture, 1521–1680.* Boston: Twayne, 1989.

———. *Theology in America: Christian Thought from the Age of the Puritans to the Civil War.* New Haven: Yale University Press, 2003.

Hood, Fred. *Reformed America: The Middle and Southern States, 1783–1837.* University: University of Alabama Press, 1980.

Horsman, Reginald. "The Indian Policy of an 'Empire of Liberty.'" In *Native Americans and the Early Republic,* ed. Frederick E. Hoxie, Ronald Hoffman, and Peter J. Albert, 37–61. Charlottesville: University Press of Virginia, 1999.

Hughes, Richard T. *Myths America Lives By.* Urbana: University of Illinois Press, 2003.

Hunter, William A. "Moses (Tunda) Tatamy, Delaware Indian Diplomat." In *A Delaware Indian Symposium,* ed. Herbert C. Kraft, 72–80. Harrisburg: Pennsylvania Historical and Museum Commission, 1974.

Icazbalceta, Joaquín García. *Don Fray Juan de Zumárraga.* 4 vols. 1881. Reprint, Mexico: Porrua, 1947.

Isenberg, Nancy, and Andrew Burstein, eds. *Mortal Remains: Death in Early America.* Philadelphia: University of Pennsylvania Press, 2003.

Jacobs, Wilbur R. "The Tip of the Iceberg: Pre-Columbian Indian Demography and Some Implications for Revisionism." *William and Mary Quarterly*, 3d ser., 31 (1974): 123–32.

Jaenen, Cornelius J. *Friend and Foe: Aspects of French-Amerindian Cultural Conflict in the Sixteenth and Seventeenth Centuries*. Toronto: McClelland and Stewart, 1976.

——. " 'Les Sauvages Ameriquains': Persistence into the 18th Century of Traditional French Concepts and Constructs for Comprehending Amerindians." *Ethnohistory* 29 (1982): 43–56.

James, Sydney V. *A People among Peoples: Quaker Benevolence in Eighteenth-Century America*. Cambridge, Mass.: Harvard University Press, 1963.

Jeffrey, David Lyle. *People of the Book: Christian Identity and Literary Culture*. Grand Rapids, Mich.: Eerdmans, 1996.

Jennings, Francis P. *The Ambiguous Iroquois Empire*. New York: Norton, 1990.

——. "Brother Miquon: Good Lord!" In *The World of William Penn*, ed. Richard S. Dunn and Mary Maples Dunn, 195–214. Philadelphia: University of Pennsylvania Press, 1986.

——. *Empire of Fortune: Crowns, Colonies, and Tribes in the Seven Years War in America*. New York: Norton, 1988.

——. *The Invasion of America: Indians, Colonialism, and the Cant of Conquest*. Chapel Hill: University of North Carolina Press, 1975.

Johnson, Eric S. "Uncas and the Politics of Contact." In *Northeastern Indian Lives, 1632–1816*, ed. Robert S. Grumet, 29–47. Amherst: University of Massachusetts Press, 1996.

Johnson, Margery Ruth. "The Mayhew Mission to the Indians, 1643–1806." Ph.D. diss., Clark University, 1966.

Kamen, Henry. *The Phoenix and the Flame: Catalonia and the Counter Reformation*. New Haven: Yale University Press, 1993.

Kamensky, Jane. *Governing the Tongue: The Politics of Speech in Early New England*. New York: Oxford University Press, 1997.

Kelsey, Rayner W. *Friends and Indians, 1655–1917*. Philadelphia: Associated Executive Committee of Friends on Indian Affairs, 1917.

Kilby, Clyde S. "David Brainerd." In *Heroic Colonial Christians*, ed. Russell T. Hitt, 151–206. Philadelphia: Lippincott, 1966.

Klingberg, Frank J. "The Indian Frontier in South Carolina as Seen by the S. P. G. Missionary." *Journal of Southern History* 5 (1939): 479–500.

Klor de Alva, J. Jorge. "Spiritual Conflict and Accommodation in New Spain: Toward a Typology of Aztec Responses to Christianity." In *The Inca and Aztec States, 1400–1800: Anthropology and History*, ed. George A. Collier, Renato I. Rosaldo, and John D. Wirth, 345–66. New York: Academic Press, 1982.

Kornfeld, Eve. "Encountering the 'Other': American Intellectuals and Indians in the 1790s." *William and Mary Quarterly*, 3d ser., 52 (1995): 287–314.

Kraft, Herbert C. *The Lenape: Archaeology, History, and Ethnography*. Newark: New Jersey Historical Society, 1986.

Kupperman, Karen Ordahl, ed. *America in European Consciousness, 1493–1750*. Chapel Hill: University of North Carolina Press, 1995.

——. *Settling with the Indians: The Meeting of English and Indian Cultures in America, 1580–1640*. Totowa, N. J.: Rowman and Littlefield, 1980.

Lach, Donald F., and Edwin J. Van Kley. *Asia in the Making of Europe*. 3 vols. Chicago: University of Chicago Press, 1965–92.

Langer, Erick, and Robert H. Jackson, eds. *The New Latin American Mission History*. Lincoln: University of Nebraska Press, 1995.

Larson, Rebecca. *Daughters of Light: Quaker Women Preaching and Prophesying in the Colonies and Abroad, 1700–1775*. New York: Alfred A. Knopf, 1999.

Leahey, Margaret J. "'Comment Peut un Muet Prescher L'Evangile?' Jesuit Missionaries and Native Languages of New France." *French Historical Studies* 19 (1995): 105–31.

Lehman, J. David. "The End of the Iroquois Mystique: The Oneida Land Cession Treaties of the 1780s." *William and Mary Quarterly*, 3d ser., 47 (1990): 522–47.

Lennox, Herbert John. *Samuel Kirkland's Mission to the Iroquois*. Chicago: University of Chicago Libraries, 1935.

Lepore, Jill. *The Name of War: King Philip's War and the Origins of American Identity*. New York: Alfred A. Knopf, 1998.

Lockhart, James. "Capital and Province, Spaniard and Indian: The Example of Late Sixteenth-Century Toluca." In *Provinces of Early Mexico: Variants of Spanish American Regional Evolution*, ed. Ida Altman and James Lockhart, 99–123. Los Angeles: UCLA Latin American Center Publications, 1976.

——. *The Nahuas after the Conquest: A Social and Cultural History of the Indians of Central Mexico, Sixteenth through Eighteenth Centuries*. Stanford, Calif: Stanford University Press, 1992.

——. *Of Things of the Indies: Essays Old and New in Early Latin American History*. Stanford, Calif: Stanford University Press, 1999.

Loskiel, George. *The History of the Moravian Mission among the Indians of North America*. 1794. London: T. Allman, 1838.

Love, W. DeLoss. *Samson Occom and the Christian Indians of New England*. Boston: Pilgrim Press, 1899.

Lovejoy, David S. "Satanizing the American Indian." *New England Quarterly* 67 (1994): 603–21.

Mackintosh, Michael Dean. "New Sweden, Natives, and Nature." In *Friends and Enemies in Penn's Woods: Indians, Colonists, and the Racial Construction of Pennsylvania*, ed. William A. Pencak and Daniel K. Richter, 3–17. University Park: Pennsylvania State University Press, 2004.

Mandell, Daniel. "'To Live More Like My Christian English Neighbors': Natick Indians in the Eighteenth Century." *William and Mary Quarterly*, 3d. ser., 48 (1991): 552–79.

——. "'Standing by His Father': Thomas Waban of Natick, circa 1630–1722." In *Northeastern Indian Lives, 1632–1816*, ed. Robert S. Grumet, 166–92. Amherst: University of Massachusetts Press, 1996.

Marietta, Jack D. *The Reformation of American Quakerism, 1748–1783*. Philadelphia: University of Pennsylvania Press, 1984.

Marsden, George M. *Jonathan Edwards: A Life*. New Haven: Yale University Press, 2003.

Martin, Joel W. *The Land Looks After Us: A History of Native American Religion*. Oxford: Oxford University Press, 2001.

——. *Sacred Revolt: The Muskogees' Struggle for a New World*. Boston: Beacon Press, 1991.

Matter, Robert Allen. "Mission Life in Seventeenth-Century Florida." *Catholic Historical Review* 67 (1981): 401–20.

McCarthy, Keely. "Conversion, Identity, and the Indian Missionary." *Early American Literature* 36 (2001): 353–69.

McDermott, Gerald R. "Jonathan Edwards and American Indians: The Devil Sucks Their Blood." *New England Quarterly* 72 (1999): 539–57.

——. *Jonathan Edwards Confronts the Gods: Christian Theology, Enlightenment Religion, and Non-Christian Faiths.* New York: Oxford University Press, 2000.

——. *One Holy and Happy Society: The Public Theology of Jonathan Edwards.* University Park: Pennsylvania State University Press, 1992.

McEwan, Bonnie G., ed. *The Spanish Missions of La Florida.* Gainesville: University Press of Florida, 1993.

McLoughlin, William G. *Cherokees and Missionaries, 1789–1839.* New Haven: Yale University Press, 1984.

McNally, Michael D. "The Practice of Native American Christianity." *Church History* 69 (2000): 834–59.

Merrell, James H. "Afterword." In *Friends and Enemies in Penn's Woods: Indians, Colonists, and the Racial Construction of Pennsylvania,* ed. William A. Pencak and Daniel K. Richter, 259–68. University Park: Pennsylvania State University Press, 2004.

——. " 'The Customes of Our Countrey': Indians and Colonists in Early America." In *Strangers within the Realm: Cultural Margins of the First British Empire,* ed. Bernard Bailyn and Philip D. Morgan, 117–56. Chapel Hill: University of North Carolina Press, 1991.

——. *The Indians' New World: Catawbas and Their Neighbors from European Contact through the Era of Removal.* Chapel Hill: University of North Carolina Press, 1989.

——. *Into the American Woods: Negotiators on the Pennsylvania Frontier.* New York: Norton, 1999.

——. "Some Thoughts on Colonial Historians and American Indians." *William and Mary Quarterly,* 3d ser., 46 (1989): 94–119.

Merritt, Jane T. *At the Crossroads: Indians and Empires on a Mid-Atlantic Frontier, 1700–1763.* Chapel Hill: University of North Carolina Press, 2003.

——. "Dreaming of the Savior's Blood: Moravians and the Indian Great Awakening in Pennsylvania." *William and Mary Quarterly,* 3d ser., 54 (1997): 723–46.

Milanich, Jerald T. "Franciscan Missions and Native Peoples in Spanish Florida." In *The Forgotten Centuries: Indians and Europeans in the American South, 1521–1704,* ed. Charles Hudson and Corwin C. Tesser, 276–303. Athens: University of Georgia Press, 1994.

Miles, Lion G. "The Red Man Dispossessed: The Williams Family and the Alienation of Indian Land in Stockbridge, Massachusetts, 1736–1818." *New England Quarterly* 67 (1994): 46–76.

Miller, Christopher L., and George R. Hamell. "A New Perspective on Indian-White Contact: Cultural Symbols and Colonial Trade." *Journal of American History* 73 (1986): 311–28.

Miller, Perry. *Errand into the Wilderness.* Cambridge, Mass.: Belknap Press of Harvard University Press, 1956.

——. *The New England Mind: From Colony to Province.* Cambridge, Mass.: Harvard University Press, 1953.

——. *The New England Mind: The Seventeenth Century.* 2d ed. Cambridge, Mass.: Harvard University Press, 1954.

Moffitt, John F., and Santiago Sebastian. *O Brave New People: The European Invention of the American Indian.* Albuquerque: University of New Mexico Press, 1996.

Morgan, Edmund S. *Visible Saints.* Ithaca, N.Y.: Cornell University Press, 1963.

Morrison, Dane. *A Praying People: Massachusett Acculturation and the Failure of the Puritan Mission, 1600–1690.* New York: Peter Lang, 1995.

Morrison, Kenneth M. *The Solidarity of Kin: Ethnohistory, Religious Studies, and the Algonkian-French Religious Encounter.* Albany: State University of New York Press, 2002.

Moss, Robert. "Missionaries and Magicians: The Jesuit Encounter with Native American Shamans on New England's Colonial Frontier." In *Wonders of the Invisible World: 1600–1900,* ed. Peter Benes, 17–33. Boston: Boston University Scholarly Publications, 1992.

Muir, Edward. *Ritual in Early Modern Europe.* Cambridge: Cambridge University Press, 1997.

Murray, David. "David Brainerd and the Gift of Christianity." *European Review of Native American Studies* 10 (1996): 23–29.

——. *Forked Tongue: Speech, Writing and Representation in North American Indian Texts.* Bloomington: Indiana University Press, 1991.

——. "Spreading the Word: Missionaries, Conversion and Circulation in the Northeast." In *Spiritual Encounters: Interactions between Christianity and Native Religions in Colonial America,* ed. Nicholas Griffiths and Fernando Cervantes, 43–64. Lincoln: University of Nebraska Press, 1999.

Naeher, Robert James. "Dialogue in the Wilderness: John Eliot and Indian Exploration of Puritanism as a Source of Meaning, Comfort, and Ethnic Survival." *New England Quarterly* 62 (1989): 346–68.

Nalle, Sara T. *God in La Mancha: Religious Reform and People of Cuenca, 1500–1650.* Baltimore: Johns Hopkins University Press, 1992.

Namias, June. *White Captives: Gender and Ethnicity on the American Frontier.* Chapel Hill: University of North Carolina Press, 1993.

Nash, Gary B. "The Concept of Inevitability in the History of European-Indian Relations." In *Inequality in Early America,* ed. Carla Gardina Pestana and Sharon V. Salinger, 267–91. Hanover, N.H.: University Press of New England, 1999.

Noll, Mark A. *America's God: From Jonathan Edwards to Abraham Lincoln.* New York: Oxford University Press, 2002.

——. *A History of Christianity in the United States and Canada.* Grand Rapids, Mich: Eerdmans, 1992.

Nouwen, Henri J. M. *The Wounded Healer: Ministry in Contemporary Society.* Garden City, N.Y.: Doubleday, 1972.

Olmstead, Early P. *Blackcoats among the Delaware: David Zeisberger on the Ohio Frontier.* Kent, Ohio: Kent State University Press, 1991.

Olson, Alison. "The Pamphlet War over the Paxton Boys." *Pennsylvania Magazine of History and Biography* 123 (1999): 31–55.

Orsi, Robert. "Everyday Miracles: The Study of Lived Religion." In *Lived Religion in America: Toward a History of Practice,* ed. David D. Hall, 3–21. Princeton: Princeton University Press, 1997.

Pagden, Anthony. *European Encounters with the New World.* New Haven: Yale University Press, 1993.

Patrick, Christine S. "The Life and Times of Samuel Kirkland, 1741–1808: Missionary to the Oneida Indians, American Patriot, and Founder of Hamilton College." Ph.D. diss., State University of New York at Buffalo, 1993.

Payne, Stanley G. *Spanish Catholicism: An Historical Overview.* Madison: University of Wisconsin Press, 1984.

Pearce, Roy Harvey. " 'The Ruines of Mankind': The Indian and the Puritan Mind." *Journal of the History of Ideas* 13 (1952): 200–217.

Pennington, Edgar Legare. "The Reverend Francis LeJau's Work among Indians and Negro Slaves." *Journal of Southern History* 1 (1935): 442–58.

Perron, Paul. "Isaac Jogues: From Martyrdom to Sainthood." In *Colonial Saints: Discovering the Holy in the Americas,* ed. Allan Greer and Jodi Bilinkoff, 153–68. New York: Routledge, 2003.

Pestana, Carla Gardina. "Martyred by the Saints: Quaker Executions in Seventeenth-Century Massachusetts." In *Colonial Saints: Discovering the Holy in the Americas,* ed. Allan Greer and Jodi Bilinkoff, 169–91. New York: Routledge, 2003.

——. *Quakers and Baptists in Colonial Massachusetts.* Cambridge: Cambridge University Press, 1991.

Pestana, Carla Gardina, and Sharon Salinger, eds. *Inequality in Early America.* Hanover, N. H.: University Press of New England, 1999.

Peterson, Jeanette Favrot. "Synthesis and Survival: The Native Presence in Sixteenth-Century Murals of New Spain." In *Native Artists and Patrons in Colonial Latin America,* ed. Emily Umberger and Tom Cummins, 14–31. Tempe: Arizona State University Press, 1995.

Pettit, Norman. "Introduction." In Jonathan Edwards, *The Life of David Brainerd,* ed. Norman Pettit, vol. 7 of *The Works of Jonathan Edwards,* 2–67. New Haven: Yale University Press, 1985.

——. "Prelude to Mission: Brainerd's Expulsion from Yale." *New England Quarterly* 59 (1986): 28–50.

Piersen, William D. "Black Arts and Black Magic: Yankee Accommodations to African Religion." In *Wonders of the Invisible World: 1600–1900,* ed. Peter Benes, 34–43. Boston: Boston University Scholarly Publications, 1995.

——. *Black Yankees: The Development of an Afro-American Subculture in Eighteenth-Century New England.* Amherst: University of Massachusetts Press, 1988.

Pigman, G. W., III. "Versions of Imitation in the Renaissance." *Renaissance Quarterly* 33 (1980): 1–32.

Pointer, Richard W. " 'Poor Indians and the Poor in Spirit': The Indian Impact on David Brainerd." *New England Quarterly* 67 (1994): 403–26.

——. "Selves and Others in Early New England: Refashioning American Puritan Studies." In *History and the Christian Historian,* ed. Ronald A. Wells, 137–58. Grand Rapids, Mich.: Eerdmans, 1998.

Poole, Stafford. "Iberian Catholicism Comes to the Americas." In Charles H. Lippy, Robert Choquette, and Stafford Poole, *Christianity Comes to the Americas,* 1–129. New York: Paragon House, 1992.

——. "Some Observations on Mission Methods and Native Reactions in Sixteenth-Century New Spain." *Americas* 50 (1994): 337–49.

Prins, Harald E. L. "Chief Rawandagan, Alias Robin Hood: Native 'Lord of Misrule' in the Maine Wilderness." In *Northeastern Indian Lives, 1632–1816,* ed. Robert S. Grumet, 93–115. Amherst: University of Massachusetts Press, 1996.

Pulsipher, Jenny Hale. *Subjects unto the Same King: Indians, English, and the Contest for Authority in Colonial New England.* Early American Studies. Philadelphia: University of Pennsylvania Press, 2005.

Raboteau, Albert J. *Slave Religion: The "Invisible Institution" in the Antebellum South.* New York: Oxford University Press, 1978.

Ricard, Robert. *The Spiritual Conquest of Mexico: An Essay on the Apostolate and Evangelizing Methods of the Mendicant Orders in New Spain, 1523–1572.* Trans.

Lesley Byrd Simpson. Berkeley and Los Angeles: University of California Press, 1966.

Richter, Daniel K. " 'Believing that many of the red people suffer much for the want of food': Hunting, Agriculture, and a Quaker Construction of Indianness in the Early Republic." *Journal of the Early Republic* 19 (1999): 601–28.

——. *Facing East from Indian Country: A Native History of Early America.* Cambridge, Mass.: Harvard University Press, 2001.

——. "Iroquois versus Iroquois: Jesuit Missions and Christianity in Village Politics, 1642–1686." *Ethnohistory* 32 (1985): 1–16.

——. *The Ordeal of the Longhouse: The Peoples of the Iroquois League in the Era of European Civilization.* Chapel Hill: University of North Carolina Press, 1992.

——. " 'Some of Them . . . Would Always Have a Minister with Them': Mohawk Protestantism, 1683–1719." *American Indian Quarterly* 16 (1992): 471–84.

——. "Whose Indian History?" *William and Mary Quarterly,* 3d ser., 50 (1993): 379–93.

Robinson, Paul A. "Lost Opportunities: Miantonimi and the English in Seventeenth-Century Narragansett Country." In *Northeastern Indian Lives, 1632–1816,* ed. Robert S. Grumet, 13–28. Amherst: University of Massachusetts Press, 1996.

Rohrer, James R. *Keepers of the Covenant: Frontier Missions and the Decline of Congregationalism, 1774–1818.* New York: Oxford University Press, 1995.

Ronda, James P. "Generations of Faith: The Christian Indians of Martha's Vineyard." *William and Mary Quarterly,* 3d ser., 38 (1981): 369–94.

——. " 'We Are Well As We Are': An Indian Critique of Seventeenth-Century Christian Missions." *William and Mary Quarterly,* 3d. ser., 34 (1977): 66–82.

Rountree, Helen C. "Powhatan Priests and English Rectors: World Views and Congregations in Conflict." *American Indian Quarterly* 16 (1992): 485–500.

Saeger, James Schofield. "*The Mission* and Historical Missions: Film and the Writing of History." In *Based on a True Story: Latin American History at the Movies,* ed. Donald F. Stevens, 63–84. Wilmington, Del.: Scholarly Resources, 1997.

Saldívar, Gabriel. *Historia de la Música en Mexico: Epocas Precortesiana y Colonial.* Mexico: Editorial "Cultura," 1934.

Salisbury, Neal. "Embracing Ambiguity: Native Peoples and Christianity in Seventeenth-Century North America." *Ethnohistory* 50 (2003): 247–59.

——. " 'I Loved the Place of My Dwelling': Puritan Missionaries and Native Americans in Seventeenth-Century Southern New England." In *Inequality in Early America,* ed. Carla Gardina Pestana and Sharon V. Salinger, 11–33. Hanover, N. H.: University Press of New England, 1999.

——. "Red Puritans: The 'Praying Indians of Massachusetts Bay and John Eliot." *William and Mary Quarterly,* 3d. ser., 31 (1974): 27–54.

——. "Squanto: Last of the Patuxets." In *Struggle and Survival in Colonial America,* ed. David G. Sweet and Gary B. Nash, 228–46. Berkeley and Los Angeles: University of California Press, 1981.

Sandos, James. *Converting California: Indians and Franciscans in the Missions.* New Haven: Yale University Press, 2004.

Sanneh, Lamin. *Translating the Message: The Missionary Impact on Culture.* Maryknoll, N. Y.: Orbis Books, 1989.

——. "Vincent Donovan's Discovery of Post-Western Christianity." In Vincent J. Donovan, *Christianity Rediscovered,* 151–59. Maryknoll, N. Y.: Orbis, [2003].

——. *West African Christianity: The Religious Impact.* Maryknoll, N. Y.: Orbis Books, 1983.

Saxton, Martha. *Being Good: Women's Moral Values in Early America.* New York: Hill and Wang, 2003.

Scalberg, Daniel A. "The French-Amerindian Religious Encounter in Seventeenth and Early Eighteenth-Century New France." *French Colonial History* 1 (2002): 101–12.

Scanlan, Thomas. *Colonial Writing and the New World, 1583–1671: Allegories of Desire.* Cambridge: Cambridge University Press, 1999.

Schattschneider, David S. "The Missionary Theologies of Zinzendorf and Spangenberg." *Transactions of the Moravian Historical Society* 22 (1975): 213–33.

Schmidt, Leigh Eric. "Practices of Exchange: From Market Culture to Gift Economy in the Interpretation of American Religion." In *Lived Religion in America: Toward a History of Practice,* ed. David D. Hall, 69–91. Princeton: Princeton University Press, 1997.

Schwartz, Stuart B., ed. *Implicit Understandings: Observing, Reporting, and Reflecting on the Encounters between Europeans and Other Peoples in the Early Modern Era.* Cambridge: Cambridge University Press, 1994.

Seeman, Erik R. "Reading Indians' Deathbed Scenes: Ethnohistorical and Representational Approaches." *Journal of American History* 88 (2001): 17–47.

Segal, Charles, and David Stineback, eds. *Puritans, Indians, and Manifest Destiny.* New York: Putnam, 1977.

Shannon, Timothy J. *Atlantic Lives: A Comparative Approach to Early America.* New York: Pearson Longman, 2004.

Shoemaker, Nancy. *A Strange Likeness: Becoming Red and White in Eighteenth-Century North America.* New York: Oxford University Press, 2004.

Shuffleton, Frank, ed. *A Mixed Race: Ethnicity in Early America.* New York: Oxford University Press, 1993.

Silverman, David J. *Faith and Boundaries: Colonists, Christianity, and Community among the Wampanoag Indians of Martha's Vineyard, 1600–1871.* Cambridge: Cambridge University Press, 2005.

——. "Indians, Missionaries, and Religious Translation: Creating Wampanoag Christianity in Seventeenth-Century Martha's Vineyard." *William and Mary Quarterly,* 3d ser., 62 (2005): 147–74.

Simmons, William S. "Cultural Bias in the New England Puritans' Perceptions of Indians." *William and Mary Quarterly,* 3d ser., 38 (1981): 56–72.

Slotkin, Richard. *Regeneration through Violence: The Mythology of the American Frontier.* Middletown, Conn.: Wesleyan University Press, 1973.

Slotkin, Richard, and James K. Folsom. *So Dreadfull A Judgment: Puritan Responses to King Philip's War, 1676–1677.* Middletown, Conn.: Wesleyan University Press, 1978.

Smaby, Beverly Prior. *The Transformation of Moravian Bethlehem: From Communal Mission to Family Economy.* Philadelphia: University of Pennsylvania Press, 1988.

Smith, Timothy L. "Religion and Ethnicity in America." *American Historical Review* 83 (1978): 1155–85.

Sobel, Mechal. *The World They Made Together: Black and White Values in Eighteenth-Century Virginia.* Princeton: Princeton University Press, 1987.

Spady, James O'Neil. "Colonialism and the Discursive Antecedents of *Penn's Treaty* with the Indians." In *Friends and Enemies in Penn's Woods: Indians, Colonists, and the Racial Construction of Pennsylvania,* ed. William A. Pencak and

Daniel K. Richter, 18–40. University Park: Pennsylvania State University Press, 2004.

Steckley, John. "The Warrior and the Lineage: Jesuit Use of Iroquoian Images to Communicate Christianity." *Ethnohistory* 39 (1992): 478–509.

Stevens, Laura M. *The Poor Indians: British Missionaries, Native Americans, and Colonial Sensibility.* Philadelphia: University of Pennsylvania Press, 2004.

Stevenson, Robert. *Music in Aztec and Inca Territory.* Berkeley and Los Angeles: University of California Press, 1968.

——. *Music in Mexico: A Historical Survey.* New York: Thomas Y. Crowell, 1952.

——. "The Music of Colonial Spanish America." In *The Cambridge History of Latin America,* ed. Leslie Bethell, 8 vols., 2:771–98. Cambridge: Cambridge University Press, 1984.

Sugrue, Thomas J. "The Peopling and Depeopling of Early Pennsylvania: Indians and Colonists, 1680–1720." *Pennsylvania Magazine of History and Biography* 116 (1992): 3–31.

Sweet, David. "The Ibero-American Frontier Mission in Native American History." In *The New Latin American Mission History,* ed. Erick Langer and Robert H. Jackson, 1–48. Lincoln: University of Nebraska Press, 1995.

Szasz, Margaret Connell. *Indian Education in the American Colonies, 1607–1783.* Albuquerque: University of New Mexico Press, 1988.

Szewczyk, David M. "New Elements in the Society of Tlaxcala, 1519–1618." In *Provinces of Early Mexico: Variants of Spanish American Regional Evolution,* ed. Ida Altman and James Lockhart, 137–53. Los Angeles: UCLA Latin American Center Publications, 1976.

Taylor, Alan. *The Divided Ground: Indians, Settlers, and the Northern Borderland of the American Revolution.* New York: Alfred Knopf, 2006.

Thayer, Theodore. "The Friendly Association." *Pennsylvania Magazine of History and Biography* 67 (1943): 356–76.

Thomas, G. E. "Puritans, Indians, and the Concept of Race." *New England Quarterly* 48 (1975): 3–27.

Thomas, Keith. *Religion and the Decline of Magic.* New York: Scribner, 1971.

Thorp, Daniel B. "Going Native in New Zealand and America: Comparing Pakeha Maori and White Indians." *Journal of Imperial and Commonwealth History* 31 (2003): 1–23.

Tiro, Karim Michel. "The People of the Standing Stone: The Oneida Indian Nation from Revolution through Removal, 1765–1840." Ph.D. diss., University of Pennsylvania, 1999.

Travers, Len. "The Missionary Journal of John Cotton, Jr., 1666–1678." *Proceedings of the Massachusetts Historical Society* 109 (1997): 52–101.

Trigger, Bruce G. *The Children of Aataentsic: A History of the Huron People to 1660.* 1976. Reprint, Kingston, Ontario: McGill-Queen's University Press, 1987.

——, ed. *Handbook of North American Indians.* Vol. 15: *Northeast.* Washington, D.C.: Smithsonian Institution, 1978.

——. *The Huron: Farmers of the North.* 2d ed. Fort Worth, Tex.: Harcourt Brace Jovanovich, 1990.

——. *Natives and Newcomers: Canada's "Heroic Age" Reconsidered.* Kingston, Ontario: McGill-Queen's University Press, 1985.

Tschoop: The Converted Indian Chief. N.p.: American Sunday School Union, 1842.

Tschoop and Shabasch, Christian Indians of North America: A Narrative of Facts. Dublin: M. Goodwin, 1824.

Usner, Daniel H., Jr. "Iroquois Livelihood and Jeffersonian Agrarianism: Reaching behind the Models and Metaphors." In *Native Americans and the Early Republic,* ed. Frederick E. Hoxie, Ronald Hoffman, and Peter J. Albert, 200–25. Charlottesville: University Press of Virginia, 1999.

Van Lonkhuyzen, Harold W. "A Reappraisal of Praying Indians: Acculturation, Conversion, and Identity at Natick, Massachusetts, 1646–1730." *New England Quarterly* 63 (1990): 396–428.

Vaughan, Alden T. "Early English Paradigms for New World Natives." American Antiquarian Society, *Proceedings* 102, pt. 1 (1992): 33–67.

——. "From White Man to Redskin: Changing Anglo-American Perceptions of the American Indian." *American Historical Review* 87 (1982): 917–53.

Vaughan, Alden T., and Daniel Richter, "Crossing the Cultural Divide: Indians and New Englanders, 1605–1763." American Antiquarian Society, *Proceedings* 90 (1980): 23–99.

Vaughan, Alden T., and Edward W. Clark. "Cups of Common Calamity: Puritan Captivity Narratives as Literature and History." In *Puritans among the Indians: Accounts of Captivity and Redemption, 1676–1724,* ed. Alden T. Vaughan and Edward W. Clark, 1–28. Cambridge, Mass.: Harvard University Press, 1981.

Wacker, Grant. "Introduction." *Church History* 72 (2003): 699–702.

Wallace, Anthony F. C. *King of the Delawares: Teedyuscung, 1700–1763.* Philadelphia: University of Pennsylvania Press, 1949.

Wallace, Paul A. W. *Conrad Weiser: Friend of Colonist and Mohawk.* Philadelphia: University of Pennsylvania Press, 1945.

Ward, Matthew C. "Redeeming the Captives: Pennsylvania Captives among the Ohio Indians, 1755–1765." *Pennsylvania Magazine of History and Biography* 125 (2001): 161–89.

Watts, Pauline Moffitt. "Hieroglyphs of Conversion: Alien Discourses in Diego Valadés's *Rhetorica Christiana.*" *Memorie Domenicane* 22 (1991): 405–33.

——. "Languages of Gesture in Sixteenth-Century Mexico: Some Antecedents and Transmutations." In *Reframing the Renaissance: Visual Culture in Europe and Latin America 1450–1650,* ed. Claire Farago, 140–51. New Haven: Yale University Press, 1995.

Weatherford, Jack. *Indian Givers: How the Indians of the Americas Transformed the World.* New York: Random House, 1989.

——. *Native Roots: How the Indians Enriched America.* New York: Random House, 1992.

Webb, Edith Buckland. *Indian Life at the Old Missions.* Los Angeles: Warren F. Lewis, 1952.

Weddle, David L. "The Melancholy Saint: Jonathan Edwards's Interpretation of David Brainerd as a Model of Evangelical Spirituality." *Harvard Theological Review* 81 (1988): 297–318.

Weddle, Meredith Baldwin. *Walking in the Way of Peace: Quaker Pacifism in the Seventeenth Century.* New York: Oxford University Press, 2001.

Wellenreuther, Hermann, and Carola Wessel, eds. "Introduction." In *The Moravian Mission Diaries of David Zeisberger, 1772–1781,* trans. Julie Tomberlin Weber, 1–87. University Park: Pennsylvania State University Press, 2005.

Weslager, C. A. "Delaware Indian Name Giving and Modern Practice." In *A Delaware Indian Symposium,* ed. Herbert C. Kraft, 135–45. Harrisburg: Pennsylvania Historical and Museum Commission, 1974.

——. *The Delaware Indians: A History.* New Brunswick, N. J.: Rutgers University Press, 1972.

Westmeier, Karl-Wilhelm. *The Evacuation of Shekomeko and the Early Moravian Missions to Native North Americans.* Lewiston, N.Y.: Edwin Mellen Press, 1994.

Wheeler, Rachel. " 'Friends to Your Souls': Jonathan Edwards' Indian Pastorate and the Doctrine of Original Sin." *Church History* 72 (2003): 736–65.

——. "Women and Christian Practices in a Mahican Village." *Religion and American Culture* 13 (2003): 27–67.

White, Richard. *The Middle Ground: Indians, Empires, and Republics in the Great Lakes Region, 1650–1815.* Cambridge: Cambridge University Press, 1991.

Wills, David W. "The Central Themes of American Religious History: Pluralism, Puritanism and the Encounter of Black and White." *Religion and Intellectual Life* 5 (1987): 30–41.

Wood, Peter H. "The Changing Population of the Colonial South: An Overview by Race and Region, 1685–1790." In *Powhatan's Mantle: Indians in the Colonial Southeast,* ed. Peter H. Wood, Gregory A. Waselkov, and M. Thomas Hatley, 35–103. Lincoln: University of Nebraska Press, 1989.

——. "North America in the era of Captain Cook: Three Glimpses of Indian-European Contact in the Age of the American Revolution." In *Implicit Understandings: Observing, Reporting, and Reflecting on the Encounters between Europeans and Other Peoples in the Early Modern Era,* ed. Stuart B. Schwartz, 484–501. Cambridge: Cambridge University Press, 1994.

Worrall, Arthur J. *Quakers in the Colonial Northeast.* Hanover, N.H.: University Press of New England, 1980.

Wright, A. D. *Catholicism and Spanish Society under the Reign of Philip II, 1555–1598, and Philip III, 1598–1621.* Lewiston, N.Y.: Edwin Mellen Press, 1991.

Wynbeek, David. *David Brainerd, Beloved Yankee.* 2d ed. Grand Rapids, Mich.: Eerdmans, 1964.

Wyss, Hilary E. *Writing Indians: Literacy, Christianity, and Native Community in Early America.* Amherst: University of Massachusetts Press, 2000.

Youngs, J. William T., Jr. "The Indian Saints of Early New England." *Early American Literature* 16 (1981/82): 241–56.

Index